United States Edition

2014 Year A

Workbook for Lectors, Gospel Readers, and Proclaimers of the Word®

Graziano Marcheschi, MA, DMIN

with Nancy Seitz Marcheschi

LTP
LITURGY
TRAINING
PUBLICATIONS

CONTENTS

WORKBOOK FOR LECTORS, GOSPEL READERS, AND PROCLAIMERS OF THE WORD® 2014, United States Edition © 2013 Archdiocese of Chicago. All rights reserved.

Liturgy Training Publications, 3949 South Racine Avenue, Chicago IL 60609, 1-800-933-1800, fax 1-800-933-7094, orders@ltp.org, www.LTP.org.

Cover art: Barbara Simcoe

As a publisher, LTP works toward responsible stewardship of the environment. We printed the text of *Workbook for Lectors, Gospel Readers, and Proclaimers of the Word®* with soy-based ink on paper certified to the SFI (Sustainable Forestry Initiative®) Certified Fiber Sourcing Standard CERT – 0048284, confirming that the paper manufacturer takes a responsible approach to obtaining fiber. The wood pulp that was required in the making of this paper was sourced from sawmill residuals or pulp logs unsuitable for other uses. A thermo mechanical pulp process in manufacturing provides 100% more efficient use of wood fiber than the conventional process.

Printed in the United States of America.

ISBN: 978-1-61671-091-0
WL14

Ordinary Time

The Authors

Graziano Marcheschi, MA, DMIN, speaks nationally on topics of liturgy and the arts, Scripture, and lay ecclesial ministry. He is the Executive Director for University Ministry at Saint Xavier University in Chicago. Formerly, he served as Director of Ministerial Resource Development for the Archdiocese of Chicago, where he also served for eighteen years as the Archdiocesan Director of Lay Ministry Formation. He has authored books on Scripture and proclamation skills, a collection of stories and poetry, and has contributed commentaries on the Pentateuch, Gospels, and Acts for the *Catholic Bible, Personal Study Edition* (Oxford University Press). Graziano holds an MA in Drama from the University of Minnesota, an MDiv from Loyola University, Chicago, and a DMIN from the University of St. Mary of the Lake, Mundelein, IL. He and his wife, Nancy, have two daughters, a son, and one grandchild.

Nancy Seitz Marcheschi, choreographer and co-director of the Anawim Players, teaches music and performing arts, and is the school liturgist at Pope John XXIII School in Evanston, Illinois.

Dedication

Per i cugini di Lucca: Candido e Maria Candida, Laura, Luca, e piccola Chiara con gratitudine e tanto amore. E per il bellissimo villaggio di S. Gennaro—the remarkable Tuscan town where my life began and where my heart still longs to be.

In accordance with c. 827, permission to publish was granted on May 14, 2013, by Reverend Monsignor John F. Canary, Vicar General of the Archdiocese of Chicago. Permission to publish is an official declaration of ecclesiastical authority that the material is free from doctrinal and moral error. No legal responsibility is assumed by the grant of this permission.

INTRODUCTION

Welcome! New in this Edition

During this liturgical year of 2014, the entire Church is celebrating the fiftieth anniversary of the first document of the Second Vatican Council: the *Constitution on the Sacred Liturgy (Sacrosanctum Concilium)*, promulgated December 4, 1963. Liturgy Training Publications was born during that time also, in response to that document, for the purpose of forming and training the faithful to participate in the liturgy. For this fiftieth anniversary year, *Workbook* introduces a few enhancements. Although the classic layout is preserved, you'll notice a fresh, clean look to the book this year—new type faces and title treatments that make it more readable and more convenient to use. *Workbook* has also added new features. Although the Responsorial Psalm is not, in best practice, the responsibility of the reader, since it should be sung and not proclaimed (*General Instruction of the Roman Missal*, [GIRM], 61; Introduction to the *Lectionary for Mass*, 20–21), the psalm is closely related to the other readings. Readers preparing to proclaim any of the other readings will find it helpful to study and pray the psalm. Now you will find the psalm included in small print for that very purpose. You will also find pointers and reminders taken from this very helpful introduction, placed in boxes, and scattered throughout the book where space allows. Among these reminders is a brief description of the ancient practice of *Lectio Divina*, a way of praying Scripture that will add a profound spiritual dimension to the preparation of your proclamation.

Workbook helps you prepare to *proclaim* your assigned reading, and it can also build your knowledge and skills when you use it every week to prepare to *hear* the readings. The commentaries deepen your understanding of Scripture and the proclamation advice in the margin notes helps you gradually absorb the skills you need to be a mature and seasoned proclaimer of the Word. *The Editor*

The Role of the Reader

As readers of the Word, we share in a sacred process in the life of the Church. "In Sacred Scripture, the Church constantly finds her nourishment and her strength, for she welcomes it not as a human word, but as what it really is, the Word of God" (1 Thessalonians 2:13; Second Vatican Council. *Dogmatic Constitution on Revelation [Dei Verbum]*, 24). "When the Sacred Scriptures are read in the Church, God himself speaks to his people, and Christ, present in his word, proclaims the Gospel. Therefore, the readings from the Word of God are to

> In the beginning was the Word, and the Word was with God, and the Word was God.

be listened to reverently by everyone, for they are an element of the greatest importance to the Liturgy" (GIRM, 29). Therefore, we who are privileged to read during the liturgy play a very important role in helping to present the Word to the assembly.

We owe this privilege, as well as the insights just expressed, to the work of the Second Vatican Council, 1962–1965, which issued the *Dogmatic Constitution on Divine Revelation (Dei Verbum)* (quoted above) and the document that has most shaped our liturgical experience: the *Constitution on the Sacred Liturgy (Sacrosanctum Concilium)*. As the Church celebrates the fiftieth anniversary of that document, we readers should celebrate it with particular joy. Among many contributions to the liturgy, it provided for a richer selection of Scripture to be read at Mass, it invited the laity into liturgical ministry, including the ministry of reader, and it urged everyone to listen attentively to the Word proclaimed, because "it is he [Christ] himself who speaks when the holy Scriptures are read in the Church" (7).

Our mission entails a great responsibility. At Mass, we serve as a bridge between the Scriptures and the faithful. In undertaking this sacred ministry, you are committing yourself to the preparation and discipline that enables Scripture to become a living Word. According to the Introduction to the *Lectionary for Mass*, this requires that "preparation must above all be spiritual, [though] . . . technical preparation is also needed." The Introduction adds that "spiritual preparation presupposes at least a biblical and liturgical formation. . . . Biblical formation is to give readers the ability to understand the readings in context and to perceive . . . the central point of the revealed message. . . . Liturgical formation ought to equip readers to have some grasp of the meaning and structure of the liturgy of the word and of its connection with the Liturgy of the Eucharist. The technical preparation should make the readers more skilled in the art of reading publicly" (55). Obviously, this responsibility requires serious effort.

Using This Book

Proclaiming the Scriptures is a ministry that involves your whole life. So make these Scriptures a part of your life every week, especially the week prior to proclaiming.

(1) Using this book, read all four Scriptures for your assigned Sunday. All were chosen for this day, so read them together. The Responsorial Psalm and Gospel can teach much about how the First Reading should be proclaimed. (2) Build your prayer for the week around the Scripture passage you will proclaim on Sunday. (3) As you are becoming familiar with your passage, read it directly from your Bible, reading also what comes before and after it to get a clear sense of its context. (4) Always read all three commentaries. Suggestions in each can help you with your own passage. As you read the commentaries, refer to the sections of the Scripture passage being discussed and make your own margin notations. (5) Read the Scriptures again using your own margin notes and those printed in the book to remind you of the commentary suggestions. (6) Always read aloud, noticing suggestions for emphasis. After several readings, alter the emphasis markings to suit your own style and interpretation.

Using Additional Resources

The better you understand the meaning of your passage, the more effectively you will proclaim it and so help the assembly to understand it. Although the commentaries in this book will help you, readers may wish to dig deeper. Also, readers need to develop a lifelong habit of turning to the Scriptures for study and prayer. Additional resources that will help you to do this are listed in a downloadable file at http://www.ltp.org/t-productsupplements.aspx.

Appropriate Dramatic Technique

Good readers use techniques from the world of theater, not to draw attention to themselves, but to draw attention to the Word. When people experience good proclamation, they forget the reader in front of them and they hear the Scripture in a powerful way. That goal is best achieved by skillful use of all the available reading techniques. Of course, when readers are overly dramatic, and more focused on *how* they proclaim than on *what* they proclaim, listeners stop believing them. Artifice (an imitation of artfulness) can become an obstacle to good proclamation.

Avoiding artifice does not mean settling for mediocrity. Often the failure to use appropriate techniques leads to a kind of mediocre reading that guarantees the Scripture will not be heard. Readers who cannot differentiate one character in a reading from another, who read too fast or too slowly, who have too little energy and don't use the colorful words of a passage, who read in a monotone without rising and falling dynamics and pacing—these readers only draw attention to themselves. The assembly cannot see beyond them. But really good proclaimers who utilize appropriate techniques for the material being read draw the assembly into the reading.

True Humility. All readers need a model of true humility as they work toward excellence in proclamation. We look to Christ who "emptied himself, taking the form of a slave . . . [and] humbled himself, becoming obedient to death, even death on a cross" (Philippians 2:7–8). Jesus, the Word, humbles himself each Sunday by making himself dependent

This is my commandment: love one another as I love you.

on us who proclaim him in the assembly. He depends on us to communicate him as a living and vital Word. Jesus, alive in every line of Scripture, is indeed obedient "unto death."

Reading as Interpretation

God's Word is "living and effective" (Hebrews 4:12) and it "goes forth from [God's] mouth . . . achieving the end for which [he] sent it" (Isaiah 55:11), yet we know that doesn't happen automatically. People must allow the Word to become a transforming influence in their lives. Before they can do that, readers must help them to hear it.

Reading is a form of interpretation. The same word spoken by two readers will not be "heard" in exactly the same way. Pacing, the words stressed, pauses, volume, tone color, and intensity are all elements that interpret the text. Your responsibility is to make sure your interpretation upholds the plain sense of the text, the author's clear intent, and that you enable the text to speak to everyone. God's Word can lose its power, beauty, and spiritual import if a reader fails to communicate the full content of a passage, which clearly consists of more than the words. Every text contains three kinds of content: intellectual-theological, emotional, and aesthetic.

The author makes certain points or shares specific details, or tells a specific story, behind which is a theological teaching or spiritual insight. That is the intellectual-theological content. Much of what we encounter in Scripture also contains emotional content. We usually call this "tone," and it is as much a part of the message as is the cognitive component. If Paul is urgent or peremptory in one of his letters but the assembly is unaware because the reader has not communicated that part of the content, then the assembly has not heard Paul's message in its entirety. Finally, every passage contains aesthetic dimensions—elements that make it beautiful. Rhythm, suspense, picturesque language, and imagery all add to the pleasure we take in fine literature. As readers, we must help our assemblies experience the beauty of the fine literature we call Scripture.

To acquire the intellectual-theological content, begin by reading the Scripture and the commentary. Next, search the text for the emotion the author is expressing: the emotional content. Finally, look for the author's aesthetic devices: repetition, simile, metaphor, irony, and so forth, the aesthetic content.

Tools of the Trade

Margin Notes. Notes may introduce new ideas or repeat information in the commentary. Often they address you as the reader ("Slowly. Build in intensity.") or offer hints about a character's feelings.

Build. "Build" refers to increasing vocal intensity as you speak a certain word or sentence. That could be done by speaking louder, but a quieter voice might produce the same effect. Sometimes "build" is achieved by speaking faster and sometimes by speaking slower. The point is to show more intensity of feeling, greater urgency, or concern. Lack of intensity is one of the great "sins" of proclamation.

Stress (Bold Print). Some words are more important than others. Some are more expressive and carry more emotion. In this book, the bolding in the

God so loved the world that he gave his only Son, so that everyone who believes in him might not perish but might have eternal life.

Scripture texts attempts to identify operative words in a sentence, the ones that convey the meaning.

Echoes. Some words are "echoes" of words that went before. For example, "You shall be a glorious crown . . . a royal diadem" (Isaiah 62:3). Here "diadem" echoes "crown" so it needs no stress. In such cases, emphasize the new idea: royal.

Words That Sound Like What They Mean. "Pop," "fizz," and "gulp" are obvious. Some are more subtle: "smashed," "vast," "in haste," "implore," "gleamed."

These words usually require special emphasis. They were chosen to convey a desired meaning, so let them do their work.

Word Value. "Shock" is always a more interesting word than "bean." "Shock" sounds like what it means and immediately conjures up vivid images. "Bean" won't even make your mouth water. Word value is also determined by context. The words "one, two, three" are neutral by themselves, but put in context they intensify: "Three seconds until lift-off! One . . . two . . . .!" If, in reading that sentence, "One, two . . . " sounds the same as when followed by "buckle my shoe" you've got work to do. Words are your medium, like a painter's brush or a sculptor's chisel. You must understand the words before you can communicate them. Most words have a dictionary meaning (denotative) and an associational meaning (connotative). "House" and "home" both mean "dwelling," yet they communicate different feelings. Be alert to subtle differences in connotative meanings and express them.

Separating Units of Thought with Pauses. Running words together blurs meaning and fails to distinguish ideas. Punctuation does not always indicate clearly what words to group together or where to pause. Identify the units of thought and use your voice to distinguish one from another. The listener depends on you for this organization of ideas. With the letters of Paul, especially, carefully identify individual ideas and share them one at a time.

Scripture in this book is arranged in sense lines, one idea per line of text. Typically, at least a slight pause should follow each line. But good reading requires you to recognize the need for other pauses within lines. Moving from one thought unit to another within a paragraph requires shifts in mood and pacing. Don't rush these transitions; honor them with a healthy pause; let the silence "speak."

Pauses are never "dead" moments. Something is always happening during a pause. Practice will teach you how often and how long to pause. Too many pauses make a reading choppy; too few cause ideas to run together. Too long a pause breaks the flow. If pauses are too short, your listeners will be struggling to keep up with you. A substantial pause always follows "A reading from . . ." and both precedes and follows "The word [Gospel] of the Lord."

Ritardando. Ritardando, an Italian word, refers to the practice, common in music, of becoming gradually slower as you approach the end of a piece. On the last line of a song you automatically slow down and expand the words. Many readings end this way—with a decreased rate but increased intensity.

Characters. Usually several characters populate the Scripture passages you will read. Do your best to distinguish one from another. Be in touch with each character's thoughts, feelings, and motivations, and suggest differences through subtle changes in pitch, pacing, or by subtly expressing each character's emotion. Differentiating between characters is the mark of a fine reader. But don't ever confuse proclamation with stage theatrics. You are suggesting characters, not "becoming" them.

Narrator. The narrator is often the pivotal role of a passage. Timbre, pitch, rate, and energy can make the same words convey very different moods or meaning. Sometimes the narrator is objective: "Jesus took Peter, James and John . . . " (Matthew 17:1; Mark 9:2). But often the narrator has great interest in the events and characters of a story: "And he was transfigured before them and his clothes became dazzlingly white" (Mark 9:2–3). Know the narrator's point of view.

Openings and Closings. First, establish eye contact with the assembly and announce, from memory, "A reading from . . . ." Then take a pause (three full beats!) before starting the reading. The correct pronunciation is "A [uh] reading from . . . " instead of "A [ay] reading . . . ." Do not vary from the prescribed introductory formula. Names of characters are often the first word of a reading. Highlight names so listeners don't miss who the subject is. Pause again (three beats!) at the end of the reading

Magnify the LORD with me; let us exalt his name together.

and establish eye contact before announcing (again, from memory) "The word [Gospel] of the Lord." Always pronounce "the" as "thuh" except before words beginning with a vowel as in "thee Acts of the Apostles." Your inflection of the reading's last line should signal that the reading is about to end. Then, after a pause to establish eye contact with the assembly, add "The word of the Lord." Maintain eye contact while the assembly makes its response.

Follow the custom of your parish, but it is recommended that a substantial period of silence follow each of the readings. Both your approach and departure from the ambo should be made with reverence, neither too fast nor too slow.

Eye Contact and Eye Expression. Eye contact is the way you connect with those to whom you minister. Look at the assembly during the middle and at the end of every thought or sentence. That means you look down at the beginning, look up in the middle, look down quickly as you approach the end, and then look up again as you finish the sentence. This "down, up, down, up" pattern must not appear mechanical or choppy. Through meaningful "eye expression" you help the listeners enter the story.

Pace. The larger the church, the larger the assembly, and the more complex the text, the slower you must read. It's better to be too slow than too fast. Your listeners have not spent time with this reading as you have. They need time to absorb it—to catch your words and comprehend what they mean.

However, too slow can also be deadly. Besides being boring and making every text sound the same, it erases the reading's natural cadences and makes it impossible to impart the passion of the author.

Blessed are the poor in spirit, for theirs is the kingdom of heaven.

You'll read more naturally if you read ideas rather than words, if you share images rather than sentences. Dialogue imitates real conversation, so it often moves faster than the rest of the passage.

Using the Microphone. Know your public address system. If it echoes, speak even more slowly. If you hear "popping," you're probably standing too close to the microphone. If you are the first reader, go to the ambo before the start of Mass to adjust the height of the microphone. If you are proclaiming the second reading or Gospel, adjust the microphone position when you reach the ambo.

Gestures and Posture. It is hard to imagine a text that requires the use of gestures. They can be distractions and should be used rarely if ever. Whether you like it or not, your body posture speaks. Make sure it says what you want it to. Don't let your face or body contradict the good news you announce. Remember, readers are allowed to smile!

Pronunciation. Pronunciation aids are provided in the margin notes (see the key at the end of this introduction). You may also find it helpful to consult the LTP publication, *Pronunciation Guide to the Lectionary*. Various Internet pronunciation guides allow you to hear the word spoken aloud. Do a simple search such as: "Bible pronunciation guide."

The Responsorial Psalm

Because preparation for proclamation requires familiarity with all the day's texts, this year's *Workbook* includes the psalm. Reflecting on it helps you see the connections among the texts and discern what to stress in your reading. In Sunday worship, the psalm should be sung, and its inclusion here is not meant to encourage its proclamation.

Literary Forms

"In texts that are to be delivered in a loud and clear voice, . . . the tone of voice should correspond to the genre of the text" (GIRM, 38). Identify the literary form of the text you are reading and remember that each form demands a different approach.

Stories. Stories must be "told," not "read." You don't have to memorize them, but you do have to tell them. You are the storyteller. Make the story yours, then share it with your listeners. Know the story and its context—what precedes and follows it. Know the significance of the events for the characters involved. Understand the chronology of the plot. Identify the climax and employ your best energy there. Use the language. Don't throw away any good words.

Settings give context for the action and usually appear at the beginning. Don't rush the description.

Characters must be believable. Understand their motivation: why they feel, act, and speak as they do. Characters are often identified in relationship to another character: "the parents of the one who had gained his sight" (John 9:18). Stress those identifying words. Create the characters as distinct individuals, changing inflection and tone of voice for each one.

Dialogue reveals character. What a character says and how are nearly infallible clues to personality. Besides subtly distinguishing one character from another with your voice, learn to let the speakers listen to and answer one another as in real conversation. Bring the dialogue to life and build suspense in the story, revealing one detail at a time.

Epistles. Epistles are simply letters. Know who wrote the letter and who received it. Many biblical resources explain the circumstances around a particular letter. Whether addressed to an individual or to a community, each epistle is also addressed to the

The LORD's word is true; all his works are trustworthy.

faithful gathered in your church. The tone of each letter may vary, but the delivery is always direct. Letters are like conversations between the writer and the person or community addressed. The purpose or intent of each letter dictates the tone. Very often Paul is the writer. As teacher and spiritual leader, he is motivated by multiple concerns: to instruct, console, encourage, chastise, warn, settle disputes, and more. When reading from one of his letters, be aware of what he's trying to accomplish. Paul is always direct and earnest; even when he exhorts, he never stops loving his spiritual children.

Go slowly in the epistles. It takes time for the assembly to catch the ideas you toss at them. Paul's theology can be tricky, and the style is often a tangle of complex sentences. Many times his mood and purpose change within a single passage. Thinking of Paul's role as teacher, disciplinarian, or "companion on the journey" will help keep you from rushing. Love your listeners and desire their good as much as Paul and the other letter-writers do.

Prophetic Writing. The intensity of emotion and degree of urgency required in proclaiming the writing of the prophets make some readers uncomfortable. But the urgency has to be there.

A pervasive theme in the Old Testament is that we are chosen. With election comes responsibility. Prophets were to remind the Chosen People about those responsibilities—not a popular task. Though not shown in the text, prophetic words are spoken with vocal exclamation points. One must work up courage to tell people what they don't want to hear.

In addition to troubling the comfortable, prophets comforted the troubled. With equal passion, the great seers spoke threat and consolation, indictment and forgiveness. You must do the same for the chosen people you call "parish."

As with the epistles, use resources to learn the situation in which a prophet ministers. Prophets vary; be attentive to style as well as content. Beware of fast transitions, instant climaxes, and the frequent lack of conclusions. Willingly or reluctantly prophets were compelled to speak for God. Don't rob them of their intensity. We need to hear their words.

Poetry. The Old Testament contains much poetry—a marvelously effective and economical form of communication. Because the carefully crafted words and images are so rich and evocative, poetry makes special demands on the proclaimer.

Take time. Poetry is gourmet food, eaten slowly and savored. Go slowly. You need to respond to images by letting yourself "hear" and "feel" as well as "see." Word choice in poetry affects meaning because it affects sound and rhythm.

Sound and meaning go hand in hand in poetry. Even in a language you don't understand, the sound of well-recited poetry should touch your emotions.

Rhythm is what distinguishes poetry from prose. It's what makes words sound like music. Compare these two verses: "In times past, God spoke in partial and various ways to our ancestors through the prophets" (Hebrews 1:1), and "For Zion's sake I will not be silent, for Jerusalem's sake I will not be quiet" (Isaiah 62:1). The first line is smooth and flat, but the second has a rhythmic beat flowing through it that makes it exciting.

Repetition abounds in poetry. Yet instead of feeling redundant, repetitions intensify our emotional experience. In Hebrew poetry, parallelism is a technique used to repeat, balance, and develop ideas in a poem. Consider this first verse of Psalm 19:

The heavens declare the glory of God;
the sky proclaims its builder's craft.

Two parallel images express one idea. Since the two thoughts mean the same thing, this is synonymous parallelism. In antithetic parallelism, opposing images express one idea. Proverbs 15:15 says:

Every day is miserable for the depressed,
but a lighthearted person has a continual feast.

Contrasting ideas make a similar point. Look for these and other forms of parallelism, and help your listeners appreciate these poetic techniques through your proclamation.

Graziano Marcheschi

A New Opportunity

The third edition of *The Roman Missal* encourages ministers of the Word to chant the introduction and conclusion to the readings ("A reading from . . . "; "The word of the Lord."). For those parishes wishing to use these chants, they are demonstrated in audio files that may be accessed either through the QR codes given here (with a smart phone) or through the URL indicated beneath the code. (This url is case sensitive, and be careful to distinguish between the letter l (lower case L) and the numeral 1.)

The first QR code contains the tones for the First Reading in both a male and a female voice.

http://bit.ly/l2mjeG

The second QR code contains the tones for the Second Reading in both a male and a female voice.

http://bit.ly/krwEYy

The third QR code contains the simple tone for the Gospel.

http://bit.ly/iZZvSg

The fourth QR code contains the solemn tone for the Gospel.

http://bit.ly/lwf6Hh

A fuller explanation of this new practice, along with musical notation for the chants, is provided in a downloadable PDF file found at http://www.ltp.org/t-productsupplements.aspx. Once you arrive at this web page, scroll until you find the image of the cover of *Workbook*, click on it, and the PDF file will appear.

Pronunciation Key

bait = bayt	thin = thin
cat = kat	vision = VIZH*n
sang = sang	ship = ship
father = FAH-ther	sir = ser
care = kayr	gloat = gloht
paw = paw	cot = kot
jar = jahr	noise = noyz
easy = EE-zee	poison = POY-z*n
her = her	plow = plow
let = let	although = ahl-THOH
queen = kween	church = cherch
delude = deh-LOOD	fun = fuhn
when = hwen	fur = fer
ice = īs	flute = floot
if = if	foot = foot
finesse = fih-NES	

Recommended Works

Find this list of recommended reading in a downloadable PDF file at http://www.ltp.org/t-product supplements.aspx.

FIRST SUNDAY OF ADVENT

LECTIONARY #1

READING I   Isaiah 2:1–5

A reading from the Book of the Prophet Isaiah

This is what **Isaiah**, son of **Amoz**,
    saw concerning **Judah** and **Jerusalem**.
    In days to come,
the **mountain** of the LORD's **house**
    shall be established as the **highest** mountain
    and **raised** above the **hills**.
All nations shall **stream** toward it;
    many **peoples** shall come and say:
"**Come**, let us **climb** the LORD's mountain,
    to the **house** of the God of **Jacob**,
that he may **instruct** us in his ways,
    and we may **walk** in his paths."
For from **Zion** shall go forth **instruction**,
    and the **word** of the LORD from **Jerusalem**.
He shall **judge** between the nations,
    and impose terms on many **peoples**.
They shall beat their **swords** into **plowshares**
    and their **spears** into **pruning** hooks;
one nation shall not raise the **sword** against another,
    nor shall they train for **war** again.
O house of Jacob, **come**,
    let us **walk** in the **light** of the LORD!

Isaiah = ī-ZAY-uh
Amoz = AY-muhz
Judah = JOO-duh

You're preparing us for a "vision," so your tone must signal the extraordinary nature of what will follow.
Jerusalem = juh-ROO-suh-lem

Start slowly, as if you were seeing the vision unfold before you.

The "peoples" are eager for God's instruction! Indeed, for millennia Israel has been a destination for the nations.

The second line of this couplet restates what was said in the first. It's a poetic devise that calls for greater emphasis on the second line.
Zion = ZĪ-ahn

This classic verse should be read slowly and with much joy and conviction.

Isaiah calls Judah, and each of us, to honor the covenant and walk in the light of God's Law.

READING I   No wonder the culture ignores Advent—it doesn't speak in the soft and gentle tones we would like. Instead, Advent speaks boldly and, one might say, with a forked tongue, for it proclaims prophecies of salvation and peace while simultaneously reminding us of the lateness of the hour and the requirement to remain ever vigilant. The more attractive message is the one that gets attention and inspires greeting cards.

Isaiah begins with a rousing message meant to encourage a people facing possible military destruction. But he also speaks to individual hearts that have lost hope and limp with failing energy. He paints a picture of the future that requires a present response: God's word will surge forth from Jerusalem and transform all it touches, but it will also call each heart to respond by yielding to the call to "walk in the light of the Lord!"

This text could (wrongly!) be read like a diplomatic dispatch explaining in seemingly sedate terms events and consequences that will unfold. But Isaiah is no diplomat. He's a prophet who speaks in poetry. And the poetry exudes joy and determination; it is a rallying cry mustering God's people to hopeful and dramatic action. As proclaimer, take your cue from the last line that sums up the tone of all that precedes it. The prophet wants to ignite the imagination, so use his images boldly, speaking with joy and conviction of the nations that will come to the house of God and of swords and spears turned into farming implements. The last line is critical, not because it is a general's marching order, but because it is a lover's summons to walk on the path of love.

For meditation and context:

RESPONSORIAL PSALM   Psalm 122:1–2, 3–4, 4–5, 6–7, 8–9

R. Let us go rejoicing to the house of the Lord.

I rejoiced because they said to me,
  "We will go up to the house of the LORD."
And now we have set foot
  within your gates, O Jerusalem.

Jerusalem, built as a city
  with compact unity.
To it the tribes go up,
  the tribes of the LORD.

According to the decree for Israel,
  to give thanks to the name of the LORD.
In it are set up judgment seats,
  seats for the house of David.

Pray for the peace of Jerusalem!
  May those who love you prosper!
May peace be within your walls,
  prosperity in your buildings.

Because of my brothers and friends
  I will say, "Peace be within you!"
Because of the house of the LORD, our God,
  I will pray for your good.

TO KEEP IN MIND

Know the purpose of the letter:
It dictates the tone. Often Paul is the writer. As teacher and spiritual leader, he is motivated by multiple concerns: to instruct, console, encourage, chastise, warn, settle disputes, and more. When reading from one of his letters, be aware of what he's trying to accomplish.

READING II   Romans 13:11–14

A reading from the Letter of Saint Paul to the Romans

Brothers and sisters:
You **know** the time;
  it is the **hour** now for you to **awake** from sleep.
For our **salvation** is nearer **now** than when we first **believed**;
  the night is **advanced**, the day is at **hand**.
Let us then throw **off** the works of **darkness**
  and put **on** the armor of **light**;
  let us conduct ourselves **properly** as in the **day**,
  not in **orgies** and **drunkenness**,
  not in **promiscuity** and **lust**,
  not in **rivalry** and **jealousy**.
But put on the Lord Jesus **Christ**,
  and make no **provision** for the **desires** of the **flesh**.

Paul's warm greeting should set the tone for your reading.

The urgency here is motivated by concern for the welfare of your listeners.

Contrast "works of darkness" with "armor of light."

Don't dwell on these items; speak of them as the waste of precious time they are.

promiscuity = proh-mis-KEW-ih-tee

Read with a slower pace here, suggesting the life and death difference Christ makes.

READING II   Why do we still heed Paul's warning that we "know the time" when Jesus insisted that such knowledge was reserved to the Father? Indeed, without predicting a particular day, Paul did, like his Christian contemporaries, anticipate Christ's return within his own lifetime. That these words remained an important part of early Christian teaching even after it became apparent that Christ's return would be delayed indicates the community found meaning beyond the literal in Paul's admonition. For every generation, Paul describes time not found on a clock or calendar but inscribed on the heart of sensible believers who understand that morning follows night, and then night comes again. The words don't speak of one particular moment but of every day, for each day draws us closer to the end—whether that be the day of Christ's return or the day of our individual entry into eternity.

Like a mother rousing a drowsy teenager, Paul urges us to wake up and to *remain* awake while daylight lingers. Living a wakeful life is no easy task, for many objects, good and bad, compete for our attention. But time moves inexorably and that awareness, once grasped, should stir us to action. First Paul lists things on which we should not waste our time, things that keep us in the grip of the darkness of our sleeping state. Move quickly, with regret rather than judgment, through his litany of negative behavior and give greater stress to the things we should do: "put on the armor of light" and "put on the Lord Jesus Christ." The first image is already striking, for we seldom speak of donning armor, but the second is positively arresting: "put on the Lord," says Paul, like a warm garment that shields us from the dangers of the flesh.

This first Sunday of Advent climaxes the eschatological themes that marked the final Sundays of the liturgical year. Subsequent Sundays will gradually shift focus to the Incarnation.

"Noah" is not meant to conjure images of playful animals but of utter destruction.

Noah = NOH-ah

Read briskly until "up to the day" then slow your pace considerably.

The examples of working in the "field" and "grinding" illustrate the parallel between Noah's time and the coming of the Son of Man.

Make eye contact and speak with authority, then continue with great significance on "for you do not."

The clear logic of this example sets up the final exhortation that follows.

This is a grand and authoritative declaration. Sustain your eye contact and speak with deep sincerity.

TO KEEP IN MIND
Slow down: The larger the church, the larger the assembly, and the more complex the text, the slower you must read.

GOSPEL   Matthew 24:37–44

A reading from the holy Gospel according to Matthew

Jesus said to his **disciples**:
"As it was in the days of **Noah**,
    so it will be at the **coming** of the Son of **Man**.
In those days before the **flood**,
    they were **eating** and **drinking**,
    marrying and **giving** in marriage,
    up to the day that Noah **entered** the **ark**.
They did not know until the flood **came** and carried them
      all **away**.
So will it be **also** at the coming of the Son of **Man**.
Two men will be out in the field;
    one will be **taken**, and one will be **left**.
Two **women** will be grinding at the mill;
    one will be taken, and one will be **left**.
Therefore, stay **awake**!
For you do not know on **which** day your Lord will come.
Be sure of **this**: if the **master** of the house
    had known the **hour** of night when the thief was **coming**,
    he would have stayed **awake**
    and **not** let his house be **broken** into.
So too, **you** also must be prepared,
    for at an hour you do not **expect**, the Son of Man will **come**."

GOSPEL   The theme of wakefulness is common in the spiritual life for it seems we humans often sleep, even when standing upright. Spoken near the end of his ministry, and taken from the great apocalyptic discourse delivered in private to his disciples, Jesus's words are meant to stir and unsettle. Chapters 24 and 25 of Matthew paint a vivid picture of the end times and call for constant watchfulness, for the Son of Man will return at a time we least expect.

Clear warnings and timetables won't characterize the Lord's return; rather, as in the days of Noah, most will go about their business as usual, the danger and destruction coming suddenly and unexpectedly upon them. The details in Jesus's analogy are striking, so don't rush his references to "eating and drinking" and "marrying," for it is just such prosaic life-moments that preoccupy us and account for our lack of attentiveness. While Jesus claims no knowledge of when the end will come, his urgency is clear. Whether it's close or far-off, the day of judgment will rush upon us like the flood that swept away Noah's generation. Jesus wants us better prepared than Noah's neighbors who "did not know" until it was too late.

The solemn pronouncement "So will it be . . . " bridges the two halves of the reading. As in the Noah reference, Jesus's details are of everyday events. Contrast the details with the warnings that bookend them and ensure that the message of vigilance for the day that will surely come is well highlighted.

SECOND SUNDAY OF ADVENT

LECTIONARY #4

READING I   Isaiah 11:1–10

Isaiah = ī-ZAY-uh;

A reading from the Book of the Prophet Isaiah

You are sharing a poetic vision of a future world made perfect by God's intervention. Speak with conviction and faith.

Begin slowly and give significance to "On that day."

Speak with the confidence and approval of one introducing a presidential candidate. Remember the couplet structure and the need to give greater stress to each couplet's second line. These are the gifts of the Spirit. Each is different and should sound different.

The same pacing throughout works against the vigor of the reading. Quicken the pace here, then slower again on "He shall strike . . . "

Remember, this is a vision of Eden's peace and serenity being restored on earth.

On that day, a **shoot** shall sprout from the stump of **Jesse**, and from his **roots** a **bud** shall blossom.
    The **spirit** of the LORD shall **rest** upon him:
        a spirit of **wisdom** and of **understanding**,
    a spirit of **counsel** and of **strength**,
        a spirit of **knowledge** and of **fear** of the LORD,
        and his **delight** shall be the fear of the LORD.
    Not by **appearance** shall he judge,
        nor by **hearsay** shall he decide,
    but he shall judge the poor with **justice**,
        and decide **aright** for the land's afflicted.
    He shall **strike** the ruthless with the rod of his mouth,
        and with the **breath** of his **lips** he shall slay the **wicked**.
    Justice shall be the band around his waist,
        and **faithfulness** a belt upon his hips.
    Then the **wolf** shall be a guest of the **lamb**,
        and the **leopard** shall lie down with the **kid**;
    the **calf** and the young **lion** shall browse **together**,
        with a little **child** to guide them.

READING I   The rich and elegant words of Isaiah we read today originally may have expressed the hope that each of Israel's kings would possess the gifts and goodness of an ideal king who would rule justly over people and land. But Israel never had such a king and so this glorious poetry came to express longing for a unique figure, the Messiah who would be Israel's savior and eternal king. Isaiah returns us to Eden with his description of harmony and peace. Wolf and lamb will dine together, natural enemies will be enemies

no more, and even the "child [shall] lay his hand on the adder's lair."

The coming of the Messiah will reverse all of sin's ill effects and restore the innocence and trust of the garden. The Messiah will be a figure imbued with God's spirit who will endow him with intellectual ("spirit of wisdom and of understanding"), practical (spirit of counsel and of strength"), and spiritual gifts ("spirit of knowledge and of fear of the Lord"). This hero will be a descendant of David, the son of Jesse. The "stump of Jesse" is a reference to the current king, Ahaz, whose reliance on political alliances rather

than on God demonstrated his lack of faith and made him an unfit king. One day, Isaiah prophesies, the stump of Jesse will sprout and blossom into a worthy descendant who will restore Israel and usher in the new age of innocence depicted in his vision of tame and peaceful animals.

This great leader will delight both God and people by the way he leads the nation. He will judge justly, not by "appearance" or "hearsay," he will defend the "poor" and "afflicted," and deal with the "wicked" with a stern and decisive hand. Note that the

The cow and the bear shall be **neighbors**,
　　together their young shall rest;
　　the **lion** shall eat hay like the **ox**.
The **baby** shall play by the **cobra's** den,
　　and the child lay his **hand** on the **adder's** lair.
There shall be no **harm** or **ruin** on all my holy mountain;
　　for the earth shall be filled with **knowledge** of the LORD,
　　as **water** covers the **sea**.
On that day, the **root** of Jesse,
　　set up as a **signal** for the nations,
the **Gentiles** shall seek out,
　　for his **dwelling** shall be **glorious**.

This could be a jarring image, so speak it with confidence and tranquility.

These final lines have a more proclamatory tone. Make good eye contact as you deliver them with boldness and joy.

Gentiles = JEN-tils

God's "dwelling" is the hearts of your listeners.

For meditation and context:

RESPONSORIAL PSALM　Psalm 72:1–2, 7–8, 12–13, 17 (7)

R. Justice shall flourish in his time, and fullness of peace forever.

O God, with your judgment endow the king,
　　and with your justice, the king's son;
he shall govern your people with justice
　　and your afflicted ones with judgment.

Justice shall flower in his days,
　　and profound peace, till the moon be
　　　no more.
May he rule from sea to sea,
　　and from the River to the ends of the earth.

For he shall rescue the poor when he
　　cries out,
　　and the afflicted when he has no one
　　　to help him.
He shall have pity for the lowly and the poor;
　　the lives of the poor he shall save.

May his name be blessed forever;
　　as long as the sun his name shall remain.
In him shall all the tribes of the earth
　　be blessed;
　　all the nations shall proclaim
　　　his happiness.

TO KEEP IN MIND

Prophets: In addition to troubling the comfortable, prophets comforted the troubled. With equal passion, the great seers spoke threat and consolation, indictment and forgiveness. You must do the same for the chosen people you call "parish."

---

text unfolds in a series of couplets, pairs of lines that state the same idea twice using slightly different images in each line. This construct typically calls for slightly greater energy and emphasis falling on the second line. Creating a rhythm of softer and greater emphasis on alternating lines will sustain interest and vitality in this long reading.

The rule of the messiah will inaugurate the bliss of Eden in the latter part of the text, so a more robust delivery in the first half should yield to a milder, more tender quality in the second half. The reading ends

with the declaration that the glory that descends upon Israel will emanate throughout the world and draw even the Gentile nations to God's holy mountain.

READING II　In this reading Paul is addressing tensions between Jewish and Gentile Christians. Struggles between groups within a community are not unknown to us today either. That is why hope is such an important theme in the Christian life. Isaiah offered hope with his grand vision of a world restored to God's rule and justice. Paul tells

us that "whatever was written previously," that is, all the words of Scripture, offers hope to anyone who embraces God's word. Hope is what sustains us in the face of mounting evidence that sin more than grace abounds. World and local conflicts challenge our faith. But when conflict invades the community of God, what little hope we have left can vanish.

Paul, for whom grace always abounds the more, won't let his spiritual children wallow in such hopelessness. He begins

READING II   Romans 15:4–9

A reading from the Letter of Saint Paul to the Romans

Brothers and sisters:
Whatever was written **previously** was written for our **instruction**,
    that by **endurance** and by the encouragement of the **Scriptures**
    we might have **hope**.
May the **God** of endurance and encouragement
    grant you to think in **harmony** with one another,
    in **keeping** with Christ **Jesus**,
    that with one **accord** you may with one **voice**
    glorify the God and Father of our Lord Jesus **Christ**.

Welcome one another, then, as Christ welcomed **you**,
    for the glory of **God**.
For I say that Christ became a minister of the **circumcised**
    to show God's **truthfulness**,
    to **confirm** the promises of the patriarchs,
    but so that the **Gentiles** might glorify God for his **mercy**.
As it is **written**:
    *Therefore, I will **praise** you among the **Gentiles***
    *and sing praises to your **name**.*

GOSPEL   Matthew 3:1–12

A reading from the holy Gospel according to Matthew

John the **Baptist** appeared, **preaching** in the desert of Judea
    and saying, "**Repent**, for the kingdom of **heaven** is at **hand**!"
It was of **him** that the prophet Isaiah had spoken when he said:
    *A voice of one **crying** out in the desert,*
    ***Prepare** the way of the Lord,*
    *make **straight** his paths.*

Establish eye contact.

Begin slowly, with a carefully reasoned argument.

Make it clear that these words are an earnest prayer for unity. Let it be your prayer as well.

What Christ did for you, you must now do for each other.

Review the commentary to recall Paul's intent that is somewhat hidden in this obscure wording.

patriarchs = PAY-tree-ahrks

Gentiles = JEN-tils

Make your reading of the ending a joyful act of praise!

The opening lines are spoken by three "voices": the narrator's, Isaiah's, and John's.

Judea = joo-DEE-uh; joo-DAY-uh

John's tone is weighty and intense.

Quoting of Isaiah calls for a shift in tone.

---

here with a reasoned, lawyer-like argument, his tone earnest but subdued, insisting that Scripture is reliable and very fertile ground for hope. But then Paul quickly assumes another role, that of pastor. Addressing the Jewish and Gentile believers, he *prays* that God will bless them with "harmony" in their life together. He follows the prayer with another piece of reasoning: welcome each other as Christ welcomed you. The contrast he draws between the "circumcised" and "Gentiles" is a bit obscure. He is asserting that God has different motives for the love poured out on

each group. Jesus's ministry to the Jews fulfilled God's promises to the patriarchs, but God owed nothing to the Gentiles. God's outreach to them, therefore, is a sign of great "mercy."

The text ends rejoicing over the Lord's name being praised "among the Gentiles." Praise is always loudest when we speak it together!

GOSPEL   As we move closer to the Incarnation we encounter the stark, stern, and riveting figure of John the Baptist. Not until Advent's fourth week will we hear of angel and virgin. This week

and next John holds the stage, and aptly so because he reminds us bluntly that this season is not about preparing for the babe in the manger but for the Christ who was born amid livestock and urine, who lived among tax collectors and prostitutes, and who died shamefully on a Cross before he rose and ascended to the Father. John's presence reminds us that we are preparing for the coming of Jesus's whole life and ministry, not just the incarnational moment in the humble stall.

John's entrance is sudden, his voice shooting forth in the darkness before our

Take time with this interesting description. John is a desert dweller free of social niceties.

Share this information with some amazement and pleasure.
Jerusalem = juh-ROO-suh-lem
Judea = joo-DEE-uh; joo-DAY-uh
Pharisees = FAYR-uh-seez

Let your tone suggest that they approached without genuine repentance.
Sadducees = SAD-yoo-seez

John's condemnation is strong, sudden, and unexpected.

You might mimic the Pharisees' defensive voices.

Farming lore recommends striking the taproot of an unproductive tree with an ax to shock it back to life.

There is rising energy in these lines as John contrasts himself with Jesus.

Contrast the humility of the previous line with the bold assertion here.

There is contrast in these final lines between comfort and challenge.

John wore clothing made of **camel's** hair
    and had a leather **belt** around his waist.
His food was **locusts** and wild **honey**.
At that time **Jerusalem**, **all** Judea,
    and the whole region around the **Jordan**
    were going **out** to him
    and were being **baptized** by him in the Jordan **River**
    as they acknowledged their **sins**.

When he saw many of the **Pharisees** and **Sadducees**
    coming to his **baptism**, he said to them, "You brood of **vipers**!
Who **warned** you to flee from the coming wrath?
Produce good **fruit** as **evidence** of your repentance.
And do not **presume** to say to yourselves,
    'We have **Abraham** as our father.'
For I **tell** you,
    God can raise up children to Abraham from these **stones**.
Even now the **ax** lies at the **root** of the trees.
Therefore every tree that does not bear **good** fruit
    will be **cut** down and thrown into the **fire**.
I am baptizing you with **water**, for **repentance**,
    but the one who is coming **after** me is **mightier** than I.
I am not worthy to carry his **sandals**.
He will baptize you with the Holy **Spirit** and **fire**.
His **winnowing** fan is in his **hand**.
He will **clear** his threshing floor
    and gather his **wheat** into his **barn**,
    but the **chaff** he will **burn** with unquenchable **fire**."

> **TO KEEP IN MIND**
> **Names** of characters are often the first word of a reading. Stress names so listeners don't miss who the subject is.

eyes can perceive him. The words are bold and uncompromising: "Repent . . . the kingdom of heaven is at hand." Immediately his ministry is identified with the prophecy of Isaiah, a daring assertion especially for one so unconventional. But in asserting John's continuity with the old Law, Matthew establishes the legitimacy of Jesus. Finally we "see" this desert dweller who is clothed in animal skins and consumes an austere desert diet.

Somehow, John's call for repentance has garnered a large response, and the whole region was going out to see him. But

John does not let his celebrity interfere with his mission. He does not compromise when speaking with hypocrites—even powerful hypocrites—whose actions belie their sincerity. In strong language he challenges them to produce "good fruit" to abandon any claim to righteousness because of their descent from Abraham. It's what's in their hearts not their bloodline that will save them from being felled like a rotten tree.

John speaks of the one who will come after him not only as "mightier" but as better able to separate true wheat from chaff. He will cleanse not with water, as John

does, but with the fire of the Spirit and with his "winnowing fan" he will separate the good and the useless and cast the latter into "unquenchable fire." Embedded in John's words is a call to conversion and to embrace the Lord whose ministry John's merely anticipates. Don't compromise the strength of John's tone or his stark judgment. Without genuine repentance we will lack the gravitas of wheat and be blown away with the chaff.

THE IMMACULATE CONCEPTION OF THE BLESSED VIRGIN MARY

LECTIONARY #689

Genesis = JEN-uh-sis

The story is economically told, so read slowly and don't waste any of the words. God's voice is non-threatening.

Adam is uncomfortable making this admission.

"He" = God. God already knows the answer. The purpose is to make Adam confront his choice.

Adam swallows hard before responding. He can feel almost justified in saying "so I ate it," if he has adequately blamed "the woman."

Take a moment for it all to "sink in" before God questions Eve. Her voice can be more confrontational than Adam's. She shows more awareness of her responsibility.

READING I   Genesis 3:9–15, 20

A reading from the Book of Genesis

After the man, **Adam**, had **eaten** of the tree,
  the LORD God **called** to the man and asked him,
    "Where **are** you?"
He answered, "I **heard** you in the garden;
  but I was **afraid**, because I was **naked**,
  so I **hid** myself."
Then he asked, "Who **told** you that you were naked?
You have **eaten**, then,
  from the tree of which I had **forbidden** you to eat!"
The man replied, "The **woman** whom you put here with me—
  she **gave** me fruit from the tree, and so I **ate** it."
The LORD God then asked the **woman**,
  "Why did you **do** such a thing?"
The woman **answered**, "The serpent **tricked** me into it, so I **ate** it."

READING I   On the day that celebrates the solution, we read first about the problem. Human choice brought sin into the world with all its consequences. Here, the divine finger points in the direction of the eventual remedy: "the woman" whose offspring will strike at the tempter's "head" while the tempter can only "strike at his heel."

Understanding why we proclaim this text helps you proclaim the meaning embedded in its words. Sin's greatest consequence is its power to alienate people from themselves, each other, and God. The innocence and harmony of the garden have been broken. The man is suddenly aware of his nakedness. In his shame, he points a finger at the woman, but he does it defensively, in accusation. The woman fares no

better, for rather than accept her responsibility, she shifts blame to the serpent that "tricked" her

Christian faith tells us Christ, the new Adam, through perfect obedience to the will of God, restored the relationship that was broken in the garden. In this economy, Mary, his mother, becomes the new Eve

God's anger is fully vented here. Brisk pacing at the start, then slower and more significantly at "I will put enmity . . . "

Slowly. Contrast the snake's *futile* strikes at "his heel" with the offspring's *damaging* blows to the serpent's "head."

Not a throwaway line nor an anticlimax, but a way to draw each of us into the drama.

For meditation and context:

Then the LORD God said to the **serpent**:
"Because you have **done** this, you shall be **banned**
    from all the **animals**
    and from all the wild **creatures**;
on your **belly** shall you crawl,
    and **dirt** shall you eat
    all the **days** of your **life**.
I will put **enmity** between you and the woman,
    and between **your** offspring and **hers**;
he will strike at your **head**,
    while **you** strike at his **heel**."

The man called his wife **Eve**,
    because she became the **mother** of all the **living**.

RESPONSORIAL PSALM   Psalm 98:1, 2–3ab, 3cd–4 (1a)

R. **Sing to the Lord a new song, for he has done marvelous deeds.**

Sing to the LORD a new song,
    for he has done wondrous deeds;
His right hand has won victory for him,
    his holy arm.

The LORD has made his salvation known:
    in the sight of the nations he has revealed
    his justice.
He has remembered his kindness and his
    faithfulness
    toward the house of Israel.

All the ends of the earth have seen
    the salvation by our God.
Sing joyfully to the LORD, all you lands;
    break into song; sing praise.

TO KEEP IN MIND
Importance of the Narrator:
The narrator is often the pivotal role of a passage. Timbre, pitch, rate, and energy can make the same words convey very different moods or meaning. Sometimes the narrator is objective, but often the narrator has great interest in the events and characters of a story.

---

who, because she was sinless from conception, also surrendered herself fully to the divine will. But God's words that the tempter will strike the heel of the woman's offspring suggest that righting the wrongs of our original parents will come at a price.

Tell the story with an awareness of the cosmic consequences involved. God's voice is not that of a parent who finds a broken dish and scattered candy on the floor. From the first uttering of the word "naked," God knows what's occurred. The dialogue reveals the minds of the man and woman; it is not a revelation of God's gradual realization of what's occurred. Use God's question "Who told you . . . ?" to coax the man into admission of what he's done. The import of God's question to Eve is, *"How could you have done such a thing?"* Here

God's anger is directed not at the humans but at the serpent. The consequences will be both immediate ("on your belly shall you crawl") and long term "he will strike at your head." End the reading on a melancholic note that addresses each of us—we who have inherited our first parents' mistake.

Ephesians = ee-FEE-zhuhnz

Establish eye contact and greet the assembly with reverence and love.

Your energy must be immediate; don't work up to exuberant praise, start with it!

"Chose" and "destined" are not familiar words to Catholic ears. Give them adequate stress.

"In love" describes God's motivation for choosing us. Don't rush past it.

Since this paragraph basically reiterates the content of the first, increase your intensity and slow your delivery to ensure everyone listening feels the words are meant for them.

Do what you say: praise God's glory!

READING II   Ephesians 1:3–6, 11–12

A reading from the Letter of Saint Paul to the Ephesians

Brothers and sisters:
Blessed be the **God** and **Father** of our Lord Jesus **Christ**,
    who has **blessed** us in Christ
    with every spiritual **blessing** in the heavens,
        as he **chose** us in him, before the **foundation** of the world,
        to be **holy** and without **blemish** before him.
In **love** he destined us for **adoption** to himself through
        Jesus **Christ**,
    in accord with the favor of his **will**,
    for the praise of the **glory** of his **grace**
    that he granted us in the **beloved**.

In him we were also **chosen**,
    destined in accord with the purpose of the **One**
    who **accomplishes** all things according to the intention
        of his **will**,
    so that we might exist for the **praise** of his **glory**,
    we who first **hoped** in **Christ**.

TO KEEP IN MIND
Openings: First, make eye contact with the assembly and announce, from memory, "A (pronounced "uh," not "ay") reading from . . ." Then pause (three full beats!) before starting the reading.

READING II A gratitude-filled hymn of blessing opens this text. God's wonderful deeds are reason for the gratefulness that explodes in the rhythmic opening sentence. We focus on beginnings, but unlike the Genesis reading, we find original blessing instead of original sin. God's loving initiative on our behalf is the theme throughout. Muster the courage to proclaim

that truth even in the face of headlines heralding death, destruction, or despair. No matter what, the Christian heart always asks, "How can I keep from singing?"

The repeated use of the expression "in Christ" highlights our oneness under Christ's leadership. Such an expression can be too easily rushed. "In Christ" means because of Christ, through Christ, as a part of Christ. So express its full weight when you speak the phrase or the words will lack impact.

Mary, the focus of this solemnity, was selected from all time to be the sinless vehicle of God's will. So give special emphasis to words and phrases like "chose," "before the foundation of the world," "holy and without blemish," and "destined." Reading I demonstrated how in the beginning human will and willfulness thwarted God's plan. Here we recognize that even *before* the "beginning" there already existed the One who would make things right again.

GOSPEL   Luke 1:26–38

A *divine* messenger comes to a *nowhere* town to find a *virgin* marrying into the *royal* house. A lot to say in one sentence, and all of it is important! Careful attention to pacing and pauses is essential.

A reading from the holy Gospel according to Luke

The angel **Gabriel** was sent from **God**
　　to a town of Galilee called **Nazareth**,
　　to a **virgin** betrothed to a man named **Joseph**,
　　of the house of **David**,
　　and the virgin's name was **Mary**.
And coming to her, he said,
　　"**Hail**, full of **grace**! The **Lord** is with you."
But she was greatly **troubled** at what was said
　　and **pondered** what sort of greeting this might be.

Mary's distress should be heard in the *narration* that speaks of it.

Then the angel said to her,
　　"Do not be **afraid**, Mary,
　　for you have found **favor** with God.

The angel's voice is energetic and authoritative without being melodramatic. Don't rush "Do not be afraid."

Behold, you will **conceive** in your womb and bear a **son**,
　　and you shall name him **Jesus**.
He will be **great** and will be called **Son** of the Most **High**,

Lift out the "royal" language ("throne, rule, house of Jacob, kingdom" that accentuates the greatness of the "son."

　　and the **Lord** God will give him the throne of **David** his **father**,
　　and he will **rule** over the house of Jacob **forever**,
　　and of his **Kingdom** there will be no **end**."

The second paragraph reprises the first, and whenever we encounter repetition we place greater emphasis on the second iteration. Your slow and measured reading of these lines can remind your listeners that when we speak of those chosen we mean not only Mary and her Son, but also each of us who has accepted Christ and honors Mary. Not only was she the "first [who] hoped in Christ," but she modeled true discipleship and now teaches us to be Church.

GOSPEL It's likely this Gospel that accounts for the generations-old assumption that the Immaculate Conception refers to Mary's virginal conception of Jesus rather than her own unique conception without the mark of Original Sin. Another truth that's often lost is that whenever the Church speaks of Mary she also speaks of Christ. It is impossible to look at Mary and not see her Son, for she is but a lens that narrows our focus onto that which truly matters: the primacy of Christ in all things and for all time.

In early Advent, as we approach the Solemnity of the Incarnation we also dwell on Mary's singular status. It's fitting that we do, for without Mary's *fiat* (her agreement) God's plan might not have unfolded. The angel's greeting creates a crisis for Mary: "Hail, full of grace!" the angel calls out, "the Lord is with you." In a culture that feared that direct encounter with God could bring death, the messenger's strange words could evoke nothing less than confusion and shock. Mary's whole life had been lived in accordance with God's will, yet

Remember, Mary is asking "how" not "if" it will happen.

This is a solemn, yet joyful, proclamation.

News of Elizabeth is meant to reassure; speak with confidence and joy.

Even if spoken softly, Mary's words convey strength and amazing boldness.

Pause, and then announce the angel's departure.

But **Mary** said to the angel,
    "**How** can this be,
    since I have no **relations** with a man?"
And the **angel** said to her in reply,
    "The Holy **Spirit** will come upon you,
    and the power of the Most **High** will overshadow you.
Therefore the **child** to be born
    will be called **holy**, the Son of **God**.
And behold, **Elizabeth**, your **relative**,
    has **also** conceived a son in her old **age**,
    and this is the **sixth** month for her who was called **barren**;
    for **nothing** will be impossible for **God**."
Mary said, "**Behold**, I am the **handmaid** of the Lord.
May it be **done** to me according to your **word**."
Then the angel **departed** from her.

TO KEEP IN MIND

Endings: Your inflection of the last line of the reading should always signal that the reading is about to end. Then pause (three beats!) and make eye contact before announcing (from memory) "The word [Gospel] of the Lord." Always pronounce "the" as "thuh" except before words beginning with a vowel.

---

even for one so singularly holy, these words set off shockwaves.

The unique moment in human history we call Jesus began in Mary's response to the angel's question. Without exaggeration, the fate of the world hung in the balance. And it was no lance-wielding warrior or wise king into whose hands human destiny was placed. It rested in the hands of a humble girl from a nowhere town whose betrothal to a son of the house of David would likely be jeopardized if she answered "yes." The angel announces, explains, and then tries to reassure the simple maiden. But the wave

of words that washes over Mary leaves her "greatly troubled" and pondering.

The angel tells Mary, "Do not be afraid," a formula that often prefaces announcements of divine intervention. But it's hard to imagine that those words alone set Mary's heart at rest. Peace will come soon enough, but not till Mary asks the angel *how* all this will come to pass. The angel's response is filled with royal, dynastic imagery that reinforces the initial assertion of the child's great dignity. Mary hears a comfort in the explanation that likely would not have sufficed for the rest of us.

If it seems puzzling that Mary's question evoked so different a response from the angel than did Zechariah's similar question, it might be that she asked "how" instead of "if." Mary knows God can do anything; what she wants to know is *how* God will turn a virgin into a mother. Gabriel reassures by asserting God's, not Mary's, role in the conception, and offers Elizabeth's pregnancy as a pledge that God can accomplish whatever he promises.

THIRD SUNDAY OF ADVENT

LECTIONARY #7

READING I   Isaiah 35:1–6a, 10

A reading from the Book of the Prophet Isaiah

The **desert** and the **parched** land will **exult**;
  the **steppe** will **rejoice** and **bloom**.
They will bloom with abundant **flowers**,
  and **rejoice** with joyful **song**.
The glory of **Lebanon** will be given to them,
  the splendor of **Carmel** and **Sharon**;
they will see the **glory** of the LORD,
  the **splendor** of our God.
Strengthen the hands that are **feeble**,
  make **firm** the knees that are **weak**,
say to those whose hearts are **frightened**:
  Be **strong**, **fear** not!
Here is your **God**,
  he comes with **vindication**;
with divine **recompense**
  he comes to **save** you.
Then will the eyes of the **blind** be **opened**,
  the ears of the **deaf** be **cleared**;
then will the lame **leap** like a stag,
  then the tongue of the **mute** will **sing**.

Isaiah = ī-ZAY-uh

Be aware of the couplet (two-line) structure of this text. Using different words, each couplet states the same idea twice. Your energy rises on the second line.

"Exult" and "rejoice" set the tone for the reading.

Don't stress "bloom" and "rejoice" the second time they occur since the repetition is just an "echo" of the first use of each word.

Lebanon = LEB-uh-nuhn

Carmel = KAHR-m*l

The *sound* of rejoicing in these lines is more important than the individual words.

Sharon = SHAYR-uhn

The tone shifts at "Strengthen the hands." Don't shy from the strong imperatives.

Imagine someone stranded, on the verge of death and you announce to them that help is on the way!

Pause before starting this final section, and then speak with conviction and strength. You are announcing miracles, not next week's "to-do" list.

READING I   In times of trial and distress, in every hardship, how we long for words like Isaiah's, encouraging us not to surrender and promising that hope will dawn like the new day. This marvelous poetry was addressed to a people cut down and in exile, served the bitter fare of conquest and the destruction of every one of their major institutions—Temple, monarchy, nation. But these words are also spoken to all who long for peace—world or domestic, for justice—global or personal, for life—the kind that rises out of loss and defeat. Because you are describing a world hoped for but not yet realized, and because you want us to believe as strongly as Isaiah, speak with a hope born of your own experiences of struggle and failure.

On this Gaudete Sunday (Gaudete means "Rejoice!"), as we draw nearer to Christmas, Isaiah announces the arrival of our God, and all of nature responds with joy and transformation. Using vivid words like "rejoice," splendor" and "glory" the reading builds to that announcement with Isaiah directing you how to proclaim: "Be strong, fear not!" Regrettably, many lectors will not do justice to the poetry of the first eight lines. Don't be one of them. Imagine lovers describing for each other what their future together will be and paint this vision with that kind of conviction.

Zion = Zī-ahn

Use ritardando (gradually slowing your delivery) on this last couplet and be as convinced as you are of your name.

For meditation and context:

TO KEEP IN MIND
Echoes: Some words echo words that went before. For example, "You shall be a glorious *crown* . . . a royal *diadem*" (Isaiah 62:3). Here "diadem" echoes "crown" so it needs no stress. In such cases, emphasize the new *idea*: "royal."

Short readings require slower delivery. Speak with authority and savor the word "precious."

Think about those who till the soil and plant. Have clear images in your mind as you speak of the patient farmer.

This line is an imperative, but you mustn't sound impatient as you deliver it.

Those whom the LORD has ransomed will **return**
    and enter Zion **singing**,
        crowned with everlasting **joy**;
they will meet with joy and **gladness**,
    sorrow and **mourning** will **flee**.

RESPONSORIAL PSALM   Psalm 146:6–7, 8–9, 9–10 (Isaiah 35:4)

R. Lord, come and save us.
or
R. Alleluia.

The LORD God keeps faith forever,
    secures justice for the oppressed,
    gives food to the hungry.
The LORD sets captives free.

The LORD gives sight to the blind;
    the LORD raises up those who were
        bowed down.
The LORD loves the just;
    the LORD protects strangers.

The fatherless and the widow he sustains,
    but the way of the wicked he thwarts.
The LORD shall reign forever;
    your God, O Zion, through all generations.

READING II   James 5:7–10

A reading from the Letter of Saint James

Be **patient**, brothers and sisters,
    until the **coming** of the Lord.
See how the farmer **waits** for the precious fruit of the earth,
    being **patient** with it
        until it receives the **early** and the **late** rains.
You **too** must be patient.
Make your hearts **firm**,
    because the coming of the Lord is at **hand**.

The next eight lines ring with imperatives. God's voice orders the people to reach out to all in need. That very effort makes God present among us, for only with our voices can God speak compassion ("fear not") and only with our hands can he come to save.

The final lines speak of the miracles that happen when we allow God to work through us: "eyes" will be "opened" and the "lame" will "leap." Your voice must quicken people's hearts with this good news so they will recognize this as the Sunday of rejoicing.

READING II James makes his only appearance in this year's Sunday readings to sound a note of patience. Whether or not it's still considered a virtue, our get-it-now culture seems to have little use for this attribute. Reading I spoke of future realities as if they were already present. James tempers that enthusiasm with a fourfold call for patience. He uses a lovely and apt image of the patient farmer waiting for spring. Even in darkest winter the seasoned farmer knows that spring *will* come. He knows the signs and doesn't get impatient because he understands he's powerless to hasten its arrival. So he waits in peace and resignation.

James's audience anticipated the Second Coming of Christ during its lifetime. The delay caused a crisis of faith for some, so James urges them to imitate the farmer

Speak like an elder advising his or her family members with confident authority.

Make eye contact and gradually slow your delivery as you approach the end of the sentence. Imagine modern-day prophets whose endurance and courage you admire.

Do not **complain**, brothers and sisters, about one another,
　　that you may not be **judged**.
Behold, the Judge is standing before the **gates**.
Take as an **example** of hardship and patience, brothers and sisters,
　　the **prophets** who **spoke** in the name of the **Lord**.

GOSPEL   Matthew 11:2–11

A reading from the holy Gospel according to Matthew

The detail of John's imprisonment is critical. Don't rush past it.

There might be some hesitancy or embarrassment for the disciples at having to ask this question.

Jesus's reply is as simple and humble as the disciples' question. Yet he wants to remove all their doubts, so speak with authority.

This is a listing of God's dramatic works, not the scores of last Sunday's games.

When John the **Baptist** heard in **prison** of the works of the **Christ**,
　　he sent his **disciples** to Jesus with this **question**,
　　　"Are you the one who is to **come**,
　　　or should we look for **another**?"
Jesus said to them in reply,
　　"**Go** and **tell** John what you **hear** and **see**:
　　the **blind** regain their **sight**,
　　the lame **walk**,
　　lepers are **cleansed**,
　　the deaf **hear**,
　　the dead are **raised**,
　　and the **poor** have the good news **proclaimed** to them.
And blessed is the one who takes no **offense** at me."

A major shift occurs here. Jesus prepares to confront the crowd.

Imagine defending someone in the parish who has been publicly wronged and shamed.

As they were **going** off,
　　Jesus began to speak to the crowds about **John**,
　　　"What did you go out to the desert to **see**?
A **reed** swayed by the wind?
Then **what** did you go out to see?
Someone dressed in fine **clothing**?
Those who **wear** fine clothing are in royal **palaces**.

---

and rest in the firm conviction that Jesus's return is assured. Waiting causes tension and often friction as well. So James warns his readers to guard against the danger of complaining about and judging each other. The prophets who, though granted visions of the coming Messiah, had to wait in patience and through much hardship for the fulfillment of their prophecies serve as models for Christian patience. Their faith and endurance instructs all of us who wait for what we know will surely come.

GOSPEL When it comes to things of God, it never hurts to get a second opinion. John the Baptist, who in last week's Gospel spoke with such authority about the one who is to come, sends emissaries to Jesus to inquire if he is "the one." John is imprisoned and lacks first-hand experience of his cousin's ministry. Jesus responds to John's question with the only evidence available. John knows Isaiah and so Jesus quotes from today's Isaiah portion: "the blind regain their sight, the lame walk . . . " and the poor hear the Good News. If these signs are the retinue of the Messiah, then surely the Messiah has come. Apparently satisfied, John's disciples depart.

　　The second half of this Gospel is more remarkable than the first. Nowhere else does Jesus speak of anyone as highly as he does of John. Addressing the crowds, Jesus's voice is filled with indignation and disappointment. Express that especially on

It is bold for Jesus to identify John with Malachi's prophecy (Malachi 3:1). Make it a strong declaration.

Speak with solemnity about John. Then surprise your listeners with Jesus's final declaration.

Then **why** did you go out? To see a **prophet**?
Yes, I tell you, and **more** than a prophet.
This is the one about whom it is **written**:
    Behold, *I am sending my* **messenger** *ahead of you;*
        he will prepare your **way** *before you.*
Amen, I say to you,
    among those born of **women**
        there has been **none** greater than John the **Baptist**;
        yet the **least** in the kingdom of **heaven** is **greater** than he."

TO KEEP IN MIND
Tell the story: The reading of Scripture is a storytelling moment. Storytellers are people of imagination. They help us to see, hear, feel, and smell the elements of the story because they themselves experience these sensory aspects of a story.

THE 4 STEPS OF *LECTIO DIVINA* OR PRAYERFUL READING

1. *Lectio:* Read a Scripture passage aloud slowly. Notice what phrase captures your attention and be attentive to its meaning. Silent pause.

2. *Meditatio:* Read the passage aloud slowly again, reflecting on the passage, allowing God to speak to you through it. Silent pause.

3. *Oratio:* Read it aloud slowly a third time, allowing it to be your prayer or response to God's gift of insight to you. Silent pause.

4. *Contemplatio:* Read it aloud slowly a fourth time, now resting in God's word.

---

the repeated question: "*What* did you go out . . . to see? . . . What *did* you go out to see?" These questions and the third ("Then *why* did you go out?") voice Jesus's frustration. The questions are rhetorical, so you needn't pause after asking each one. Instead, focus on delivering Jesus's vigorous reply to his own questions.

The love and admiration Jesus had for his cousin is profound. Don't fail to convey it. Increase your intensity steadily from "and more than a prophet" through "John the Baptist." Announce the remarkable uniqueness of John, then pause, look right at the congregation, and slowly proclaim the even more remarkable status freely given to each of us who follows the Lord whom John so anxiously sought.

FOURTH SUNDAY OF ADVENT

LECTIONARY #10

Isaiah = ī-ZAY-uh;

Speak the opening sentence as Isaiah would have delivered it to Ahaz, with confidence and authority.

Ahaz = AY-haz

The hyperbole is saying, ask for whatever you want!

Ahaz is hiding his true motives, making his tone all the more righteous.

Frustration and irritation are clearly evident in Isaiah's question.

Let Isaiah's pronouncement ring with confident hope and authority.

Speak the name "Emmanuel" with great tenderness.

Emmanuel = ee-MAN-y<u>oo</u>-el

For meditation and context:

READING I   Isaiah 7:10–14

A reading from the Book of the Prophet Isaiah

The LORD spoke to **Ahaz**, saying:
Ask for a **sign** from the LORD, your God;
　　let it be **deep** as the netherworld, or **high** as the sky!
But Ahaz answered,
　　"I will **not** ask! I will not **tempt** the LORD!"
Then **Isaiah** said:
　　Listen, O house of David!
Is it not **enough** for you to weary **people**,
　　must you also weary my **God**?
Therefore the Lord **himself** will **give** you this sign:
　　the **virgin** shall **conceive**, and bear a **son**,
　　and shall name him **Emmanuel**.

RESPONSORIAL PSALM   Psalm 24:1–2, 3–4, 5–6 (7c, 10b)

R. Let the Lord enter; he is king of glory.

The LORD's are the earth and its fullness;
　　the world and those who dwell in it.
For he founded it upon the seas
　　and established it upon the rivers.

Who can ascend the mountain of the LORD?
　　or who may stand in his holy place?
One whose hands are sinless, whose heart
　　is clean,
　　who desires not what is vain.

He shall receive a blessing from the LORD,
　　a reward from God his savior.
Such is the race that seeks for him,
　　that seeks the face of the God of Jacob.

READING I The text of this passage is easy to proclaim. The subtext is another matter. Short readings always require a slower pace, but here you have another reason to go slowly: the rapid mood and character shifts you must make. Faced with political and military disaster, Ahaz is prepared to join forces with a hated enemy. Isaiah comes to say (in other words), "Trust in God rather than the strength of your Assyrian ally; if you want proof of God's fidelity, just ask for a sign. Go ahead. No matter how spectacular, God will give you what you ask."

Ahaz demurs, hiding behind false humility. "Oh no," he protests, "I can't ask the great God to bother with giving me a sign!" He's lying. Let your voice reveal his lack of faith. Ahaz would rather put his trust in human military resources than in divine power. No wonder God is fed up! Speaking for the Lord, Isaiah (in other words) says, "Listen, you wear down everybody with your lack of faith; must you also wear down my God? Whether you want it or not, God *will* give you a sign."

Some scholars believe that Ahaz was hearing in Isaiah's words a prophecy of the birth of Ahaz's own son, Hezekiah, who would become a great king of Judah. But we Christians hear in them an announcement of what will be the ultimate sign of God's faithfulness: a "son" born (in a stable) of a "virgin" (Mary) who will be called "Emmanuel." Read Isaiah's words with a confidence that says: This sign will be enough to persuade you, finally, to put all your trust in God's love for you."

Paul's style is especially challenging today. Read slowly, remembering the multiple points he makes with his string of thought units. Keep the tone upbeat.

You can keep the "balls in the air" if you vary your pacing and renew energy when you come to a new thought. Maintaining a steady, unvaried rhythm as if everything were equally important will be deadly. Note: + = more important and slower; - = less important and faster: "+The gospel about his Son -descended from David -according to the flesh, +but established as Son of God . . . " Paul asserts his calling as an Apostle.

Make sure your assembly hears that they, too, are called.

This is a prayer and a verbal embrace.

TO KEEP IN MIND
Units of Thought: Running too many words together blurs meaning and fails to distinguish ideas. Punctuation does not always indicate clearly what words to group together or where to pause. Identify *units of thought* and use your voice to distinguish one from another.

READING II Romans 1:1–7

A reading from the Letter of Saint Paul to the Romans

Paul, a slave of Christ **Jesus**,
 called to be an **apostle** and **set** apart for the gospel of God,
 which he promised previously through his **prophets** in the
  holy **Scriptures**,
the gospel about his **Son**, descended from **David** according
  to the **flesh**,
 but established as Son of God in **power**
 according to the Spirit of holiness
 through resurrection from the dead, Jesus **Christ** our **Lord**.
Through **him** we have received the grace of **apostleship**,
 to bring about the obedience of **faith**,
 for the sake of his **name**, among all the **Gentiles**,
 among whom are **you** also, who are called to **belong**
  to Jesus Christ;
 to all the beloved of God in **Rome**, called to be **holy**.
Grace to you and **peace** from God our **Father**
 and the **Lord** Jesus **Christ**.

 This is the very beginning of Paul's Letter to the Romans and, as such, it is all salutation. But Paul is rarely satisfied with doing only one thing at a time. He might simply have said: "Greetings from Paul to all in Rome." But like a juggler floating five balls in the air and one on his head, he inserts a long parenthetical statement that attempts to tell us a) he is an Apostle, b) chosen to preach the Gospel, c) which was announced by the prophets, d) and recorded in Scripture; e) this Gospel concerns Jesus, f) a descendant of David, g) who was "established as"

Son of God, h) by being raised from the dead; i) Jesus made Paul an Apostle to the Gentiles, j) which, by the way, includes all of us—and all this while saying "Hello!" Luckily there is one period in the midst of all that, but obviously you'll need to read slowly to avoid running his thoughts together.

In the second sentence Paul refers to his status as Apostle. He speaks humbly but asserts his credibility. He also conveys a fatherly concern for those in whom he seeks to "bring about the obedience of faith." Through good eye contact, tell your

assembly that "among whom are you" applies to them as well as the Gentiles of Paul's day.

The closing line must convey energetic sincerity. Paul's words serve as both a prayer and an embrace for loved ones far away.

GOSPEL This is one of our foundational stories that, as such stories do, continues to nurture and sustain us and to tell us who we are. Like the stories we tell our children of their birth, this story gives more than details of where and

GOSPEL   Matthew 1:18–24

A reading from the holy Gospel according to Matthew

This is how the **birth** of Jesus Christ came about.
When his mother **Mary** was betrothed to **Joseph**,
    but before they **lived** together,
    she was found with **child** through the Holy **Spirit**.
Joseph her **husband**, since he was a **righteous** man,
    yet **unwilling** to expose her to **shame**,
    decided to divorce her **quietly**.
Such was his **intention** when, **behold**,
    the **angel** of the Lord appeared to him in a **dream** and said,
    "**Joseph**, son of **David**,
    do not be **afraid** to take Mary your wife into your home.
For it is through the Holy **Spirit**
    that this child has been **conceived** in her.
She will bear a **son** and you are to name him **Jesus**,
    because he will **save** his people from their **sins**."
All this took place to **fulfill** what the Lord had said through
        the **prophet**:
*Behold, the **virgin** shall **conceive** and bear a **son**,
and they shall name him **Emmanuel**,*
    which means "God is **with** us."
When Joseph **awoke**,
    he **did** as the angel of the Lord had commanded him
    and took his **wife** into his **home**.

Remember you are telling a story. The opening line sets the scene.

betrothed = bee-TROTHD

"But before . . . " is an important qualifier.

Note that it's the "righteousness" of Joseph that would require him to expose Mary. Contrast that virtue with his unwillingness to harm her.

The word "behold" slows everything down. The angelic apparition is a vision, so give it an otherworldly feel.

Joseph is hearing these words for the first time. They won't make sense to him if rushed. Take time.

Help him understand that the impossible is possible with God.

Matthew makes a direct link between Isaiah's prophecy and its fulfillment in Jesus.

Emmanuel = ee-MAN-yoo-el

Take time with the name's translation.

Conclude the story simply and sustain your eye contact for a moment after speaking the name "Jesus."

---

when. Birth stories tell us who we came from, why we're here, who wanted us, and how we can turn our history into our legacy. In short, they help us understand who we are. All this and more is found in the story of Jesus's birth. Like other miracles that enter life when least expected, this story begins by relating a rather ordinary situation: life is going on, a young woman is betrothed, and then she is found to be pregnant, but "through the Holy Spirit." That last detail is mentioned so matter-of-factly we might miss it. Then, despite the mention of divine intervention, the story surprisingly goes on to talk of "shame" and "divorce." Not till the mention of the angel does the story suddenly slow down.

You are describing a delicate situation, so speak of it delicately. There is good news and bad about "his mother Mary": she is pregnant and unmarried, but it's a miracle! Communicate Joseph's sensitivity by taking time with the "righteous man" clause and by inserting a brief pause before the word "quietly." The angel reassures a probably hurt and frightened Joseph that there is more here than meets the eye, so he should "not be afraid." Persuasion shifts to proclamation when you assume the prophet's voice to announce the coming of Emmanuel. Matthew reinterprets Isaiah's words to demonstrate how they are fulfilled in Jesus. The closing sentences are somewhat anticlimactic but convey important information. Marvel at Joseph's ability to awaken and immediately do "as the angel of the Lord had commanded him." In the final sentence Mary, as Joseph's wife, enters his home where they will raise Jesus as a member of the house of David.

THE NATIVITY OF THE LORD (CHRISTMAS): VIGIL

LECTIONARY #13

READING I   Isaiah 62:1–5

A reading from the Book of the Prophet Isaiah

Isaiah = ī-ZAY-uh;

Zion = ZĪ-ahn

This is long-awaited news that can be announced loudly with great energy, or softly with real but muted zeal.

In Isaiah's couplets an idea is stated in the first of a pair of lines then immediately repeated, in slightly different words, in the second ("not be silent . . . "/ "not be quiet . . . "; "vindication . . . like the dawn"/ "victory like a burning torch"; "Nations shall behold your vindication . . . " / "kings your glory"; "glorious crown . . . "/ "royal diadem . . . "). Use this literary device to achieve emphasis by increasing energy from the first to the second line.

diadem = DĪ-uh-dem.

Contrast "Forsaken" and "Desolate"—the former times that will be no more, with "My Delight" and "Espoused"—Israel's new status. Your tone might convey their former hopelessness or continue on the dominant note of joy.

Note the spousal imagery of the last four couplets: in each pair the second line receives greater stress. The passionate/ tender marriage language suggests God's enduring covenant with the Chosen People whose repeated infidelities are transformed into the innocence of a "virgin" bride.

> For **Zion's** sake I will not be **silent**,
>   for **Jerusalem's** sake I will not be **quiet**,
> until her **vindication** shines forth like the **dawn**
>   and her **victory** like a burning **torch**.
>
> **Nations** shall **behold** your vindication,
>   and all the **kings** your **glory**;
> you shall be called by a **new** name
>   pronounced by the mouth of the **Lord**.
> You shall be a glorious **crown** in the hand of the Lord,
>   a **royal** diadem held by your God.
> No more shall people call you "**Forsaken**,"
>   or your land "**Desolate**,"
> but you shall be called "My **Delight**,"
>   and your land "**Espoused**."
> For the Lord **delights** in you
>   and makes your land his **spouse**.
> As a young **man** marries a **virgin**,
>   your **Builder** shall marry **you**;
> and as a bridegroom **rejoices** in his bride
>   so shall your **God** rejoice in **you**.

READING I The people of Israel endured centuries of waiting; if it had not been for the prophets, they might have despaired. Voices like Isaiah's sustained them with hopeful images of God's plan for those who remained faithful.

Isaiah is the poet of Christmas and Advent; his songs adorn the liturgies of both seasons. In God's voice, he announces deliverance from exile and Israel's restoration. The people will be vindicated for the indignities they suffered; kings will behold the might and mercy of Israel's God.

Isaiah's words are not like the exhortations of motivational speakers who assert: "If you can imagine it, you can make it happen." The miracle of reconciliation with God will not result from the people's effort, but from God's. He is the initiator, the bridegroom in eager pursuit of his beloved. The Chosen People (and all humanity) will have a new accord with God when his promises are fulfilled in the coming of the Messiah.

Using colorful imagery, Isaiah states every idea twice. This repetition won't sound redundant if you render the lines with varied inflection, color, and energy. By stressing different parts of the parallel structures and placing greater stress on the second line than the first, you will achieve both emphasis and variety.

Using images of a grand coronation and a joyous wedding feast, Isaiah describes a new, intimate bond between God and the people in the messianic age. God will give them a "new name" and will hold them in his own hands. Isaiah spotlights this great reversal by contrasting it with the former "forsaken" and "desolate" state that God has now blotted out.

For meditation and context:

RESPONSORIAL PSALM   Psalm 89:4–5, 16–17, 27, 29 (2a)

R. Forever I will sing the goodness of the Lord.

I have made a covenant with my chosen one,
    I have sworn to David my servant:
forever will I confirm your posterity
    and establish your throne for all
        generations.

Blessed the people who know the joyful
        shout;
    in the light of your countenance, O Lord,
        they walk.
At your name they rejoice all the day,
    and through your justice they are exalted.

He shall say of me, "You are my father,
    my God, the rock, my savior."
Forever I will maintain my kindness
        toward him,
    and my covenant with him stands firm.

TO KEEP IN MIND

Tell the story: The reading of Scripture is a storytelling moment. Storytellers are people of imagination. They help us to see, hear, feel, and smell the elements of the story because they themselves experience these sensory aspects of a story.

READING II   Acts of the Apostles 13:16–17, 22–25

A reading from the Acts of the Apostles

When **Paul** reached **Antioch** in **Pisidia** and entered the **synagogue**,
    he **stood** up, motioned with his **hand**, and said,
        "Fellow **Israelites** and you **others** who are God-fearing, **listen**.
The God of this people **Israel** chose our **ancestors**
    and **exalted** the people during their sojourn in the land
        of **Egypt**.
With uplifted **arm** he led them **out** of it.
Then he removed **Saul** and raised up **David** as **king**;
    of him he **testified**,
    'I have found **David**, son of **Jesse**, a man after my own **heart**;
he will carry out my every **wish**.'

Antioch = ANN-tee-ahk

Pisidia = pih-SID-ee-uh

"Motioned with his hand . . . " he's asking them for silence.

Paul speaks with authority. Setting is important here: Paul is in a synagogue, a setting not unlike yours.

Recount the history keeping in mind where you're headed . . . Jesus! It's not history for its own sake.

Speak of David with affection and pride, but remember, he's not the main focus of the passage. Mention of "kings" evokes God's care of Israel.

The last three couplets express God's love and commitment to the people with tender nuptial language ("spouse," "marries," "bridegroom"). God's covenant with the Chosen People endures; he transforms their repeated infidelities into the innocence of a "virgin" bride.

READING II   The great missionary Paul, impelled by his passion to make Christ known to the world, arrives in Antioch and immediately heads for the synagogue to announce the Good News that transformed his life. That news takes the

form of a story. A consummate theologian, Paul retells the story of God's intervention in human history through the radical relationship he established with the Hebrew people. He makes no apologies to the God-fearing non-Israelites in his audience for his claim that God *chose* "our ancestors" and made them his special possession. The God of the Bible is embarrassingly concrete. While contemporary theologies imagine a God who makes no distinctions and plays no favorites, the Bible tells a story in which God chooses Israel over all the other nations and chooses David over Saul.

Paul rose to speak in response to the officials' invitation that anyone with an exhortation for the people should address them. We don't hear that exhortation today because our reading ends where the exhortation begins. Instead, Paul delivers a review of salvation history to introduce the more impassioned comments that will follow. Though less zealous than in other passages (note, he must quiet the people), Paul still wants these strangers who've not heard him before to recognize his authority, so your tone must portray a man of substance and influence. He is reviewing information

This is the climax of the text. Greater energy. Take a pause before "Jesus."

Imagine John speaking these lines. It's a powerful witness to the importance of Jesus.

As if watching Jesus standing on the opposite shore, speak the last line simply and sincerely. A long pause after will allow these famous words to echo in your listeners' minds.

From this man's **descendants** God, according to his **promise**,
  has brought to Israel a **savior**, **Jesus**.
John **heralded** his coming by proclaiming a **baptism** of **repentance**
  to all the people of **Israel**;
  and as John was **completing** his course, he would say,
  'What do you suppose that I **am**? I am not **he**.
Behold, one is coming **after** me;
  I am not **worthy** to unfasten the **sandals** of his **feet**.'"

GOSPEL   Matthew 1:1–25

A reading from the holy Gospel according to Matthew

The book of the **genealogy** of Jesus **Christ**,
  the son of **David**, the son of **Abraham**.

Abraham became the father of **Isaac**,
  Isaac the father of **Jacob**,
  Jacob the father of **Judah** and his brothers.
Judah became the father of **Perez** and **Zerah**,
  whose **mother** was **Tamar**.
Perez became the father of **Hezron**,
  Hezron the father of **Ram**,
  Ram the father of **Amminadab**.
Amminadab became the father of **Nahshon**,
  Nahshon the father of **Salmon**,
  Salmon the father of **Boaz**,
  whose **mother** was **Rahab**.
Boaz became the father of **Obed**,
  whose **mother** was **Ruth**.
Obed became the father of **Jesse**,
  Jesse the father of **David** the **king**.

Don't rush the "litany" of names. Rehearse (but don't obsess over) the pronunciations.

genealogy = jee-nee-OL-uh-jee

Renew energy every few lines.

Abraham = AY-bruh-ham

Isaac = Ī-zik

Judah = JOO-duh

Perez = PAYR-ez

Zerah = ZEE-rah

Tamar = TAY-mahr: see Genesis 38.

Hezron = HEZ-ruhn

Ram = ram

Amminadab = uh-MIN-uh-dab

Nashon = NAH-shun

Salmon = SAL-muhn

Boaz = BOH-az

Rahab = RAY-hab: see Joshua 2:1-7

Obed = OH-bed

Ruth was the great-grandmother of King David.

Jesse = JES-ee

his Jewish listeners already know. Your assembly knows it too, but like Paul's audience, they will benefit from the organization Paul gives the material and the salvation thread he pulls through the events.

Paul's reference to "David" reminds the people that the monarchy was a sign of God's care for them. Speak of David with affection and pride, but with more reserve than if David were the focus of the passage. All this talk of David leads to the climactic sentence that follows: Israel's history culminates in the coming of its "savior, Jesus."

At the conclusion of Advent it's appropriate that we hear again of John, the herald

who prepared the way, the remarkable figure who straddles the Old and New Testaments by personifying the spirit of Israel's prophets and who focuses their collective light on Jesus. Because he's in such continuity with the Israelite prophetic tradition, John's bow to Jesus is a powerful testimony. If John is "not worthy to unfasten [Jesus's] sandals," then Jesus is special indeed. Paul gives John the last word, so speak the final lines in John's voice as he did, to convince followers that he is not what they "suppose," for "someone greater"—the fulfillment of the messianic promise—is coming after him.

GOSPEL   Many will try to resolve the problem of this long and seemingly tedious listing of obscure names by using the shorter form of the reading. But consider the value in rendering the text just as the Evangelist presents it. While the names *will* be obscure, still the litany can have a positive and powerful impact.

The whole history of the Hebrew people is here, and most of salvation history with it. Matthew's implication, like Paul's in Reading II, is that to fully understand the Lord of history, we must understand the history from which he sprang. Liturgically, the lengthy listing conjures up the protracted,

Uriah = yoo-RĪ-uh. His "wife" is Bathsheba: 2 Samuel 11:1–27.

Rehoboam = ree-huh-BOH-uhm

Abijah = uh-BĪ-juh

Asaph = AY-saf

Jehoshaphat = jeh-HOH-shuh-fat

Joram = JOHR-uhm

Uzziah = yuh-ZĪ-uh: Struck with leprosy for usurping role of priests: 2 Chronicles 26:16–20.

Jotham = JOH-thuhm

Ahaz = AY-haz

Hezekiah = hez-eh-KĪH-uh: One of the few "good" kings; a reformer.

Manasseh = muh-NAS-uh: The nation's worst king.

Josiah = joh-SĪ-uh: One of Judah's best kings; a reformer. Ascended the throne at age eight.

The exile was the nation's greatest trial.

Jechoniah = jek-oh-NĪ-uh

Shealtiel = shee-AL-tee-uhl

Zerubbabel = zuh-ROOB-uh-b*l

Abiud = uh-BĪ-uhd

Eliakim = ee-LĪ-uh-kim

Azor = AY-sohr

Zadok = ZAD-uhk

Achim = AH-kim

Eliud = ee-LĪ-uhd

Eleazar = el-ee-AY-zer

Matthan = MATH-uhn

"Fourteen" is a deliberate redundancy. Stress each recurrence.

David became the father of **Solomon**,
    whose **mother** had been the wife of **Uriah**.
Solomon became the father of **Rehoboam**,
    Rehoboam the father of **Abijah**,
    Abijah the father of **Asaph**.
Asaph became the father of **Jehoshaphat**,
    Jehoshaphat the father of **Joram**,
    Joram the father of **Uzziah**.
Uzziah became the father of **Jotham**,
    Jotham the father of **Ahaz**,
    Ahaz the father of **Hezekiah**.
Hezekiah became the father of **Manasseh**,
    Manasseh the father of **Amos**,
    Amos the father of **Josiah**.
Josiah became the father of **Jechoniah** and his brothers
    at the time of the Babylonian **exile**.

After the Babylonian exile,
    Jechoniah became the father of **Shealtiel**,
    Shealtiel the father of **Zerubbabel**,
    Zerubbabel the father of **Abiud**.
Abiud became the father of **Eliakim**,
    Eliakim the father of **Azor**,
    Azor the father of **Zadok**.
Zadok became the father of **Achim**,
    Achim the father of **Eliud**,
    Eliud the father of **Eleazar**.
Eleazar became the father of **Matthan**,
    Matthan the father of **Jacob**,
    Jacob the father of **Joseph**, the husband of **Mary**.
Of her was born **Jesus** who is called the **Christ**.

Thus the total number of **generations**
    from **Abraham** to **David**
    is **fourteen** generations;
    from **David** to the Babylonian **exile**,

often painful waiting that proceeded the time of fulfillment. Through centuries of corrupt leadership, political shame, and military oppression, the nation persevered; infidelities multiplied, but within an overall context of faithfulness that led to the birth of the Messiah.

The names you will read belong to sinners and saints, heroes and traitors, but each is a flesh and blood human being who reminds us God works in and through our frail humanity to accomplish divine objectives. It's a perfect message for celebrating the Incarnation. Wonderfully, God will work

through the mortal flesh of Jesus to bring the world the gift of everlasting life. Beating all the odds, the genealogical line is unbroken, reminding us of God's constancy—a divine fidelity to the covenant, unmerited by the sinful nation to which it was sworn.

But most of all, the genealogy speaks of God's willingness to work through concreteness and particularity. Individual men and women helped advance salvation history to its terminus in Christ. No surprise for us, but in an ancient culture the inclusion of five women—all of them Gentiles

(except Mary) and one of them a harlot!— showed God's ability to break limits and surmount prejudices to achieve the divine will. Finally, the genealogy traces a family, both nuclear and universal. Besides being the lineage of Abraham and David, this listing names the ancestors of all people of faith who descend from Abraham, the "father of all believers." The genealogy must be read with that awareness.

Each name need not stand out as distinct. In fact, the opposite may be desirable. A rhythmic repetition creates a chant-like litany, but let the familiar names

fourteen generations;
from the Babylonian exile to the **Christ**,
fourteen generations.

Now this is how the **birth** of Jesus Christ came about.
When his mother **Mary** was betrothed to Joseph,
    but before they **lived** together,
    she was found with **child** through the Holy **Spirit**.
Joseph her **husband**, since he was a **righteous** man,
    yet unwilling to expose her to **shame**,
    decided to divorce her **quietly**.
Such was his **intention** when, **behold**,
    the **angel** of the Lord appeared to him in a **dream** and said,
    "**Joseph**, son of **David**,
    do not be **afraid** to take Mary your **wife** into your **home**.
For it is through the Holy **Spirit**
    that this child has been **conceived** in her.
She will bear a **son** and you are to name him **Jesus**,
    because he will **save** his people from their **sins**."
All this took place to **fulfill**
    what the Lord had said through the **prophet**:
      *Behold, the **virgin** shall **conceive** and bear a **son**,*
        *and they shall name him **Emmanuel**,*
    which means "**God** is **with** us."
When Joseph **awoke**,
    he **did** as the angel of the Lord had **commanded** him
    and took his **wife** into his **home**.
He had no **relations** with her until she bore a **son**,
    and he **named** him **Jesus**.

[Shorter: Matthew 1:18–25]

Matthew stresses details of Jesus's conception and the role of Joseph.

Deliver the words "before they lived together" with care about the delicacy of the situation.

Stress "righteous man." Insert a brief pause before the word "quietly."

The angelic encounter asserts Jesus's divine origin and his messianic destiny.

Take time with the translation of the name "Emmanuel," which climaxes the reading.

Make a subtle vocal shift for the quotation.

Sustain eye contact after speaking "Jesus."

TO KEEP IN MIND
Practice pronunciation!

---

slow you down as images from these characters' lives color the way you name them.

The proclamation changes radically at the birth narrative. This needs to sound like a good story. The account is full of divine activity: Mary conceives through "the *Holy Spirit*," Joseph is counseled by an "*angel*." Matthew's careful attention to the details of the conception ("betrothed" but "before they lived together") suggests disputes over Jesus's legitimacy. Speak with sensitivity to the delicacy of the situation.

In Matthew's account, Joseph receives some rare attention that serves the Evangelist's theological agenda. While Luke focuses on Mary, Matthew spotlights Joseph, through whom Jesus derives his Davidic lineage (another good reason to include the genealogy). We're told Joseph is "righteous." That very virtue precipitates a crisis for this groom who's apparently been cuckolded. Virtue demanded that he set aside this seemingly unfaithful woman he loves. Here the angel exhorts Joseph, not Mary, with "do not be afraid," signaling God's saving intervention. The angel's

words comfort Joseph; they also reassert Jesus's divine origin and messianic destiny, in which this humble carpenter will now play a central role.

The familiar quote from the prophet Micah announces the coming of "*Emmanuel*," the name that describes what Jesus was and is—God with us. Matthew's well-designed text reminds us that, in Jesus, God came among us in a unique and unimaginable way, but that miracle was made possible by generations of believers who cherished hope and never abandoned faith.

THE NATIVITY OF THE LORD (CHRISTMAS): NIGHT

LECTIONARY #14

READING I   Isaiah 9:1–6

A reading from the Book of the Prophet Isaiah

Isaiah = ī-ZAY-uh;

Tonight's liturgy gives us a Christian perspective on this ancient prophecy.

"Light" is the operative word. Contrast it with "darkness" and "gloom" as you slowly increase the energy and pacing of your reading.

The line is clearer if you imagine the sentence without the first "as."

Build energy on each successive phrase ("yoke . . . pole . . . rod"). All three lead to "smashed."

Quicken your pacing on this line.

Midian = MID-ee-uhn

Return to a slower pace until "will be burned."

Speak tenderly, with growing dignity. Know of whom you speak.

The titles can be spoken with either a bold or quiet energy.

The people who walked in **darkness**
    have seen a great **light**;
upon those who dwelt in the land of **gloom**
    a **light** has **shone**.
You have brought them abundant **joy**
    and great **rejoicing**,
as they rejoice before you as at the **harvest**,
    as people make **merry** when dividing **spoils**.
For the **yoke** that **burdened** them,
    the **pole** on their **shoulder**,
and the **rod** of their **taskmaster**
    you have **smashed**, as on the day of **Midian**.
For every **boot** that tramped in **battle**,
    every **cloak** rolled in **blood**,
    will be **burned** as fuel for **flames**.
For a **child** is born to us, a **son** is given us;
    upon his shoulder **dominion** rests.
They name him **Wonder-Counselor**, **God-Hero**,
    Father-Forever, **Prince** of **Peace**.

READING I   The familiar and tender words of Isaiah envelop us in images of darkness made resplendent, of the merriment that follows an abundant harvest, and of the celebration that erupts after military victory. During Israel's centuries of longing for the Messiah, the crowning of each new king reawakened the hope that perhaps *this* was the promised one who would fulfill their hopes. The "light" of his reign would dispel the "darkness" and "gloom" that visited each prior generation. The arrival of the Messiah would turn night into day, gloom into rejoicing, and oppression into glorious freedom.

Isaiah's poetry teems with contrasts and transformations. The "rod" of defeat, the burden of conquest, and the "yoke" of exile are utterly destroyed. Oppression yields to celebration, and a time of fulfillment and liberation follows. Isaiah personifies this idyllic future in the most unexpected image: a "child . . . a son" who will wear the titles formerly reserved to kings at their time of coronation: "Wonder-Counselor," "Prince of Peace."

In this Christmas liturgy, Isaiah's words are a promise kept and a prophecy fulfilled. Suddenly, we are drawn into his oracle and recognize ourselves as those who "walked in darkness" and on whom "great light . . . has shone." The dark land of our exile was sin; the Savior who freed us, Christ the Lord.

The sense of this sentence is: his dominion, (which he exercises) from David's throne and over (David's) kingdom, (and) which he confirms and sustains by judgment and justice both now and forever, is vast and forever peaceful.

This is a strong, climactic statement that must be spoken with authority.

For meditation and context:

His dominion is **vast**
　　and forever **peaceful**,
from **David's** throne, and over his **kingdom**,
　　which he **confirms** and **sustains**
by **judgment** and **justice**,
　　both **now** and **forever**.
The **zeal** of the Lord of **hosts** will **do** this!

RESPONSORIAL PSALM　Psalm 96:1–2, 2–3, 11–12, 13 (Luke 2:11)

R. Today is born our Savior, Christ the Lord.

Sing to the Lord a new song;
　　sing to the Lord, all you lands.
Sing to the Lord; bless his name.

Announce his salvation, day after day.
　　Tell his glory among the nations;
　　among all peoples, his wondrous deeds.

Let the heavens be glad and the earth rejoice;
　　let the sea and what fills it resound;
　　let the plains be joyful and all that is
　　　　in them!
Then shall all the trees of the forest exult.

They shall exult before the Lord,
　　for he comes;
　　for he comes to rule the earth.
He shall rule the world with justice
　　and the peoples with his constancy.

> **TO KEEP IN MIND**
> **Slow down**: The larger the church, the larger the assembly, and the more complex the text, the slower you must read.

Titus = TĪ-tuhs

READING II　Titus 2:11–14

A reading from the Letter of Saint Paul to Titus

Beloved:
The **grace** of **God** has appeared, saving **all**
　　and **training** us to reject **godless** ways and **worldly** desires
　　and to live **temperately**, **justly**, and **devoutly** in this age,
　　as we await the blessed **hope**,
　　the **appearance** of the glory of our great **God**
　　and **savior** Jesus **Christ**,
　　who **gave** himself for us to **deliver** us from all **lawlessness**
　　and to **cleanse** for himself a people as his **own**,
　　eager to do what is **good**.

Note the tender greeting.

Avoid an exaggerated reading by aiming for sincerity rather than drama. Avoid: "The grace / of God / has appeared." Try instead: "The grace of God / has appeared / saving all /."

Don't rush the listing of virtues. Call your assembly to live each one.

Our "blessed hope" is Christ's glorious return.

In your tone, model the eagerness to which you call your listeners.

The joy of deliverance is often proportionate to the misery that preceded it. Isaiah gives you strong language to convey the hardship of exile: "darkness," "gloom," "yoke," "pole," and "rod." Unless you contrast painful past with transcendent future, the text's meaning will be diluted. Most of all, persuade us that the child whose birth we celebrate will indeed transform human lives—including the lives of those sitting before you. It's a solemn promise made, not by you, but by "the Lord of hosts."

READING II Getting things in proper order is essential in the affairs of daily life *and* in the spiritual life. Those who focus first on the responsibilities of the Christian life might easily conclude that Christianity is all about rules that were invented to limit our fun. Only when we see what came *first* can we understand why Christianity indeed makes legitimate claims on us. The author's first line gives us all we need: "The grace of God has appeared." God took the initiative. God took on human flesh. God became one of us in order to bear the weight of our sins and transform darkness into the glory of salvation offered to all.

The rest is gratitude and a response consistent with the gift we were given. If you receive silver, you must polish it regularly so that it retains its luster. If you receive a car, you must change the oil regularly or

GOSPEL   Luke 2:1–14

A reading from the holy Gospel according to Luke

In those days a **decree** went out from Caesar **Augustus**
    that the whole **world** should be **enrolled**.
This was the **first** enrollment,
    when **Quirinius** was governor of **Syria**.
So all went to be **enrolled**, each to his own **town**.
And **Joseph** too went up from **Galilee** from the town of
        Nazareth
    to **Judea**, to the city of **David** that is called **Bethlehem**,
    because he was of the **house** and **family** of David,
    to be enrolled with **Mary**, his **betrothed**, who was with **child**.
While they were there,
    the **time** came for her to have her **child**,
    and she gave **birth** to her firstborn **son**.
She wrapped him in **swaddling** clothes and laid him in a **manger**,
    because there was no **room** for them in the **inn**.

Now there were **shepherds** in that region living in the **fields**
    and keeping the **night** watch over their **flock**.
The **angel** of the Lord **appeared** to them
    and the **glory** of the Lord **shone** around them,
    and they were struck with great **fear**.
The angel **said** to them,
    "Do not be **afraid**;
    for **behold**, I proclaim to you good **news** of great **joy**
    that will be for **all** the people.
For **today** in the city of **David**
    a **savior** has been born for you who is **Christ** and **Lord**.
And this will be a **sign** for you:
    you will find an **infant** wrapped in **swaddling** clothes
    and lying in a **manger**."

Don't let overfamiliarity with the story cause you to overlook the important details and contrasts.

This is an elegant and momentous beginning.

Caesar = SEE-zer; Augustus = aw-GUHS-tuhs; Quirinius = kwih-RIN-ee-uhs

Syria = SEER-ee-uh

Bethlehem = BETH-luh-hem

Jesus's royal lineage comes through his adoptive father, Joseph. Don't rush the names.

Judea = joo-DEE-uh; joo-DAY-uh;

The text takes an important turn here. Speak simply so the words can do their work.

Nazareth = NAZ-uh-reth; Galilee = GAL-ih-lee

Cherish these familiar but tender images.

betrothed = bee-TROTHD
swaddling = SWAHD-ling

Use a bit faster pacing to suggest the sudden appearance and the shepherds' fearful reaction. Though lowly in social status, *many* biblical heroes are shepherds.

"Do not be afraid" is a biblical formula that signals the announcement of God's saving intervention. The angel calms fear by announcing "good news of great joy." What does that suggest about your tone and energy?
Stress "savior," "Christ," and "Lord."

---

the engine may seize up. One doesn't resent those responsibilities because they are just a way of maintaining the gift that was given. The grace of God is of course far greater than silver or an automobile. To retain its luster within us we must "reject godless ways." We must be proactive in our care for the grace we've received by living "temperately, justly, and devoutly." Our fidelity and right-living are but a prelude to another great gift of God: the "appearance" of Christ when he returns in glory.

These lines are full of the joy of this Christmas day. They comprise less a morality lesson than a lesson in gratitude; what God has done for us makes us "eager to do what is good."

GOSPEL | There's a fulcrum in this reading on which the text turns, and once we hear it, everything changes. Luke's telling of the birth of Jesus begins with details that name civil authorities ("Caesar," "Quirinius"), establish time and place ("first enrollment," "Nazareth," "Galilee," and most of all "Bethlehem"), speak of betrothal and pregnancy, and assert the Davidic lineage of Joseph—a lineage that will be critical in establishing Jesus's own identity. Once these important details are established, we hear the phrase: "While they were there . . . ."

In short order, the mundane becomes extraordinary. A child is born in circumstances unusual even for that time, for he's

Don't rush, and don't waste a single word describing the awe-filled scene!

Help your listeners hear the connection between these words and the "Glory to God" sung in the liturgy.

And **suddenly** there was a **multitude** of the heavenly host with
    the angel,
  praising God and saying:
    "**Glory** to God in the **highest**
      and on **earth peace** to those on whom his **favor** rests."

THE 4 STEPS OF *LECTIO DIVINA* OR PRAYERFUL READING

1. *Lectio:* Read a Scripture passage aloud slowly. Notice what phrase captures your attention and be attentive to its meaning. Silent pause.

2. *Meditatio:* Read the passage aloud slowly again, reflecting on the passage, allowing God to speak to you through it. Silent pause.

3. *Oratio:* Read it aloud slowly a third time, allowing it to be your prayer or response to God's gift of insight to you. Silent pause.

4. *Contemplatio:* Read it aloud slowly a fourth time, now resting in God's word.

born without the attention of midwife or family members, and his first cradle is an animal's feed trough. An angel appears and announces the birth to an unlikely audience—people of dubious character tending sheep on the hillside. The "good news" proclaimed to these lowly shepherds suddenly explodes into praise as a chorus of heavenly voices sings God's glory and rains peace upon the earth.

The humble circumstances of Christ's birth and the lowly figures who first hear of it are key aspects of Luke's telling. This God-child who is known to the angelic hosts comes to live among both the poor—like the shepherds who greet him—and the mighty—who rule the world into which he's born. But throughout his life he will continue to resemble the poor and continually challenge the power of the mighty.

THE NATIVITY OF THE LORD (CHRISTMAS): DAWN

LECTIONARY #15

READING I   Isaiah 62:11–12

A reading from the Book of the Prophet Isaiah

See, the LORD proclaims
    to the **ends** of the **earth**:
say to daughter **Zion**,
    your **savior** comes!
Here is his **reward** with him,
    his **recompense** before him.
They shall be called the **holy** people,
    the **redeemed** of the LORD,
and you shall be called "**Frequented**,"
    a city that is **not forsaken**.

RESPONSORIAL PSALM   Psalm 97:1, 6, 11–12

R. A light will shine on us this day: the Lord is born for us.

The LORD is king; let the earth rejoice;
    let the many isles be glad.
The heavens proclaim his justice,
    and all peoples see his glory.

Light dawns for the just;
    and gladness, for the upright of heart.
Be glad in the LORD, you just,
    and give thanks to his holy name.

Isaiah = i-ZAY-uh

Short readings require slower pacing. But don't pause after every word—learn to group words that comprise a thought unit and pause after the unit, not the individual words.

Proclaim the word "See" as if it were "Behold."

It is God's voice speaking from here to the end.

Zion = Zi-ahn

Stress the words "reward" and "recompense," not the prepositions.

"Redeemed" requires even more energy than "holy people."

"Frequented" is unusual and unexpected. Stress it with a joyful inflection, then use ritardando (gradual slowing to the end).

For meditation and context:

READING I   Babylon has opened her gates to allow the Chosen People to return to their beloved land of Israel. The exile is over, and great rejoicing issues from the hearts and lips of all the people. A hopeless situation has become the very icon of hope, for enslavement has turned into freedom and a people who were spurned and rejected will now be called "the redeemed of the Lord." The shame of being forsaken is stripped away and the home to which the exiles return receives a new name—"Frequented" because all the nations of the world will seek her out.

Such reversals are not rare. We see them in the grand sweep of world politics where empires fall and unexpected revolutions sweep tyrants from their thrones; and in the ebb and flow of everyday life when sickness recedes, relationships mend, and lost jobs turn into new jobs. In all these instances, both grand and small, the hidden hand of God is at work. Sometimes the impact is local and unseen, but sometimes it reaches to the very "ends of the earth."

On this Christmas morning, the announcement that "your savior comes" speaks to us of the birth of Jesus. The salvation he brings is final and complete for he saves us from the slavery of sin and frees us to inherit the gift of eternal life. He exalts our dignity by naming us "holy people," the Lord's "redeemed."

This brief poetic text requires careful pacing. Like music, poetry stretches words so they fill more time than prose speech. The words are few, so use them all ("daughter," "savior," "recompense", "redeemed," "frequented") and render them with the intensity and joy that characterize this Christmas morning.

Titus = TĪ-tuhs

Announce salvation, then the reason why.

Use ritardando (gradual slowing to the end) on the words "of his mercy."

Vocally connect the first clause ("When the kindness . . . appeared") with the third clause ("he saved us through . . . the Holy Spirit). The parenthetical clause in between is also important, so don't rush.

Pause after the word "Spirit" and vocally build from one clause to the other, slowing on the words "hope of eternal life."

Make your joy and gratitude apparent, for you, too, are announcing the birth of Christ.

TO KEEP IN MIND
"Ritardando" refers to the practice, common in music, of becoming gradually slower and expanding the words as you approach the end of a piece. Many readings end this way — with a decreased rate but increased intensity.

READING II   Titus 3:4–7

A reading from the Letter of Saint Paul to Titus

Beloved:
When the **kindness** and generous **love**
    of God our **savior** appeared,
not because of any righteous **deeds** we had done
    but because of his **mercy**,
he **saved** us through the **bath** of **rebirth**
    and **renewal** by the Holy **Spirit**,
whom he richly **poured** out on us
    through Jesus **Christ** our **savior**,
so that we might be **justified** by his grace
    and become **heirs** in hope of eternal **life**.

READING II | God the Father showers the gift of the Holy Spirit upon us through Jesus Christ, who is our Lord and Savior. Thus, at every moment, divine life surrounds us. God's "kindness and generous love" appeared in the person of Jesus. Through the "bath" of Baptism, God's life penetrated us and continues to animate and renew us. This is the wonderful, good news the author of Titus is announcing. His style is more precise than elegant, but the ideas are as comforting as they are revolutionary.

It was not our merit that caused God to make a home among us. No, it was God's own mercy and nothing more that prompted that initiative. And that mercy was not a one-time event, for Baptism continues to invite and initiate any willing heart into the new life made possible by God's Spirit. The divine life of God that we call "grace"—showered upon us and working within us—makes us "heirs" of all the riches God possesses. These riches God apportions freely

and generously for the very same reason that the "savior" appeared: not our merit, but God's ever-abounding mercy.

Though there's no mention of manger and shepherds, this brief text is as much an announcement of the birth of Jesus and the salvation he brought as is today's Gospel. With profound joy and gratitude, you are proclaiming that "grace," "hope," and "eternal life" came this day to transform the world forever.

From the start, convey the marvel of the awesome appearance that is just concluding. These are not clouds vanishing in the sky, but angels!

Speak the shepherds' dialogue with eagerness and energy!

Pause after "Mary and Joseph;" then speak "and the infant" as if suddenly seeing the child. (It's only the "*infant*" who's lying in the manger!)
Don't rush: speak as if these words are still sinking in and astonishing you.

An earlier translation rendered "kept" as "treasured." Give "kept" that nuance, and don't rush the line. Pause between "these things" and "reflecting."

Mood shifts to the joy of the shepherds. Differentiate "heard" (expectation) and "seen" (fulfillment).

TO KEEP IN MIND
Careful preparation expresses your reverence for the Word.

GOSPEL   Luke 2:15–20

A reading from the holy Gospel according to Luke

When the **angels** went **away** from them to **heaven**,
    the **shepherds** said to one another,
    "Let us go, then, to **Bethlehem**
    to **see** this thing that has taken place,
    which the Lord has made **known** to us."
So they went in **haste** and found **Mary** and **Joseph**,
    and the **infant** lying in the **manger**.
When they **saw** this,
    they made known the **message**
    that had been **told** them about this child.
All who heard it were **amazed**
    by what had been **told** them by the shepherds.
And Mary **kept** all these things,
    reflecting on them in her **heart**.
Then the shepherds **returned**,
    glorifying and **praising** God
    for all they had **heard** and **seen**,
    just as it had been **told** to them.

GOSPEL   The "hopes and fears of all the years" might easily have soared right past the simple manger where the helpless child lay. Could this be the fulfillment of centuries of longing? Even the lowly shepherds who are the first to witness the fulfillment of God's greatest promise could have been sorely disappointed. Angelic voices and eyes of faith persuaded them that history was indeed culminating in this little town of Bethlehem.

Often despised and mistrusted in their day, shepherds bookend this text where they first are told of what God has done and then, having seen it for themselves, go off to announce it with great joy and hearts full of praise. They announce not only what they have seen but also what they have *believed* about the child in the manger. Even an angelic announcement doesn't *compel* faith: many could have looked upon this child and left unimpressed. The shepherds leave with full and welling hearts because faith has provided what eyes could never see.

And immediately they become what all who encounter Christ are called to be—evangelists who announce to others the good news that they have both received and understood. These simple witnesses go about sowing the awe that filled their hearts till "all" are filled with amazement. As we contemplate the child who came under such unexpected circumstances and whose birth was announced to such an unlikely audience, we can do no better than to proclaim that world-altering event with the same conviction and joy that filled the hearts of those first witnesses.

THE NATIVITY OF THE LORD (CHRISTMAS): DAY

LECTIONARY #16

READING I   Isaiah 52:7–10

A reading from the Book of the Prophet Isaiah

How **beautiful** upon the **mountains**
　are the **feet** of him who brings glad **tidings**,
announcing **peace**, bearing good **news**,
　announcing **salvation**, and saying to **Zion**,
　"Your **God** is **King**!"

Hark! Your sentinels raise a **cry**,
　together they shout for **joy**,
for they see **directly**, before their **eyes**,
　the LORD **restoring** Zion.
Break out together in **song**,
　O **ruins** of Jerusalem!
For the LORD **comforts** his people,
　he **redeems** Jerusalem.
The LORD has **bared** his holy arm
　in the sight of all the **nations**;
all the ends of the **earth** will behold
　the **salvation** of our **God**.

Isaiah = ī-ZAY-uh

Proclaim slowly, but joyfully with mounting energy. "Feet" is a synecdoche, a poetic device using a part to represent the whole person.

Don't speed up: distinguish each unique thought by visualizing a different image for "peace," "good news," and "salvation."

Don't overstress the word "Hark." Concentrate on enthusiasm and sincerity.

sentinels = SEN-tih-nuhlz

The words "directly" and "before their eyes" are an intentional redundancy. Stress *both* expressions.

The chorus of joy widens. Stress "ruins" and "redeems" instead of "Jerusalem."

bared = bayrd

The last four lines are a summary and a promise, reminding us of what God has done and what God will do. Sustain eye contact and remember, "salvation" is the child in the manger. That should color your tone.

READING I   The expression "don't shoot the messenger" is born of the human tendency to identify the bearer with the news he brings. In today's text from Isaiah, the messenger brings news so revolutionary that the very sight of him sends swells of joy through the hearts of all who see him. Even the "feet" that bear him are made beautiful by the news he brings—news longed for during many years of languishing in Babylonian exile.

God has triumphed. Any doubts about his sovereignty are removed, for God has given victory to Babylon's enemies, the Persians. The rod of oppression is smashed, and now Babylon tastes the defeat that it once inflicted on God's Chosen People. Eyes accustomed to darkness can only gradually take in light, so the message is stated and restated in a swirl of images that speak of "peace" and "salvation," of restoration and rejoicing, and of a mighty God taking charge and proving to the "ends of the earth" that those who hope in the Lord will never be disappointed, for with God nothing is impossible.

Because context is missing from today's reading, you must rely as much on the sound of the proclamation as on the words themselves to convey the meaning of the text. It must be obvious you are proclaiming joyous news of salvation and that tragedy and misery have turned to peace, comfort, and deliverance. You are the messenger who must be identified with the message; therefore, you must exude joyful fulfillment. But this does not give you license for excess and showiness. This joy is deep, stirring within the recesses of

For meditation and context:

RESPONSORIAL PSALM   Psalm 98:1, 2–3, 3–4, 5–6 (3c)

R. All the ends of the earth have seen the saving power of God.

Sing to the LORD a new song,
  for he has done wondrous deeds;
his right hand has won victory for him,
  his holy arm.

The LORD has made his salvation known:
  in the sight of the nations he has revealed
his justice.
He has remembered his kindness
  and his faithfulness
  toward the house of Israel.

All the ends of the earth have seen
  the salvation by our God.
Sing joyfully to the LORD, all you lands;
  break into song; sing praise.

Sing praise to the LORD with the harp,
  with the harp and melodious song.
With trumpets and the sound of the horn
  sing joyfully before the King, the LORD.

TO KEEP IN MIND
Read through all three readings and commentaries for your assigned Sunday. All three were chosen for this day, and each commentary has suggestions that can help you with your own passage.

Remember, it's Christmas, so give this businesslike opening a warmer tone.

"Partial" means "incomplete." Distinguish "partial" from "various."
Contrast "in these last days" with "In times past" and "prophets" with "Son." The mood intensifies at the mention of "these last days."
Probably based on a liturgical hymn of praise. Continue building intensity to the end of the paragraph.

"Accomplished purification" means he accomplished *our* salvation—not *his* purification—through his Death on the Cross.

Speak with conviction, asserting the superiority of Christ over the angels and the uniqueness of Christ's relationship with God.

You are quoting three separate texts here; make that evident and speak the quotes with authority and love. The last line describes what happened on Christmas day and what the angels continue to do for all eternity. Speak with joyous energy.

READING II   Hebrews 1:1–6

A reading from the Letter to the Hebrews

Brothers and sisters:
In times **past**, God spoke in **partial** and **various** ways
  to our **ancestors** through the **prophets**;
  in these **last** days, he has spoken to us through the **Son**,
  whom he made **heir** of all **things**
  and **through** whom he created the **universe**,
  who is the **refulgence** of his **glory**,
    the very **imprint** of his **being**,
  and who **sustains** all things by his mighty **word**.
When he had accomplished purification from **sins**,
he took his **seat** at the **right** hand of the **Majesty** on high,
as far **superior** to the **angels**
as the **name** he has inherited is more **excellent** than theirs.

For to **which** of the angels did God ever say:
  You are my **son**; *this day I have* **begotten** *you?*
Or again:
  I will be a **father** *to him, and he shall be a* **son** *to me?*
And again, when he leads the **firstborn** into the world, he says:
  Let all the **angels** *of God* **worship** *him.*

---

hearts and lives once marked by depression and despair. It's not the giddiness of a national championship but the spontaneous relief and joy of learning a loved one has survived dangerous surgery or that a long and bloody war has ended.

On this Christmas day these words, most of all, speak to us of what God has done in Christ, who came to reign and to restore, to redeem and to comfort; and who saved us not just from the oppression of others but from the darkness and terrible weight of our own sins.

READING II God is always reaching out to humanity, seeking ways to reveal divine truth and life. But like a growing child, humanity could only be given what it had the capacity to understand. So in ages past, God used many, varied, and "partial," or incomplete, ways to reveal himself. Only in the fullness of time did God choose the most complete and excellent way—"the Son" who is everything the Father is. This Son God made "heir of all things;" through him God created the "universe"; he is the "refulgence," that is,

the "brilliance," of God's glory; and he "sustains all things by his mighty word." By saying the Son is "the very imprint of God's being," the unknown author of Hebrews is telling us what Jesus himself often said, "Whoever has seen me has seen the Father" (John 14:9).

Liturgical time is different from time on a clock. In liturgy, all truths are present and celebrated simultaneously. So on this day when the crèches in our churches present Jesus as a helpless child in Mary's arms, the author of Hebrews gives us a fuller, grander vision of who this child really is. Though he suffered the degradation of

Using staircase parallelism (where the last word of one line becomes the first or key word of the following line) John introduces the dominant themes of his presentation of the Gospel: Christ's pre-existence, life, light and darkness, the world, and witness. Stress those topics which will dominate the life and ministry of the Word who was made flesh.

Give these classic lines your best reading. The echoes of Genesis are obvious.

"Life" indicates *all* of life, including yours.

Shift your tone to signal a new subject.

Stress the word "testimony" but not the first "testify." Testimony inspires faith in others.

The supremacy of Christ over the Baptist is clearly asserted here.

Speak without judgment.

Stress in awe and gratitude what Christ made possible: becoming children of God.

The "not," "nor," and "but" phrases require growing intensity.

GOSPEL   John 1:1–18

A reading from the holy Gospel according to John

In the **beginning** was the **Word**,
   and the **Word** was with **God**,
   and the Word **was** God.
He was in the **beginning** with God.
All things came to be **through** him,
   and without him **nothing** came to be.
What came to be through him was **life**,
   and this life was the **light** of the human race;
the light **shines** in the **darkness**,
   and the darkness has not **overcome** it.
A man named **John** was sent from **God**.
He came for **testimony**, to testify to the **light**,
   so that all might **believe** through him.
He was not the light,
   but came to **testify** to the light.
The **true** light, which enlightens **everyone**,
   was coming into the world.
He was **in** the world,
   and the world came to **be** through him,
   but the world did not **know** him.
He came to what was his **own**,
   but his own people did not **accept** him.

But to those who **did** accept him
   he gave power to become **children** of God,
   to those who **believe** in his name,
   who were born not by **natural** generation
   nor by human **choice** nor by a **man's** decision
   but of **God**.

---

the Cross in winning our salvation, he is now the sovereign Lord who sits at God's right hand and over all the ranks of angels.

Only gradually did the Church come to a complete understanding of the identity of Jesus. His superiority to the angels was not always assumed, for angels were believed to be mediators of God's covenant with Israel. Was Jesus just another mediator or something more? The author of Hebrews leaves no doubt in a final paragraph that asks but *one* question: did God ever speak of angels the way he has spoken of the Son? What follows are three statements,

(all declarative sentences, not *questions*) that assert the uniqueness of Christ and contrast him with the angels: "You are my son"; "I will be a father to him"; "Let all the angels of God worship him." By citing these Old Testament texts, Hebrews presents a full and clear understanding of the human child in the manger: he is God's divine Son who existed before the angels, and even they must bow down and worship him.

| GOSPEL | John often gifts us with a different perspective than the synoptics, a perspective that views the

precious jewel of the Good News from an angle that reveals a new and brilliant facet. The image of the manger is so pervasive during the Christmas season that John's telling of the Incarnation might seem drab and lean. But on close examination, we find one of Scripture's most sublime texts, which expresses with the brevity, density, and elegance of poetry, the deep mystery of God becoming human.

Beginning with the same words as the Old Testament, John creates a cosmic backdrop for the fusion of humanity and divinity. God came into the darkness of

Speak as if you were witnessing the birth. Perhaps the feeling is the joy mixed with fear we call "awe," or maybe it is assertive testimony declaring God's willingness to live "among us."

This is another aside regarding John. Speak with conviction, but slowly.

Moses = MOH-zis, MOH-ziz

Recall gratefully the "fullness" of which you and your parish have partaken.

"Grace in place of grace" refers to the fulfillment of the former covenant by the new covenant.

"Law" and "Moses" contrast with "grace" and "Jesus." Avoid a didactic tone; instead, stress the good fortune of having received the revelation of God in Jesus.

The closing speaks of the deep relationship between the Father and Son.

And the **Word** became **flesh**
  and made his **dwelling** among us,
  and we saw his **glory**,
  the glory as of the Father's only **Son**,
  full of **grace** and **truth**.
John **testified** to him and cried out, saying,
  "**This** was he of whom I said,
  'The one who is coming **after** me ranks **ahead** of me
  because he existed **before** me.'"
From his **fullness** we have **all** received,
  grace in place of **grace**,
  because while the **law** was given through **Moses**,
  grace and **truth** came through Jesus **Christ**.
No one has ever **seen** God.
The only **Son**, **God**, who is at the Father's **side**,
  has **revealed** him.

[Shorter: John 1:1–5, 9–14]

TO KEEP IN MIND

Endings: Your inflection of the last line of the reading should always signal that the reading is about to end. Then pause (three beats!) and make eye contact before announcing (from memory) "The word [Gospel] of the Lord." Always pronounce "the" as "thuh" except before words beginning with a vowel.

---

human experience as "life" and "light." Though some rejected the light, others embraced it and became "children of God." In John, more than in the synoptics, we see that God did not simply appoint some worthy human to undertake humanity's salvation. It is the preexistent Christ, through whom the world that now needs saving was first created, who takes on human flesh in a unique and unrepeatable moment in time. "The Word became flesh" and made a home among us, rendering the invisible God both visible and tangible, one with us in all things but sin.

The two mentions of John the Baptist inserted within the more poetic lines don't detract from the elegance of the Evangelist's exposition. The Baptist's presence serves not only to assert Christ's supremacy but also to argue the necessity of every Christian doing what John did: giving constant witness to Christ and calling others to Christ through the example of their own daily commitment.

The Evangelist speaks of the Word becoming flesh as if he were watching the birth of a child. It is one of *the* classic lines of Scripture, not because of the elegance of the language, though it has that, but because it expresses ineffable truth in few, accessible, and memorizable words. Whether you speak them with joy, pride, or gratitude, employ the same emotion later to characterize the Baptist's assertion that "the one who is coming after me ranks ahead of me."

Great poetry invites us back into its chambers over and over again. The poetry of this prologue loses nothing from being familiar; only our lack of confidence in its power and beauty could diminish its ability to move and inspire.

THE HOLY FAMILY OF JESUS, MARY, AND JOSEPH

Sirach = Sī-ruhk; SEER-ak

Avoid a didactic or preachy tone and instead communicate respect for beloved elders.

Note that the reading is comprised of two-line couplets that often repeat in the second line what was stated in the first. When that's the case, reserve the greater energy for the second line.

Equal dignity is accorded to "father" and "mother."

Convey the serenity and joy created by right relationship with parents.

The text jumps to a new section here, so pause before you begin.

Speak of the care of elderly parents with the compassion you would want accorded to your own parents.

The final lines are a promise you must announce to your assembly with conviction. "Firmly planted against" means "will be *credited* to you against." "Kindness" to parents builds a "house" of "justice" for devout children.

LECTIONARY #17

READING I   Sirach 3:2–6, 12–14

A reading from the Book of Sirach

God sets a **father** in **honor** over his children;
  a **mother's** authority he **confirms** over her sons.
Whoever **honors** his father atones for **sins**,
  and **preserves** himself from them.
When he **prays**, he is **heard**;
  he stores up **riches** who reveres his **mother**.
Whoever honors his father is gladdened by **children**,
  and, when he **prays**, is **heard**.
Whoever **reveres** his father will live a long **life**;
  he who **obeys** his father brings **comfort** to his **mother**.

My **son**, take **care** of your father when he is **old**;
  grieve him **not** as **long** as he lives.
Even if his mind **fail**, be **considerate** of him;
  revile him not all the **days** of his life;
kindness to a father will not be **forgotten**,
  firmly **planted** against the **debt** of your **sins**
  —a house raised in **justice** to you.

READING I Interestingly, this book that offers much advice for family living and was written about 180 years before Christ, was translated into Greek some fifty years later by the original author's grandson. Family life has always provided the foundations of society, but the modern world defines family more narrowly than ancient cultures where living with and caring for extended family was the norm. Modern life makes it possible to consign the care of aging parents to others, but in the ancient world parents relied, of necessity, on family members for their physical and emotional welfare.

The author, known as Jesus son of Sirach, connects respect for parents and caring for them in their dotage with the will of God. Love of parents is not an option but is writ into the very character of a godly person. Honoring parents is clearly mandated by the fourth of the Ten Commandments, but rather than prescribing a duty, the commandment prescribes a relationship between parent and child. Some of the ways of living out that relationship are enumerated here.

The deeper the relationship with parents, the deeper the relationship with God, for God hears, forgives, and blesses those who honor their parents. Indeed, our human relationships disclose the quality of our relationship with God. Is it possible, after all, to love and honor our heavenly Father, to forge a true and meaningful relationship with him, if we are unable or unwilling to honor the parents God has given us here on earth?

The key to proclaiming this text is to avoid a moralistic tone. Sirach calls us to clearer vision and deeper understanding,

For meditation and context:

RESPONSORIAL PSALM   Psalm 128:1–2, 3, 4–5 (1)

R. Blessed are those who fear the Lord and walk in his ways.

Blessed is everyone who fears the LORD,
    who walks in his ways!
For you shall eat the fruit of your handiwork;
    blessed shall you be, and favored.

Your wife shall be like a fruitful vine
    in the recesses of your home;
your children like olive plants
    around your table.

Behold, thus is the man blessed
    who fears the LORD.
The LORD bless you from Zion:
    may you see the prosperity of Jerusalem
    all the days of your life.

> **TO KEEP IN MIND**
> **Names** of characters are often the first word of a reading. Stress names so listeners don't miss who the subject is.

Colossians = kuh-LOSH-uhnz

Since you begin with an instruction, establish eye contact before you speak.

Distinguish each virtue from the others as if you were naming sacred vestments.

Renew your energy for this line that tells us what the sum of the other virtues is.

Stress "peace' only the first time it occurs.

Note that "And be thankful" is a separate sentence. Set it off vocally with slow pacing and adequate emphasis.

Be sure to stress the "word of Christ" and the importance of *teaching* one another.

Read this instruction slowly for it sets the context for the directions that follow for husbands and wives: everything must be done "in the name of the Lord Jesus."

READING II   Colossians 3:12–21

A reading from the Letter of Saint Paul to the Colossians

Brothers and sisters:
Put on, as God's **chosen** ones, **holy** and **beloved**,
    heartfelt **compassion**, **kindness**, **humility**, **gentleness**,
      and **patience**,
    bearing with one another and **forgiving** one another,
    if one has a **grievance** against another;
    as the **Lord** has forgiven **you**, so must you **also** do.
And over all these put on **love**,
    that is, the bond of **perfection**.
And let the **peace** of Christ control your **hearts**,
    the **peace** into which you were also called in one body.
And be **thankful**.
Let the word of Christ dwell in you **richly**,
    as in all **wisdom** you **teach** and **admonish** one another,
    singing **psalms**, **hymns**, and spiritual **songs**
    with **gratitude** in your hearts to God.
And **whatever** you do, in **word** or in **deed**,
    do **everything** in the name of the Lord **Jesus**,
    giving **thanks** to God the **Father** through him.

---

to love and conversion, more than to obedience. Obedience comes when the heart sees, and what it needs to see is not the individual virtue of parents who may have failed us through their faults and limitations. The clarity of vision Sirach calls for sees beyond frailty of mind and weakness of character and recognizes a divine paradigm in our relationship with those who gave us life. Sirach calls us to love as God does, that is, as God loves *us*.

READING II | The early Church began in the homes of the first believers; therefore, the governance of the home was important not only for family peace but also for the welfare of the embryonic Christian faith. The community at Colossae had been disrupted by teachings regarding the importance of angels, dietary regulations, and other ascetical practices. These disruptions so threatened the faith of the community members that they sought advice from the imprisoned Paul. His advice is as clear as it is inspiring:

nothing must compete with Christ as the source of our salvation. The asceticism of the true Christian lies not in dietary disciplines but in uprooting the weeds of sin in our hearts and in embracing the love of neighbor that Christ modeled by giving up his life for us.

Paul urges us to put on virtues in the way we might put on our finest clothing. Don't save those luxurious garments for special occasions to strut them before others. Our finest selves must be evident in all

Don't rush these lines or overemphasize the roles of husband, wife, etc. Instead, stress the call to love that's common among the four family roles.

Don't rush these lines or overemphasize the roles of husband, wife, etc. Instead, stress the call to love that's common among the four family roles.

Make eye contact and stress the *consequence* of each injunction.

Wives, be subordinate to your **husbands**,
    as is **proper** in the Lord.
Husbands, **love** your wives,
    and avoid any **bitterness** toward them.
Children, **obey** your parents in **everything**,
    for this is **pleasing** to the Lord.
Fathers, do not **provoke** your children,
    so they may not become **discouraged**.

[Shorter: Colossians 3:12–17]

GOSPEL   Matthew 2:13–15, 19–23

The narrator quotes the angel; carefully distinguish one from the other through pauses and subtle vocal shifts.

A reading from the holy Gospel according to Matthew

When the **magi** had **departed**, behold,
    the **angel** of the Lord appeared to **Joseph** in a **dream** and said,
    "**Rise**, take the **child** and his **mother**, flee to **Egypt**,
    and **stay** there until I **tell** you.

The angel warns of real and imminent danger.

Herod = HAYR-uhd

Joseph is setting out for an unknown and foreign land; don't make it sound like he's packing for a family vacation.

Herod is going to **search** for the child to **destroy** him."
Joseph **rose** and took the child and his mother by **night**
    and **departed** for Egypt.
He stayed there until the **death** of Herod,
    that what the Lord had said through the **prophet** might
        be **fulfilled**,
Out of **Egypt** *I* **called** *my* **son**.

Give proper stress to the fulfillment of prophecy.

Stress the *confirmation* of the death: "When Herod *had* died."

When Herod had **died**, behold,
    the **angel** of the Lord appeared in a dream
    to Joseph in **Egypt** and said,
    "**Rise**, take the **child** and his **mother** and go to the land
        of **Israel**,
    for those who sought the child's **life** are **dead**."

Distinguish the angel's voice from the narrator's.

we do and with everyone we know. It is not the stranger or the occasional acquaintance who needs our forgiveness but those with whom we live our lives; it is those who annoy, hurt, disappoint, and even betray us that we must learn to forgive.

Paul offers three keys to unlock the treasure of living the devout Christian life. First is love that bonds all the other virtues and perfects them. Second is God's word, which we must take in like the rich food of a lavish banquet so it can nourish and sustain us. Last is the gift of the community that teaches and admonishes us so we

don't forget the path of righteousness. If we do everything in the name of the Lord and exclude behavior that we could not do in his name, we will have nothing to fear when we stand before "God the Father."

The final instructions focus on the network of love that flows among family members as it does among the persons of the Trinity. If husbands love their wives and "avoid any bitterness," if wives are subject to their husbands only "as is proper in the Lord," and if children obey their parents while parents avoid provoking and discouraging their children, then the domestic

Church will be a sacrament of the larger Church, which is a sacrament of Christ.

GOSPEL   Originally instituted by Leo XIII, the Solemnity of the Holy Family was inserted into the universal liturgical calendar in 1921 during the papacy of Benedict XV. Then and now, this solemnity focuses us on the family of Nazareth as a model for all Christian families. These readings, selected to provide moral edification, do more than teach right behavior. They make present within the worshipping assembly the healing power of

Convey the trust and courage required of Joseph to respond to God's command.

Archelaus = ahr-kuh-LAY-uhs

Joseph's own intuition kicks in.

The dream confirms Joseph's suspicions.

The fulfillment of Scripture is an important detail.

Nazorean = naz-uh-REE-uhn

He **rose**, **took** the child and his **mother**,
  and **went** to the land of Israel.
But when he heard that **Archelaus** was ruling over Judea
  in place of his father **Herod**,
  he was **afraid** to go back there.
And because he had been **warned** in a **dream**,
  he departed for the region of **Galilee**.
He went and dwelt in a town called **Nazareth**,
  so that what had been spoken through the **prophets** might be
    fulfilled,
  He shall be called a **Nazorean**.

TO KEEP IN MIND

Importance of the Narrator: The narrator is often the pivotal role of a passage. Timbre, pitch, rate, and energy can make the same words convey very different moods or meaning. Sometimes the narrator is objective, but often the narrator has great interest in the events and characters of a story.

God and bring us into the presence of God's own Spirit who offers visions of family life lived in accord with God's perfect will.

In patterning family life on the family of Nazareth, each family becomes a domestic church consecrated to God. Becoming a domestic church is not about roles or rituals but about doing what Joseph does in this Gospel text—making Jesus the center of family life and the Lord of all choices. The text is redolent of Christmas as it speaks of magi and King Herod. But unlike the visitors from the east, the jealous king poses imminent danger to the child and so Joseph takes action to safeguard the boy and his mother. Clearly, God is working through Jesus's human father to ensure the safety of the Holy Family.

Although Joseph is the instrument for its unfolding, a divine plan is plainly at work: three times an angelic messenger intervenes through a dream to provide divine instruction that guides the family away from danger and to places of safety. What Joseph models most of all is a willingness to trust God and to follow wherever God leads. Such trust does not magically emerge, but has to be carefully nurtured over a lifetime. It requires the ability to recognize the voice of God from among the many others that offer advice, and to discern the Spirit of God from those that would lead one astray.

Matthew's allusions remind us that God is not only offering divine guidance that safeguards the Holy Family, but is also fulfilling Old Testament prophecy that the Messiah would come "out of Egypt" and be "called a Nazorean."

MARY, THE HOLY MOTHER OF GOD

Avoid a slow monotone or over-articulated delivery of this classic prayer. The lines that introduce and follow the blessing reinforce the prevailing mood of graciousness and compassion.

The reading is short, so don't start till the assembly is well settled.

Allowing yourself to pray this cherished text will keep you from reading too fast or too slowly. Too slow a reading robs the words of power as surely as too fast a delivery. Keep in mind that each invocation is distinct.

Your tempo slows on "and give you peace," as when ending a song.

Stress the word "name," not "my." This is God's commentary and not part of the blessing. Use ritardando on "I will bless them."

For meditation and context:

TO KEEP IN MIND

Always read Scriptures aloud, noting suggestions for stresses and pauses. After several readings, alter the stress markings to suit your style and interpretation.

LECTIONARY #18

READING I   Numbers 6:22–27

A reading from the Book of Numbers

The Lord said to **Moses**:
    "Speak to **Aaron** and his **sons** and **tell** them:
    This is how you shall **bless** the Israelites.
Say to them:
    The Lord **bless** you and **keep** you!
    The Lord let his face **shine** upon
        you, and be **gracious** to you!
    The Lord look upon you **kindly** and
        give you **peace**!
So shall they invoke my **name** upon the Israelites,
    and I will **bless** them."

RESPONSORIAL PSALM   Psalm 67:2–3, 5, 6, 8 (2a)

R. May God bless us in his mercy.

May God have pity on us and bless us;
    may he let his face shine upon us.
So may your way be known upon earth;
    among all nations, your salvation.

May the nations be glad and exult
    because you rule the peoples in equity;
    the nations on the earth you guide.

May the peoples praise you, O God;
    may all the peoples praise you!
May God bless us,
    and may all the ends of the earth
        fear him!

READING I   When we can't attend a significant event, we send expressions of regret. But God sends no regrets, for God is never absent. When we gather and invoke God's holy name, God is truly present. No symbol need *represent* God's presence, for God is there. Biblical understanding of names differs from ours. For us a name is a symbol, but in biblical times a name was synonymous with the person. To invoke the sacred name of God was to invoke God's very being, making him present among those blessed.

So read with the awareness that you are not just speaking *about* God's presence but *invoking* it within your assembly. The blessing formula three times calls upon God's name in unintended but striking anticipation of our Trinitarian invocations. It won't be enough to read slowly. Too slow a reading will drain life from these noble words. Read with energy and fervor, stressing only one word in each phrase. In each invocation, the conjunction "and" connects two units of thought; don't pause within the units, but only at the "and" between them.

Though given to Moses, the blessing is to be used by his brother Aaron and Aaron's sons, the ancestors of all of Israel's future priests. The words are like soothing ointment placed upon a wound or a warm mantle laid upon one's shoulders, so speak them with tenderness and authority, as if addressing a child leaving home or comforting a friend facing hardship. Note the invocations' subtle differences: the first asks the Lord to shelter and sustain; the second that God's face shine its saving light upon us; and the last asks again for God to

Galatians = guh-LAY-shuhnz

READING II   Galatians 4:4–7

A reading from the Letter of Saint Paul to the Galatians

Brothers and sisters:
When the **fullness** of time had come, God sent his **Son**,
   born of a **woman**, born under the **law**,
   to **ransom** those under the law,
   so that we might receive **adoption** as **sons**.
As **proof** that you are sons,
   God sent the **Spirit** of his Son into our **hearts**,
   crying out, "**Abba**, **Father!**"
So you are no longer a **slave** but a **son**,
   and if a **son** then also an **heir**, through **God**.

"Fullness of time" means God's timing. Pause after "Son" and mentally insert "who was born"

Jesus was human and subject to the Law, all for the sake of *saving* us from the Law.

Read gently, slowly, and most of all joyfully. Note the exclamation point, and remember "Daddy" is a better translation of Abba than "Father."

Pause between the words "Abba" and "Father" using the same inflection for both words.

Offer the last sentence as a gift of good news, speaking with joy and gratitude.

For additional insights on this reading, please refer to the commentary for Nativity of the Lord (Christmas): Dawn.

GOSPEL   Luke 2:16–21

A reading from the holy Gospel according to Luke

The shepherds went in **haste** to Bethlehem and found **Mary**
   and **Joseph**,
   and the **infant** lying in the **manger**.
When they **saw** this,
   they made known the **message**
   that had been **told** them about this child.
All who heard it were **amazed**
   by what had been **told** them by the shepherds.
And Mary **kept** all these things,
   reflecting on them in her **heart**.

The text contains four scenes with four moods: a) the arrival of the shepherds (energetic excitement); b) Mary's pondering (quiet peace) ; c) the departure of the shepherds (joyful praise); d) the eighth day (solemn).

Bethlehem = BETH-luh-hem

Proclaim slowly here. Suggest the depth of her pondering.

"look" upon us and grant a "peace" only God can give.

READING II The Bible assigns causality to everything, for God is always in charge, guiding human destiny. So it was in "the *fullness* of time," that is, God's *perfect* time, that God sent his Son to be born "of a woman" and "under the law." Though he was the Son of God, Jesus shared fully in our humanity and fully accepted human limitations and the demands of human society. Though he

came to set humanity free from the constraints of the Law, Jesus himself submitted to it fully, as demonstrated by his submission to circumcision in today's Gospel.

Paul uses a formula he probably borrowed from an early creed to announce that "God sent his son . . . that *we* might receive *adoption* as sons." A great mystery, the meaning of this solemnity, and the heart of the Good News all rest within Paul's simple formula: the Son of God became one of us that we might become children of God. Christmas is not just the story of a baby's birth, but of the beginning

of our salvation in Christ. Our response can be no less than to follow the Spirit's lead and call God "Abba!"

Paul manages both to teach and inspire in this brief text. His teaching will emerge only if you pay close attention to commas and pauses and communicate ideas, not just words, as you wend your way through the maze of the six clauses that comprise the first sentence. Inspiration flows from the final sentence, reminding us that Christ blotted out our former status as slaves. Now each of us is a member of God's family, a "son" and "heir" who receives an

Increase energy for the words "Then the shepherds . . . " with a faster pace on the middle lines and a slower pace at the end.

Then the shepherds **returned**,
  glorifying and **praising** God
  for all they had **heard** and **seen**,
  just as it had been **told** to them.

Pause here. Time has elapsed. Stress the role of the angel in naming Jesus.

circumcision = ser-kuhm-SI-zhuhn

When eight days were **completed** for his circumcision,
  he was named **Jesus**, the name given him by the **angel**
  before he was **conceived** in the **womb**.

> **TO KEEP IN MIND**
> **Tell the story**: The reading of Scripture is a storytelling moment. Storytellers are people of imagination. They help us to see, hear, feel, and smell the elements of the story because they themselves experience these sensory aspects of a story.

> **THE 4 STEPS OF *LECTIO DIVINA* OR PRAYERFUL READING**
>
> 1. *Lectio:* Read a Scripture passage aloud slowly. Notice what phrase captures your attention and be attentive to its meaning. Silent pause.
>
> 2. *Meditatio:* Read the passage aloud slowly again, reflecting on the passage, allowing God to speak to you through it. Silent pause.
>
> 3. *Oratio:* Read it aloud slowly a third time, allowing it to be your prayer or response to God's gift of insight to you. Silent pause.
>
> 4. *Contemplatio:* Read it aloud slowly a fourth time, now resting in God's word.

equal share of the bountiful inheritance God intends for all his children.

GOSPEL At the center of this reading sits Mary, reflecting in her heart on many things. Activity swirls around her as shepherds arrive in haste to verify what was told them by the angels. As soon as they see, they announce, and when they announce, those who hear are amazed. The world begins to waken from a deep slumber on this night. Hope arises that a long-awaited promise has been fulfilled,

that a dream some had abandoned and others forgotten has indeed come true.

A new year can rouse us from our quotidian slumber and inspire a resolve to be more awake in the coming months than in those just ended. Faith, more than anything, is what enables us to embrace newness. Today's text from Galatians insists that in Christ our whole identity changed. But that makes no sense without faith. The shepherds hear that "a savior" is born, but only faith can persuade them that the child in a manger is more than he seems. Mary gives birth, but without faith could she rec-

ognize the Lord of life in the eyes of her son? Mary sits serenely pondering, but is she also working out the calculus of where these events will lead and what changes they will wreak?

The naming of Jesus connects the Gospel with the First Reading. The blessing of Aaron prays that God's presence might shine upon us. The holy name of Jesus reminds us that God doesn't shine on us from afar, but from within and among us. Mary's title, Mother "of God," names Jesus one way; the angel used a different name: Emmanuel—God with us.

THE EPIPHANY OF THE LORD

LECTIONARY #20

READING I   Isaiah 60:1–6

A reading from the Book of the Prophet Isaiah

Rise up in **splendor**, Jerusalem! Your **light** has **come**,
    the **glory** of the Lord **shines** upon you.
See, **darkness** covers the earth,
    and thick **clouds** cover the **peoples**;
but upon **you** the LORD **shines**,
    and **over** you appears his **glory**.
Nations shall walk by your **light**,
    and **kings** by your shining **radiance**.
Raise your eyes and **look** about;
    they all **gather** and **come** to you:
your **sons** come from **afar**,
    and your **daughters** in the arms of their **nurses**.

Then you shall be **radiant** at what you see,
    your **heart** shall throb and **overflow**,
for the **riches** of the sea shall be emptied out **before** you,
    the **wealth** of nations shall be **brought** to you.
Caravans of camels shall **fill** you,
    dromedaries from **Midian** and **Ephah**;
all from **Sheba** shall come
    bearing **gold** and **frankincense**,
    and proclaiming the **praises** of the LORD.

Isaiah = ī-ZAY-uh;

Highlight and *contrast* references to light and darkness. Notice the synonymous parallelism (see the Introduction) used in almost every couplet (paired lines) in which the second line of the couplet repeats, balances, or develops what was stated in the first. Though ideas are repeated, they are not redundancies; each time, build energy from the first to the second line.

Don't let the series of couplets lure you into a sing-song delivery. Focus on each line's meaning to avoid that trap.

These are tender images. Don't waste them.

First pause, and then start this section with renewed energy. "Riches . . . wealth" require growing intensity for variety.

"Dromedaries" are single-humped camels.

Midian = MID-ee-uhn

Ephah = EE-fah

Sheba = SHEE-buh

"Gold and frankincense" tie this text to the Gospel. The reading begins and ends in joyful praise!

| READING I | This ancient solemnity, which predates the celebration of Christmas, is part of a fourfold manifestation of the Christ that begins with the shepherds, and continues with the magi, Jesus's baptism in the Jordan, and his first miracle at Cana. Today's celebration focuses on Christ's manifestation to the nations, an unnerving aspect of the Gospel message, especially as articulated by St. Paul, who was the first to understand that Jesus came not just for Israel but for the world. That's an obvious insight in our day, but not in Paul's.

Had Paul's contemporaries remembered their Scriptures, however, they might not have been unsettled. The gorgeous words of Isaiah in the First Reading already anticipate the diffusion of Israel's light to all the nations of the earth. Israel's exile will end, says Isaiah, and the darkness of their circumstances and in their hearts will be shattered by the "light" that is God's very presence. No flame of a star will brighten their night, but the Lord himself will shine upon them. The "glory" of God will guide Israel and draw the *nations* to Israel's land.

Isaiah paints pictures of wild, impossible things—people's hearts will "throb and overflow"; their children will be carried to Israel by the Gentiles in whose lands they had been exiled; within the land of Israel, foreigners will sing the praises of Israel's God. Human hearts resist God's light and

For meditation and context:

TO KEEP IN MIND

Pauses are never "dead" moments. Something is always happening during a pause. Practice will teach you how often and how long to pause. Too many pauses make a reading choppy; too few cause ideas to run into one another.

RESPONSORIAL PSALM   Psalm 72:1–2, 7–8, 10–11, 12–13 (11)

R. Lord, every nation on earth will adore you.

O God, with your judgment endow the king,
　　and with your justice, the king's son;
he shall govern your people with justice
　　and your afflicted ones with judgment.

Justice shall flower in his days,
　　and profound peace, till the moon
　　　be no more.
May he rule from sea to sea,
　　and from the River to the ends of the earth.

The kings of Tarshish and the Isles shall
　　offer gifts;
　　the kings of Arabia and Seba shall
　　　bring tribute.
All kings shall pay him homage,
　　all nations shall serve him.

For he shall rescue the poor when he cries out,
　　and the afflicted when he has no one to
　　　help him.
He shall have pity for the lowly and the poor;
　　the lives of the poor he shall save.

Ephesians = ee-FEE-zhuhnz

Paul is saying: For your benefit, I was given a grace from God; that is, a *mystery* was made known to me by *revelation*. Read slowly so this sentence won't become obscure.

Use "namely" to draw focus on what follows.

The "revelation" isn't named yet. Former generations were denied it, but now apostles (like Paul) have glimpsed it.

These last three lines name the hidden truth that's now revealed. You have three distinct images: "coheirs," "same body," "copartners." Distinguish them by speaking slowly and deliberately.

It's your joyful privilege to announce that salvation is available to *all*.

Gentiles = JEN-tīls
coheirs = coh-ayrs

READING II   Ephesians 3:2–3a, 5–6

A reading from the Letter of Saint Paul to the Ephesians

Brothers and sisters:
You have **heard** of the **stewardship** of God's **grace**
　　that was **given** to me for your **benefit**,
　　　namely, that the **mystery** was made **known** to me
　　　　by **revelation**.
It was not made known to people in **other** generations
　　as it has **now** been revealed
　　to his holy **apostles** and **prophets** by the **Spirit**:
　　that the **Gentiles** are **coheirs**, **members** of the same **body**,
　　and **copartners** in the promise in Christ **Jesus** through
　　　the **gospel**.

---

spend more time in darkness than in God's radiance. That's why we proclaim these texts again and again, so our feeble memories and our eyes that prefer night to light will be roused and filled again with hope. God never stops dispelling darkness and causing hearts to throb.

READING II Paul claimed the name "Apostle" and fiercely defended his right to that title. But he never lost sight of the fact that he did not enter the ranks of Apostles or the ranks of

Christian disciples for that matter, through normal channels. He came in the back door and received what he knew of Christ not from Jesus during his time on earth, but through divine "revelation." Paul believed he was given a special task—sowing the seed of the Gospel among the *Gentiles*. It took time and the guidance of the Spirit to teach the earliest followers of Jesus, all of whom were Jewish, that the Good News was meant to travel to the ends of the

earth. Paul was the indisputable champion of that cause, and all of us who love Jesus today can thank Paul for his diligence and uncompromising commitment to this goal.

Paul's message troubled those who first heard it: Israel's enemies are now members of the family. There is no more "us" and "them," but only "us." This truth was not *fully* revealed to past generations; only *now* does God's Spirit plant it in the hearts of "apostles and prophets," like Paul. The special, chosen status of the Israelites

GOSPEL   Matthew 2:1–12

A reading from the holy Gospel according to Matthew

When **Jesus** was born in **Bethlehem** of **Judea**,
   in the days of King **Herod**,
     behold, **magi** from the **east** arrived in **Jerusalem**, saying,
    "Where is the newborn **king** of the **Jews?**
We saw his **star** at its **rising**
   and have come to do him **homage**."
When King Herod **heard** this,
   he was greatly **troubled**,
   and all Jerusalem **with** him.
Assembling all the chief **priests** and the **scribes** of the people,
   he **inquired** of them where the **Christ** was to be **born**.
They said to him, "In **Bethlehem** of **Judea**,
   for thus it has been written through the **prophet**:
     *And you, Bethlehem, land of **Judah**,*
      *are by no means **least** among the rulers of Judah;*
     *since from you shall come a **ruler**,*
      *who is to **shepherd** my people **Israel**."*
Then Herod called the magi **secretly**
   and **ascertained** from them the **time** of the star's appearance.
He sent them to **Bethlehem** and said,
   "Go and search **diligently** for the child.
When you have **found** him, bring me **word**,
   that I **too** may go and do him **homage**."
After their **audience** with the king they **set** out.

Bethlehem = BETH-luh-hem

Judea = joo-DEE-uh; joo-DAY-uh

Herod = HAYR-uhd.

Before anything else, this is a story. Proclaim it as such.

"East" suggests the magi's foreign, exotic identity. They are astrologers, and their dialogue is spoken with eagerness and sincerity.

"Herod" introduces an undercurrent of threat.

Your tone can suggest Herod's anxiety and evil intent.

The quote comes from Micah 5:1, but it is altered by Matthew.

Judah = JOO-duh

Note of danger sounds again. Speak the line in Herod's "voice."

King Herod is cunning, but don't overdo it in your delivery.

TO KEEP IN MIND
Posture speaks: Make sure it says what you want it to. Don't let your face or body contradict the good news you announce. Remember, readers are allowed to smile!

---

is no longer exclusive. From the very beginning, it turns out, God envisioned a family of innumerable sisters and brothers. Thus we too are "coheirs" and "copartners" in the promises of God. But the most jarring truth is that we are also "members of the same *body*." The categories of friend, neighbor, stranger, and foe are obliterated. All believers are bonded by the Good News and have the same blood of the Gospel coursing through our veins!

GOSPEL   An epiphany is a manifestation. And what's manifested in today's Gospel is a child who is God among us. Gentile kings seek and find him; they offer gifts and prostrate themselves in worship before him. Gentiles, too, then go forth to bring their news to distant lands. But Matthew wants most of all to demonstrate that Jesus's life fulfills the ancient prophecies and that the provident hand of God protects and guides Jesus from birth to death.

The story itself is compelling: magi from the East seek a child they believe to be a king; the reigning monarch immediately senses threat and is driven by fear to plot treachery against the child. Not only Herod, but "all Jerusalem" feel the tremors that emanate from Bethlehem. These leaders have strayed so far from the promises of the patriarchs, they've invested so completely in the things of this world, that they feel compelled to plot against the very will of God. But their intrigue cannot threaten God's plan.

Here is familiar, comforting imagery.

"House" is unexpected. They find him with Mary.

Suggest the significance of these dignitaries prostrating before the child.

Express both the relief and derision found in this sentence: in the nick of time (relief!) the necessary information was kept from Herod (delight!).

And **behold**, the star that they had seen at its rising
    preceded them,
until it came and **stopped** over the place where the **child** was.
They were **overjoyed** at seeing the star,
    and on entering the **house**
    they saw the **child** with **Mary** his **mother**.
They **prostrated** themselves and did him **homage**.
Then they opened their **treasures**
    and offered him gifts of **gold**, **frankincense**, and **myrrh**.
And having been **warned** in a dream not to **return** to Herod,
    they **departed** for their country by another **way**.

TO KEEP IN MIND
Tell the story: The reading of Scripture is a storytelling moment. Storytellers are people of imagination. They help us to see, hear, feel, and smell the elements of the story because they themselves experience these sensory aspects of a story.

Their malice *will* cause much harm and suffering, but the child who exalts Bethlehem over the grander "rulers of Judah" will be found and worshipped and known to Jew and Gentile as God's ultimate gift.

Images both familiar and disturbing populate this text. The familiar, comforting words are obvious: "magi," "Bethlehem," "star," "shepherd," "gold, frankincense, and myrrh." But Herod's presence deeply disturbs. His intrigue presages the threat that will haunt Jesus throughout his ministry and foreshadows his Passion. The blend of disturbing and familiar lends depth and power to this rich text.

THE BAPTISM OF THE LORD

LECTIONARY #21

READING I   Isaiah 42:1–4, 6–7

Isaiah = Ī-ZAY-uh

These are exalted lines. Don't rush. Stress God's initiative and choice.

This is not wishful thinking, but a prophecy of what God *will* accomplish through his servant.

God delights in the servant.

"Until he establishes" refers to the two clauses that precede it. "Coastlands will wait . . . " stands alone as a new thought. Here, "until" is like the "until" in "he won't give up *until* he wins," which means he'll *never* give up. So "reed" and "wick" will never be abused.

Pause to transition to a more personal tone. Stress the verbs ("called," "grasped," "formed") that suggest the fullness with which the servant is infused with God's spirit. Blend tenderness and strength.

Jesus used similar words to describe his own ministry.

Because the Gospel leans on this "servant song," your reading should ready our ears for the subtle echoes that will follow.

A reading from the Book of the Prophet Isaiah

Thus says the Lord:
Here is my **servant** whom I **uphold**,
   my **chosen** one with whom I am **pleased**,
upon whom I have put my **spirit**;
   he shall bring forth **justice** to the nations,
not **crying** out, not **shouting**,
   not making his voice heard in the **street**.
A **bruised** reed he shall not break,
   and a **smoldering** wick he shall not **quench**,
until he establishes **justice** on the earth;
   the coastlands will **wait** for his teaching.

I, the Lord, have **called** you for the **victory** of **justice**,
   I have **grasped** you by the **hand**;
I **formed** you, and set you
   as a **covenant** of the people,
   a **light** for the nations,
to **open** the eyes of the **blind**,
   to bring out **prisoners** from **confinement**,
   and from the **dungeon**, those who live in **darkness**.

READING I While the Christian West more often focused on the historical aspects of the events surrounding Christmas, the East stressed their theological significance. By placing the Feast of the Baptism of the Lord at the end of Christmas Time, the Church enables us to conclude the Christmas cycle of feasts with a theological reflection on the manifestation of God in the incarnate Jesus.

Elements of this First Reading are embedded in the Gospel story where we hear the same sentiment ("with whom I am well pleased") addressed to Jesus as is here addressed to God's "servant" as "one with whom I am pleased." Four sections of the Book of Isaiah are known as songs of the "Suffering Servant," poetic sections that pay tribute to a "chosen one" whose mission is to bring justice, but whose fidelity to God's will brings him great suffering. Scholars still ponder the identity of this Servant: is it Isaiah himself, the nation, a future Messiah? But today's liturgy clearly identifies the Suffering Servant with Jesus, and Jesus himself saw his life as the embodiment of these prophecies.

The opening lines read like a job description for God's Suffering Servant, but of course they are much more. They are a blessing that becomes a self-fulfilling prophecy, as the positive expectations we place on children draw the best out of them. Speak these lines with the same parental tone you hear in the Gospel's voice from heaven.

In the second paragraph, God no longer talks *about* the Suffering Servant but *to* him. "I . . . have called you," says the Lord, to be light, to open eyes, to free prisoners! These lines, similar to words Jesus quotes

For meditation and context:

Cornelius = kohr-NEEL-yuhs

Peter is in the home of a Gentile who, without Baptism, has received the Holy Spirit.

"In truth, I see" suggests Peter's growing awareness, which comes slowly at first, then gradually builds momentum.

Stress the words that convey the universality of salvation: "*no* partiality," "in *every* nation," "Lord of *all*."

These words tell us God is working in and through Jesus. Speak them with conviction.

Jesus is the supreme instrument of God's saving action in the world. Peter understands and proclaims this truth.

Let this be your own statement of faith. Speak "for God was with him" with a gradually slowing pace.

RESPONSORIAL PSALM   Psalm 29:1–2, 3–4, 3, 9–10 (11b)

R. The Lord will bless his people with peace.

Give to the LORD, you sons of God,
   give to the LORD glory and praise,
Give to the LORD the glory due his name;
   adore the LORD in holy attire.

The voice of the LORD is over the waters,
   the LORD, over vast waters.
The voice of the LORD is mighty;
   the voice of the LORD is majestic.

The God of glory thunders,
   and in his temple all say, "Glory!"
The LORD is enthroned above the flood;
   the LORD is enthroned as king forever.

READING II   Acts of the Apostles 10:34–38

A reading from the Acts of the Apostles

Peter proceeded to speak to those gathered
   in the house of **Cornelius**, saying:
   "In **truth**, I see that God shows no **partiality**.
Rather, in **every** nation whoever **fears** him and acts **uprightly**
   is **acceptable** to him.
You know the word that he sent to the **Israelites**
   as he proclaimed **peace** through Jesus **Christ**, who is **Lord** of all,
   what has happened all over **Judea**,
   beginning in **Galilee** after the baptism
   that **John** preached,
   how God anointed **Jesus** of **Nazareth**
   with the Holy **Spirit** and **power**.
He went about doing **good**
   and **healing** all those oppressed by the **devil**,
   for **God** was with him."

---

to describe his own ministry, convey God's encouragement and commissioning of the Servant for a ministry of healing and hope. Speak them with a blend of tenderness and strength.

READING II | Peter briefly alludes to Jesus's baptism in this short text and presents Christ as *the* sacrament of God to the world, the manifestation and the implementation of God's will among people. He understands that what Isaiah said would be accomplished through the Suffering Servant, God has achieved in Christ.

But this same Peter, who knew Jesus well and speaks of him so powerfully, continues learning the full meaning of the Jesus event he had been so privileged to experience. Only by reading the entire tenth chapter of Acts, which provides the context, will you appreciate the meaning of the discourse presented here. A God-given vision has brought Peter to the home of the Gentile Cornelius, where he discovers that God plays no favorites. Formerly an adamant proponent of Jesus only for the Jews, Peter suddenly recognizes the error of his ways. He now realizes that Jesus is not

Israel's exclusive possession, but the embodiment of God's infinite love sent and meant for all humanity. It is that realization he speaks when he states, "In truth, I see . . ."

Speaking to a Gentile who, even before Baptism, has received the gift of the Holy Spirit, humbles Peter and colors his tone. "You *know* the word that he sent . . . " indicates he is reviewing the ministry of Jesus less with the didactic tone of a teacher and more with the joy of a fellow believer speaking to new friends about his old friend, Jesus.

This text presents a moment of high drama that's presented in few and simple words. Read slowly, using the words and images to paint the significant encounters between the cousins and between Father and Son.

Galilee = GAL-ih-lee

Suggest John's discomfort with Jesus's request. John is so sure of his position that he tries to "prevent" the baptism.

Jesus's tone is authoritative but compassionate.

With this line, you might suggest lingering reluctance in John.

Is Jesus already in deep communion with God when the skies open?

Suggest the profound awe of a great miracle. The better you visualize the scene the better we'll see it with you.

The voice of God speaking of a "beloved Son" may call less for thunder than for tenderness. Simple and sincere serve best, as long as your energy says this is a moment of great significance.

TO KEEP IN MIND
Who really proclaims: "When the Sacred Scriptures are read in the Church, God himself speaks to his people, and Christ, present in his word, proclaims the gospel" (#29 GIRM).

GOSPEL   Matthew 3:13–17

A reading from the holy Gospel according to Matthew

Jesus came from Galilee to **John** at the **Jordan**
    to be **baptized** by him.
John tried to **prevent** him, saying,
    "**I** need to be baptized by **you**,
    and yet **you** are coming to **me**?"
Jesus said to him in reply,
    "**Allow** it now, for thus it is **fitting** for us
    to fulfill all **righteousness**."
Then he **allowed** him.
After Jesus was **baptized**,
    he came up from the **water** and **behold**,
    the heavens were **opened** for him,
    and he saw the **Spirit** of God descending like a **dove**
    and coming **upon** him.
And a **voice** came from the heavens, saying,
    "This is my **beloved Son**, with whom I am well **pleased**."

GOSPEL Already in Advent we heard John's self-abasement: "One who is coming after me is mightier than I." There he addressed the crowds in order to heighten expectancy over the coming of the Messiah. Today, his self-abasement is spoken to Jesus, whose presence fills John with conviction that he stands in the presence of someone far greater than himself. Yet Jesus seeks to submit to John's baptism. The early Church witnessed some tension between the followers of Jesus and those of John, whom some believed to be greater than Jesus. In that context, Jesus's baptism posed a problem, for Jesus seems to be submitting to John as if he were the greater. The odd dialogue between cousins is Matthew's answer to the problem: Jesus did submit, but it was "to fulfill all righteousness," not to concede superiority. Jesus submits as does the Suffering Servant of the First Reading, and thus the baptism establishes the servant character of Jesus's messianic ministry.

Matthew's account differs in a subtle but significant way from Mark's and Luke's. In the latter tellings, the voice from heaven speaks directly to Jesus ("*You* are my beloved,") in an intimate moment between Father and Son that is equally a moment of high drama and high Christology. But in Matthew, God addresses the crowd ("*This is my beloved*,") making the baptism more a manifestation of Jesus's true identity as God's Son and God's faithful servant who henceforward will move inexorably toward his destiny.

Since this baptism eventually leads to the Cross, perhaps the voice from heaven should sound like the voice that spoke to Mary years before: "Do not be afraid. You have found favor with God."

SECOND SUNDAY IN ORDINARY TIME

LECTIONARY #64

READING I   Isaiah 49:3, 5–6

Isaiah = ī-ZAY-uh

The servant's voice introduces God's words. The Lord speaks to vindicate the servant, who has been shamed in the eyes of the world.

God's endorsement does not make the servant vain. Instead, aim for confidence that flows from knowledge of God's unfailing support.

"Jacob" and "Israel" are used synonymously, so stress "gathered" rather than "Israel."

A verse is left out here, and God's voice returns, so pause before you begin this sentence. God declares to the servant (and to us) that mercy and salvation have no limits. You might try a strong tone and volume on the first three lines and a hushed tone for the surprising news of the last two lines.

A reading from the Book of the Prophet Isaiah

The LORD said to me: You are my **servant**,
    Israel, through whom I show my **glory**.
Now the LORD has **spoken**
    who **formed** me as his servant from the **womb**,
that Jacob may be brought **back** to him
    and Israel **gathered** to him;
and I am made **glorious** in the sight of the LORD,
    and my God is now my **strength**!
It is too little, the LORD says, for you to be my **servant**,
    to raise up the tribes of **Jacob**,
    and restore the survivors of **Israel**;
I will make you a **light** to the **nations**,
    that my **salvation** may reach to the **ends** of the **earth**.

TO KEEP IN MIND

Openings: First, make eye contact with the assembly and announce, from memory, "A (pronounced "uh," not "ay") reading from . . ." Then pause (three full beats!) before starting the reading.

READING I   Relationships define us. Knowing to whom we matter gives us a sense of who we are. One can forego many things on a hard and perilous journey, but woe to the would-be explorer or missionary who lacks a clear sense of identity. Scholars debate the identity of the Suffering Servant (was he Israel, the prophet himself, the future Messiah?), but the Servant himself is clear about who he is: he is God's spokesperson, chosen from the womb to serve the Lord.

Thus far, God's service has been neither easy nor successful. The Servant has endured suffering and shame. But he has not yielded to discouragement for he understands the nature of his task and who it is asking him to undertake it. The world will define us if we let it; it will say that success matters most and that who we are depends on it. But the Servant knows better. "I am made glorious in the sight of the *Lord*," he announces. In other words, it's not my success that gives me strength, but "my *God.*"

But now God offers a further and greater task that will be even more challenging than what the Servant has done before. It is not *enough* for you to bring my word to Israel, God tells him, "I will make you a light to the *nations*." That God's mercy and "salvation" would be offered to the entire world was a stunning truth for Israel, one she wasn't ready to hear. Despite hardship, however, the Servant will indeed bring that message to the nations and, eventually, they will embrace his word. The salvation of God continues to stretch to the "ends of the earth." It but needs our willingness to also embrace the task God gave the Suffering Servant.

For meditation and context:

RESPONSORIAL PSALM   Psalm 40:2, 4, 7–8, 8–9, 10 (8a, 9a)

R. Here am I, Lord; I come to do your will.

I have waited, waited for the LORD,
   and he stooped toward me and heard
     my cry.
And he put a new song into my mouth,
   a hymn to our God.

Sacrifice or offering you wished not,
   but ears open to obedience you gave me.
Holocausts or sin-offerings you sought not;
   then said I, "Behold I come."

"In the written scroll it is prescribed for me,
   to do your will, O my God, is my delight,
     and your law is within my heart!"

I announced your justice in the vast assembly;
   I did not restrain my lips, as you,
     O LORD, know.

We will read from I Corinthians five of the next six Sundays.

When a name opens a passage, speak it slowly and with emphasis so listeners won't miss who the subject is. Suggest the weight and authority carried by Paul's name.

Corinthians = kohr-IN-thee-uhnz
Sosthenes = SOS-thuh-neez

Paul's parenthetical identifiers are important. They are part of his style of packing many units into one package.

Make strong eye contact here. The greeting is also a prayer.

Corinth = KOHR-inth

READING II   1 Corinthians 1:1–3

A reading from the first Letter of Saint Paul to the Corinthians

Paul, called to be an **apostle** of Christ Jesus by the will of **God**,
   and **Sosthenes** our brother,
     to the church of God that is in **Corinth**,
     to you who have been **sanctified** in Christ Jesus,
       called to be **holy**,
     with all those **everywhere** who call upon the **name** of our
       Lord Jesus Christ, **their** Lord and **ours**.
Grace to you and **peace** from God our **Father**
   and the **Lord** Jesus **Christ**.

> **TO KEEP IN MIND**
> **Slow down**: The larger the church, the larger the assembly, and the more complex the text, the slower you must read.

READING II   Today's text may seem little more than a salutation, but Paul always packs a great deal into whatever he says. While greeting, Paul also reminds us that he was called to be an Apostle, that the Corinthians are consecrated in Christ, that they were "called," and that Jesus is Lord of all who call on him. This complex sentence is a perfect example of why we proclaim "thought units" rather than "sentences" since sentences may contain several units which, when heard, can be distinguished from one another *only by your voice.*

Corinth was known for its reckless licentiousness. But Paul indicates by his greeting that Christians are not party to that behavior. They have submitted themselves to Christ, not to the flesh. They have been "sanctified" and "called to be holy." If that sounds like predictable biblical jargon, remember Paul's letters weren't Scripture when he wrote them. He wrote as an elder to his spiritual children who, at great personal cost, had bonded themselves to Christ and one another, and had willingly branded themselves with "the name" of the Lord Jesus Christ.

Paul alludes to issues he will address more fully later—exhortations to holiness and right conduct we'll read during five of the next six Sundays. Read slowly, carefully distinguishing each idea from every other, stressing in a cheerful and authoritative tone Paul's subtle references to the topics he will later expand. His asides out of the way, Paul comes to his formal greeting. Authority yields to affection as Paul prays: "grace . . . and peace" for the young community he fathered in Corinth.

Take time to set the scene and establish the players.

In other translations John's declaration ends with an exclamation point. But don't rush. Proclaim Jesus's singular role in God's plan of salvation.

His testimony is the sigh of relief of one who has finally solved a great mystery.

John's description of the descent of the Spirit is the corroborating sign that John had been told to expect. It may add to his chagrin at having been unable to "know him."

John is saying, essentially: now I *have* seen despite my earlier blindness. From John's seeing comes his testimony; if your testimony comes from the same conviction, you can say with John, this *is* the Son of God.

> **TO KEEP IN MIND**
> **Pray the Scriptures**: Make reading these Scriptures a part of your prayer life every week, and especially during the week prior to the liturgy in which you will proclaim.

GOSPEL   John 1:29–34

A reading from the holy Gospel according to John

John the **Baptist** saw **Jesus** coming toward him and said,
  "**Behold**, the **Lamb** of **God**, who takes away the **sin**
    of the world.
He is the one of whom I said,
  'A man is coming **after** me who ranks **ahead** of me
  because he existed **before** me.'
I did not **know** him,
  but the **reason** why I came baptizing with **water**
  was that he might be made **known** to Israel."
John testified **further**, saying,
  "I saw the **Spirit** come down like a **dove** from **heaven**
  and **remain** upon him.
I did not **know** him,
  but the one who **sent** me to baptize with water **told** me,
  'On whomever you see the **Spirit** come down and **remain**,
  he is the one who will **baptize** with the Holy **Spirit**.'
Now I have **seen** and **testified** that he is the **Son** of **God**."

GOSPEL   Each year, this Second Sunday of Ordinary Time offers a text from John instead of the designated Evangelist for that year. In presenting pericopes that continue to focus on the manifestation of Jesus—using accounts of John the Baptist and the wedding at Cana—this Sunday provides a transition from Christmas and Epiphany to Ordinary Time.

The Evangelist's use of John the Baptist is calculated to shed light on Jesus without overemphasizing the Baptist's role. The Evangelist does not want to fuel any erroneous thinking about John's superiority over Jesus. So, without directly describing the baptism, John comments on the theological truth it reveals, which is Christ's unique identity as God's Son. Upon seeing Jesus, John makes a profound declaration about Jesus's identity while also confessing his prior ignorance about the one whose way he was preparing.

John stares in the face of the future, his and ours. The dawn of the day of Jesus means the eclipse of his own day. "He must increase; I must decrease," John will later say (3:30). He does not regret the termination of his time at center stage, for a greater player has entered the scene. His confession that he announced him but "did not know him" is simple and sincere.

By declaring Jesus the "Lamb of God" who will bear the world's sin, John asserts the central dimension of Jesus's mission. Even this close to Christmas we can hear hammers pounding at Calvary, an intuition not lost on medieval artists. One master depicts Joseph and Mary adoring the child in the manger; doves and angels hover overhead, and on the wall behind Joseph hangs a crucifix.

THIRD SUNDAY IN ORDINARY TIME

LECTIONARY #67

Isaiah = Ī-ZAY-uh

Zebulun = ZEB-y<u>oo</u>-luhn

Naphtali = NAF-tuh-lī

You have multiple opportunities to highlight contrasting images: "degraded" and "glorified," "darkness" and "light," and "gloom" and "light." Your *tone* will be the key to understanding.

The prophet's rejoicing climaxes here.

Pause and shift tone before beginning the "People who walked" section.

Joyfully stress "light" both times it occurs.

Harvesting and dividing spoils are examples of the kind of rejoicing God has brought the people.

The tempo slows down here and the energy builds on the three successive lines and is released (without exaggeration) on the word "smashed."

The "day of Midian" refers to Israel's iconic victory over the Midianites led by Gideon and his army of only 300 soldiers.

Midian = MID-ee-uhn.

READING I   Isaiah 8:23—9:3

A reading from the Book of the Prophet Isaiah

First the L<small>ORD</small> **degraded** the land of Zebulun
   and the land of Naphtali;
   but in the **end** he has **glorified** the seaward road,
   the land west of the **Jordan**,
   the District of the **Gentiles**.

Anguish has taken **wing**, **dispelled** is darkness:
   for there is no **gloom** where but **now** there was **distress**.
The people who walked in **darkness**
   have seen a great **light**;
upon those who dwelt in the land of **gloom**
   a **light** has shone.
You have brought them abundant **joy**
   and **great** rejoicing,
as they **rejoice** before you as at the harvest,
   as people make **merry** when dividing **spoils**.
For the yoke that burdened them,
   the **pole** on their **shoulder**,
and the **rod** of their **taskmaster**
   you have **smashed**, as on the **day** of **Midian**.

READING I

Here on the Third Sunday in Ordinary Time, we meet again this reading we heard during Christmas Time, demonstrating the versatility of Scripture and the ability of texts to teach us in different ways depending on the context. Whereas earlier this text was associated with Jesus's birth, today's Gospel links it with the inauguration of his ministry.

The lands of "Zebulun" and "Napthali" were parts of the Northern Kingdom of Israel that had been invaded by and subsumed into the Assyrian empire. Isaiah recalls the pain and shame of that conquest and prophesies a future time of restoration and glory for these lands that eventually became the land of Galilee, west of the Jordan River.

Even if you were familiar with all the historical and political events that first "degraded" and later "glorified" the geographical areas mentioned, your listeners would not be. So *mood* is the key to the first part of this reading. When you speak of Zebulun and Naphtali, your listeners should hear *gloom* that turns to *joy*. Speak of the two provinces as you might speak of your own children who had been mistreated by

bullies. Then immediately add that the children were vindicated, in fact "glorified," for all to see. "There is *no* gloom," you say, "where but now there was *distress*."

What has brought about this turn of events? Light, "a *great* light!" Speak of the light as you'd speak of anything that brought a joyous reversal into your life—a job offer after a recent layoff, recovery from a near fatal illness, reconciliation with a loved one. Such joy infuses the remainder of the passage, especially the phrases "a light has shone," "great rejoicing," "as people make merry when dividing spoils."

For meditation and context:

RESPONSORIAL PSALM   Psalm 27:1, 4, 13–14 (1a)

R. The Lord is my light and my salvation.

The Lord is my light and my salvation;
    whom should I fear?
The Lord is my life's refuge;
    of whom should I be afraid?

One thing I ask of the Lord;
    this I seek:
to dwell in the house of the Lord
    all the days of my life,
that I may gaze on the loveliness of the Lord
    and contemplate his temple.

I believe that I shall see the bounty
    of the Lord
    in the land of the living.
Wait for the Lord with courage;
    be stouthearted, and wait for the Lord.

Corinthians = kohr-IN-thee-uhnz

READING II   1 Corinthians 1:10–13, 17

A reading from the first Letter of Saint Paul to the Corinthians

The tone is direct and urgent from the start.

Make and sustain good eye contact.

Let "mind" and "purpose" suggest two different agendas.

Shift to a more serious tone and slower pace as you address the divisions that scar them.

Chloe = KLOH-ee ; Apollos = uh-POL-uhs;
Cephas = SEE-fuhs.
Don't try to "mimic" the voices of the various factions. You needn't stress "I" each time, but do stress the name of each leader.

Ask the questions with power. A "yes" reply would be unthinkable.

In no way was Paul a source of distraction from the Gospel. Instead, his weakness manifested God's strength. Words to live by for any reader of the Word!

I **urge** you, brothers and sisters, in the name of our
    Lord Jesus **Christ**,
    that all of you **agree** in what you say,
    and that there be no **divisions** among you,
    but that you be united in the same **mind** and in the
        same **purpose**.
For it has been **reported** to me about you, my brothers and sisters,
    by **Chloe's** people, that there are **rivalries** among you.
I mean that each of you is saying,
    "I belong to **Paul**," or "I belong to **Apollos**,"
    or "I belong to **Cephas**," or "I belong to **Christ**."
Is Christ **divided**?
Was **Paul** crucified for you?
Or were you baptized in the **name** of Paul?
For Christ did not send me to **baptize** but to preach the **gospel**,
    and not with the **wisdom** of human **eloquence**,
    so that the **cross** of Christ might not be **emptied** of its **meaning**.

These repeated references to joy suggest the tone you will need to proclaim in the spirit of Isaiah.

Recalling your own experiences of oppression—illness, loss of job—will give the words "yoke," "pole," and "rod" added power and will enable you to speak the word "smashed" with appropriate intensity and joyous relief.

READING II The Corinthians are Paul's spiritual children and they're having problems. The most serious problem, it seems, is a spirit of rivalry and

discord within the Christian family. So Paul wastes no time and minces no words. "I urge you," he says, in the name of Jesus to get along. Notice, he doesn't ask that they try but that they do it. Already, it seems, Paul senses that the greatest scandal the Church can give is dissension among its members.

Paul is far away in Ephesus when, from various sources, he receives the distressing news about Corinth. He's not concerned that some project of his is being undone, but that the Corinthians have lost sight of the meaning of their Baptism. They

were baptized in Christ's name, not in Paul's or that of any of the other early Christian leaders, including Peter. Only Christ died for them, and only he rose from the grave.

From the first line, we sense the pain with which Paul addresses the difficult topic of their quarrels. And what a thing to quarrel about! Paul's tone (and yours) says this shouldn't be happening. His "I belong to . . . " litany indicates Paul has little patience for this kind of gamesmanship. The lines of division are drawn in predictable ways: Apollos, who was a fine orator,

GOSPEL   Matthew 4:12–23

A reading from the holy Gospel according to Matthew

When **Jesus** heard that **John** had been **arrested**,
  he withdrew to **Galilee**.
He left **Nazareth** and went to live in **Capernaum** by the sea,
  in the region of **Zebulun** and **Naphtali**,
  that what had been said through **Isaiah** the prophet
  might be **fulfilled**:
*Land of **Zebulun** and land of **Naphtali**,*
  the way to the sea, beyond the Jordan,
  ***Galilee** of the **Gentiles**,*
*the people who sit in **darkness** have seen a great **light**,*
*on those dwelling in a land **overshadowed** by **death***
  ***light** has arisen.*
From **that** time on, Jesus began to **preach** and say,
  "**Repent**, for the kingdom of heaven is at **hand**."

As he was walking by the Sea of **Galilee**, he saw two **brothers**,
  Simon who is called **Peter**, and his brother **Andrew**,
  casting a **net** into the sea; they were **fishermen**.
He **said** to them,
  "Come **after** me, and I will make you fishers of **men**."
At once they **left** their nets and **followed** him.
He walked along from there and saw two **other** brothers,
  James, the son of Zebedee, and his brother **John**.
They were in a **boat**, with their father Zebedee, mending
  their **nets**.

Don't rush past this significant detail that motivates Jesus's move to the land of the Gentiles. Galilee = GAL-ih-lee
Nazareth = NAZ-uh-reth

Share this information with significance; Jesus is not just moving to the sea, but fulfilling prophecy.

Vocal shift is needed when quoting the prophecy. The naming of the geographic locations can move more quickly, though the tone is lofty. For the balance of the quote, employ a slower pace using a muted voice to hauntingly remind us that the truth of another age has become the truth of every age. Sustain good eye contact.
Pause briefly after "repent." Then a longer pause after "at hand."

Employ a brighter, livelier tone for this section. Name the Apostles with familiarity and affection.

Stress the disciples' willingness to abandon all they had and knew.
Zebedee = ZEB-uh-dee

Mention of their "father" who shortly will be left behind adds poignancy to the narrative.

---

gained the allegiance of the *intelligentsia*; Cephas (Peter) drew the loyalty of the *Jewish* members of the community, while many *pagan* converts and the poor adhered to Paul. But Paul does not want to win a popularity contest that's wrong from the start, and so he boasts of his weakness instead—apparently Paul's eloquence paled in comparison with Apollos's.

Paul vents his frustration through his three not-so-rhetorical questions. Try scanning a different part of your assembly with each question. Paul is unashamed to profess that he preaches the Gospel without worldly eloquence and depends on God's power to bring good from his efforts. What reader of the Word can fail to take comfort in that posture? It is the Cross of Jesus that saves us, not any human effort. Paul affirms that truth. Your spirited proclamation can do the same.

GOSPEL   A great light comes to the lands of Zebulun and Naphtali. Scripture is fulfilled, but the only one who understands that truth has just been cast into prison. Ironically, the imprisonment of John sets the stage for Jesus's proclamation of the reign of God. It's as if John's exit were the cue for Christ's entrance. Jesus moves to Capernaum in Galilee, a land of prophecy and fulfillment, and also a land of the Gentiles. Here among Gentiles, not in Judea where he was born, Jesus begins his ministry. Matthew heralds the universality of the Good News from the first note of his symphonic narrative that announces Jesus as the Messiah, whom the Gentiles embrace but his own reject.

John's arrest at the start of Jesus's ministry foreshadows Jesus's own dire destiny. But the quote from Isaiah establishes a

Treat each of these short declarative phrases as a sentence, taking a good pause in between them. There is a grand quality to this narration. Speak with pride and confidence in Jesus's mission of teaching and healing.

He **called** them, and immediately they **left** their boat
and their **father**
and **followed** him.
He went around all of **Galilee**,
teaching in their synagogues, proclaiming the **gospel**
of the **kingdom**,
and **curing** every **disease** and **illness** among the people.

[Shorter: Matthew 4:12–17]

TO KEEP IN MIND

Endings: Your inflection of the last line of the reading should always signal that the reading is about to end. Then pause (three beats!) and make eye contact before announcing (from memory) "The word [Gospel] of the Lord." Always pronounce "the" as "thuh" except before words beginning with a vowel.

tone of expectancy and fulfillment, for in Jesus something long awaited finally arrives. Jesus undertakes his ministry announcing the advent of the Kingdom. Like John, Jesus shouts the call for "reform!" The coming of the Kingdom is not a neutral event; it calls for repentance and for genuine, lasting conversion.

The Kingdom will need laborers, and Jesus immediately sets out to find them. Remarkably, they are right under his nose. He neither scours the countryside nor summons from the hilltops, but walks along the shore and calls those he sees. He first sum-

mons two sets of brothers, all of them fishermen. The truly remarkable aspect of the call of these first Apostles is that they respond "immediately" and leave *everything* behind—nets, boats, even their father. Jesus enters people's lives and instantly turns them upside down. A quiet telling from you will provide a good counterpoint to the personal upheaval Jesus asks of those he calls.

Jesus immediately undertakes the activity that will characterize his ministry: "teaching," "proclaiming," and "curing." The Kingdom is here among us and it changes

the objective order. The clearest signs of its presence and power are the healings "of every disease and illness among the people." Remember that liturgical proclamation is never simply a retelling of a past event, but an experience in the now of God's saving love made present among us.

THE PRESENTATION OF THE LORD

LECTIONARY #524

READING I   Malachi 3:1–4

Malachi = MAL-uh-kī

The introductory phrase sets a solemn tone for the quote that follows.

"Lo" means "See" or "Behold." The first two lines carry a tone of warning.

The mood intensifies here. The "Lord" and "the messenger of the covenant" are the same person.

Ask this important question while sustaining good eye contact.

These images are strong and intimidating, but let the images create a sense of threat, not a melodramatic tone from you.

"Sons of Levi" refers to the negligent priests.

"Then" signals a tone shift. Now you describe the consequence of the prophesied purification: sacrifice that pleases the Lord.

A reading from the Book of the Prophet Malachi

Thus **says** the Lord **GOD**:
Lo, I am sending my **messenger**
  to prepare the **way** before me;
And suddenly there will come to the **temple**
  the **LORD** whom you seek,
And the **messenger** of the covenant whom you **desire**.
  Yes, he is **coming**, says the **LORD** of hosts.
But who will **endure** the day of his coming?
  And who can **stand** when he appears?
For he is like the refiner's **fire**,
  or like the fuller's **lye**.
He will sit **refining** and **purifying** silver,
  and he will purify the **sons** of **Levi**,
Refining them like **gold** or like **silver**
  that they may offer due **sacrifice** to the **LORD**.
Then the sacrifice of **Judah** and **Jerusalem**
  will **please** the **LORD**,
  as in the days of **old**, as in **years** gone **by**.

> **TO KEEP IN MIND**
> **Careful preparation** expresses your reverence for the Word.

READING I   In older understandings of the liturgical year, today's feast, forty days after Christmas, brought the celebration of the Nativity to a formal conclusion. Previously, this day was known as the Purification of the Blessed Virgin Mary and focused on Mary's observance of the Jewish legal requirements for purification after childbearing. That perspective is gone, and today the feast celebrates another manifestation of Jesus. The Epiphany marked Jesus's manifestation to the Gentile nations, but on this day Jesus is manifest among his own people as the ful-

fillment of their messianic hopes. So, in effect, today is another sort of Epiphany.

The First Reading comes from a somber prophetic book, the last book of the Old Testament, written at a time when Israel's faith was at low tide and even its priests, the "sons of Levi," had grown negligent in their observance of the Law. So the prophet warns of what he later calls "the great and terrible Day" (3:23), a day of reckoning that few will endure. God will send a "messenger" in anticipation of that day who will prepare the way for the "Lord" who will appear unexpectedly in "the temple." Matthew iden-

tifies John the Baptist with this messenger. The selection of this text for today's liturgy confirms Matthew's understanding and further identifies Jesus with Malachi's "Lord."

The coming of the Lord will be awe-inspiring and terrifying. "Who will endure the day of his coming?" asks the prophet. His coming will be overwhelming because he comes to purify, and the images used to describe the nature of the purification are powerful. He will be like "fire" that melts and purifies metals and like "lye" that bleaches even the roughest cloth. This purification will cause the people to finally offer

For meditation and context:

This will not be an easy reading to follow for those who are hearing with no preparation. So read slowly, lifting out the meaning for your listeners.

Contrast "children" and "Jesus."

This is not the place for a neutral tone. Celebrate Jesus's victory over the "devil."

As you contrast "angels" and "descendants of Abraham," rejoice that Jesus chose to come to our aid.

Again, don't settle for a neutral tone here, but rejoice that Jesus helps us who are put constantly to the "test."

RESPONSORIAL PSALM　Psalm 24:7, 8, 9, 10 (8)

R. Who is this king of glory? It is the Lord!

Lift up, O gates, your lintels;
　reach up, you ancient portals,
　　that the king of glory may come in!

Who is this king of glory?
　The Lord, strong and mighty,
　the Lord, mighty in battle.

Lift up, O gates, your lintels;
　reach up, you ancient portals,
　　that the king of glory may come in!

Who is this king of glory?
　The Lord of hosts; he is the king of glory.

READING II　Hebrews 2:14–18

A reading from the Letter to the Hebrews

Since the children share in **blood** and **flesh**,
　Jesus **likewise** shared in them,
　that through **death** he might **destroy** the one
　who has the **power** of death, that is, the devil,
　and **free** those who through **fear** of death
　had been subject to **slavery** all their life.
Surely he did not help **angels**
　but rather the descendants of **Abraham**;
　therefore, he had to become like his brothers and sisters
　in **every way**,
　that he might be a **merciful** and **faithful** high priest before God
　to expiate the **sins** of the people.
Because he himself was **tested** through what he **suffered**,
　he is able to **help** those who are being tested.

worthy sacrifices, not the blemished, second rate offerings they have been putting before the Lord. Right worship will lead to righteousness before the Lord.

In today's Second Reading and Gospel we will see that the prophesied Lord who comes to the Temple will become both "high priest" and also the "due sacrifice" that truly pleases God and replaces all the offerings of former times.

 READING II　In coming to faith, one may encounter many stumbling blocks. One of the largest of those obsta-

cles can be the humanity of Jesus, and especially the suffering he endured. Early converts to the faith had to struggle with the notion that Jesus was human like us, a mortal subject to the unavoidable suffering and death of earthly life. It would have made more sense to embrace a god who saves by being impervious to the limitations of the flesh and who would vanquish death not by experiencing it, but by being exempt from it. As always, the ways of God are not our ways and the Lord chose the very path that human sense would banish.

In the verses preceding today's passage, the author of Hebrews argues that Jesus accepted human existence and for a time lived "'lower than the angels'" (2:7); but now Jesus reigns in heavenly glory above all creatures, including the angels. Jesus's suffering prepared him for the role of high priest, an intermediary between God and humanity. The perfection he achieved through his suffering enables Jesus to perfect us, his disciples.

Since siblings share "blood and flesh," Jesus, our true brother, also had to share in them. By entering human experience

GOSPEL   Luke 2:22–40

A reading from the holy Gospel according to Luke

When the days were completed for their **purification**
     according to the law of **Moses**,
     Mary and **Joseph** took **Jesus** up to **Jerusalem**
     to **present** him to the **Lord**,
     just as it is written in the **law** of the Lord,
     *Every **male** that opens the womb shall be **consecrated***
          to the Lord,
     and to offer the **sacrifice** of
     *a pair of **turtledoves** or two young **pigeons**,*
     in accordance with the **dictate** in the law of the Lord.

Now there was a man in Jerusalem whose name was **Simeon**.
This man was **righteous** and **devout**,
     awaiting the **consolation** of Israel,
     and the Holy **Spirit** was upon him.
It had been **revealed** to him by the Holy Spirit
     that he should not see **death**
     before he had seen the **Christ** of the Lord.
He came in the **Spirit** into the temple;
     and when the parents brought in the child **Jesus**
     to perform the custom of the **law** in regard to him,
     He took him into his **arms** and **blessed** God, saying:

     "**Now**, Master, you may let your servant **go**
          in **peace**, according to your **word**,
     for my eyes have **seen** your **salvation**,
          which you prepared in the sight of all the **peoples**:
     a **light** for revelation to the **Gentiles**,
          and **glory** for your people **Israel**."

Speak in a brisk and upbeat tone as if relating a story about family members to family members.

"Every male . . . " requires a vocal shift since here we move from narration to quotation of the Law.

Two doves or pigeons is the poor woman's substitution for a lamb.

Pause briefly before starting this section and begin with renewed energy.

Simeon = SIM-ee-uhn

Speak in a softer, more familiar tone as if sharing privileged information.

Don't overlook the detail of Simeon taking Jesus in his arms.

Simeon's words have become a beloved canticle used daily in the Church's prayer.

---

and accepting the ultimate destiny of all mortal life—the grave—Jesus was able to destroy the power of the primordial gravedigger, "the devil." The one with the power to impose death on humanity is rendered powerless by the perfect obedience of Jesus.

Jesus came to help "the descendants of Abraham," and the happy consequence is a perfect high priest who, on our behalf, offers the perfect sacrifice (himself!) for the remission of our sins. This will be a central theme throughout the Letter to the Hebrews. Jesus was "tested" and did not fail, so now

and for all time he intercedes for those who continue to be tested—us. In today's Gospel reading we see this "high priest" being brought to the Temple of sacrifice for the very first time and we hear a prophecy that foretells the testing he will have to endure for our sake.

GOSPEL   Malachi's prophetic words find ultimate fulfillment in the events narrated in this Gospel text. Jesus is presented in the Temple where a spirit-filled man recognizes him as the fulfillment of prophecy. Simeon alludes to

Isaiah's second song of the Suffering Servant when he speaks of Jesus as "a light for . . . the Gentiles." Given his own prophecy that he will soon share, the Servant allusion is very apt and begins the process of turning our focus away from the manger and toward the hill of Calvary.

Faithful adherence to the prescripts of the Law brings Joseph and Mary to the Temple precincts where they purchase the offerings of the poor, two turtledoves or pigeons, to present as a sin offering to the Lord. These gifts are necessary, not because of individual sin on the part of the Holy

Suggest both their amazement and their pride.

Though this is Simeon's more sober message, don't overdramatize the prophetic words. State them seriously and without hesitation.

Pause briefly before introducing Anna. The details of her marriage and widowhood add to the family narrative feel of the text.

Phanuel = FAN-yoo-el; fuh-NYOO-uhl

These are fascinating details.

Scan your assembly as you speak these lines.

Pause before this final sentence. Speak with pride and admiration.

The child's father and mother were **amazed** at what was **said**
        about him;
    and Simeon **blessed** them and said to Mary his **mother**,
    "**Behold**, this child is destined
    for the **fall** and **rise** of many in Israel,
    and to be a sign that will be **contradicted**
    —and you yourself a **sword** will pierce—
    so that the thoughts of many **hearts** may be **revealed**."
There was also a **prophetess**, **Anna**,
    the daughter of Phanuel, of the tribe of Asher.
She was **advanced** in years,
    having lived seven years with her **husband** after her marriage,
    and then as a **widow** until she was **eighty-four**.
She never **left** the temple,
    but worshiped **night** and **day** with **fasting** and **prayer**.
And coming forward at that very **time**,
    she gave **thanks** to God and spoke about the **child**
    to all who were awaiting the **redemption** of **Jerusalem**.

When they had fulfilled all the **prescriptions**
    of the law of the Lord,
    they **returned** to Galilee, to their own town of **Nazareth**.
The child **grew** and became **strong**, filled with **wisdom**;
    and the favor of **God** was **upon** him.

[Shorter: Luke 2:22–32]

TO KEEP IN MIND
Eye contact is your means of connecting with those to whom you minister. You should look at the assembly during the middle and at the end of every thought or sentence.

Family, but because by entering the human condition Jesus immerses himself in the grime of the human condition we call sin.

Besides Simeon, another elder inhabits the Temple area, and she, too, is given the great grace of an encounter with the Lord. (When first observed in the East, this feast was known as "The Encounter.") Anna recognizes Jesus as the hope of Israel and the savior of Jerusalem and becomes a font of praise for this marvelous child. In this encounter, Luke presents what amounts to a second Epiphany, this time to representatives of Jesus's own people rather than to those of the Gentile nations.

The narrative dimension of the text has all the elements of a classic family story. Besides the details of how the Law was strictly observed and how the infant child embarks on his first journey to the city of his ultimate destiny, we have the colorful characters of Simeon and Anna, spirit-filled elders who have lived the old Law so faithfully that they are given the vision to recognize the embodiment of the new Law. While Anna's response is all light and praise, Simeon's casts a shadow over the otherwise celebratory event. His penetrating vision sees how the child he holds in his arms will one day bring turmoil and dissension and how his mother's heart will be pierced.

But first the boy must grow, and acquire wisdom, and bask in the "favor of God."

FIFTH SUNDAY IN ORDINARY TIME

LECTIONARY #73

READING I   Isaiah 58:7–10

A reading from the Book of the Prophet Isaiah

Thus says the LORD:
Share your **bread** with the **hungry**,
   shelter the **oppressed** and the **homeless**;
clothe the naked when you see them,
   and do not turn your back on your **own**.
Then your **light** shall break forth like the **dawn**,
   and your **wound** shall quickly be **healed**;
your **vindication** shall go before you,
   and the **glory** of the LORD shall be your rear **guard**.
Then you shall **call**, and the LORD will **answer**;
   you shall **cry** for help, and he will say: **Here** I am!
If you **remove** from your midst
   oppression, false **accusation** and malicious **speech**;
if you bestow your bread on the **hungry**
   and **satisfy** the afflicted;
then **light** shall rise for you in the **darkness**,
   and the **gloom** shall become for you like **midday**.

Isaiah = ī-ZAY-uh

"Thus says the Lord" always requires a solemn tone.

You begin with imperatives, but not with an overbearing tone. Making eye contact with individual members of the assembly will help soften the directives.

We are to show mercy both to the stranger *and* the neighbor.

Here you announce the joyful consequences of embracing God's instruction.

As you continue to proclaim the rewards of just behavior, let your energy build and your tone fill with the joy of knowing God's mercy.

Slow your tempo and soften your volume as you remind us that the aforementioned blessings will come only "if" we heed God's call for just behavior.

The if/then clause is completed here as you declare again that we manifest God's light when we live God's love.

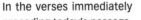 In the verses immediately preceding today's passage, God poses a key question to the community that has just returned from exile: what spiritual discipline truly pleases me? God's answer is clear: it is not ritual fasting, but doing justice and tending to the needs of the poor. God requires *positive* action that demonstrates genuine concern for the needy in our midst.

Our treatment of others manifests the quality of our relationship with God. Right behavior makes our light shine "like the dawn," an image that connects this text with today's Gospel where Jesus calls his disciples "the light of the world." The theme of epiphany (manifestation) continues in today's readings, reminding us that we are called to become living manifestations of God's love in the same way Jesus was a living sacrament of God, manifesting divine love by surrendering his very life.

Addressed to the survivors of the exile, Isaiah's words offer hope that the nation can be rebuilt and recover its former glory. Dramatic images of healing, vindication, and God's vigilant solicitude paint a compelling picture of this future. But it will come only "*if*" they embrace God's justice and mercy. "If" must be stressed both times it appears, for the cause-effect relationship is strongly stated.

Note that "light" replaces "gloom" not only because of grand gestures, like removing poverty and oppression from society, but also because of small gestures, like retracting our pointed fingers and taming our tongues. God offers a choice: saying no deepens the gloom around us; saying yes makes us living sacraments and transforms our darkness to radiant light.

For meditation and context:

RESPONSORIAL PSALM   Psalm 112:4–5, 6–7, 8–9 (4a)

R. The just man is a light in darkness to the upright.
or
R. Alleluia.

Light shines through the darkness for the
   upright;
  he is gracious and merciful and just.
Well for the man who is gracious and lends,
  who conducts his affairs with justice.

He shall never be moved;
  the just one shall be in everlasting
    remembrance.
An evil report he shall not fear;
  his heart is firm, trusting in the LORD.

His heart is steadfast; he shall not fear.
  Lavishly he gives to the poor;
his justice shall endure forever;
  his horn shall be exalted in glory.

Corinthians = kohr-IN-thee-uhnz

Establish eye contact before you begin, and then read slowly as this text begins in the middle of things.

He's not beating himself up; he's saying there is something more persuasive than eloquent speech: our crucified Lord.

His "weakness" and "fear" are manifestations of his reverence and his awe before almighty God, not fear of the Corinthians.

Speak with confidence of the pillar of our faith: not human wisdom but the "power of God."

READING II   1 Corinthians 2:1–5

A reading from the first Letter of Saint Paul to the Corinthians

When I **came** to you, brothers and sisters,
   proclaiming the **mystery** of God,
   I did not come with **sublimity** of words or of **wisdom**.
For I resolved to know **nothing** while I was with you
   except Jesus **Christ**, and him **crucified**.
I came to you in **weakness** and **fear** and much **trembling**,
   and my **message** and my **proclamation**
   were not with persuasive words of **wisdom**,
   but with a demonstration of **Spirit** and **power**,
   so that your **faith** might rest **not** on human wisdom
   but on the **power** of **God**.

READING II   A weaker man might have sought a stronger argument; but no one has ever accused Paul of being weak (except himself, as we shall see). So he takes up the great stumbling block regarding Christianity and makes it the foundation of his argument: yes, the Son of God was crucified, the Messiah came in weakness and vulnerability and endured the ignominy of the Cross. That is Paul's teaching delivered in simple, unadorned language that lacks the sophistication of eloquent oratory, but never lacks the power of truth, or the Spirit and the power of God.

Whether Paul had tried and failed or whether he knew that his oratorical skills were eclipsed by evangelists like Apollos we cannot say with certainty. What we know for sure is that Paul chooses to imitate in his own demeanor the "weakness" of his crucified Lord. But Paul's language is metaphorical, for in his life he faced beatings, imprisonment, and even death with great valor. What he means is that his life and teaching are imbued with the virtue we call "fear of the Lord," a healthy and respectful fear that flows from awareness of God's awesome majesty. Though some contemporary spirituality looks askance at notions of reverential fear, Paul endorses it as a chief means of working out our salvation.

Paul's self-effacement regarding his lack of "persuasive words of wisdom" is his way of teaching that human wisdom cannot save us; but the power of the Cross cannot fail.

Establish eye contact and speak the introductory phrase slowly, so your listeners will be fully focused before you begin quoting Jesus.

It's difficult to stress both "you" and "salt." Stressing "you" says, "It is you who are salt, not someone else!" Emphasis on "salt" says, "Be aware of what you are!"

These strong words hint at the eternal destiny of those who squander their privileged status.

Remind your assembly of their status with confidence and gratitude. Then call them to responsibility as you speak of the need to let our light shine.

Having made his argument, Jesus concludes with vigor, calling all to selfless practice of virtue for the glory of God and the sake of others.

TO KEEP IN MIND

Names of characters are often the first word of a reading. Stress names so listeners don't miss who the subject is.

GOSPEL   Matthew 5:13–16

A reading from the holy Gospel according to Matthew

Jesus said to his **disciples**:
   "You are the **salt** of the **earth**.
But if salt loses its **taste**, with what can it be **seasoned**?
It is no longer good for **anything**
   but to be **thrown** out and **trampled** underfoot.
You are the **light** of the **world**.
A city set on a **mountain** cannot be **hidden**.
Nor do they light a **lamp** and then put it under a **bushel** basket;
   it is set on a **lampstand**,
   where it gives **light** to all in the house.
Just so, **your** light must **shine** before others,
   that they may **see** your good deeds
   and **glorify** your heavenly Father."

GOSPEL   The Church is a sacrament of Christ who is a sacrament of God. That geometry is unequivocal and its logic makes "epiphany" a perpetual feast. Before anything else, Christian faith is about manifesting Christ, and we do it first of all not by what we do but through who we are.

Jesus's words in this text are not equivocal; he does not say we will be light "*if*" or that we will be salt "*when*." Because of our Baptism, we are incorporated into Christ and that status *makes* us salt and light. Our very being is now sacramental and we go forth evincing Christ with every breath, for we are his body. A married couple does not strive to *become* a sacrament of God's love; they are made a sacrament when, in love, they bind themselves to each other. What remains for them is to grow in their ability to show forth God's love for the Church through their ever deepening love for each other.

Perhaps Matthew is suggesting that the role of being the light of the world has now passed to the Gentile nations. Understanding and prizing our status as "salt," "light," and "a city built on a mountain" does not exempt us from the responsibility of manifesting who we are. Duties flow from identity, not the other way around. Once we know who we are we begin to intuit what we should do. So, we must not lose our flavor nor hide our light under a basket. And we must do "good deeds," not to glorify ourselves but to glorify God and to cast light onto God's mercy in a way that draws others into deep relationship with him.

SIXTH SUNDAY
IN ORDINARY TIME

LECTIONARY #76

Sirach = Sĭ-ruhk; SEER-ak

READING I   Sirach 15:15–20

A reading from the Book of Sirach

Strong eye contact is essential to effective proclamation of this passage.

If you **choose** you can **keep** the commandments, they will
>   **save** you;
>   if you trust in **God**, you too shall **live**;
> he has set before you **fire** and **water**;
>   to whichever you **choose**, stretch forth your hand.
> Before man are **life** and **death**, **good** and **evil**,
>   whichever he **chooses** shall be **given** him.
> **Immense** is the wisdom of the LORD;
>   he is **mighty** in power, and all-**seeing**.
> The eyes of God are on those who **fear** him;
>   he **understands** man's every deed.
> **No** one does he command to act **unjustly**,
>   to **none** does he give license to sin.

The sense is, you can reach out and pick whichever you want.

Again, the emphasis is on one's ability to choose, even if the choice is counter to God's will.

The latter part of the text focuses on God's sovereign power that remains despite human freedom. God is not neutral regarding human choice for he keeps an eye "on those who fear him."

For meditation and context:

RESPONSORIAL PSALM   Psalm 119:1–2, 4–5, 17–18, 33–34 (1b)

R. Blessed are they who follow the law of the Lord!

Blessed are they whose way is blameless,
   who walk in the law of the LORD.
Blessed are they who observe his decrees,
   who seek him with all their heart.

You have commanded that your precepts
   be diligently kept.
Oh, that I might be firm in the ways
   of keeping your statutes!

Be good to your servant, that I may live
   and keep your words.
Open my eyes, that I may consider
   the wonders of your law.

Instruct me, O LORD, in the way
   of your statutes,
   that I may exactly observe them.
Give me discernment, that I may observe
   your law
   and keep it with all my heart.

TO KEEP IN MIND
Eye contact is your means of connecting with those to whom you minister. You should look at the assembly during the middle and at the end of every thought or sentence.

READING I   Today's text, taken from this book that the Church uses regularly for the ongoing instruction of the faithful, focuses on human freedom and human responsibility. After creating humanity, God left us free to make our own choices; therefore, we can choose whether or not to obey the commandments; we can even choose "life" or "death" and "good" or "evil." A superficial reading of this text might persuade us that human freedom is absolute and that doing what we do is simply a matter of choice. It would seem that Sirach leaves no room for ambiguity: if you want to do good, you can. Period. But to make such a claim would overlook a fundamental conviction of the Christian faith. The sin of Adam and Eve left us fundamentally flawed and inclined toward sin. In Romans (7:14–25) Paul describes the tension of not doing what he *wants* to do and instead doing what he does *not* want to do.

But Scripture is as complex as human life. Unless we consider all of Scripture we will easily and quickly be led astray. The fact is that Paul and Sirach are both right. Because of the hold original sin has on us, like Paul, we often fail to do the good we desire to do. But at the same time we remain essentially free to choose. If we claim the power of grace, we can indeed follow the commandments and choose good over evil.

But Sirach does not so much want to debate the extent of human freedom as to assert that if there is evil in the world, it is not God's doing. Some might joke that "The devil made me do it," but Sirach isn't buying it. And certainly he won't accept anyone trying to put the blame for their sin on God. God never has and never will "command

READING II   1 Corinthians 2:6–10

A reading from the first Letter of Saint Paul to the Corinthians

Brothers and sisters:
We speak a wisdom to those who are **mature**,
 not a wisdom of **this** age,
 nor of the **rulers** of this age who are passing away.
Rather, we speak **God's** wisdom, **mysterious**, **hidden**,
 which God **predetermined** before the ages for our **glory**,
 and which none of the rulers of this age **knew**;
 or, if they **had** known it,
 they would not have **crucified** the Lord of glory.
But as it is written:
 What **eye** *has not* **seen**, *and* **ear** *has not* **heard**,
  and what has not **entered** *the human* **heart**,
 what God has **prepared** *for those who* **love** *him*,
  this *God has revealed to* **us** *through the Spirit.*

For the Spirit **scrutinizes** everything, even the **depths** of **God**.

Corinthians = kohr-IN-thee-uhnz

"Mature" means those who understand and embrace the full Christian mystery, which includes the Cross.

"Rulers of this age" may refer to Pilate and Herod or perhaps the demonic powers that influenced those temporal leaders. "Mysterious," "hidden," and "predetermined" all describe "God's wisdom," but each word is different, so don't run them together. Take a slight pause after "God's wisdom." Speak this line with great conviction.

This announcement deserves great energy and sincerity. Read slowly. The three clauses build one upon the other and culminate on the word "this" that summarizes them all: "*This* (what has just gone before) is what God has *revealed* to us."

This final line and the one just above communicate great joy and gratitude.

GOSPEL   Matthew 5:17–37

A reading from the holy Gospel according to Matthew

Jesus said to his **disciples**:
 "Do not think that I have come to abolish the **law**
  or the **prophets**.
I have come not to **abolish** but to **fulfill**.
Amen, I say to you, until heaven and earth pass **away**,
 not the smallest **letter** or the smallest **part** of a letter
 will pass from the law,
 until all things have taken place.

As homilist you will have much to explain about this passage; as reader your concern is animating the character of Jesus and communicating his uncompromising standard of righteousness, while not losing his compassion.

The Law remains in force during the time of Jesus' ministry, but his Death and Resurrection will usher in a new age when the Old Law will be fulfilled as in the antitheses that follow.

anyone to act unjustly" and God never gives "license to sin." At great cost God has entrusted us with the power to choose; whether we use that freedom to build up or to destroy, the responsibility rests squarely and only on our own shoulders.

READING II Just last week, Paul was downgrading human wisdom and denying having any of his own. Now he asserts that wisdom may in fact have an appropriate role in the life of the Christian. The wisdom of which he speaks, however, is of a radically different nature than what the world is used to and very different from the Gnostic brand to which members of the Corinthian community subscribed.

The wisdom to which Paul refers is the only one deserving of the name, and it is reserved to the "spiritually mature." Paul appropriates a word often used in the Gnostic sects; for them, "maturity" was a special privilege that came automatically, bestowed on them from above at Baptism. Part of the attraction of Gnosticism was its claim that special knowledge or wisdom was conferred on its members—wisdom others were denied.

But Paul intends a different kind of wisdom—the Cross of Jesus, for which the Gnostics had little use. The great hidden mystery about which Paul is truly excited is the one the Gnostics fail to see: the *crucified* one is the Lord of heaven and earth. Paul is not creating spiritual castes, but asserting that some are spiritual children while others have grown into spiritual adults. Christian adulthood requires being able to understand the supreme and lasting significance of the Cross. To relegate

Jesus is not endorsing legalism but love of God's will as manifested in the Law.

Pharisees = FAYR-uh-seez

Set up a contrast between the "You have heard . . . " and "But I say . . . " sections.

Raqa = ree-KAY; ree-kuh. The word means "idiot" or "dimwit."

Sanhedrin = san-HEE-druhn
Gehenna = geh-HEN-nah

Your voice can reflect the growing seriousness of the offenses.

Make eye contact and speak very deliberately to your assembly.

Give these lines the feel of solid brotherly or neighborly advice.

Therefore, whoever **breaks** one of the **least** of these commandments
   and teaches **others** to do so
   will be called **least** in the kingdom of **heaven**.
But whoever **obeys** and **teaches** these commandments
   will be called **greatest** in the kingdom of heaven.
I tell you, unless your righteousness **surpasses**
   that of the scribes and Pharisees,
   you will not **enter** the kingdom of heaven.

"You have heard that it was said to your ancestors,
   *You shall not **kill**; and whoever kills will be liable to **judgment**.*
But **I** say to you,
   whoever is **angry** with his brother
   will be liable to judgment;
   and whoever says to his brother, '**Raqa**,'
   will be answerable to the **Sanhedrin**;
   and whoever says, 'You **fool**,'
   will be liable to fiery **Gehenna**.
Therefore, if you bring your **gift** to the altar,
   and there recall that your brother
   has anything **against** you,
   leave your gift there at the altar,
   go first and be **reconciled** with your brother,
   and **then** come and offer your gift.
Settle with your opponent **quickly** while on the **way** to court.
Otherwise your opponent will hand you over to the **judge**,
   and the judge will hand you over to the **guard**,
   and you will be thrown into **prison**.
Amen, I say to you,
   you will not be **released** until you have paid the **last penny**.

"You have heard that it was said,
   *You shall not commit **adultery**.*

the Cross to the scrap heaps of history and focus only on the Resurrection is to miss the core of the Christian faith. And that is precisely what some of the Corinthians were doing.

   Paul concludes rejoicing that what the human eye has not seen, what the human ear has not heard, and what has not yet entered the human heart, are nonetheless revealed to us "through the *Spirit*." Through that Spirit we gain access even to the "depths of God." If you used appropriate energy in the forgoing lines, the last two sentences will feel momentous.

GOSPEL   Addressing the crowds he has called "blessed," Jesus teaches them how to live as the "salt" and "light" we heard about last week. His listeners are the eager crowd and the disciples, not those he calls "hypocrites." That awareness can focus your tone. Six times Jesus quotes the Law and then comments, "But I say," in seeming opposition to the teaching of the Law. While Jesus's sayings are known as "antitheses," his tone needs no hostility. He is sharing truth that, in the context of the Kingdom, speaks for itself. It can be stated simply, lovingly, in a way that reveals

the truth's deep beauty. Truth's innate beauty is compelling; when it sounds harsh, it becomes a bitter pill.

   The last sentence is the key to the first paragraph. Jesus wants his followers to enter the Kingdom, but he knows they won't unless they embrace his new, higher standard of morality. Three of his six antitheses *expand* the demands of the Mosaic Law while three call disciples to a new and *higher* standard. Jesus's call for adherence to the Old Law may not be as literal as it sounds. The passing of "heaven and earth" may refer to the new order ushered in by

Don't pull back from Jesus's unequivocal stance.

This is metaphoric language that needs a more nuanced delivery.

An "unlawful" marriage refers to incestuous relationships, as between a son and stepmother, which were not true marriages and therefore not an exception to Jesus's absolute prohibition against divorce.

Nothing that manifests God can be used as a substitute for the divine name in an oath. One should be able to rely on the honesty of a Christian disciple.

Jesus is straightforward: "Say, 'Yes' when you mean 'Yes' and 'No' when you mean 'No.'"

Because they presuppose the human weakness of lying, oaths are "from the evil one."

But **I** say to you,
    everyone who looks at a woman with **lust**
    has **already** committed adultery with her in his **heart**.
If your right **eye** causes you to sin,
    tear it out and **throw** it away.
It is better for you to **lose** one of your members
    than to have your whole **body** thrown into Gehenna.
And if your right **hand** causes you to sin,
    cut it off and **throw** it away.
It is better for you to **lose** one of your members
    than to have your whole **body** go into **Gehenna**.

"It was **also** said,
    *Whoever **divorces** his **wife** must give her a **bill** of divorce.*
But **I** say to you,
    whoever divorces his wife—unless the marriage is **unlawful**—
    causes her to commit **adultery**,
    and whoever **marries** a divorced woman commits adultery.

"Again you have heard that it was said to your ***ancestors***,
    *Do not take a **false** oath,*
    *but make **good** to the Lord all that you **vow**.*
But **I** say to you, do not swear at **all**;
    not by **heaven**, for it is God's **throne**;
    nor by the **earth**, for it is his **footstool**;
    nor by **Jerusalem**, for it is the city of the great **King**.
Do not swear by your **head**,
    for you cannot make a single **hair** white or black.
Let your '**Yes**' mean '**Yes**,' and your '**No**' mean '**No**.'
Anything **more** is from the **evil** one."

[Shorter: Matthew 5:20–22a, 27–28, 33–34a, 37]

TO KEEP IN MIND
Slow down: The larger the church, the larger the assembly, and the more complex the text, the slower you must read.

---

his Death and Resurrection, rather than the end of the physical order.

The old Law forbade murder, but Jesus forbids all that leads to it: anger and disparaging language. Quote the old Law with authority, but then speak Jesus' antithesis as a superior truth that's offered for the good of all. The consequences ("the Sanhedrin," "Gehenna") grow more serious in proportion to the injuries given. Jesus's warnings highlight the primacy of reconciliation, making settling with opponents a necessity, not an option.

Jesus's teaching flows from his awareness of sin's dire consequences. Adultery can be committed in the heart, not only the bedroom. So, it is better to lose part of the body than to let it lead us into sin. It's like the motivation that causes a father to slap the hand of a child who's approaching an electric outlet with a hairpin. Jesus exaggerates (gouge out your eye, cut off your hand!) because like most parents he'd rather overreact than risk seeing children hurt.

Jesus offers no qualifiers when presenting obviously hard teachings. He is straightforward and makes no apologies for the truth. His injunction against divorce is unequivocal.

We are not to swear by "God" or anything related to God ("heaven" or "earth") because in the Kingdom honesty should be a given and oaths unnecessary, and we are to say what we mean and mean what we say. Imitating Jesus's directness will give this passage its greatest power.

SEVENTH SUNDAY
IN ORDINARY TIME

LECTIONARY #79

READING I   Leviticus 19:1–2, 17–18

A reading from the Book of Leviticus

The LORD said to **Moses**,
   "**Speak** to the whole Israelite community and **tell** them:
   Be **holy**, for I, the LORD, your **God**, am holy.

"You shall not bear **hatred** for your brother or sister in your heart.
Though you may have to **reprove** your fellow citizen,
   do not incur **sin** because of him.
Take no **revenge** and cherish no **grudge** against any of your people.
You shall love your **neighbor** as **yourself**.
I am the LORD."

Leviticus = lih-VIT-ih-kuhs

But for the introductory phrase, the entire reading is spoken in the voice of God.

Israelite = IZ-ree-uh-līt; IZ-ray-uh-līt

This is not a "do it or else" admonition, but a call to be what we are—holy children of a holy God.

Continue in the compassionate tone of a parent who instructs children on what will bring them joy and abundant life.

This is a loving word of warning that says revenge is like drinking poison we thought would kill the *other* person.

God means business.

For meditation and context:

RESPONSORIAL PSALM   Psalm 103:1–2, 3–4, 8, 10, 12–13 (8a)

R. The Lord is kind and merciful.

Bless the LORD, O my soul;
   and all my being, bless his holy name.
Bless the LORD, O my soul,
   and forget not all his benefits.

He pardons all your iniquities,
   heals all your ills.
He redeems your life from destruction,
   crowns you with kindness and compassion.

Merciful and gracious is the LORD,
   slow to anger and abounding in kindness.
Not according to our sins does he deal
   with us,
   nor does he requite us according
     to our crimes.

As far as the east is from the west,
   so far has he put our transgressions
     from us.
As a father has compassion on his children,
   so the LORD has compassion on those who
     fear him.

> **TO KEEP IN MIND**
> **Read through all three readings and commentaries** for your assigned Sunday. All three were chosen for this day, and each commentary has suggestions that can help you with your own passage.

READING I Short readings provide no time to "warm up" or "ease in"; you've got to be ready to deliver your best right from the start, as you would in a hundred-yard dash. But unlike a race, short readings challenge your ability to go slowly. Understand the tone of the reading and let your posture and facial expression convey it even before you speak the first word.

A loving God calls for uncompromising efforts to "be holy." The import of God's command is not, "If I can do it, you can do it." God is God and we are not; no amount of trying will change that. God is saying, *because* I, your God, am a holy God, you *can* be holy, too. We were created in God's image and likeness, which gives us an attainable destiny: to be an embodiment of the love that is God.

In the second paragraph God explains what holiness looks like, and all of it requires courage and humility. If we want to emulate the holiness of God, here is the agenda: surrender hatred; correct one another, but in a way that doesn't make us as bad as those we wish to correct (the primordial antecedent of the familiar admonition, "Don't stoop down to their level!"); hold no grudges; and love others as we love ourselves. This is a formula for sanctity, for the saints often did no more than this—every day and in all circumstances. It's no easy task, and God knows it. Your tone, more pleading than command, should reflect that. The last line is challenging. Pause after "I," then speak "am the Lord" as much to reassure your listeners that God loves them as to insist that God means business.

Corinthians = kohr-IN-thee-uhns

Establish eye contact on the greeting and sustain it through the first sentence. This is so obvious, you say, please see it!

"Holy" means "belonging to God."

This is a directive. Speak it with authority.

Note carefully where "wise" should and should not be stressed.

Set off the Scripture quotations from the rest of the text.

The list that begins with "Paul" and ends with "the future" names the human realities in which we should *not* seek our sense of importance.
He's saying: "All belongs to you . . . Paul, Apollos, . . . the future . . . *all* (of this) belongs to *you*."
Apollos = uh-POL-uhs
Cephas = SEE-fuhs
The final line contains great profundity; speak it slowly and with considerable weight.

READING II   1 Corinthians 3:16–23

A reading from the first Letter of Saint Paul to the Corinthians

Brothers and sisters:
Do you not know that you are the **temple** of **God**,
 and that the **Spirit** of God **dwells** in you?
If anyone **destroys** God's temple, God will destroy that **person**;
 for the temple of God, which you **are**, is **holy**.

Let no one **deceive** himself.
If any one among you considers himself **wise** in this age,
 let him become a **fool**, so as to **become** wise.
For the **wisdom** of this world is **foolishness** in the eyes of God,
 for it is written:
  God *catches the wise in their own **ruses**,*
 and again:
  The Lord knows the thoughts of the wise,
   *that they are **vain**.*
So let no one **boast** about human beings, for everything **belongs**
   to you,
 Paul or **Apollos** or **Cephas**,
 or the **world** or **life** or **death**,
 or the **present** or the **future**:
 all belong to **you**, and you to **Christ**, and Christ to **God**.

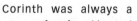 **READING II** Corinth was always a source of profound joy and profound frustration for Paul. Prone to high drama and deep divisions, the Christians of Corinth seemed often to miss the boat and focus more on personalities like Apollos and Peter than on the heart of the Gospel. So Paul tries once again to put them in touch with their core: the risen Jesus.

When something obvious hits you in the face, the frustration doubles if others can't see it. That is Paul's dilemma. He has tried other comparisons—a "body," a

"building"—to drive home the truth of who believers are. Now he calls them God's holy *temple* and pities anyone who fails to understand. Christ is the *true* temple, but we are his body, so we make up the temple of God. Imagine speaking the first paragraph to a child you love. As if looking in the child's eyes, speak with conviction when you say "the temple . . . which you *are*, is holy." See this truth with such clarity that not seeing it strikes you as incomprehensible and tragic.

In recent weeks, Paul has been speaking on the theme of wisdom. Here he juxtaposes worldly and Godly wisdom, saying the worldly pales in comparison to the Godly. His contrasts are almost playful, but intensify your delivery when quoting the Scripture passages, building to the conclusion that there should be no boasting about "human beings." The items in the litany of the final lines comprise a single thought, so you don't need to stress or distinguish them. Paul's point is that everything belongs to Christ—everything, including us. We are truly Christ's, and Christ is fully God's.

GOSPEL   Matthew 5:38–48

A reading from the holy Gospel according to Matthew

Jesus said to his **disciples**:
  "You have heard that it was said,
  An **eye** *for an* **eye** *and a* **tooth** *for a* **tooth**.
But **I** say to you, offer no **resistance** to one who is evil.
When someone strikes you on your **right** cheek,
  turn the **other** one as well.
If anyone wants to go to **law** with you over your **tunic**,
  hand over your **cloak** as well.
Should anyone **press** you into service for **one** mile,
  go for **two** miles.
Give to the one who **asks** of you,
  and do not turn your **back** on one who wants to **borrow**.

  "You have heard that it was said,
  You shall **love** *your neighbor and* **hate** *your enemy*.
But I say to you, love your **enemies**
  and **pray** for those who **persecute** you,
  that you may be **children** of your heavenly **Father**,
  for he makes his sun rise on the **bad** and the **good**,
  and causes **rain** to fall on the **just** and the **unjust**.
For if you love those who love **you**, what **recompense** will
    you have?
Do not the **tax** collectors do the same?
And if you greet your **brothers** only,
  what is **unusual** about that?
Do not the **pagans** do the same?
So be **perfect**, just as your heavenly **Father** is perfect."

This pericope begins in the middle, so start slowly, with a proclamatory tone that helps set the unstated scene: Jesus teaching in the midst of the large crowd.

Give due weight to Jesus's "But I say . . ."

In the next two sentences, pause at the comma, then surprise the listeners with Jesus's instruction: "turn . . . " "hand over . . . "

Deliver this instruction forcefully, then pause and begin with renewed energy.

When you know people will think you're crazy, you have to look into their eyes and speak with an earnestness that at least gets you a hearing, if not agreement.
Imagine your listeners turning away from your unnerving words. You must hold them, and your voice is the rope that binds them.

Jesus is not holding back and he is working hard.

These questions are painful to hear.

The final declaration must be more a seduction than a command. Because you know God's love and the divine grace God gives, you know perfection is possible.

GOSPEL Jesus knows his ideas will stretch the understanding, even the tolerance, of his listeners. The last two of Jesus's six antitheses affect our relationship with our neighbor and require dramatically challenging behavior: turning the other cheek and loving our enemy. Jesus's teaching directly contradicts, though in his language it "*fulfills*," the "Law of talion"—a law that seemed to offer license to retaliate. In reality, the Law limited one's response to injustice, stipulating that if an eye was taken no *more* than an eye could be taken in return. The Law specified the kind of compensation one could receive when wronged; now the "fulfill-ment" Jesus offers is no compensation at all, just forgiveness.

But Jesus isn't finished; not only does he forbid retaliation, he orders love of those who harm us. We are to abandon the path of "resistance to . . . evil" and instead embrace the love of enemies and persecutors because that is the only path to becoming children of God. Anyone can do what comes naturally, Jesus says; even scoundrels go home and kiss their babies.

But Jesus's rhetorical questions are spoken with regret that his followers often do no better than pagans. Jesus won't settle for that. He asks for nothing short of heroism and perfection, loving with the divine Father's love. If, as Mother Teresa said, rec-ognizing Christ in the face of the other is what Jesus means by perfection, then Jesus's call is not an impossible goal. It is Jesus's earnest plea that we surrender our skepticism and adopt his divinely mad game plan.

EIGHTH SUNDAY IN ORDINARY TIME

LECTIONARY #82

READING I   Isaiah 49:14–15

Isaiah = ī-ZAY-uh

Short reading = Slow reading.

Zion = Zī-ahn

Zion insists she is "forsaken" though she should know better.

Pause before and after the question, and "fill" both pauses, looking at the assembly.

We know this happens often today; yet God will *never* forget us!

A reading from the Book of the Prophet Isaiah

Zion said, "The LORD has **forsaken** me;
  my Lord has **forgotten** me."
Can a **mother** forget her **infant**,
  be without **tenderness** for the child of her **womb**?
Even should **she** forget,
  I will **never** forget you.

For meditation and context:

RESPONSORIAL PSALM   Psalm 62:2–3, 6–7, 8–9 (6a)

R. Rest in God alone, my soul.

Only in God is my soul at rest;
  from him comes my salvation.
He only is my rock and my salvation,
  my stronghold; I shall not be disturbed
  at all.

Only in God be at rest, my soul,
  for from him comes my hope.
He only is my rock and my salvation,
  my stronghold; I shall not be disturbed.

With God is my safety and my glory,
  he is the rock of my strength; my refuge is
  in God.
Trust in him at all times, O my people!
  Pour out your hearts before him.

TO KEEP IN MIND

Pauses are never "dead" moments. Something is always happening during a pause. Practice will teach you how often and how long to pause. Too many pauses make a reading choppy; too few cause ideas to run into one another.

READING I   When even the smallest stone is placed in a well-crafted setting, its beauty shines and brings delight. Today's short reading will shine *if* you provide a well-crafted setting. Despite its unexpected brevity, this gem of a reading stuns us with a single powerful image—a mother who abandons her child.

A devastated Zion had languished long in exile. But verse thirteen of this same text orders heaven and earth to rejoice because God "comforts his people and shows mercy to his afflicted." Indeed, exile's end had been mandated by King Cyrus and was

coming to fruition. In the Bible, verse fourteen begins, "But Zion said . . . " Because the Lectionary omits the word "but," we could miss knowing that this passage is not focused on Israel's distress, but on her reluctance to trust God and rejoice as she was commanded.

Like a wounded lover after an argument, Israel can't believe the Lord's avowal of forgiveness, and blurts out a desperate "you don't love me anymore!" But by conjuring a moving image—the love of a mother for her child—God makes the idea of abandoning the Chosen People unimaginable.

Picture an expectant mother when you question the assembly, your head shaking "no" even as you ask, "Can a mother forget . . . be without tenderness?" It goes without saying that you must read s-l-o-w-l-y. If you proclaim in less than thirty seconds you're not conveying the drama and poignancy of the passage. Much of today's message resides in the silence between the words. Pause after God's question. Then, with solemn assurance, speak God's promise that even if the unthinkable were to happen, "I will *never* forget you."

For proper context, review the sections of I Corinthians read over the last seven weeks.

Corinthians = kohr-IN-thee-uhnz

Take a good pause at the colon and read slowly so the point that leaders are "servants" is not lost.

Avoid a businesslike tone; instead, suggest that leadership is based on relationship.

These lines convey confidence, not arrogance. Keep the tone conversational.

The point is that only God's judgment matters!

Use a slower and more considered delivery here, for this is what flows from the previous advice; that is, make no judgments until Christ comes, for only by his light will we see the truth.

With sustained eye contact, convey the happy news that the faithful will receive God's praise.

READING II   1 Corinthians 4:1–5

A reading from the first Letter of Saint Paul to the Corinthians

Brothers and sisters:
Thus should one regard us: as **servants** of **Christ**
     and **stewards** of the mysteries of **God**.
Now it is of course **required** of stewards
     that they be found **trustworthy**.
It does not concern me in the **least**
     that I be **judged** by you or any **human** tribunal;
     I do not even pass judgment on **myself**;
     I am not conscious of **anything** against me,
     but I do not thereby stand **acquitted**;
     the one who **judges** me is the **Lord**.
Therefore do not make any judgment before the appointed **time**,
     until the Lord **comes**,
     for he will bring to light what is hidden in **darkness**
     and will manifest the **motives** of our hearts,
     and **then** everyone will receive **praise** from God.

GOSPEL   Matthew 6:24–34

A reading from the holy Gospel according to Matthew

Jesus said to his **disciples**:
     "No one can serve **two** masters.
He will either **hate** one and **love** the other,
     or be **devoted** to one and **despise** the other.
You cannot serve **God** and **mammon**.

"Therefore I tell you, do not **worry** about your life,
     what you will **eat** or **drink**,
     or about your **body**, what you will **wear**.

Pause at the colon.

Jesus's tone through the first half of the reading conveys warning, not judgment.

It's as if Jesus flips on a light to prevent anyone's falling into the trap of thinking they can serve both God and "mammon."

Jesus understands our anxiety; communicate that rather than a scolding tone.

READING II Paul's been at this for six of the past seven weeks, so reading the passages that lead up to today's portion will put Paul's argument in clearer context. Your listeners, however, will only hear today's five verses that climax Paul's efforts to reconcile the Corinthian community and end their bickering.

Rivalries existed even in the early Church and concern about status and reputation could as readily distract the "stewards" of the Gospel then as it does now. When we give our lives to God, the forces of evil quickly assemble against us and often their best weapon is our own ego. Paul was ever guarding himself against ego's tug and encouraging others to resist its sway. Rather than diplomacy, Paul employs blunt language to make his point. "Look," he says, "people need to see us as servants; our chief concern must be our trustworthiness, not others' judgments." Then he points to himself, saying "As for me, I don't care if people judge me. I don't even judge myself." His attitude is relaxed and his tone sincere. He continues, "It's not that I have anything to feel guilty about, (though that doesn't mean I think my hands are completely clean, either), but it's no one's business to pass judgment. Only the Lord judges; so let's leave it to him!"

After making that point, Paul speaks of what will happen at "the appointed time" when the Lord returns: darkness will yield to light, hearts will be bared, and everyone will receive praise from the only source that really matters—God.

GOSPEL Human life is riddled with pain. Much of it is real and results from tragic events and difficult choices. But often we experience psychic

But as he progresses, we hear frustration that his own disciples fail to put their trust in God's mercy.

Is not **life** more than **food** and the **body** more than **clothing**?
Look at the **birds** in the sky;
    they do not **sow** or **reap**, they gather nothing into **barns**,
    yet your heavenly Father **feeds** them.
Are not you more **important** than they?
Can any of you by **worrying** add a single **moment**
      to your life-span?

The question is pointed; the elaboration, however, is full of poetry that summons hope and elicits trust.

Why are you anxious about **clothes**?
Learn from the way the wild **flowers** grow.
They do not **work** or **spin**.
But I tell you that not even **Solomon** in all his **splendor**
    was clothed like one of **them**.

For Jesus the conclusion is obvious and he expects his disciples to see what he sees.

If God so clothes the **grass** of the **field**,
    which grows **today** and is thrown into the oven **tomorrow**,
    will he not much **more** provide for **you**, O you of little **faith**?

"Do not worry" means "Do not waste your life over these concerns, but trust God instead!"

So do not **worry** and say, 'What are we to **eat**?'
    or 'What are we to **drink**?' or 'What are we to **wear**?'
All these things the **pagans** seek.
Your heavenly Father **knows** that you need them all.

Here is Jesus's remedy: seek and do God's will and all else will follow.

But seek **first** the **kingdom** of **God** and his **righteousness**,
    and all these things will be **given** you besides.
Do not worry about **tomorrow**; tomorrow will take care of **itself**.
Sufficient for a day is its own **evil**."

Having reached the climax of the reading, we can almost hear Jesus sigh before he offers his final admonition about "tomorrow." If spoken with a smile, what he says about "today" won't sound depressing, and may even provoke a smile in return.

THE 4 STEPS OF *LECTIO DIVINA* OR PRAYERFUL READING

1. *Lectio:* Read a Scripture passage aloud slowly. Notice what phrase captures your attention and be attentive to its meaning. Silent pause.

2. *Meditatio:* Read the passage aloud slowly again, reflecting on the passage, allowing God to speak to you through it. Silent pause.

3. *Oratio:* Read it aloud slowly a third time, allowing it to be your prayer or response to God's gift of insight to you. Silent pause.

4. *Contemplatio:* Read it aloud slowly a fourth time, now resting in God's word.

---

pain that results from focusing on the past or future rather than on the present. We mourn what "might have been" as if regret could change the past, or we obsess over what might be as if worry could alter the future. Jesus often urges "be not afraid" because he knows that fear turns tomorrow into a worrisome monster that fogs our vision.

On retreats designed to help participants experience each moment as it comes, clocks are covered, schedules withheld, and questions like "What's next?" are ignored. The retreat master knows the

answers, but letting go of such concerns teaches participants to live in the moment. Jesus's goal is the same: to teach us trust and help us see the larger picture. So he tells us to stop focusing on anxiety and learn from the "birds" and "wild flowers."

But first he gives a solemn warning: "do not worry about your life" because concern for "mammon" prevents us from serving "God." His conviction that tragic consequences follow efforts to "serve two masters" animates the second half of the reading.

Jesus calls for more trust than most can muster, but the alternative is a life of fruitless worry, so his tone grows ever more insistent as he uses the analogies of birds and flowers. "You of little faith" is more lament than indictment, but Jesus shows little patience for anxiety that replaces trust in God. Love God and seek the Kingdom, then you'll have what truly matters, he announces. Though cognizant of human struggle and pain, Jesus's last line is not without humor—can one toss away worry with anything but a smile?

ASH WEDNESDAY

LECTIONARY #219

READING I   Joel 2:12–18

A reading from the Book of the Prophet Joel

Even **now**, says the LORD,
    return to me with your **whole heart**,
    with **fasting**, and **weeping**, and **mourning**;
Rend your hearts, not your **garments**,
    and **return** to the LORD, your **God**.
For **gracious** and **merciful** is he,
    slow to anger, **rich** in kindness,
    and **relenting** in **punishment**.
Perhaps he will **again** relent
    and leave behind him a **blessing**,
Offerings and **libations**
    for the LORD, your **God**.

Blow the **trumpet** in **Zion**!
    proclaim a **fast**,
    call an **assembly**;
Gather the **people**,
    notify the congregation;
Assemble the elders,
    gather the **children**
    and the **infants** at the **breast**;
Let the bridegroom **quit** his room
    and the **bride** her **chamber**.

Joel = JOH-*l

"Even now . . . " = "Even in the midst of this terrifying plague." Make eye contact so your assembly knows these words are also meant for them.

In this season of repentance there are two categories of words to stress: 1) words of call and command: "return," "rend," "blow," "proclaim," "gather," "notify," "assemble" and 2) words encouraging repentance: "gracious and merciful," "kindness," "relenting," "blessing," "spare," "pity."

Slower pace. Offer hope in a caring and persuasive tone.

After a pause, speak these lines with energy and urgency. Quicker pace.

Zion = ZĪ-ahn

"Children," "bride," and "bridegroom" signal the importance of the entire community's response. Your tone says, yes, even bride and groom must forgo their pleasure to join the priests in petitioning God.

READING I   The great gift that is Lent begins with Ash Wednesday's clarion call to abandon the ways of death and embrace those of life. The Bible sees sin primarily as an obstacle to love—and love's obstacles are many. We can see how they work within our own life histories as easily as in the history of Israel: disobedience and infidelity lead to some impending danger, danger leads to repentance, and repentance reveals God's merciful pardon. Despite the many times we've mounted that treadmill, we walk it still. We return to God promising never to stray again. But then we do.

So today God's voice commands "return to me" and calls us to emerge from a spiritual winter's sleep to embrace spring's revitalization and growth. The people of Israel often saw natural disaster as a sign of God's disfavor and experienced it as punishment for their sins or as warning to change their ways. In Joel's day, a devastating plague of locusts was the clanging bell that roused the nation from the drowsiness of sin. For Joel the plague was a dire sign that the fearful "Day of the Lord" was drawing near. So, to avert disaster, he calls for repentance through prayer and fasting.

The entire community is called to respond and no one is exempt—not the infant, not the elders, not the bride or groom. But the people are motivated by more than fear. Joel reminds them their God is "gracious and merciful" and "slow to anger." They are less panicked than hopeful for God may again "relent" and leave a blessing instead of punishment.

There are three clear moments in this text: call, response, and consequence. The

Between the **porch** and the **altar**
     let the **priests**, the **ministers** of the LORD, **weep**,
And say, "**Spare**, O LORD, your **people**,
     and make not your **heritage** a **reproach**,
     with the nations **ruling** over them!
Why should they say among the **peoples**,
     '**Where** is their **God**?' "

Then the LORD was stirred to **concern** for his land
     and took **pity** on his people.

Don't overdo this plea, but make it sound like a prayer.

Imagine scoffing non-believers speaking these lines.
First pause, then slowly announce God's decision to forgive. These crucial lines are spoken by the prophet and remind us that repentance brings forgiveness.

For meditation and context:

TO KEEP IN MIND
"Ritardando" refers to the practice, common in music, of becoming gradually slower and expanding the words as you approach the end of a piece. Many readings end this way — with a decreased rate but increased intensity.

RESPONSORIAL PSALM   Psalm 51:3–4, 5–6ab, 12–13, 14 and 17 (3a)

R. Be merciful, O Lord, for we have sinned.

Have mercy on me, O God, in your goodness;
     in the greatness of your compassion wipe
          out my offense.
Thoroughly wash me from my guilt
     and of my sin cleanse me.

For I acknowledge my offense,
     and my sin is before me always:
"Against you only have I sinned,
     and done what is evil in your sight."

A clean heart create for me, O God,
     and a steadfast spirit renew within me.
Cast me not out from your presence,
     and your Holy Spirit take not from me.

Give me back the joy of your salvation,
     and a willing spirit sustain in me.
O Lord, open my lips,
     and my mouth shall proclaim your praise.

READING II   2 Corinthians 5:20—6:2

A reading from the second Letter of Saint Paul to the Corinthians

Brothers and sisters:
We are **ambassadors** for **Christ**,
     as if **God** were **appealing** through us.
We **implore** you on behalf of **Christ**,
     be **reconciled** to God.
For **our** sake he made him to **be** sin who did not **know** sin,
     so that we might become the **righteousness** of God in **him**.

Corinthians = kohr-IN-thee-uhnz

Memorize the first line and read slowly or the assembly will miss the main point. You tell us 1) who we are and 2) what God is doing through us.

Don't "implore" like a beggar, but with the dignity of God's spokesperson.

A new beat. This is a marvel announced with awe: God allowed Christ to bear the consequences of our sins! Stress that it was done "for our sake."

---

first paragraph presents God's call to repentance and the hope of mercy and forgiveness. "Blow the trumpet" describes the people's fervent response, which is communal, not individual. Their cry is "spare your people," not "spare me." They even appeal to God's pride by saying, "Why should foreigners look at us and wonder where our God is!" The consequence is found in the last sentence that announces God's decision to spare the people yet again. The word "pity" suggests how to speak of the compassionate God who listens and forgives.

READING II | Before anything else, we need to know who we are. Christianity doesn't provide an agenda but an identity; when we know who we are, the agenda takes care of itself. Christianity is about being in relationship with the man Jesus Christ, who was also the divine Son of God. Today Paul points clearly to one aspect of our Christian identity—being "ambassadors for Christ," for we present and represent Christ in all we do.

This seminal and ancient concept somehow got lost along the centuries only to be fully recovered at the Second Vatican Council, which reminded every Christian we have a mission entrusted to us by Christ himself. We are heralds and evangelists; sometimes we preach with words, but more often through our actions. Christ takes a great risk in naming us "ambassadors," for what the world will know of him it will largely know through us.

To ensure that we communicate Christ effectively, Paul gives but one command: "Be reconciled to God." Don't go your own way and claim to speak for God; don't envy your neighbor or hate your sister or brother and expect to represent the Lord of love.

Paul urges us not to waste the gift purchased at so great a price!

Don't lessen your intensity on the quotation.

The second "now" requires more energy and conviction than the first! Employ ritardando (slowing toward the end).

This text is sometimes called the "Lector's Prayer" because of the proclaimer's role as God's spokesperson.

Remember to avoid an overly harsh or judgmental tone.

Throughout, the text achieves emphasis through contrast, juxtaposing the behavior of hypocrites with that of true disciples.

alms = olms; ahmz

Let your tone convey the futility of this behavior.

hypocrites = HIP-uh-krits

synagogues = SIN-uh-gog

Is Jesus speaking from anger or frustration?

Don't vary the stress on the occurrences of this thrice-repeated refrain, but emphasize those same three words each time.

Resist the temptation to adopt the superior attitude of the hypocrites as you speak these lines.

Working **together**, then,
    we **appeal** to you **not** to receive the **grace** of God in **vain**.
For he **says**:

    In an **acceptable** time I **heard** you,
        and on the day of **salvation** I **helped** you.

Behold, **now** is a very **acceptable** time;
    behold, **now** is the **day** of salvation.

GOSPEL   Matthew 6:1–6, 16–18

A reading from the holy Gospel according to Matthew

Jesus said to his **disciples**:
    "Take **care** not to perform righteous **deeds**
    in order that people may **see** them;
    otherwise, you will have no **recompense** from your
        heavenly **Father**.
When you give **alms**,
    do not blow a **trumpet** before you,
    as the **hypocrites** do in the **synagogues** and in the **streets**
    to win the praise of **others**.
Amen, I **say** to you,
    they have **received** their reward.
But when **you** give alms,
    do not let your **left** hand know what your **right** is **doing**,
    so that your **almsgiving** may be **secret**.
And your **Father** who **sees** in secret will **repay** you.

"When **you** pray,
    do not be like the **hypocrites**,
    who love to **stand** and pray in the **synagogues** and on **street**
        corners
    so that others may **see** them.

"Be reconciled" is the heart of the Gospel and the heart of Lent. Speaking it boldly is your mission today.

In Christ's name, Paul "*implores*" us to worthily wear the name of Christ, for Christ made that possible by taking all human sin upon himself. By paying sin's price, Jesus won for us what we could never achieve on our own: "the righteousness (the very holiness and justice of) God." Because we remain free agents able to surrender or hold back, Paul "appeals" to us not to let Christ's great sacrifice be fruitless in our lives.

Quoting Isaiah, he reminds us that we live in an eternal "now," in an "acceptable time" that was present then when he wrote and that will be present when you announce his words to your assembly. Through you, God calls; and as the assembly listens and reflects on that word, the time for responding is upon them! Be the voice of Paul as you remind your hearers that the work Christ left to his Church sits squarely upon their shoulders.

GOSPEL   We often misuse the term "hypocrite" thinking it refers to people who "don't live by their convictions." But that's the definition of a "sinner," a category to which we all belong. True hypocrites profess what they don't really *believe*—they are people who, as André Gide observed, have become so deluded that they don't recognize their deception and lie with great sincerity, even to themselves.

Why does Jesus demonstrate such rancor toward the religious hypocrites of his day who, after all, were ostensibly

Here Jesus offers the better way that leads to life.

Stress the same words as before.

Do you hear sarcasm or regret in these lines?

Once again, be sure you don't sound as arrogant as the hypocrites and note the third recurrence of the "Father sees/repays" refrain.

Slow down as you speak the words "who sees . . . will repay you." Our growth in humility and holiness will be its own reward.

Amen, I say to you,
    they have **received** their reward.
But when **you** pray, go to your **inner** room,
    close the door, and pray to your Father in **secret**.
And your Father who **sees** in secret will **repay** you.

"When **you** fast,
    do not look **gloomy** like the **hypocrites**.
They **neglect** their appearance,
    so that they may **appear** to others to be **fasting**.
Amen, I say to you, they have **received** their reward.
But when **you** fast,
    anoint your head and **wash** your face,
    so that you may **not** appear to be fasting,
    except to your **Father** who is **hidden**.
And your Father who **sees** what is hidden will **repay** you."

TO KEEP IN MIND
Endings: Your inflection of the last line of the reading should always signal that the reading is about to end. Then pause (three beats!) and make eye contact before announcing (from memory) "The word [Gospel] of the Lord." Always pronounce "the" as "thuh" except before words beginning with a vowel.

---

behaving in the manner endorsed by the prophet Joel? Because the communal and public penance Joel called for had devolved by Jesus's day into empty posturing meant to impress the crowds rather than please the Lord.

But if that were the extent of the harm caused by religious hypocrisy, the leaders would be more the objects of pity than of scorn. Jesus holds nothing back in his verbal lashing because he sees full well the damage to self and others wrought by the hollow piety of the hypocrites. Jesus came to bring sight to the blind and set prisoners

free, yet the leaders imprisoned the people in their own human laws and *clung* to blindness because the light of Jesus's truth was more than they would bear.

Jesus seeks true piety that reflects a humble heart; in that posture prayer, fasting, and almsgiving become spiritual practices that change the world as well as us. If you make the opinion of others your god, you'll worship often at that altar, gaining nothing but chaff for your efforts. Jesus tells us to seek only God's approval, privately and with clean faces. Anything else is its own reward.

Calling people to abandon pride requires humility. Our culture views hypocrisy as the unpardonable sin, but Jesus is playing teacher here, not judge, for he loves even the hypocrites. No sin is unforgiveable, though some are harder to shake off. Jesus would rejoice if the leaders cast off their self-inflicted blindness, because he loves *all* his listeners and his mercy is available to everyone willing to listen—hypocrites included.

FIRST SUNDAY OF LENT

LECTIONARY #22

READING I   Genesis 2:7–9; 3:1–7

A reading from the Book of Genesis

The Lord God formed **man** out of the **clay** of the **ground**
and **blew** into his nostrils the **breath** of **life**,
and so **man** became a living **being**.

Then the Lord God planted a **garden** in Eden, in the **east**,
and placed there the **man** whom he had formed.
Out of the **ground** the Lord God made various **trees** grow
that were **delightful** to look at and good for **food**,
with the tree of **life** in the **middle** of the garden
and the tree of the **knowledge** of **good** and **evil**.

Now the **serpent** was the most **cunning** of all the animals
that the Lord God had made.
The serpent asked the **woman**,
"Did God **really** tell you not to eat
from any of the **trees** in the garden?"
The woman **answered** the serpent:
"We **may** eat of the fruit of the trees in the garden;
it is only about the fruit of the tree
in the **middle** of the garden that God said,
'You shall not **eat** it or even **touch** it, lest you **die**.'"
But the serpent said to the woman:
"You certainly will **not die**!
No, God knows well that the moment you **eat** of it

Genesis = JEN-uh-sis

Remember this is the story of God's creation of humans and humans' creation of sin.
God's relationship with his creatures is intimate and loving.

Eden = EE-d*n

The tone is joyous and hopeful.

Your tone should immediately signal a sinister presence.

Eve appears naïve, not sensing the serpent's intent.

But Eve does know the rules! Speak God's instruction with a tone of warning.

The serpent entices Eve into eating the fruit with a silky, compelling voice that masks its sinister motives.

READING I A story about origins is no ordinary story, and one that speaks of human responsibility for the origin of sin requires telling with a parent's love and prayerful humility. Like today's Gospel, this text presents a suspenseful tale that is both privilege and challenge to read. Privilege because of its favored status within our religious imagination; challenge because its familiarity leads some to think, "I already know this one."

To keep everyone listening you must get reacquainted with the characters—sinuous Satan, innocent Eve, the omniscient God—to ensure the story is new for you. But avoid stereotyping the characters by staying focused on the *details* that carry the narrative.

Subtly vary your vocal quality—the tempo, pitch, and color of your voice—for each character. Don't waste the words, for each communicates something new: the tree was "good . . . pleasing . . . desirable."

Create suspense by revealing details one at a time, and giving life to the dialogue.

As narrator, your voice sets the mood like a film's musical score. When danger threatens or the villain appears, a movie score alerts the audience. Your tone can signal that the snake's entrance brings something menacing into the scene, and that Eve's naiveté makes her easy prey. When she quotes God, her voice reveals ignorance about the significance of the "tree"

This is the real moment of temptation, when Eve "sees" the fruit for all that it is. There is much subtext here, so don't rush.

Again, much is said with few words. The critical moment of disobedience is brief, but your narration should suggest the lasting consequences.

They now know what they've done. Their nakedness symbolizes their guilt and shame; that's what they're trying to cover with loincloths, not their bodies.

For meditation and context:

your eyes will be **opened** and you will be like **gods**
who know what is **good** and what is **evil**."
The woman saw that the tree was **good** for **food**,
     pleasing to the eyes, and **desirable** for gaining **wisdom**.
So she **took** some of its fruit and **ate** it;
     and she also gave some to her **husband**, who was with her,
     and **he** ate it.
Then the **eyes** of both of them were **opened**,
     and they **realized** that they were **naked**;
     so they sewed **fig** leaves together
     and made **loincloths** for themselves.

RESPONSORIAL PSALM   Psalm 51:3–4, 5–6, 12–13, 17 (3a)

R. Be merciful, O Lord, for we have sinned.

Have mercy on me, O God, in your goodness;
     in the greatness of your compassion wipe
          out my offense.
Thoroughly wash me from my guilt
     and of my sin cleanse me.

For I acknowledge my offense,
     and my sin is before me always:
"Against you only have I sinned,
     and done what is evil in your sight."

A clean heart create for me, O God,
     and a steadfast spirit renew within me.
Cast me not out from your presence,
     and your Holy Spirit take not from me.

Give me back the joy of your salvation,
     and a willing spirit sustain in me.
O Lord, open my lips,
     and my mouth shall proclaim your praise.

TO KEEP IN MIND

Know the purpose of the letter:
It dictates the tone. Often Paul is the writer. As teacher and spiritual leader, he is motivated by multiple concerns: to instruct, console, encourage, chastise, warn, settle disputes, and more. When reading from one of his letters, be aware of what he's trying to accomplish.

Be ready to read slowly and to lead your listeners through these complex sentences.

though = even though; accounted = reckoned

READING II   Romans 5:12–19

A reading from the Letter of Saint Paul to the Romans

Brothers and sisters:
Through **one** man **sin** entered the world,
     and through **sin**, **death**,
     and thus death came to **all** men, inasmuch as all **sinned**—
     for up to the time of the **law**, sin was in the world,
     though sin is not **accounted** when there is **no** law.

---

but also clear understanding that God meant business by saying, "Don't touch!"

     "The woman saw that the tree was good . . . So she . . . ate it" can be spoken in the voice of Eve, as if she is trying to convince herself that it's all right to eat the desirable fruit. Narrate from Adam's point of view on the line "and she also gave . . . and *he* ate it." Speak of their eyes being opened and of their nakedness as if the narration were *dialogue* spoken by the couple.

The contrasting moods of the text's opening and closing frame the story and enhance its impact. If you conveyed intimacy between God and the creatures God forms from the clay of the ground, then the sublime beauty of that relationship will heighten the sense of loss in the last sentence as the man and woman, recognizing their defiance and loss of innocence, sew "loincloths" to hide their shame.

READING II Paul's message forms a nice bridge between the First Reading and the Gospel, where Jesus, too, is tempted. Paul compares Adam and Jesus and the condemnation and salvation that resulted from their respective responses to temptation. Paul's convoluted language, especially in this translation, obscures rather than illumines his important message. So, consult at least one other translation to better understand his reasoning. For

"Even over those . . . " = Death reigned even over people who had not sinned by breaking a specific command, like Adam did. Adam prefigures the one who will come to set things right: Jesus.

Use different tone colors for "gift" (positive) and "transgression" (negative).

What resulted from Jesus's obedience is not at all like what resulted from Adam's sin.

acquittal = uh-KWIT-*l

"How much more" calls for a very upbeat and joyous tone.

Speak with authority, like a teacher reviewing to ensure students have understood.

Each statement is spoken with conviction.

The passage ends with the good and hopeful news that Christ's obedience has brought righteousness to "the many."

But **death** reigned from **Adam** to **Moses**,
    even over those who did **not** sin
    after the pattern of the trespass of Adam,
    who is the **type** of the one who was to come.

But the **gift** is not like the **transgression**.
For if by the transgression of the **one**, the **many** died,
    how much more did the **grace** of **God**
    and the gracious **gift** of the one man Jesus **Christ**
    overflow for the **many**.
And the gift is not like the **result** of the one who sinned.
For after **one** sin there was the **judgment** that brought
        condemnation;
    but the **gift**, after **many** transgressions, brought **acquittal**.
For if, by the transgression of the **one**,
    death came to reign through that one,
    how much **more** will those who receive the abundance
        of **grace**
    and of the gift of **justification**
    come to **reign** in life through the one Jesus **Christ**.
In **conclusion**, just as through **one transgression**
    condemnation came upon **all**,
    so, through **one righteous** act,
    acquittal and **life** came to **all**.
For just as through the **disobedience** of the one man
    the many were made **sinners**,
    so, through the **obedience** of the one,
    the many will be made **righteous**.

[Shorter: Romans 5:12, 17–19]

TO KEEP IN MIND

Tell the story: The reading of Scripture is a storytelling moment. Storytellers are people of imagination. They help us to see, hear, feel, and smell the elements of the story because they themselves experience these sensory aspects of a story.

---

greater clarity, speak the opening sentence as if there were a period after "inasmuch as all sinned." You'll need to read slowly, sharing one thought unit at a time, to adequately communicate Paul's ideas.

The first paragraph begins with the bad news that original sin tainted all of God's creation. Paul inserts a quick aside that says sin *was* in the world even before the Law of Moses, but he quickly adds that you can't technically speak of "sin" when there are no laws. The word, "but" signals a

shift to better news. Reason slowly, balancing Paul's parallel ideas and structures: the "one man" Adam contrasts with the "one man" Christ; "gift" contrasts with "result," "condemnation" with "acquittal"; "death" with "life." Paul's concluding summary is especially well balanced: a single "transgression" brought "condemnation" while a single "righteous act" brought "acquittal and life." "Obedience" balances "*dis*obedience" and "sinners" balances "righteous."

Your tone color should shift according to whether you are speaking about the consequences of Adam's sin or the "gift" that

flows from Christ's obedience. Despite your best efforts, some will remain confused by this passage. So do two things: make sure they remember your enthusiastic and joyful attitude when you speak of the "one man, Jesus," and make sure they hear and remember the last line.

GOSPEL   Despite the brief narrative and few details, this story looms large in our religious imagination. But because the story is very familiar, there's always the danger that by the time

GOSPEL   Matthew 4:1–11

A reading from the holy Gospel according to Matthew

At that time **Jesus** was led by the **Spirit** into the **desert**
    to be **tempted** by the **devil**.
He **fasted** for forty **days** and forty **nights**,
    and afterwards he was **hungry**.
The **tempter** approached and said to him,
    "If you are the **Son** of **God**,
    command that these **stones** become loaves of **bread**."
He said in reply,
    "It is written:
*One does not **live** on bread **alone**,*
    *but on every **word** that comes forth*
    *from the mouth of **God**."*

Then the devil took him to the holy **city**,
    and made him stand on the **parapet** of the **temple**,
    and said to him, "If you **are** the Son of God, **throw**
    yourself down.
For it is written:
*He will command his **angels** concerning you*
    *and with their **hands** they will **support** you,*
*lest you dash your **foot** against a **stone**."*
Jesus answered him,
    "Again it is **written**,
*You shall not put the Lord, your God, to the **test**."*

Sidebar notes (left margin):

Make good use of the words that set the scene. You tone should signal the cosmic clash that's coming.

This is not normal hunger. Give the forty days and nights proper emphasis.

Signal the approach of evil.

The tempter thinks himself the equal of Jesus.

Jesus is not teaching Satan, but holding up armor that shields him from the tempter's wiles.

Your tone should signal that this is an unusual and dangerous setting.

The tempter's confidence has grown; he cites Scripture intentionally and without reserve.

Jesus's strength grows. Of whom is he speaking when he says, "You shall not put . . . God to the test?"

---

you reach "command these stones" many will have begun daydreaming of the meal awaiting them at home.

But you are narrating the clash of cosmic forces—two powerful characters engaged in a contest of wills. That will never cease to fascinate if you tell it with conviction. Remember: before you can preach, you have to tell the story. You'll do that well by taking time to visualize the scene and deciding how to use the few words you have to paint this encounter between obedience and rebellion.

Hungry and weakened to the point of collapse, a vulnerable Jesus waits in the desert. The tempter does not waste the opportunity. In a voice laced with concern and in a tone that epitomizes reason and persuasion, he urges Jesus to satisfy his need. Don't speak Jesus's reply too quickly, nor the two that follow, for if Jesus didn't consider Satan's offer, they wouldn't be temptations. After "He said in reply," pause to imagine what saying "yes" might mean, but then shake off the temptation as he begins his response.

Don't rush the few words you are given to identify the three locations, for the settings reveal much about the action of each scene. The desert, like Jesus, is hot, parched, and barren, and perhaps calls for narration delivered in an intense whisper. Next, Satan enters the "holy city" and perches atop God's own house to put God "to the test," quoting the very Scriptures that echo daily in the Temple area. Confident and puffed-up, Satan speaks in a voice that mocks the sincerity of true worshippers.

This is the grandest scene; describe it with the gusto of the tempter.

Clearly, the tempter offers something he himself could not resist.

Jesus need not shout the dismissal. Controlled anger is better.

Is Satan being reminded of what caused his fall from grace?

Pause after "the devil left him," and then announce the angels' appearance.

TO KEEP IN MIND

Posture speaks: Make sure it says what you want it to. Don't let your face or body contradict the good news you announce. Remember, readers are allowed to smile!

Then the devil took him up to a very high **mountain**,
  and showed him all the **kingdoms** of the world in their
    magnificence,
  and he said to him, "All these I shall **give** to you,
  if you will **prostrate** yourself and **worship** me."
At this, Jesus **said** to him,
  "Get **away**, Satan!
It is **written**:
  *The Lord, your **God**, shall you worship*
    *and him **alone** shall you **serve**."*

Then the devil **left** him and, behold,
  angels came and **ministered** to him.

Finally, on the "very high mountain" that offers a view of all the world's kingdoms and where Satan tempts through clenched jaws so as not to overplay his hand, Jesus finally asserts his authority, dismisses Satan, and affirms that God alone is king.

Jesus's energy grows with each response, but he saves his best for last. Jesus's strong rebuke of Satan contrasts with the milder dismissal in Luke's rendering. After he dismisses Satan, Jesus collapses into the arms of "angels." His voice remains strong throughout the encounter, and we wonder if perhaps he is talking as much to himself as to Satan, dismissing his own urges as well as the devil's promptings.

As narrator, sustain the tension and suspense till the end. Then, in a tone that's as comforting as the angels' hands, express relief that the struggle is over.

SECOND SUNDAY OF LENT

LECTIONARY #25

Genesis = JEN-uh-sis

Abram = AY-br*m

Your *tone* conveys the emotional content of the passage more clearly than the actual words. Keep it upbeat and hopeful.

God's voice is authoritative, but it speaks promise and hope, not the barkings of a drill sergeant.

Twice the words "great" and "blessing" are closely associated, suggesting what constitutes true greatness.

God is saying, "*I* will bless *you* and *you* will bless *others*."

"I . . . will curse . . . ": this hyperbolic statement ascribes to God human sentiments that reflect the culture of the time.

Read slowly this reminder of Abram's fidelity to God's command.

> **TO KEEP IN MIND**
> **Importance of the Narrator**: The narrator is often the pivotal role of a passage. Timbre, pitch, rate, and energy can make the same words convey very different moods or meaning. Sometimes the narrator is objective, but often the narrator has great interest in the events and characters of a story.

READING I   Genesis 12:1–4a

A reading from the Book of Genesis

The LORD said to **Abram**:
    "**Go** forth from the land of your **kinsfolk**
    and from your father's **house** to a land that I will **show** you.

    "I will make of you a great **nation**,
        and I will **bless** you;
I will make your name **great**,
        so that **you** will be a **blessing**.
I will **bless** those who bless **you**
        and **curse** those who **curse** you.
All the communities of the **earth**
        shall find **blessing** in you."

Abram **went** as the LORD **directed** him.

READING I | Israel's history begins when the seventy-five-year-old Abram agrees to leave everything he knows and loves for a promised land he's never seen. Today, men of that age are considering "reverse-mortgages" or heeding funeral industry exhortations to make "pre-need" plans. But Abram's advanced age broadcasts an unmistakable message: only God could give this old man his new beginning. A new moment in human history begins with Abram's "yes" to God, but it comes at God's initiative. Abram need only cooperate; God will make his name great.

Unlike the builders of Babel who wanted to settle and make a name for *themselves*, Abram agrees to uproot and seek out Canaan. His obedience blesses *him* and makes him a blessing for *others*, for all peoples will look at him and yearn for the special relationship with God that he enjoys. Abram's privileged role is further underscored by the fact that God will "bless those who bless" and "curse those who curse" him.

God's decree, coming at the beginning of today's reading, should echo with hope and promise. The minute the assembly hears your voice they should know you are speaking of a major moment that will change history. God's voice sings a song of blessing over Abram, a blessing that assures Abram he won't regret heeding God's command to "go forth." Pray the blessing as over a newly baptized infant or a bridal couple setting out to seek their destiny. The final narration resounds with pride, reminding us again of Abram's obedience.

READING II | It's a hard saying: "Bear your share of hardship for the gospel." Some may not have gotten the

For meditation and context:

RESPONSORIAL PSALM   Psalm 33:4–5, 18–19, 20, 22 (22)

R. Lord, let your mercy be on us, as we place our trust in you.

Upright is the word of the LORD,
    and all his works are trustworthy.
He loves justice and right;
    of the kindness of the LORD the earth
    is full.

See, the eyes of the LORD are upon those
    who fear him,
    upon those who hope for his kindness,
to deliver them from death
    and preserve them in spite of famine.

Our soul waits for the LORD,
    who is our help and our shield.
May your kindness, O LORD, be upon us
    who have put our hope in you.

TO KEEP IN MIND
Know the purpose of the letter:
It dictates the tone. Often Paul is the writer. As teacher and spiritual leader, he is motivated by multiple concerns: to instruct, console, encourage, chastise, warn, settle disputes, and more. When reading from one of his letters, be aware of what he's trying to accomplish.

READING II   2 Timothy 1:8b–10

A reading from the second Letter of Saint Paul to Timothy

Beloved:
Bear your share of hardship for the gospel
    with the **strength** that comes from **God**.

He **saved** us and called us to a **holy** life,
    not according to our **works**
    but according to his own **design**
    and the grace **bestowed** on us in Christ **Jesus** before time **began**,
    but now made **manifest**
    through the **appearance** of our savior Christ **Jesus**,
    who destroyed **death** and brought **life** and **immortality**
    to **light** through the **gospel**.

Paul's salutation greets both Timothy and us with tenderness and love.

Read slowly, so the weight of this exhortation is not lost.
God did two things: "saved us" and "called us." Don't rush.

Here the magnanimity of God is asserted. It was God's plan to save us from the beginning, but in Christ it was finally made manifest.

A new idea: Christ destroyed the greatest enemy, death. So now we can walk by the Gospel's saving light.

---

memo that living the Gospel inevitably leads to suffering. Don't be afraid to let these words surprise, even unsettle your listeners. Hard truths are sometimes the most valuable. And hard does not mean bad news. Certainly Paul doesn't see it that way. He's in prison, anticipating death, so he knows about suffering. And yet he echoes boldly the message of today's First Reading: all the good in our lives comes at God's initiative. God even provides the "strength" we need to bear our suffering.

Writing to the much younger Timothy, whom he calls "my dear child," Paul urges

the young bishop to live with the same firmness of faith that has sustained him through all his trials. He reminds Timothy (and us) that *God* saved us, and not because of our own good "works" but because of his own purposes. Perhaps Paul's most important lesson is the strength he draws from Christ's Resurrection. How does one facing death approach it as philosophically as Paul? Remember, Paul was never naïve, for though he was a Roman citizen, he was also a double minority—Jew and Christian. This made him quite expendable within the

empire. So Paul harbors no illusions about his fate.

But Christ has already "destroyed death" and offered immortality to all who believe in him! Because Paul walks by the light of the Gospel, no darkness can ever overcome him. Announce this with great conviction and joy.

GOSPEL   A great truth of Christian spirituality declares that "life is not about you." It's a hard lesson to master and one even Peter learned only over time. This brief episode is comprised

GOSPEL   Matthew 17:1–9

A reading from the holy Gospel according to Matthew

Jesus took **Peter**, **James**, and John his **brother**,
   and led them up a high **mountain** by **themselves**.
And he was **transfigured** before them;
   his face **shone** like the **sun**
   and his clothes became **white** as **light**.
And behold, **Moses** and **Elijah** appeared to them,
   conversing with him.
Then **Peter** said to Jesus in reply,
   "**Lord**, it is **good** that we are here.
If you **wish**, I will make three **tents** here,
   one for **you**, one for **Moses**, and one for **Elijah**."
While he was still **speaking**, **behold**,
   a bright cloud cast a **shadow** over them,
   then from the cloud came a **voice** that said,
   "This is my beloved **Son**, with whom I am well **pleased**;
   listen to him."
When the disciples **heard** this, they fell **prostrate**
   and were very much **afraid**.
But Jesus came and **touched** them, saying,
   "**Rise**, and do not be **afraid**."
And when the disciples raised their **eyes**,
   they saw no one **else** but Jesus **alone**.

As they were coming **down** from the mountain,
   Jesus **charged** them,
   "Do not tell the vision to **anyone**
   until the Son of Man has been **raised** from the **dead**."

You have but one sentence to set the scene. Give the mountaintop setting an air of mystery.

Because this moment occurs immediately, read it slowly and with significance.

Be sure to say "Moses and Elijah," not "MosesandElijah." Remember their symbolic significance.
Moses = MOH-ziz; MOH-zi
Elijah = ee-Lī-juh
Don't make Peter bumbling; but possibly self-absorbed.

Your tone should signal the presence of the divine.

Speak these words with dignity and affection.

Spend more time relating Jesus's effort to relieve their fear than the fear itself. This is one of many instances where Jesus says, "Do not be afraid."

Don't narrate the disappearance as if it were some magic trick; it is the denouement of a life-altering experience.

Jesus's words are strong. Discussing this revelation would only hasten his Death—which waits its appointed time.

> **TO KEEP IN MIND**
> **Careful preparation** expresses your reverence for the Word.

---

of several beats—the ascent, the transfiguration, the appearance of Moses and Elijah, Peter's response, the cloud theophany, the Apostles' panic, Jesus's comforting gesture, and the descent. Though each beat is significant, they all orbit the pivotal moment when Jesus is revealed in transcendent glory. The only appropriate response to such a manifestation is the *second* reaction of which we hear. The first is Peter's offer to set up camp and give Moses, Elijah, and Jesus their own tents. God interrupts Peter's emoting and silences him with the thundering voice from the cloud.

A miracle has occurred, and Peter has begun thinking about how he could make it better. He's so absorbed in his idea of what will be an appropriate response that he neglects to make an appropriate response, which would be to fall on his face in awe. The three privileged disciples are given a unique opportunity to glimpse Jesus in his fullness and accompanied by icons of the two great pillars of the old covenant: Moses and Elijah, one representing the Law and the other the prophets. On this high mountain, the typical biblical place of divine revelation,

Peter is given a gift that he almost becomes too preoccupied to fully appreciate.

But Jesus is tolerant and touches them in order to calm their fears. If they hadn't yet realized how fortunate they were to be with Jesus at this special moment, the disciples should certainly understand when Jesus instructs them to tell no one about the vision. But the final line sounds a somber note, for Jesus echoes an earlier prediction of his Death and Resurrection that turns our gaze to another mountaintop—Calvary.

THIRD SUNDAY
OF LENT

LECTIONARY #28

Exodus = EK-suh-duhs
Moses = MOH-ziz; MOH-zis

READING I   Exodus 17:3–7

A reading from the Book of Exodus

Start slowly. The people's thirst for water is essential information; so is the fact that they complain.

When you grumble, do you express anxiety by becoming more strident or quietly intense?

In those days, in their **thirst** for **water**,
    the people **grumbled** against Moses,
    saying, "**Why** did you ever make us leave **Egypt**?
Was it just to have us die here of **thirst**
    with our **children** and our **livestock**?"

Moses is angry, but at whom—the people, God, both?

So Moses **cried** out to the LORD,
    "What shall I **do** with this people?
A little **more** and they will **stone** me!"
The LORD **answered** Moses,

Like a frustrated parent, be angry at first but then melt into a tone of reassurance. Remember, love is behind all the words.

    "Go over there in **front** of the people,
    along with some of the **elders** of Israel,
    holding in your **hand**, as you go,
    the **staff** with which you struck the **river**.
I will be standing there in **front** of you on the rock in **Horeb.**

Horeb = HOHR-eb

Strike the rock, and the water will **flow** from it
    for the people to **drink**."

"This Moses did": let your tone suggest that the miracle occurred.

This Moses **did**, in the **presence** of the elders of Israel.
The place was called **Massah** and **Meribah,**
    because the Israelites **quarreled** there
    and **tested** the LORD, saying,

The way you speak the names "Massah" and "Meribah" should tell us this was not a proud moment in Israel's history.

The closing question can be read with the people's anxiety or with the narrator's regret at their apparent lack of faith.

    "Is the LORD in our **midst** or **not**?"

READING I The references to "thirst," "drink," and "water" we encounter here will become key elements of the Gospel story as well, so help us hear them as central to today's liturgy. Even independent of the Gospel, the Exodus story contains a compelling lesson. Recently freed from the shackles and shame of slavery, the Israelites wander the desert on their protracted journey to the land God promised so long ago to Abraham. But as soon as things become difficult, the people long for the fleshpots of Egypt. Lack of water generates panic among the people,

and their grumbling might be excusable if they had not so recently witnessed wonders and the reliability of God's strong arm when they were delivered from Pharaoh's chariots.

This all-too-human characteristic is tiresome for Moses. He has helped deliver Israel but he has little patience left for a people whose memory and trust last no longer than the morning dew. But ironically, when he cries out to God in fear of his own life he betrays his own lack of confidence. He will wander forty years before his own

faith becomes as solid as the rock he will soon strike at God's command.

God orders that "elders of Israel" come as witnesses of the wonder and mercy he is about to bestow on the people. Using the same staff with which he struck the river in Egypt, turning its water to blood and rendering it undrinkable, Moses is to strike the rock at Horeb. The same staff that deprived Egypt of water will now supply it for Israel. If the people were deserving, this episode would be less surprising. But despite the people's mean-spirited taunt to God's prophet—essentially "Why

For meditation and context:

RESPONSORIAL PSALM   Psalm 95:1–2, 6–7, 8–9 (8)

R. If today you hear his voice, harden not your hearts.

Come, let us sing joyfully to the LORD;
    let us acclaim the Rock of our salvation.
Let us come into his presence with
        thanksgiving;
    let us joyfully sing psalms to him.

Come, let us bow down in worship;
    let us kneel before the LORD who made us.
For he is our God,
    and we are the people he shepherds,
        the flock he guides.

Oh, that today you would hear his voice:
    "Harden not your hearts as at Meribah,
    as in the day of Massah in the desert.
Where your fathers tempted me;
    they tested me though they had seen
        my works."

TO KEEP IN MIND

Eye contact is your means of connecting with those to whom you minister. You should look at the assembly during the middle and at the end of every thought or sentence.

READING II   Romans 5:1–2, 5–8

A reading from the Letter of Saint Paul to the Romans

Brothers and sisters:
Since we have been **justified** by **faith**,
    we have **peace** with God through our Lord Jesus **Christ**,
    through whom we have gained **access** by faith
    to this **grace** in which we stand,
    and we **boast** in hope of the glory of **God**.

And hope does not **disappoint**,
    because the **love** of God has been poured out into our **hearts**
    through the Holy **Spirit** who has been given to us.
For **Christ**, while we were still **helpless**,
    died at the appointed time for the **ungodly**.
Indeed, only with **difficulty** does one die for a **just** person,
    though perhaps for a **good** person one might even find **courage**
        to die.
But God **proves** his love for us
    in that while we were still **sinners** Christ **died** for us.

Establish eye contact.

Don't read this like abstract theology, for the text announces hope, love, and joy!

Paul describes the workings of faith, hope, and love, moving effortlessly from one to the other: faith brings peace and access to grace; this leads to a hope that will not disappoint. Note: we don't "speak" of hope, we "boast"! There are three distinct ideas in this sentence.

Assume the diction of a teacher making an important point.

Yes, it would be unusual to willingly die for a just person.

But more unusual is what God did: dying for us while we were still in sin! Speak with joy and awe.

---

did we ever listen to you?"—God still meets their needs and threatens no punishment. Be sure to narrate "This Moses did . . . " in a positive tone, so we understand that he *succeeded* in making the water flow.

  This event will remain a significant marker in the history of Israel, always reminding them of their petulance and evanescent faith, so a tone of regret should characterize the final narration. A people who should have known better, put their God to the test, something we were reminded in a recent Lenten Gospel that we should never do. On our Lenten journey

we pray for confidence that God is always "in our midst."

READING II These words from Paul express the very sentiment that might have helped the wandering Israelites of today's First Reading. Paul insists that "hope does not disappoint," but that's a slippery concept that's hard to hold onto. It gets away from us because hope is based on faith, and faith is the "evidence of things not *seen*" (Hebrews 11:1). When evidence is right before us, we *know*; and therefore we don't need to *believe*. But

people of faith must believe without seeing. Faith is our "evidence." And on that evidence we base our hope. Without faith there is no hope, and without hope it's difficult to love.

  Paul weaves faith and hope with love and demonstrates their inseparability. The evidence of God's love was made powerfully and insuperably evident in Christ's willing Death on the Cross. That manifestation of love strengthens our faith and gives us reason to hope. Everything we build, we build on that foundation. Paul reasons out the logic of God's love. Only with great

Narrate as if you were one of the Samaritans who is converted at the end of the story: it's your own town you're describing; the woman is your neighbor; this incident changed your life.

Samaria = suh-MAYR-ee-uh
Sychar = SĪ-kahr

Speak of this ancient holy place with familiarity.

Slower pacing helps suggest Jesus's tiredness.

Jesus asks matter-of-factly.

She is stunned that he would ask her for a favor.

Samaritans = suh-MAYR-uh-tuhnz

Keep the dialogue conversational, not theological.

She bluntly challenges him and his *chutzpah*.

Contrast his tone with the woman's.

GOSPEL   John 4:5–42

A reading from the holy Gospel according to John

(1) **Jesus** came to a town of **Samaria** called **Sychar**,
    near the plot of land that **Jacob** had given to his son **Joseph**.
Jacob's **well** was there.
Jesus, tired from his journey, sat **down** there at the well.
It was about **noon**.

(2) A **woman** of Samaria came to draw **water**.
Jesus said to her,
    "Give me a **drink**."
His **disciples** had gone into the town to buy **food**.
The Samaritan woman said to him,
    "How can **you**, a **Jew**, ask me, a Samaritan **woman**, for a **drink**?"
—For Jews use nothing in **common** with Samaritans.—
(3) Jesus answered and **said** to her,
    "If you knew the **gift** of God
    and **who** is saying to you, 'Give me a drink,'
    you would have asked **him**
    and he would have given you **living** water."
The woman **said** to him,
    "**Sir**, you do not even have a **bucket** and the cistern is **deep**;
    where then can you **get** this living water?
Are you **greater** than our father **Jacob**,
    who **gave** us this cistern and drank from it **himself**
    with his **children** and his **flocks**?"
(4) Jesus answered and **said** to her,
    "Everyone who drinks **this** water will be **thirsty** again;
    but whoever drinks the water **I** shall give will **never** thirst;
    the water I shall give will become in him
    a **spring** of water **welling** up to eternal **life**."

reluctance, he says, would one die for a "just person," though heroic people do give up their lives for "good" people, that is, people who are good and generous to others. But God's greatest generosity to us was given "while we were still sinners." We had nothing to recommend us; no righteousness or goodness of our own. God wasn't waiting for us to merit salvation, for it would always have to be an act of God's pure and unconditional love.

That is why the opening verses speak of "peace with God through . . . Christ." In Paul's day, personal trials and tragedies

were seen as punishment from God for sin. So Paul assures his readers that God bears no ill will, for Christ has established perfect peace. In fact, Christ's sacrifice gives us unrestricted access to the throne of God. And that, like all the good in our lives, came at God's initiative. We were the ones who did wrong, yet God took the first step at reconciliation.

Without direct experience of God's personal love for us—what the Samaritan woman experiences in today's Gospel—it is impossible to turn Paul's theology into words to live by. As part of your prepara-

tion, reflect on the gifts that God has lavished on you—especially the gift of love and salvation. If *you're* convinced of this, then perhaps you can convince your friends and neighbors.

GOSPEL Jesus continues his self-revelation here to Samaritans who were considered only "half-Jews." In John's account, Jesus's every choice reveals some new insight about himself. For example, he chooses a dialogue partner who is a double outcast, with whom he converses openly without another

The **woman** said to him,
>"**Sir**, **give** me this water, so that I may not be **thirsty**
>or have to keep **coming** here to draw water."

(5) Jesus said to her,
>"Go call your **husband** and come **back**."

The woman answered and said to him,
>"I do not **have** a husband."

Jesus answered her,
>"You are **right** in saying, 'I do not have a husband.'

For you have had **five** husbands,
>and the one you have **now** is not your **husband**.

What you have said is **true**."

(6) The woman said to him,
>"Sir, I can see that you are a **prophet**.

Our ancestors worshiped on this **mountain**;
>but you people say that the place to worship is in **Jerusalem**."

Jesus said to her,
>"**Believe** me, woman, the **hour** is coming
>when you will worship the Father
>neither on this **mountain** nor in **Jerusalem**.

You people worship what you do not **understand**;
>**we** worship what we **understand**,
>because **salvation** is from the **Jews**.

But the **hour** is coming, and is now **here**,
>when **true** worshipers will worship the Father in **Spirit**
>   and **truth**;
>and indeed the Father **seeks** such people to worship him.

God is **Spirit**, and those who **worship** him
>must worship in **Spirit** and **truth**."

She's eager for this amazing water.

Speak evenly, with no hint of judgment.

Is her tone wholly transformed, or is this a final brusque reply?

Jesus is blunt here, but not harsh.

His prescient knowledge impresses her, but she abruptly changes the subject.

Here, too, despite the teaching, maintain a conversational tone.

Don't let these words sound accusatory or prideful.

This section of his discourse takes on a less personal and more universal quality.

Punctuate this final instruction.

TO KEEP IN MIND
Names of characters are often the first word of a reading. Stress names so listeners don't miss who the subject is.

---

male present and then asks to drink from her bucket, a vessel rendered ritually impure by the very fact that it belongs to a ritually unclean Samaritan. Thus, Jesus tutors us about who is and is not unclean and who can and cannot be a disciple.

With obvious baptismal imagery, this story speaks powerfully to the elect preparing for initiation. The iconic "woman at the well" looms large in our imaginations because of her boldness, her conversion, and her knack at evangelization. There is no part of the story that isn't worth telling, so be sure to tell it in its entirety. The first of

this drama's three acts is by far the longest. Besides the pointed and ironic repartee between Jesus and the woman, this section contains clear statements about Jesus's identity. The return of the Apostles, characterized by their surprise and confusion and Jesus's urgency, comprises the second act. Finally, the woman's unexpectedly effective proselytizing concludes the story.

(1,2) Jesus chooses to pass through Samaria on his way to Galilee, not because it is the shortest route, for faithful Jews regularly bypassed this shortcut, but because it provides an opportunity to make

a theological statement. The woman comes to the well when the other townswomen are absent to avoid their scorn. In the noontime heat, Jesus approaches and wastes no time asking a favor, though his request shatters a strong taboo. The woman can't believe that a man who is also a rabbi would speak to her. She, on the other hand, is already an outcast with nothing to lose. She has lived with men to whom she was not married and is unafraid to take on this man who, she's convinced, already feels superior to her.

She begins to sense who stands before her.

(7) The woman said to him,
"I know that the **Messiah** is coming, the one called the
Christ;
when he **comes**, he will tell us **everything**."
Jesus said to her,
"I am **he**, the one **speaking** with you."

His self-identification is a gesture of love to the woman.

The second act begins here. The return of disciples shatters the mood. They seem suspicious.

(8) At that moment his disciples **returned**,
and were **amazed** that he was talking with a **woman**,
but still no one said, "What are you **looking** for?"
or "Why are you **talking** with her?"
The woman **left** her water jar
and went into the **town** and said to the people,
"Come **see** a man who told me **everything** I have done.
Could he possibly be the **Christ**?"
They **went** out of the town and **came** to him.

The woman undertakes her missionary journey. Speak the phrase "Could he be . . . ?" with expectant joy.

(9) Meanwhile, the disciples **urged** him, "Rabbi, **eat**."
But he said to them,
"I have **food** to eat of which you do not **know**."
So the disciples said to one another,
"Could someone have **brought** him something to eat?"
Jesus said to them,
"My **food** is to do the **will** of the one who **sent** me
and to **finish** his work.

The disciples are prodding: "Rabbi, EAT!" His response summarizes his ministry.
Rabbi = RAB-ī

(10) Do you not **say**, 'In four **months** the **harvest** will be here'?
I tell you, **look** up and see the fields **ripe** for the harvest.
The reaper is **already** receiving payment
and gathering crops for eternal **life**,
so that the **sower** and **reaper** can rejoice **together**.
For here the saying is **verified** that 'One **sows** and another **reaps**.'

Note the ample harvest imagery.

Jesus is urging them to open their eyes and see.

sower = SOH-er

TO KEEP IN MIND
Pray the Scriptures: Make reading these Scriptures a part of your prayer life every week, and especially during the week prior to the liturgy in which you will proclaim.

(3) Jesus refers to himself as "the gift of God," insinuating his identity as the source of "living water," but the woman misses that cloaked reference and takes him literally. This exchange is central to the story. Jesus means "water of life," but she hears, "flowing water" as opposed to *stagnant* well water. She mocks Jesus's naiveté, but in doing so she only mocks herself, for what she presumes impossible—that Jesus could be greater than Jacob—is the very truth she'll shortly learn.

(4) Jesus's argument is persuasive and evokes great interest from the woman, but mostly because she misunderstands. Contrast is the key to Jesus's dialogue: everyone who drinks *this* water will thirst *again;* but those who drink the water *I* shall give will *never* thirst. Jesus will be water that requires no bucket, for he will bubble up like a "spring" within the believer's heart. The woman's demonstration of naiveté sets the stage for the disarming crisis that follows.

(5) Knowingly, Jesus instructs her to "Go, call your husband." But his feigned ignorance has a benign purpose—her conversion. The woman lays aside her contentiousness and readily acknowledges her lifestyle. She even accepts Jesus's blunt assertion of her sinfulness, suggesting that his honesty is tempered with compassion.

(6) Rather than becoming defensive, the woman acknowledges Jesus as "prophet," then moves quickly to a theological (and less embarrassing) topic. Jesus is clearly more interested in *how* than in *where* one worships. Both "mountain" and "Jerusalem" will soon be replaced by a new universalism where worship transcends place.

(7) Jesus's words conjure dreams of the Messiah in the woman. When she

I sent you to reap what you have not **worked** for;
    others have done the work,
    and you are sharing the **fruits** of their work."

(11) Many of the **Samaritans** of that town began to **believe** in him
    because of the **word** of the woman who testified,
    "He told me **everything** I have done."
When the Samaritans **came** to him,
    they invited him to **stay** with them;
    and he stayed there two **days**.
Many **more** began to believe in him because of his **word**,
    and they said to the **woman**,
    "We no longer believe because of **your** word;
    for we have heard for **ourselves**,
    and we know that this is **truly** the **savior** of the world."

[Shorter: John 4:5–15, 19b–26, 39a, 40–42]

This is the final act. The woman's testimony generates high energy.

Stress that point and speak "He told me everything . . . " in her excited voice.

They are urging him to remain with them.

There should be joy and gratitude in their comment to the woman who is responsible for their faith. Place special emphasis on the title given to Jesus.

TO KEEP IN MIND
Read through all three readings and commentaries for your assigned Sunday. All three were chosen for this day, and each commentary has suggestions that can help you with your own passage.

---

speaks with confidence and longing of the Messiah's coming, Jesus rewards her by revealing himself to her. Echoes of the divine "I am" sound in his self-identification.

(8) The return of the disciples alters the mood and returns us to the realm of the mundane. The disciples are surprised to find Jesus with the woman; their unasked questions reveal confusion, and even hint at disapproval. But the transformed woman, now freed of shame, runs to share her discovery with the townspeople.

(9,10) Now it is the disciples who misunderstand, taking literally Jesus's reference to food. Their confusion is probably best spoken is a hushed tone, contrasting with the urgency of their appeal to "eat." But Jesus does not let them linger in confusion. His "food," he says, is doing God's will. In one sentence Jesus summarizes his ministry and our mission. Employing rich harvest imagery, Jesus speaks urgently on the theme of evangelization.

(11) The Samaritans believe "because of the word of the woman" about the way Jesus plumbed the secrets of her heart.

They open their homes as well as their hearts to Jesus. But soon others hear Jesus's words directly and, through their own experience, believe that he is the "savior of the world." The hope of every Christian is to be able to make the same faith-filled proclamation!

FOURTH SUNDAY OF LENT

LECTIONARY #31

READING I   1 Samuel 16:1b, 6–7, 10–13a

A reading from the first Book of Samuel

The LORD said to **Samuel**:
    "**Fill** your horn with **oil**, and be on your **way**.
I am sending you to **Jesse** of **Bethlehem**,
    for I have chosen my **king** from among his **sons**."

As Jesse and his sons came to the **sacrifice**,
    Samuel looked at **Eliab** and thought,
    "**Surely** the LORD's anointed is **here** before him."
But the LORD said to Samuel:
    "Do not judge from his **appearance** or from his lofty **stature**,
    because I have **rejected** him.
Not as **man** sees does **God** see,
    because man sees the **appearance**
    but the LORD looks into the **heart**."
In the same way Jesse presented **seven** sons before Samuel,
    but Samuel said to Jesse,
    "The LORD has not chosen any **one** of these."
Then Samuel **asked** Jesse,
    "Are these **all** the sons you have?"
Jesse replied,
    "There is still the **youngest**, who is tending the **sheep**."
Samuel said to Jesse,
    "**Send** for him;
    we will not begin the sacrificial banquet until he **arrives** here."

Samuel = SAM-yoo-uhl

Let us hear who's speaking to whom.

Jesse = JES-ee
Bethlehem = BETH-luh-hem

God's command moves briskly until "for I have chosen . . . "

Speak the balance of God's command more slowly and with great significance.

Take a slight pause to indicate the scene shift.

Eliab = ee-LĪ-uhb

Speak Samuel's inner thoughts in a hushed tone.

The tone of God's dialogue is strong; God shakes Samuel out of his own way of seeing.

Don't give these lines a harsh tone; God is instructing Samuel, not scolding him.

Your tone should suggest passage of time and the frustration of not finding the "chosen" one among the seven sons.

Express Samuel's puzzlement as you speak this line.

Jesse's tone suggests no hope that David will be the "one."

Samuel, on the other hand, sees hope in this news. His tone is authoritative.

READING I   Most peoples can look back upon some seminal leader whose personality and service left a deep and lasting impact on the nation, and the final words of this portion from I Samuel certainly indicate that such was the case with David. But that is not the point of this selection, especially as it is used in today's liturgy. The Gospel will narrate a story of sight rendered to a blind man; here we read that God does not *see* as people see. In both instances, we encounter challenges about what we see when we look at things.

The Pharisees of Jesus's day saw a sinner when they looked at the blind man. David's family saw only a young sheepherder where God saw a future king.

The story of David is important both today and in the history of Israel because it so clearly demonstrates the power of God to raise up and transform, to establish and tear down. David's success will be the work of God who has chosen him despite his lack of credentials. The Spirit of God that rushes mightily upon David will transform this boy into Israel's greatest king. So, from the start, read with the awareness that God is teaching an object lesson here. We have an enacted parable of sorts through which God demonstrates quite vividly that our expectations do not correspond with his. The details of Samuel's preparation and journey to Bethlehem, his interview of Eliab, the procession of six more brothers, his frustrated question ("Are these *all* the sons you have?"), and the final demand that David be summoned work together to set up the surprise that the least likely is

Take a slight pause before describing David, whose presence immediately makes an impact!

Speak this last sentence with solemnity, as if you were narrating while watching it happen. That "the spirit of the Lord rushed upon David" is a great and significant line. Don't waste it.

For meditation and context:

TO KEEP IN MIND
Pauses are never "dead" moments. Something is always happening during a pause. Practice will teach you how often and how long to pause. Too many pauses make a reading choppy; too few cause ideas to run into one another.

Ephesians = ee-FEE-zhuhnz
The good news contained in the opening and closing sentences undergirds your teaching tone throughout the body of the reading.

Contrast the tone of "you were once darkness" and "you are light."

Darkness = being without Christ; Light = possessing him.

Notice the imperative verbs: "Live," "Try," "Take."

Jesse **sent** and had the young man **brought** to them.
He was **ruddy**, a youth **handsome** to behold
 and making a **splendid** appearance.
The LORD said,
 "**There**—**anoint** him, for **this** is the one!"
Then **Samuel**, with the horn of **oil** in hand,
 anointed **David** in the presence of his **brothers**;
 and from that day on, the **spirit** of the LORD **rushed**
 upon David.

RESPONSORIAL PSALM   Psalm 23:1–3a, 3b–4, 5, 6 (1)

R. The Lord is my shepherd; there is nothing I shall want.

The LORD is my shepherd; I shall not want.
 In verdant pastures he gives me repose;
beside restful waters he leads me;
 he refreshes my soul.

He guides me in right paths
 for his name's sake.
Even though I walk in the dark valley
 I fear no evil; for you are at my side
with your rod and your staff
 that give me courage.

You spread the table before me
 in the sight of my foes;
you anoint my head with oil;
 my cup overflows.

Only goodness and kindness follow me
 all the days of my life;
and I shall dwell in the house of the LORD
 for years to come.

READING II   Ephesians 5:8–14

A reading from the Letter of Saint Paul to the Ephesians

Brothers and sisters:
You were once **darkness**,
 but **now** you are **light** in the **Lord**.
Live as **children** of light,
 for light produces every kind of **goodness**
 and **righteousness** and **truth**.
Try to learn what is **pleasing** to the Lord.

the chosen one. David becomes a living embodiment of one of the features of the Kingdom of God—"the last shall be first."

READING II   All lives are marked by physical, emotional, and intellectual growth. But Paul's keen sense of human anthropology focuses on yet another area of growth: the spiritual. Think of the time and great effort required to make progress in any one of these areas as you read Paul's comments about the

Christian's vocation to move from "darkness" to "light." The message is clear and stark: once you were a child, but now you're an adult; once you were ignorant, but now you know; once you were without Christ, but now you have him. And Paul's tone seems to add, "So act like it! Be an adult, use your knowledge, *live* like a Christian." Of the many roles Paul assumes in his writing, today's is most obvious: he is playing the teacher.

Paul explains *why* we should live like children of light: because "goodness and righteousness and truth" grow in the light and they are what "is pleasing to the Lord." Make no mistake about it! The tragedy of child sexual abuse illustrates only too well the grip of darkness that can envelop even those who have been raised in brilliant light. So with energy and urgency Paul admonishes his readers to "take no part" in the "shameful" things done "in secret." If you were speaking to young people who

Don't rush this long sentence about exposing shameful things. Your tone can suggest that the pain of bringing secrets to light is like life-saving cancer surgery.

Pause before "Therefore it says" and muster a hushed intensity which erupts on the word "Awake." "It" refers to the hymn from which these last words were likely taken. Let them resound with joy.

Stress "blind from birth" for it is later questioned.

Rabbi = RAB-ī

Jesus's answer is unexpected and new. Don't rush. The second half of his reply prepares the way for the miracle.

Enjoy the graphic details!

Siloam = sih-LOH-uhm

Relate the miracle with a sense of awe. Then pause to shift to the new scene.

Take no part in the **fruitless** works of **darkness**;
   rather **expose** them, for it is shameful even to **mention**
   the things done by them in **secret**;
   but everything **exposed** by the light becomes **visible**,
   for everything that becomes **visible** is **light**.
Therefore, it says:
   "**Awake**, O sleeper,
   and **arise** from the **dead**,
   and **Christ** will give you **light**."

GOSPEL   John 9:1–41

A reading from the holy Gospel according to John

(1) As **Jesus** passed by he saw a man **blind** from **birth**.
His **disciples** asked him,
   "Rabbi, who **sinned**, this man or his **parents**,
   that he was born **blind**?"
Jesus answered,
   "Neither **he nor** his parents sinned;
   it is so that the works of **God** might be made **visible**
     through him.
We have to do the works of the one who **sent** me while it is **day**.
Night is coming when **no** one can work.
While I am in the **world**, I am the **light** of the world."
(2) When he had **said** this, he **spat** on the ground
   and made **clay** with the saliva,
   and **smeared** the clay on his **eyes**, and said to him,
   "Go **wash** in the Pool of **Siloam**"—which means **Sent**—.
So he went and **washed**, and came back able to **see**.

(3) His **neighbors** and those who had **seen** him earlier
   as a **beggar** said,
   "Isn't this the one who used to **sit** and **beg**?"

were away from home for the first time, you would find the energy and intensity to remind them to use their new-found freedom responsibly, and to warn that shameful behavior—no matter how dark the cloak of darkness that conceals it—eventually comes to light.

A distinctive tone infuses the last three lines of the text. Having focused on the dangers of living in the dark, Paul now sings an invitation to embrace the light which is Christ. Probably part of an early Christian hymn, "Awake, O sleeper . . . " is a rousing call to action followed by the joyous promise that "Christ will give you light." It's the same promise embraced by the blind man of today's Gospel, and by all of us who once were in darkness.

GOSPEL Again we have a long Gospel and again a classic story. If you recognize and value the literary beauty of John's writing and the power of the narrative form, you won't want to shorten this very significant Gospel story.

(1) The emotional involvement of the narrator is especially important in this long narrative. Through the several parenthetical asides we get the feeling that the narrator is an eyewitness turned believer, now relating this seminal story to other believers. You might imagine a grandfather speaking to his wide-eyed grandchildren about an amazing event he once witnessed.

The disciples' question innocently reflects the accepted wisdom that presumed that some sin, either of the individual or his parents, was the root cause of physical hardships like blindness. John uses

The man is insistent: "I am"!

He relates the details joyfully.

It suddenly dawns on him that he doesn't know Jesus's whereabouts. Pause, then new scene.

Pharisees = FAYR-uh-seez

"So then the Pharisees . . . ": your tone hints where they're going with this.

"He put clay" is spoken in a matter-of-fact, but joyful, manner.

In speaking the words of the Pharisees, note that one voice is angry, the other reasonable.

He must decide if he will make this confession of faith, and then does it boldly.

They feel they've been duped, so they look further.

Their speech is guarded; they say only what they must.

Some said, "It **is**,"
　　but **others** said, "**No**, he just **looks** like him."
He said, "I **am**."
So they said to him, "How were your eyes **opened**?"
He replied,
　　"The man called **Jesus** made **clay** and **anointed** my eyes
　　　　and told me, 'Go to **Siloam** and **wash**.'
So I **went** there and **washed** and was able to **see**."
And they said to him, "Where **is** he?"
He said, "I don't **know**."

(4) They brought the one who was once blind to the **Pharisees**.
Now Jesus had made clay and opened his eyes on a **sabbath**.
So then the Pharisees **also** asked him how he was able to see.
He **said** to them,
　　"He put **clay** on my eyes, and I **washed**, and now I can **see**."
So some of the **Pharisees** said,
　　"This man is not from **God**,
　　because he does not keep the **sabbath**."
But **others** said,
　　"How can a **sinful** man do such **signs**?"
And there was a **division** among them.
So they said to the blind man again,
　　"What do **you** have to say about him,
　　　　since he opened **your** eyes?"
He said, "He is a **prophet**."

(5) Now the Jews did not **believe**
　　that he had been blind and gained his **sight**
　　until they summoned the **parents** of the one who had gained
　　　　his sight.
They **asked** them,
　　"Is this your **son**, who you say was **born** blind?
How does he now **see**?"
His parents answered and said,
　　"We **know** that this is our **son** and that he was born **blind**.

their ignorance to set up one of his misunderstanding / illumination sequences that reveals his insight that Jesus is the Light of the World. The disciples' question should be posed without arrogance or hostile judgment. They already "know" the cause was sin; they just want to know who the "sinner" was. Jesus's surprising reply requires a forceful delivery to overcome their predisposition to assign blame. Jesus knows that the time for him to "do the works" of God is growing short. So, with urgency and hope,

he speaks of the advance of night "when *no one* can work."

(2) Deliver the pungent clay/saliva narration one phrase at a time, but with energy. Jesus's authority prompts the beggar's immediate compliance; his instruction to wash may be a test of faith which the man gladly accepts. Interestingly, the meaning of "Siloam" refers back to Jesus's self-description as one "sent" by the Father. The wonder of the crowd marveling at a blind man returning "able to see" infuses that narration.

(3) The neighbors are instantly astounded and each becomes an authority claiming to know the truth. The beggar responds to their skepticism by stating the facts without editorial comment, finally revealing his excitement on "and was able to see." His awareness will grow, but at this point Jesus, whom he has yet to "see," is still part of his former world of darkness.

(4) A note of threat is heard in the narration about "the Pharisees" and the "sabbath." Both suggest Jesus has run straight

Offer this aside as an excuse for the parent's behavior.

We do **not** know how he **sees** now,
  nor do we know **who** opened his eyes.
Ask **him**, he is of **age**;
  he can speak for **himself**."
His parents said this because they were **afraid**
  of the Jews, for the Jews had already **agreed**
  that if anyone **acknowledged** him as the **Christ**,
  he would be **expelled** from the **synagogue**.
For this **reason** his parents said,
  "He is of **age**; question **him**."

Suggest the exasperation of the leaders who may be speaking as if through clenched teeth.

The tone of his response is: "Don't entangle me in your politics. All I know is I'm healed!"

(6) So a **second** time they called the man who had been blind
  and said to him, "Give God the **praise**!
We **know** that this man is a **sinner**."
He replied,
  "If he is a **sinner**, I do not **know**.
One thing I **do** know is that I was **blind** and now I **see**."
So they said to him,
  "What did he **do** to you?
  How did he open your eyes?"
He answered them,
  "I told you **already** and you did not **listen**.
Why do you want to hear it **again**?
Do **you** want to become his disciples, **too**?"

He's becoming impatient and bold, even sarcastic!

They **ridiculed** him and said,
  "**You** are that man's disciple;
  we are disciples of **Moses**!
We know that God spoke to **Moses**,
  but we do not know where this one is **from**."

The leaders' anger mounts.

The man **answered** and said to them,
  "This is what is so **amazing**,
  that you do not know where he is **from**, yet he **opened** my **eyes**.
We know that God does **not** listen to **sinners**,
  but if one is **devout** and does his **will**, he **listens** to him.
It is **unheard** of that anyone ever **opened** the eyes of a person
      born **blind**.

First he's openly mocking. Then, he instructs.

into a religious quagmire, and your tone can signal the anticipated controversy. Because of the perceived danger, the beggar remains guarded, enumerating the facts without emotion. Like the crowd, the Pharisees take sides, some calling Jesus "sinner" while others suggest "such signs" reveal a godly foundation. Stressing their sharp division avoids caricaturing the Pharisees as uniformly sinister. The skeptics question the beggar hoping to hear something with which to discredit Jesus.

Despite the risk, he goes ahead and calls Jesus a prophet, a confession that suggests he has reached a new level of illumination.

(5) The judgment Jesus later levels at the religious leaders stems largely from belligerence in this scene. Fearing deception, they probe and bully. The parents fear for their safety, so say only what they must and volunteer nothing. Because fear causes much unexplainable behavior the narrator's parenthetical statement explains why the parents seemed so uncaring, though it probably alludes to a reality that actually occurred only after the Resurrection, when

Christians, in fact, were sometimes expelled from synagogues.

(6) The second summons is born of anger and frustration, so the energy builds. That Jesus is a sinner is now spoken as a given. But the beggar won't have it. "What I do know is this," he says. "The man made me see!" As the tension mounts, the beggar unleashes some sarcasm. His response to their ridicule is, "This is . . . amazing!" Openly mocking at first, he unwittingly launches into a sincere lecture bringing a swift, severe response upon himself.

They take refuge in the false assumption that his blindness was the result of sin. Pause before the final scene with Jesus.

As yet, he has not seen Jesus but is anxious to do so.

Pause after "he said" to suggest the beggar's moment of decision.

Jesus's tone attracts the attention of the Pharisees.

Jesus's language is strong and uncompromising, but it is motivated by his desire that they truly "see."

If this man were **not** from God,
   he would not be able to do **anything**."
They answered and said to him,
   "**You** were born totally in **sin**,
   and are you trying to teach **us**?"
Then they **threw** him out.

(7) When Jesus **heard** that they had thrown him out,
   he **found** him and said, "Do you **believe** in the Son of **Man**?"
He answered and said,
   "Who **is** he, sir, that I may **believe** in him?"
Jesus said to him,
   "You have **seen** him,
   and the one **speaking** with you is **he**."
He said,
   "**I do** believe, Lord," and he **worshiped** him.
Then Jesus said,
   "I came into this world for judgment,
   so that those who do **not** see **might** see,
   and those who **do** see might become **blind**."

Some of the **Pharisees** who were with him **heard** this
   and said to him, "Surely **we** are not also blind, **are** we?"
Jesus said to them,
   "If you **were** blind, you would have no **sin**;
   but now you are saying, 'We **see**,' so your sin **remains**."

[Shorter: John 9:1, 6–9, 13–17, 34–38]

TO KEEP IN MIND
Tell the story: The reading of Scripture is a storytelling moment. Storytellers are people of imagination. They help us to see, hear, feel, and smell the elements of the story because they themselves experience these sensory aspects of a story.

---

(7) As usual, Jesus plays the Good Shepherd seeking out the sheep. His question to the beggar is an invitation into relationship with "the Son of Man." The man is not too exhausted to eagerly desire to learn about and "see" the one who healed him. Jesus gently and tenderly obliges. Perhaps it's the recognition of Jesus's voice that sends the beggar to his knees to worship him, a reference that occurs only a handful of times in the Gospels.

This compassionate Jesus is never naïve. He knows some will reject him. And in doing so, some will bring judgment upon themselves. The Good Shepherd shares that truth, not to condemn, but motivate, so that no sheep is lost.

Sustained energy, variety, and careful attention to the very real characters of this story will make its telling effective and rewarding. In taking the time to prepare well, you, too, will be a shepherd of the sheep.

FIFTH SUNDAY OF LENT

Ezekiel = ee-ZEE-kee-uhl

It will be God, not the prophet, who speaks.

"O my" is like a single sound, with the emphasis going to "people."

Try a faster pace for "and have you rise from them."

Don't diminish your energy on this second iteration.

This section is more intense and intimate. Imagine looking into the eyes of one who needs these promises.

Take a long pause before announcing, "The word of the Lord."

For meditation and context:

LECTIONARY #34

READING I   Ezekiel 37:12–14

A reading from the Book of the Prophet Ezekiel

Thus says the LORD **God**:
 O my **people**, I will **open** your **graves**
 and have you **rise** from them,
 and bring you **back** to the land of **Israel**.
Then you shall know that I am the LORD,
 when I **open** your graves and have you **rise** from them,
 O my people!
I will put my **spirit** in you that you may **live**,
 and I will **settle** you upon your land;
 thus you shall **know** that I am the LORD.
I have **promised**, and I will **do** it, says the LORD.

RESPONSORIAL PSALM   Psalm 130:1–2, 3–4, 5–6, 7–8 (7)

R. With the Lord there is mercy and fullness of redemption.

Out of the depths I cry to you, O LORD;
 LORD, hear my voice!
Let your ears be attentive
 to my voice in supplication.

If you, O LORD, mark iniquities,
 LORD, who can stand?
But with you is forgiveness,
 that you may be revered.

I trust in the LORD;
 my soul trusts in his word.
More than sentinels wait for the dawn,
 let Israel wait for the LORD.

For with the LORD is kindness
 and with him is plenteous redemption;
and he will redeem Israel
 from all their iniquities.

TO KEEP IN MIND

Openings: First, make eye contact with the assembly and announce, from memory, "A (pronounced "uh," not "ay") reading from . . ." Then pause (three full beats!) before starting the reading.

READING I The striking imagery of God raising the Israelites from their graves clearly links this reading to today's Gospel. Though we must realize that the "graves" to which Ezekiel alludes are metaphorical, not literal like the tomb of Lazarus, still there was a deep sense among the Chosen People that God had abandoned the covenant and relegated Israel to tombs of exile and desolation. The monarchy was lost, the Temple destroyed, and the people languished in exile. Israel indeed had undergone death as a nation and faced what seemed a hopeless situation.

But God speaks directly and urgently to the people. The exclamation "O my people" frames God's first promise, which also is twice stated in the two opening sentences. "I will open your graves" is a promise to restore the nation and prove decisively that God has not forsaken the covenant. The Berlin Wall and the wall of apartheid posed similarly hopeless situations that proved in our own day God's power to restore and make new!

Speak God's strange words slowly and significantly so their impact will not be lost. Quicken the pace on "and have you rise . . ." to awaken hope in your listeners. Deliver the rest of the sentence more slowly, your tone confident and assuring. God is saying, "When I have given you this great sign, you shall know who I am!" There is neither arrogance nor anger in God's words, only a burning love that seeks to comfort the people, not vindicate God. Your energy should not diminish when you refer for a second time to open graves and rising from them.

God's second promise—"I will put my spirit in you"—is even more significant than

98

READING II   Romans 8:8–11

A reading from the Letter of Saint Paul to the Romans

Brothers and sisters:
Those who are in the **flesh** cannot **please** God.
But **you** are not in the flesh;
   on the **contrary**, you are in the **spirit**,
   if only the Spirit of God **dwells** in you.
Whoever does not have the Spirit of **Christ** does not **belong**
    to him.
But if **Christ** is in you,
   although the body is **dead** because of **sin**,
   the spirit is **alive** because of **righteousness**.
If the **Spirit** of the one who **raised** Jesus from the dead **dwells**
    in you,
   the One who raised **Christ** from the dead
   will give life to **your** mortal bodies **also**,
   through his **Spirit dwelling** in you.

Begin soberly. Paul's statement is stark and unflinching.

With eye contact, tell your listeners they don't belong to the category you just named.

Life in the spirit is not "automatic"; we must *allow* the Spirit to dwell in us.

Renew your energy, and speak with conviction that your hearers indeed possess the Spirit of Christ.

Though Paul is employing logical reasoning, allow the Good News to ring in his words.

Gradually slow your delivery on this last line and pause before announcing, "The word of the Lord."

TO KEEP IN MIND
Know the purpose of the letter:
It dictates the tone. Often Paul is the writer. As teacher and spiritual leader, he is motivated by multiple concerns: to instruct, console, encourage, chastise, warn, settle disputes, and more. When reading from one of his letters, be aware of what he's trying to accomplish.

---

the first. You might imagine how you would speak to a battered wife or abused children who are huddled in fear. How might you use your words to reassure the victims they can believe you will be their strength and their protection if they dare face life again? "I have promised, and I will do it . . . " is a very personal and direct assurance from a loving God to a beloved people. You'll need a substantial pause at the end of the reading before you break the mood to announce, "The word of the Lord." Remember, many wounded hearts long to hear these words of comfort.

READING II   Paul offers a message of hope and promise that echoes the words of Ezekiel in Reading I. A single theme unites this Sunday's readings that proclaim a message of resurrection and new life. Paul starts with bad news: those in the "flesh" can't please God. But immediately he qualifies: "you are not" part of that bad news. He then announces the good news of life in the Spirit. For Paul "flesh" is all those things that focus us on self rather than on God and others. It is the existence we had prior to Baptism into Jesus's Death and Resurrection. The Paschal

Mystery opened up a whole new life for believers—a life in the Spirit that frees us from enslavement to sin and enables us to surrender our wills to God's.

Of course, Christians still live life in the flesh, but the flesh no longer defines us. Now our identity is found in God's Spirit. And that same Spirit who makes it possible for us to pursue and achieve holiness will also make it possible for us to rise from our tombs on that great and terrible day when Christ returns in glory.

Without diminishing your enthusiasm, move slowly through this passage as you

GOSPEL   John 11:1–45

A reading from the holy Gospel according to John

Lazarus = LAZ-uh-ruhs

Bethany = BETH-uh-nee

For the narrator, these are familiar names and places. Speak of the anointing and of Mary with tenderness.

(1) Now a man was **ill**, **Lazarus** from **Bethany**,
　　the village of **Mary** and her sister **Martha**.
Mary was the one who had **anointed** the Lord with perfumed **oil**
　　and dried his **feet** with her **hair**;
　　it was her **brother** Lazarus who was ill.
So the sisters sent **word** to Jesus saying,
　　"**Master**, the one you **love** is **ill**."
When Jesus **heard** this he said,
　　"This illness is not to end in **death**,
　　but is for the **glory** of **God**,
　　that the **Son** of God may be **glorified** through it."

With the word "Master" convey the anxiety of the sisters.

Don't get philosophical. Keep the tone low-key and conversational.

Proclaim the words "Jesus loved" very slowly. Everything else builds on this.

(2) Now Jesus **loved** Martha and her sister and Lazarus.
So when he **heard** that he was ill,
　　he **remained** for two days in the place where he **was**.
Then **after** this he said to his **disciples**,
　　"Let us go back to **Judea**."
The disciples said to him,
　　"**Rabbi**, the Jews were just trying to **stone** you,
　　and you want to go **back** there?"
Jesus answered,
　　"Are there not **twelve** hours in a day?
If one walks during the **day**, he does not **stumble**,
　　because he sees the **light** of this world.
But if one walks at **night**, he **stumbles**,
　　because the light is not **in** him."
He said this, and then told them,
　　"Our friend **Lazarus** is **asleep**,
　　but I am going to **awaken** him."

Judea = joo-DEE-uh; joo-DAY-uh

The disciples are immediately anxious and incredulous. They're asking: "Do you really want to go back there?"

Rabbi = RAB-ī

Again, avoid a lofty tone and keep it conversational.

Remember the special significance in John of "day" and "night."

Say it like you would if really going to wake a sleeping friend.

---

present Paul's careful reasoning: "You are not in the *flesh* (because) you are in the *spirit* (and that is true because) the Spirit of God dwells in you." You rejoice that those to whom you speak are not trapped in a self-centeredness that leads to death.

Use Paul's contrasting words to make and emphasize his points, especially contrasting "body," "dead," and "sin" with "spirit," "alive," and "righteousness." Life in the Spirit calls us to embrace the challenge of constantly denying the evil desires of the flesh in order to live a joyful life in the Spirit—a life only God can make possible.

GOSPEL Every Gospel story speaks both of then and now. Then God acted powerfully in the life of Jesus, turning darkness into light, despair into hope, and death into life. The value of those stories is the hope they engender that God still can act, lives still can be transformed, and twisted limbs and twisted hearts still can be restored. Almost daily death finds us. Whether in the guise of a failed relationship or a great loss, we drink life's pain and enter dark tombs with large stones rolled across them. But Christian faith insists that Jesus comes today as he did then to call us

out of those tombs. Your listeners will hear that message only if the Jesus story is well told. Only when we can "see" what happened then, can we believe that the grace that flowed then can flow again. And if you're going to be a storyteller, tell the whole story (the long form) remembering that the telling is a sacramental moment that makes the Word present. Such sacred moments should not be edited.

(1) The narrator is not someone who watches these events unfold before him, but a believer who relates the story after it has taken place, telling the tale with the

Speak the line as if saying, "Master . . . you're not making sense!"

So the disciples said to him,
"**Master**, if he is **asleep**, he will be **saved**."
But Jesus was talking about his **death**,
while **they** thought that he meant **ordinary** sleep.
So then Jesus said to them **clearly**,

With some gravity, but not sadness.

"Lazarus has **died**.
And I am **glad** for you that I was not **there**,
that you may **believe**.
Let us **go** to him."

He's willing to pay the price of discipleship.

So **Thomas**, called **Didymus**, said to his fellow disciples,
"Let us **also** go to **die** with him."

(3) When Jesus **arrived**, he found that Lazarus
had already been in the **tomb** for **four days**.

"Four days" reflects the Jewish belief that the spirit left the body after three days; hence, Lazarus is "fully" dead.

Now Bethany was near **Jerusalem**, only about two miles away.
And many of the **Jews** had come to Martha and Mary
to **comfort** them about their brother.
When Martha heard that **Jesus** was coming,
she went to **meet** him;
but **Mary** sat at home.
Martha said to Jesus,

Martha exhibits mixed emotions: disappointment and hopefulness.

"**Lord**, if you had **been** here,
my brother would not have **died**.
But even **now** I know that **whatever** you ask of God,
God will **give** you."
Jesus said to her,
"Your brother will **rise**."
Martha said to him,
"I **know** he will rise,
in the **resurrection** on the last **day**."

Martha has missed his point. Jesus's explanation and self-identification are the key points of this Gospel passage.

Jesus told her,

Speak these lines slowly. This parallels the "light of the world" pronouncement in last week's Gospel.

"**I** am the resurrection and the **life**;
whoever **believes** in me, even if he **dies**, will **live**,
and everyone who **lives** and believes in me will **never** die.

advantage of hindsight. Aware of the powerful story he is about to relate, the narrator speaks familiarly of the people and village and of perfume and hair-dried feet. The sisters' message conveys Mary and Martha's concern but lacks panic, for they know Jesus can heal. Jesus makes a low-key response, knowing full well the disciples won't comprehend his declaration that this "illness" will achieve a divine purpose.

(2) Despite the declaration of Jesus's love for Mary and Martha, Jesus responds to the news of Lazarus's illness by intentionally and inexplicably delaying his departure—a

detail that should rouse questions in your listeners. The Apostles don't hide their fear of what awaits in Jerusalem and seem to think Jesus's decision to go there is irresponsible. But Jesus answers like one who knows his wisdom surpasses that of his followers. He employs the familiar Johannine motif of day and night in which "day" refers to the time of Jesus's earthly ministry—a time for doing God's work fearlessly, because "if one walks during the *day*, he does not stumble." Jesus announces Lazarus's death without emotion (simplicity often works better to suggest depth of feel-

ing). The disciples remain and misunderstand Jesus's use of "asleep," so Jesus speaks plainly and reiterates the divine purpose at work in these events. Thomas demonstrates fierce loyalty and valor in his willingness to face death with Jesus.

(3) Jesus's arrival in Bethany confronts us with the stark physical reality of Lazarus's death. Suddenly, the town is abuzz with activity, and we hear important details about the reaction of the two sisters. Energy climbs as Martha, seemingly hurt and possibly angry, runs to meet Jesus. "But even now . . . " is not an abrupt

Do **you** believe this?"
She said to him, "**Yes**, Lord.
I have come to believe that you are the **Christ**, the Son of **God**,
    the one who is **coming** into the **world**."

> Quieter tone. Martha may have been coaxing Mary to go, but now Mary goes eagerly.

(4) When she had **said** this,
    she went and called her sister Mary **secretly**, saying,
    "The **teacher** is here and is **asking** for you."
As soon as she **heard** this,
    she rose **quickly** and **went** to him.

> Again, Jesus seems to be delaying.

For Jesus had not yet come into the **village**,
    but was still where Martha had **met** him.
So when the **Jews** who were with her in the house **comforting** her
    saw Mary get up quickly and go out,

> Keep the story moving; no need for strong emphases here.

    they **followed** her,
    presuming that she was going to the **tomb** to **weep** there.
When Mary came to where **Jesus** was and **saw** him,
    she **fell** at his feet and said to him,

> Her line echoes Martha's, but vary the delivery for variety. Note that she pays homage before she complains.

    "**Lord**, if you had **been** here,
    my brother would not have **died**."
When Jesus saw her **weeping** and the Jews who had **come** with
        her weeping,

> Jesus experiences genuine sorrow. A note in the NAB says that in Greek this is rendered as a startling image: "He snorted in spirit."

    he became **perturbed** and deeply **troubled**, and said,
    "Where have you **laid** him?"
(5) They said to him, "**Sir**, come and **see**."

> Jesus also says "come and see" to John's disciples at the start of his ministry.

And Jesus **wept**.
So the Jews said, "See how he **loved** him."
But some of them said,

> Convey the contrasting moods of the crowd.

    "Could not the one who opened the eyes of the **blind** man
    have **done** something so that this man would not have **died**?"

So **Jesus**, perturbed **again**, came to the **tomb**.

> Speak these simple but dramatic statements slowly.

It was a **cave**, and a **stone** lay across it.
Jesus said, "Take away the **stone**."

---

change in mood but a declaration that Jesus can and *should* do something. Jesus's response is intentionally cryptic and *not* what Martha wants to hear. From intimate conversation between Jesus and Martha we shift to Jesus's public proclamation that he is the source of life, prompting Martha to lay aside her agenda and make a clear declaration of faith.

(4) Martha's whispered message to Mary initiates a scene of mounting intensity and excitement. Amid the buzzing of the crowd, Mary jumps to her feet and rushes to

see Jesus, eager to lay upon him responsibility for Lazarus's death and her deep loss. That grief, mixed with the mourning of the crowd, sparks a rare show of emotion from Jesus. "Where have you laid him?" Jesus asks. And like every time you visit a funeral home, Jesus is told, "Come and see."

(5) The detail from this narrative that most puzzles readers is Jesus's tears. Why does he weep when he knows he is about to raise his friend? Is it their lack of faith, the reality of human suffering and death, or perhaps the knowledge that he, too, will soon be swallowed by a tomb that pries the

tears from Jesus's eyes? Some of the crowd speculate it's love of Lazarus; but others demonstrate the human inclination to douse profundity with pettiness. "It was a cave" is the haunting introduction to the place of reversal and victory. Jesus speaks with authority, but Martha's concern ("by now there will be a stench") betrays a lack of confidence, so he reproaches her gently.

(6) Ever the teacher, Jesus prays "because of the crowd," addressing the Father with confidence and gratitude, and asking that the crowds be brought to faith.

Martha expresses a very practical concern about the stench.

Jesus expresses a mild reproach.

Jesus prays for others here, not himself.

The command is spoken with great authority.

See commentary for possible phrasing of this line.

Again, Jesus's voice is full of authority.

Hearing this Gospel should arouse deeper faith in the assembly.

Martha, the dead man's **sister**, said to him,
  "Lord, by **now** there will be a **stench**;
  he has been dead for four **days**."
Jesus said to her,
  "Did I not **tell** you that if you **believe**
  you will see the **glory** of **God**?"
So they **took** away the stone.
(6) And Jesus raised his **eyes** and said,
  "**Father**, I **thank** you for **hearing** me.
I know that you **always** hear me;
  but because of the **crowd** here I have said this,
  that they may **believe** that you **sent** me."
(7) And when he had said this,
  he **cried** out in a **loud voice**,
  "**Lazarus**, come **out**!"
The **dead** man **came** out,
  tied hand and foot with **burial** bands,
  and his **face** was wrapped in a **cloth**.
So Jesus said to them,
  "**Untie** him and let him **go**."

(8) Now **many** of the Jews who had come to **Mary**
  and **seen** what he had done began to **believe** in him.

[Shorter: John 11:3–7, 17, 20–27, 33b–45]

TO KEEP IN MIND
Importance of the Narrator: The narrator is often the pivotal role of a passage. Timbre, pitch, rate, and energy can make the same words convey very different moods or meaning. Sometimes the narrator is objective, but often the narrator has great interest in the events and characters of a story.

Nowhere else in the Gospel accounts is Jesus's authority better manifested. Throughout, he has been in charge, controlling, not yielding to the circumstances. In John, this event finally prompts the religious leaders to move against him.

(7) Speak "Lazarus" as if it were the name of those most in need of renewed life: your city's homeless poor, an oppressed nation, a friend suffering from depression, a long-dead part of you. Lazarus's appearance can be narrated without much inflection. Underplaying the drama will allow your listeners to do the work of witnessing the event. But help them by carefully pacing your delivery, perhaps like this: "The dead man/ came out/ bound/ hand/ and foot/ with burial bands/ and his face/ was wrapped in a cloth." Practice till it sounds and feels right.

(8) Build on each phrase of the final sentence. Unlike the story of the blind man, "*many*" come to faith in Bethany. This dramatic narrative allows us to glimpse a side of Jesus we rarely see. The Lord of life, who healed the blind and raised the dead, was one of us, mourning the death of a friend, comforting his family, shedding real tears.

PALM SUNDAY OF THE PASSION OF THE LORD

LECTIONARY #37

GOSPEL AT THE PROCESSION   Matthew 21:1–11

A reading from the holy Gospel according to Matthew

When **Jesus** and the **disciples** drew near **Jerusalem**
   and came to **Bethphage** on the Mount of **Olives**,
   Jesus sent two **disciples**, saying to them,
   "Go into the village **opposite** you,
   and immediately you will find an ass tethered,
   and a **colt** with her.
Untie them and **bring** them here to me.
And if anyone should **say** anything to you, reply,
   'The **master** has **need** of them.'
Then he will send them at **once**."
This happened so that what had been spoken through the prophet
   might be **fulfilled**:
Say to daughter Zion,
"Behold, your king comes to you,
   meek and riding on an ass,
   and on a colt, the foal of a beast of burden."
The disciples **went** and did as Jesus had ordered them.
They **brought** the ass and the colt and laid their **cloaks** over them,
   and he **sat** upon them.
The very large crowd spread their **cloaks** on the **road**,
   while others cut **branches** from the trees
   and strewed them on the road.

Let your tone suggest the expectant mood of the crowd.

Bethphage = BETH-fuh-jee

Jesus, too, is hopeful and full of anticipation.

Keep the dialogue upbeat, but don't give these instructions an overly serious tone.

Deliver this line with a knowing sense of authority.

Serve Matthew's purpose by giving due emphasis to his Old Testament citation.

Zion = Zī-ahn

The revelation is of a humble king who comes upon a lowly beast.

Don't be distracted by Matthew's misunderstanding about the ass and the colt.

The crowd's energy starts building here and doesn't climax till the last sentence.

PROCESSION GOSPEL Even though the events narrated in today's two Gospel texts occurred some days apart, it still stretches credulity that a crowd so adoring could so soon turn lethal. But that reversal may not have surprised Jesus, who'd probably read enough Isaiah to understand that a faithful servant is typically a suffering servant, and glory comes to such servants only at God's hands, not from admiring crowds.

It also shouldn't surprise us who witness almost daily the stunning reversals of the capricious human heart. The hidden, wounded ego that often drives us seeks heroes to raise up, then just as gladly tears them down. We easily and readily identify with the exultant crowd that welcomes Jesus amid shouts of adulation; but the inclination to identify shuts down when that same crowd turns sinister and calls for his execution. Such is human blindness.

Addressed to a Jewish audience who needed to believe Jesus was the fulfillment of their prophetic tradition, the Gospel according to Matthew strives to illustrate Jesus's continuity with Old Testament prophecy. But, here, Matthew tries so hard that he takes literally what's meant to be a poetic redundancy in Zechariah: "A just savior is he, meek and riding *on an ass, on a colt, the foal of an ass*" (Zechariah 9:9). By failing to understand that "ass" and "colt" refer to the same animal, Matthew ends up suggesting that Jesus rode two animals at the same time. Luke and Mark make no reference to Zechariah's prophecy in their narratives, but Matthew takes pains to point out this important biblical allusion.

Still stirred by the healing of the blind man, the crowd may well be expecting another miraculous display. After the blind

The crowds preceding him and those following
    kept crying out and saying:
      "Hosanna to the Son of David;
        blessed is he who comes in the name of the Lord;
      hosanna in the highest."
And when he entered Jerusalem
    the whole city was shaken and asked, "Who is this?"
And the crowds replied,
    "This is Jesus the prophet, from Nazareth in Galilee."

The crowds are quoting Psalm 118:26. It is both a cry of welcome and a prayer.

Don't gloss over the detail that the city was "shaken."

This is not simply factual information, but a declaration of faith!

READING I   Isaiah 50:4–7

A reading from the Book of the Prophet Isaiah

Isaiah = ī-ZAY-uh

The Lord's servant is speaking with gratitude despite much suffering.

Be aware of the multivalent meaning of "weary" as you speak the word.

God has been persistent and faithful.

Communicate pride and gratitude for the God-given strength to endure.

Don't gloss over these graphic details. Give them their due. "Plucked my beard" is a grave insult in that culture. The past tense lessens the intensity of the pain described.

Here is the voice of hope in the face of adversity.

Speak with rock-like confidence and strength.

The Lord God has **given** me
    a **well**-trained **tongue**,
that I might **know** how to **speak** to the **weary**
    a word that will **rouse** them.
Morning after **morning**
    he **opens** my ear that I may **hear**;
and I have not **rebelled**,
    have not **turned** back.
I gave my **back** to those who **beat** me,
    my **cheeks** to those who plucked my **beard**;
my **face** I did not **shield**
    from **buffets** and **spitting**.

The Lord God is my help,
    therefore I am not **disgraced**;
I have **set** my face like **flint**,
    knowing that I shall **not** be put to **shame**.

---

man's healing, the hearts of the leaders turned dark. Jesus's condemnation of their leadership provoked them, so their malice turned against him. Seeming to sense that his time is short, Jesus focuses entirely on his entry into Jerusalem, a spectacle that will push the leaders' buttons yet again.

The Mount of Olives not only situates the scene, it also names the spot prophesied in Zechariah 14:4 as the place from which the Anointed One would come to deliver Jerusalem from her enemies. Jesus makes no effort to stifle the excitement of the crowd and allows himself to be caught in its flow, evinced by his rapid instructions to the disciples. Whatever he may sense about the future, Jesus remains upbeat and fully absorbed in the crowd's adulation.

When he instructs the disciples, Jesus anticipates every detail but makes no great show of his foreknowledge. Deliver his lines calmly and with confidence, as you would direct someone to a corner of your home to find a needed item.

Drop your voice to explain *why* "this happened" and let your tone suggest its significance. Still subdued, but with greater intensity, speak the prophecy that predicts a humble king who comes upon a lowly beast.

Your rate and energy build as you become a mouthpiece for the exultant crowd. The crowd surrounds their hero Jesus. Hosannas fill the air and branches are laid in his path. The crowd's energy grows and their infatuation seems unbounded for "the whole city" feels the profound impact of Jesus's presence. Shaken to the point of turmoil, a question burns within them: "Who is this?" Join your faith to the crowd's as you confess that "This is Jesus the prophet, from Nazareth in Galilee." And now everyone knows what "good" can come from there.

For meditation and context:

Philippians = fih-LIP-ee-uhnz

Begin slowly, but with solid energy.

Speak the name of the Lord with reverence.

"Rather" signals a shift. As important as what he rejected, what Christ humbly embraced is even more important.

Speak with gratitude that Christ became one of us, also of the great pain he endured.

Another significant shift: tempo quickens. You can get louder, or softer but more intense.

RESPONSORIAL PSALM   Psalm 22:8–9, 17–18, 19–20, 23–24 (2a)

R. My God, my God, why have you abandoned me?

All who see me scoff at me;
   they mock me with parted lips, they wag
     their heads:
"He relied on the LORD; let him deliver him,
   let him rescue him, if he loves him."

Indeed, many dogs surround me,
   a pack of evildoers closes in upon me;
they have pierced my hands and my feet;
   I can count all my bones.

They divide my garments among them,
   and for my vesture they cast lots.
But you, O LORD, be not far from me;
   O my help, hasten to aid me.

I will proclaim your name to my brethren;
   in the midst of the assembly I will
     praise you:
"You who fear the LORD, praise him;
   all you descendants of Jacob, give glory
     to him;
   revere him, all you descendants of Israel!"

READING II   Philippians 2:6–11

A reading from the Letter of Saint Paul to the Philippians

Christ **Jesus**, though he was in the form of **God**,
   did not regard **equality** with God
   something to be **grasped**.
Rather, he **emptied** himself,
   taking the form of a **slave**,
   coming in **human** likeness;
   and found human in **appearance**,
   he **humbled** himself,
   becoming **obedient** to the point of **death**,
   even death on a **cross**.
Because of this, God greatly **exalted** him
   and **bestowed** on him the **name**
   which is above **every** name,
   that at the name of **Jesus**
   every **knee** should **bend**,

READING I	A proclaimer of the Word who encounters this text

may discern within it a powerful lesson in the ministry of proclamation. God trains the tongue of those who speak for him, for their service is to utter rousing words of hope to a people grown weary with suffering and the hard labors of daily life.

The context of these words is the third of Isaiah's Suffering Servant songs, in which God's servant is depicted as one who embraces a thankless ministry that's doomed to failure. And yet, the words constitute a prayer of thanks for a ministry that is privilege as well as burdensome respon-

sibility. Seeing with the eyes of faith, Isaiah's servant prays in gratitude for God's special call, a call that's bittersweet because it trains him in obedience but does so through endurance of great pain and indignity. The servant seeks to awaken hope in a people who languish in exile and have grown tired of promises of deliverance that remain unfulfilled.

With awareness of the daily hardship that characterizes his ministry, the servant declares God has tutored him to speak to the "weary" a word that will "rouse" them. The "weary" sit before us every Sunday burdened with physical or emotional chal-

lenges, with the random or enduring sorrows that find their way into every life. These are heartened and healed with nothing more than God's Word—today spoken through you. But God's Word is not magic. It rouses listless spirits only when it is heard and embraced, and to be heard, it must be spoken with conviction.

It is easy to understand why the early Church saw a connection between Isaiah's Suffering Servant and the suffering Jesus of the Gospel. "Morning after morning" God opens the prophet's ear to hear God's Word. The servant neither resists nor resents God's persistence and asserts his

Slowly—stress *"heaven," "earth,"* and *"under the earth."* The hymn is citing Isaiah 45:23.

Your greatest energy goes to the acclamation of Christ, followed by a slightly lower key delivery of the final line.

of those in **heaven** and on **earth** and **under** the earth,
and every **tongue confess** that
Jesus Christ is **Lord**,
to the **glory** of God the **Father**.

GOSPEL   Matthew 26:14—27:66

The Passion of our Lord Jesus Christ according to Matthew

Judas = JOO-duhs
Iscariot = ih-SKAYR-ee-uht
Stress Judas's identity as "one of the Twelve."

There's tension in his voice that betrays his ambivalence.

"From that time on" the payment deepens his resolve.

(1) One of the **Twelve**, who was called **Judas Iscariot**,
    went to the chief **priests** and said,
    "What are you willing to **give** me
    if I hand him **over** to you?"
They paid him **thirty** pieces of **silver**,
    and from **that** time on he looked for an opportunity
        to **hand** him over.

The tone of the disciples is upbeat.

(2) On the first day of the Feast of Unleavened **Bread**,
    the disciples **approached** Jesus and said,
    "**Where** do you want us to prepare
    for you to eat the **Passover**?"
He said,
    "Go into the **city** to a certain man and tell him,
    'The **teacher** says, "My appointed time draws **near**;
    in **your** house I shall celebrate the **Passover** with
        my **disciples**."'"

Speak without melancholy, in a straightforward, confident tone.

This line can suggest the disciples' desire to care for Jesus through these preparations.

The disciples then **did** as Jesus had ordered,
    and **prepared** the Passover.

openness to God's discipline, saying: "I have not *rebelled*, have *not* turned my back." He offers graphic images of being beaten and spat upon that anticipate the cruel treatment Jesus himself will endure.

The last four lines profess trust in God's ultimate vindication, for God will not allow him to be "put to shame." So with a face of flint he stands strong and confident, and ready for God to start making sparks.

 READING II   Christian faith always sees Jesus's suffering and Death through the filter of his glorious Resurrection

and Ascension. The Church's liturgy never requires lopsided emphasis on agony, for the song of Resurrection pervades our every prayer and celebration. So the magnificent hymn of praise and exultation that comprises the Philippians text provides notes of joy that harmonize with the music of the Passion that follows.

The structure of the hymn is the key to its meaning: the first half (up to "death on a cross") refers exclusively to Christ, telling us *who* he is—equal with God, born as a man, humble, and obedient! But in the second half the subject becomes God, and we learn

what God has done for Christ: exalted him, given him the name above every other, that all might worship him. Though the theology of the preexistent Christ elaborated here is essential, it is the poetry that commands your attention as reader. The hymn first lauds Christ for humbling himself to become human, then suddenly changes key and tempo and swells to symphonic praise.

The text entreats us to imitate Christ who in humble obedience embraced the cruelest of deaths. But it also reminds us that God's Kingdom is a place of reversals where emptying leads to filling and humility

Use the reference to fading light to set the scene for the betrayal.

Speak slowly. Jesus's emotions are held in check.

The disciples are fearful and defensive.

Sharing the dish is a privilege reserved for a friend or honored guest.

This sad and solemn pronouncement must be stressed.

Contrast Judas's calm denial with the others' agitation.

Rabbi = RAB-ī

Calm pervades the scene. Speak these sacred words as if for the first time, not as ritual prayer but as words shared with friends.

Keep the mood upbeat since Jesus is focused on the coming of the Kingdom.

The mood remains one of intimacy and friendship.

Don't let their singing go unnoticed.

(3) When it was **evening**,
　　he reclined at **table** with the Twelve.
And while they were **eating**, he said,
　　"**Amen**, I say to you, **one** of you will **betray** me."
Deeply **distressed** at this,
　　they began to say to him one after **another**,
　　"Surely it is not **I**, Lord?"
He said in reply,
　　"He who has dipped his hand into the **dish** with me
　　is the one who will **betray** me.
The Son of Man indeed **goes**, as it is **written** of him,
　　but **woe** to that man by whom the Son of Man is **betrayed**.
It would be **better** for that man if he had never been **born**."
Then **Judas**, his **betrayer**, said in reply,
　　"Surely it is not **I**, Rabbi?"
He answered, "You have **said** so."

(4) While they were eating,
　　Jesus took **bread**, said the **blessing**,
　　broke it, and **giving** it to his disciples said,
　　"**Take** and **eat**; this is my **body**."
Then he took a **cup**, gave **thanks**, and **gave** it to them, saying,
　　"**Drink** from it, all of you,
　　for this is my **blood** of the **covenant**,
　　which will be **shed** on behalf of **many**
　　for the **forgiveness** of sins.
I **tell** you, from now on I shall not **drink** this fruit of the vine
　　until the day when I drink it with you **new**
　　in the **kingdom** of my **Father**."
Then, after singing a **hymn**,
　　they went out to the Mount of **Olives**.

to glorification. Begin with conviction and a tone guided by the emptying and humbling of which you speak. The hymn stresses Christ's oneness with humanity, but "death on a cross" asserts what makes him unique.

That Christ accepted the most humiliating form of death imaginable leads to the heart of the reading. "Because of this" is the hinge that shifts the mood and tempo of the hymn. Like Isaiah's servant, Jesus is not put to shame but "exalted," and exalted not only on "earth," but also in "heaven," and "under the earth." "Exalted" colors all that follows: it either softens the tone while intensifying the feeling, or it brightens the

proclamation. Whichever way you express those final lines, convey joy and gratitude for what God has done for Christ. And note that the lordship of Jesus is a beacon that shines its light on "God the Father."

PASSION　Each Holy Week the Church gifts us with two different Passion narratives—one from John, the other from one of the synoptics. By looking at the same reality from two perspectives we acquire an understanding of the whole no one narrative could convey. Two people's opinions of the same friend may yield very different portraits, with the truest

image being a combination of the two. John's Jesus is royal and self-assured. His destiny is in his own hands. He does not shrink from his fate and at the appropriate time he hands over his life, announcing almost triumphantly, "It is finished."

Matthew's Jesus is distinctive and his narrative so characteristic of the paradoxical reversals that distinguish this day. Unlike John's Jesus whose kingship is acknowledged by Pilate in three languages, Matthew's Lord receives recognition only after his Death, when a Roman centurion declares, "Truly this was the son of God." God does hear and answer prayer, we

Jesus's tone is persuasive, but not angry.

(5) Then Jesus said to them,
"This night **all** of you will have your faith in me **shaken**,
for it is **written**:
*I will strike the **shepherd**,*
*and the **sheep** of the flock will be **dispersed***;
but after I have been **raised** up,
I shall go before you to **Galilee**."
Peter said to him in reply,
"Though **all** may have their faith in you shaken,
mine will **never** be."
Jesus said to him,
"**Amen**, I say to you,
this very **night** before the cock **crows**,
you will **deny** me three **times**."
Peter said to him,
"Even though I should have to **die** with you,
I will not **deny** you."
And all the disciples spoke **likewise**.

Galilee = GAL-ih-lee

Peter really believes he won't fail Jesus and says so adamantly.

Jesus is not trying to convince Peter, but prepare him for what will surely happen.

Probably wounded, Peter nonetheless remains confident and full of love in these exclamations.

Read slowly to set the somber mood.

Gethsemane = geth-SEM-uh-nee

Zebedee = ZEB-uh-dee

Jesus's grief is contained and muted.

(6) Then Jesus came with them to a place called **Gethsemane**,
and he said to his disciples,
"**Sit** here while I go over there and **pray**."
He took along **Peter** and the two sons of **Zebedee**,
and began to feel **sorrow** and **distress**.
Then he said to them,
"My soul is **sorrowful** even to **death**.
Remain here and keep **watch** with me."
He advanced a little and fell prostrate in **prayer**, saying,
"My **Father**, if it is **possible**,
let this cup **pass** from me;
yet, not as **I** will, but as **you** will."
When he **returned** to his disciples he found them **asleep**.

Jesus is not playacting. He truly wishes to avoid this fate.

learn, but often it's when we least expect it. And for Jesus this reversal comes only after total abandonment by his friends and supporters. In contrast with last year's Passion from Luke, the disciples come off very badly: they fall asleep three times while Jesus prays; they all desert him; Judas betrays him; and Peter denies him amid oaths and curses. From the Cross, rather than Lucan forgiveness for his persecutors and compassion for the thief, Jesus speaks only words of abandonment: "My God, my God, why have you forsaken me?" This is a sadder Passion than Luke's or John's. In no other Gospel account is there

greater sorrow than in Matthew's garden scene. Your reading should heighten these moments of abandonment, for all that sadness makes Jesus's ultimate vindication a more striking reversal.

From the earliest days of Christianity, the Passion was told as one continuous story, not in episodic pieces like the rest of the Gospel. Like Jesus's seamless garment, the Passion is a narrative that cannot be divided into parts, for each section needs the others to be complete. A longer telling like this manifests more visibly and powerfully the ability of a story to "make present." Liturgical storytelling is not simply a

function of remembering. Important as that is, a remembered event remains in the past with little power to touch us. But in liturgy, past events are made present, not just remembered. The Lord of life comes among us with his healing love and saving power, and we are no further removed from his saving activity than were those men and women who walked the dusty roads of Galilee two thousand years ago. As proclaimer, let this story first work its magic on you by being the first to be moved by the events and emotions you describe. Then read with the awareness that you are witnessing and describing the original event

He said to **Peter**,
  "So you could not keep watch with me for one **hour**?
Watch and **pray** that you may not undergo the **test**.
The **spirit** is **willing**, but the **flesh is weak**."
Withdrawing a **second** time, he prayed **again**,
  "My **Father**, if it is not **possible** that this cup pass
  without my **drinking** it, **your** will be done!"
Then he returned once **more** and found them **asleep**,
  for they could not keep their eyes **open**.
He **left** them and withdrew again and prayed a **third** time,
  saying the **same** thing **again**.
Then he **returned** to his disciples and said to them,
  "Are you still **sleeping** and taking your **rest**?
Behold, the **hour** is at hand
  when the Son of Man is to be **handed** over to **sinners**.
Get up, let us **go**.
Look, my **betrayer** is at hand."

(7) While he was still speaking,
  Judas, one of the Twelve, arrived,
  accompanied by a large **crowd**, with **swords** and **clubs**,
  who had come from the chief **priests** and the **elders**
    of the people.
His betrayer had arranged a **sign** with them, saying,
  "The man I shall **kiss** is the **one; arrest** him."
Immediately he went over to Jesus and said,
  "**Hail**, Rabbi!" and he **kissed** him.
Jesus answered him,
  "**Friend**, do what you have **come** for."
Then stepping forward they laid **hands** on Jesus and **arrested** him.
And **behold**, one of those who **accompanied** Jesus
  put his hand to his **sword**, **drew** it,
  and **struck** the high priest's **servant**, cutting off his **ear**.

Margin notes (left column):

Jesus is clearly disappointed in the three disciples. He warns them, but without anger.

Don't rush this classic line.

After "without my drinking it" pause for a moment of decision.

Matthew makes a feeble excuse for the exhausted disciples.

Jesus is now resigned and ready.

Contrast "one of the Twelve" with "swords and clubs." It's painful to admit one of his own betrayed him.

Try subtly suggesting a conspiratorial whisper.

Take a slight pause before and after "Rabbi."

Jesus won't play his game.

Suggest the fury of the sword wielder.

---

that is mysteriously and solemnly made present in the telling.

(1) The Prologue. Jesus's fate is sealed from the beginning of the narrative. Betrayal is inevitable, but the fact that it comes from "one" of "the Twelve" makes it more painful. Though his question about how much he would be paid introduces a greed motive for Judas's betrayal, his decision must have been fraught with ambivalence. He is still conflicted when he asks "What are you willing to give me?" The priests' reply, however, solidifies his resolve to look "for an opportunity to hand him over."

(2) Preparation for the Passover. Upbeat and filled with festival excitement, the disciples choose to forget Jesus's recent prediction of his Passion. Jesus answers their question without melancholy. Apparently Jesus has spoken to this "certain man" in the city before, and now the prearranged signal is sent: "My appointed time draws near." He speaks with assurance, knowing that neither the disciples nor this "man" can sense the great privilege being conferred.

(3) The Betrayer. The word "evening" sets the tone for this section. The light of

day is waning, and a night of shadows that makes it hard to find one's way is fast approaching. The narration provides three valuable pieces of information: when it was ("evening"), where he was ("at table"), and who he was with ("the Twelve"). Narrate slowly, then drop the shocking news: "One of you will betray me." Jesus is resigned, his emotions in check. But he's dropped a bomb and immediately there follows shock and confusion condensed into the repeated question: "Surely, it is not I, Lord?" Jesus silences them with the solemn assurance

Jesus speaks with confidence and shames them for their cowardice.

Then Jesus said to him,
  "Put your **sword** back into its **sheath**,
    for all who **take** the sword will **perish** by the sword.
Do you think that I cannot call upon my **Father**
    and he will not **provide** me at this moment
    with more than twelve **legions** of **angels**?
But then how would the Scriptures be **fulfilled**
    which say that it **must** come to pass in this **way**?"

Jesus does not spare the crowds who have followed him and benefited from his merciful ministry.

At that hour Jesus said to the **crowds**,
  "Have you come out as against a **robber**,
    with swords and clubs to **seize** me?
Day after day I sat **teaching** in the **temple** area,
    yet you did not **arrest** me.
But all this has come to **pass**
    that the writings of the **prophets** may be **fulfilled**."

There is great irony in this line following the previous narration.

Then all the disciples **left** him and **fled**.

Your tone should signal the approaching danger.
Caiaphas = KAY-uh-fuhs; KĪ-uh-fuhs

The sound of your voice can suggest Peter's hesitance and fear.

(8) Those who had **arrested** Jesus led him away
    to **Caiaphas** the high **priest**,
    where the **scribes** and the **elders** were assembled.
Peter was following him at a **distance**
    as far as the high priest's **courtyard**,
    and going **inside** he sat down with the **servants** to see
      the **outcome**.

Sanhedrin = san-HEE-drin.

The chief priests and the entire **Sanhedrin**
    kept trying to obtain false **testimony** against Jesus
    in order to put him to **death**,
    but they found **none**,

As narrator, enjoy their frustration and failure to find corroborating witnesses.

    though many false **witnesses** came forward.
Finally **two** came forward who stated,

The witnesses quote Jesus in slow cadences.

  "This man said, 'I can **destroy** the temple of God
    and within **three** days **rebuild** it.'"

that his betrayer is, in fact, one of those with whom he shares this final meal.

Starkly and without melodrama, Jesus's voice reveals his pain and disappointment. The condemnation of the betrayer is the most severe found in any of the Gospel accounts. Christianity asserts that being equals goodness. Saying that it would have been better for Judas if he had never been born hints at his bitter fate. Jesus's whole being, it seems, wishes it had not been one of his own who betrayed him. But though Judas calmly and smoothly feigns innocence, Jesus responds with a pointed "You have said so."

(4) The Lord's Supper. Speak the narration and Jesus's dialogue slowly. Jesus knows his words will ring strangely in the disciples' ears. With the taste of betrayal still on his lips, Jesus focuses on the meal that will be his last. Knowledge and fear of what lies ahead are also on the table, but Jesus's focus is entirely on the bread and wine that will become the mysterious way of remaining one with his friends. The sense of loss in "I shall not drink . . . " quickly yields to a confident prediction of renewed fellowship in his Father's Kingdom. Jesus joins his friends in singing psalms, but the

joy is muted by the knowledge that these singing friends will soon desert him.

(5) Peter's Denial Foretold. Jesus leads the men to the Mount of Olives, the same place where David fled during Absolom's revolt and where he wept at discovering that he'd been betrayed by a trusted counselor (2 Samuel 15:13-31). Here, Jesus predicts abandonment and denial by his most trusted friends, speaking forcefully, but without anger or self-pity, for he must convince them that they *will* do the unthinkable. He ends on a note of hope, prophesying Resurrection and reunion, but Peter, naively thinking himself incapable of infidelity,

The high priest takes charge, attempts to provoke Jesus and is amazed by his silence.

The high priest rose and **addressed** him,
    "Have you no **answer**?
What are these men **testifying** against you?"
But Jesus was **silent**.
Then the high **priest** said to him,
    "I **order** you to tell us under oath before the living **God**
    whether you are the **Christ**, the **Son** of God."
Jesus said to him in reply,

Jesus's silence is enigmatic.

They heighten the stakes in an effort to provoke a response.

Jesus is calm, confident and regal in his response.

    "**You** have said so.
But **I** tell you:
    From now on you will **see** the 'Son of Man
        seated at the **right** hand of the **Power**'
        and 'coming on the clouds of **heaven**.'"
Then the high priest **tore** his robes and said,
    "He has **blasphemed**!
What further **need** have we of **witnesses**?
You have now **heard** the blasphemy;
    what is your **opinion**?"
They said in reply,
    "He deserves to **die**!"

They are all convinced Jesus is a liar and blasphemer.

Then they **spat** in his face and **struck** him,
    while some **slapped** him, saying,
    "**Prophesy** for us, Christ: who **is** it that **struck** you?"

Once the sentence is spoken, their hatred turns violent.

This scene is fraught with tension throughout.

(9) Now **Peter** was sitting outside in the **courtyard**.
One of the **maids** came over to him and said,
    "You **too** were with Jesus the Galilean."
But he **denied** it in front of everyone, saying,
    "I do not know what you are **talking** about!"
As he went out to the gate, **another** girl saw him
    and said to those who were there,
    "**This** man was with Jesus the **Nazorean**."
Again he denied it with an **oath**,
    "I do not **know** the man!"

Her assertion is sparked by simple curiosity.
Galilean = gal-ih-LEE-uhn

Peter can't escape scrutiny.

Nazorean = naz-uh-REE-uhn

Now he adds an oath to his denial.

responds with unadulterated confidence. So Jesus speaks bluntly, but Peter responds with even more bravado, inspiring the like in the rest of the disciples.

(6) The Agony in the Garden. In the company of his closest intimates, Jesus readily confesses his heavyhearted mood. As narrator, imagine you are telling the story of a loved one who is greatly distressed, letting your tone match the heaviness of the situation. For once, Jesus asks help of his friends: "Remain here and keep watch." Matthew is less kind than Luke to the disciples for he offers but a weak

excuse for the three (they "could not keep their eyes open") while Luke claims that they were "exhausted with grief." But Jesus offers no rebuke and instead exhorts them to pray that they not face a test they can't pass. He needs no one to tell him that he'll walk the road to Calvary alone. Jesus's prayer reveals that his love of God weighs heavier in his heart than the fear of what awaits him on Calvary's hill. He returns from his third prayer time prepared to face the "hour" that is upon him, though the disciples' lack of vigilance draws a disapproving comment. Motivate his sudden order to

"get up!" by pausing and looking up to "see" the approaching mob led by "my betrayer."

(7) The Betrayal and Arrest. Judas's identification as "one of the Twelve" reminds us of the intimacy between Jesus and his betrayer and underscores the depth of Judas's treachery. But don't too easily caricature Judas. The pain of knowingly betraying a friend should be heard in his voice, both in his instructions to the priests and in his greeting. Jesus poignantly calls him "friend," and before that word has even stopped echoing, the leaders fall upon Jesus. The narration of the sudden sword

The bystanders are adamant.

A little later the **bystanders** came over and said to Peter,
　"Surely you **too** are one of them;
　even your **speech** gives you away."
At that he began to **curse** and to **swear**,
　"I do not **know** the man."

Peter is in a rage, cursing.

And immediately a **cock crowed**.
Then Peter **remembered** the words that Jesus had spoken:
　"Before the cock **crows** you will **deny** me **three** times."
He went **out** and began to weep **bitterly**.

Deliver these lines as a haunting memory.
Underplay the emotions: as if remembering tears, not shedding them.
The story continues to unfold. Tell it as the sympathetic narrator, not as one of the Sanhedrin.

(10) When it was **morning**,
　all the chief **priests** and the elders of the people
　took **counsel** against Jesus to put him to **death**.
They **bound** him, **led** him away,
　and handed him over to **Pilate**, the **governor**.

Pilate = Pī-luht

(11) Then **Judas**, his **betrayer**, seeing that Jesus had
　　been **condemned**,
　deeply **regretted** what he had done.

Suggest Judas's desperate regret.

He **returned** the thirty pieces of silver
　to the chief priests and elders, saying,
　"I have **sinned** in betraying **innocent** blood."
They said,

Their tone is mocking.

　"What is that to **us**?
　Look to it **yourself**."
Flinging the money into the **temple**,
　he **departed** and went off and **hanged** himself.

Pause before announcing his fate.

The chief **priests** gathered up the **money**, but said,
　"It is not **lawful** to deposit this in the **temple** treasury,
　for it is the price of **blood**."

The conversation is all practicality, void of guilt or remorse.

After **consultation**, they used it to buy the **potter's** field
　as a **burial** place for **foreigners**.
That is why that field even today is called the Field of **Blood**.

---

play quickens the pace, but Jesus's strong command to resheathe the sword brings that action to a halt. His deliberate reflection on how violence begets violence and his mention of the army of angels who could be summoned to his aid serves to reinforce the voluntary nature of Jesus's sacrifice. This is not a sudden development in his life, but a long-anticipated consequence of his unfaltering commitment to the Father's all-consuming will.

He addresses the mob, not in an effort to dissuade them but to reproach their cowardice for seeking him in darkness rather than the light of day. Color the stark narration of the disciples' desertion with the regret that must have filled their hearts once they realized what they'd done.

(8) Jesus before the Sanhedrin. Jesus faces a decidedly hostile group led by a high priest who exudes malice. Matthew's purpose is to present Jesus as wholly innocent of all the charges leveled against him, a victim of manipulative leaders who nonetheless are motivated by real concern for preserving the system they see Jesus threatening. These men are not driven by evil, but by their conviction that Jesus is a charlatan. This text does not call for an objective, disinterested narrator. Instead, the narration brims with bias for Jesus. Imagine the early tellers of this narrative as disciples who loved this man who had become their hero and read with the conviction and familiarity of such a partisan. Angered by Jesus's silence, the high priest demands a reply. And Jesus does not disappoint, though he gives a more cryptic response here than in Mark where his answer is a clear yes. The priests have what they need; lest he can recant, they spring

Again, Matthew points out the fulfillment of prophecy.

Jeremiah = jayr-uh-MĪ-uh

Israelites = IZ-ree-uh-līts; IZ-ray-uh-līts

At first, Pilate is more annoyed than curious, but Jesus's calm demeanor captures Pilate's attention.

Jesus's silence is not petulance, but confidence that amazes Pilate.

Your tone betrays the hope that things might turn out differently this time.

Pilate asks a leading question.

The detail about Pilate's wife adds great texture to this scene.

Pilate is seeking a way out for Jesus.

Then was **fulfilled** what had been said through **Jeremiah**
    the prophet,
    *And they took the **thirty** pieces of silver,*
    *the value of a man with a **price** on his head,*
    *a price set by some of the **Israelites**,*
    *and they paid it out for the **potter's** field*
    *just as the **Lord** had **commanded** me.*

(12) Now Jesus stood before the **governor**, and he questioned him,
    "Are you the **king** of the **Jews**?"
Jesus said, "**You** say so."
And when he was **accused** by the chief priests and elders,
    he made no **answer**.
Then Pilate said to him,
    "Do you not **hear** how many things they are **testifying**
        against you?"
But he did not answer him one **word**,
    so that the governor was greatly **amazed**.

(13) Now on the occasion of the **feast**
    the governor was accustomed to **release** to the crowd
    one prisoner whom they **wished**.
And at that time they had a notorious prisoner called **Barabbas**.
So when they had **assembled**, Pilate said to them,
    "**Which** one do you want me to **release** to you,
    Barabbas, or **Jesus** called **Christ**?"
For he knew that it was out of **envy**
    that they had handed him over.
While he was still seated on the **bench**,
    his **wife** sent him a **message**,
    "Have nothing to **do** with that righteous **man**.
I **suffered** much in a **dream** today because of him."
The chief priests and the elders **persuaded** the crowds
    to **ask** for **Barabbas** but to **destroy Jesus**.
The governor said to them in reply,
    "Which of the **two** do you want me to **release** to you?"

the charge of blasphemy and pass judgment. As narrator you spoke with pride of Jesus's courageous silence. Now speak with sadness of how they hit and spit at him.

(9) Peter's Denial. In the courtyard Peter undergoes a trial of his own. Both in content and intensity his triple denial grows, from simple avoidance to careful lying to loud cursing. Fearful and panicked, his denials become as urgent and impassioned as his earlier claims of unfailing loyalty. The bystanders, whose energy is fueled by Peter's denials, at first make simple observations, but soon become determined to

pin him down. His vehement denials culminate in Peter's intense sorrow. The sound of the cock slaps Peter to his senses, but it's too late. What's said is said, and he can but go and try to cry the guilt out with the tears.

(10) The Sentence. As day dawns, the situation grows darker. The assembled Sanhedrin makes short shrift of Jesus for they know they must turn to the civil authorities to rid themselves of him. Your tone as narrator is not that of a loyal partisan but more like that of a court official dispassionately reporting the day's deliberations.

Neither Peter's tears that preceded nor the pleas of Judas that will follow will dissuade the leaders from delivering Jesus to his destiny.

(11) The Death of Judas. Judas's treachery is somewhat mitigated by his deep regret. As narrator, imagine the tone of a first-century storyteller telling a group of converts how even this traitor recognized his tragic error. Frantically, desperately, Judas tries to stop what he has started, but mockery is his reward and his response is to angrily fling his blood money into the Temple. The contrast between

Barabbas = buh-RAB-uhs

Pilate appears weak and indecisive.

They answered, "**Barabbas**!"
Pilate said to them,
  "Then what shall I do with **Jesus** called **Christ**?"
They all said,
  "Let him be **crucified**!"
But he said,
  "**Why**? What **evil** has he done?"
They only shouted the **louder**,
  "Let him be **crucified**!"
When Pilate **saw** that he was not succeeding at **all**,
  but that a **riot** was breaking out instead,
  he took **water** and **washed** his hands in the sight of the crowd,
  saying, "I am **innocent** of this man's blood.

He complies angrily, as if saying, "All right, have it your way!"

Look to it **yourselves**."
And the whole **people** said in reply,
  "His **blood** be upon **us** and upon our **children**."
Then he released **Barabbas** to them,
  but after he had Jesus **scourged**,
  he handed him over to be **crucified**.

They speak the words, but do they know what they're saying?

Without melodrama, make Christ's pain your own as you narrate the ensuing scenes.

(14) Then the **soldiers** of the governor took Jesus
    inside the **praetorium**
  and gathered the whole **cohort** around him.
They **stripped** off his clothes
  and threw a scarlet military **cloak** about him.
Weaving a **crown** out of **thorns**, they placed it on his **head**,
  and a **reed** in his right hand.

Your empathy with the mocked Jesus is evident as you speak these lines. He will be stripped of all dignity before he is put to death!

And **kneeling** before him, they **mocked** him, saying,
  "**Hail**, **King** of the Jews!"
They **spat** upon him and took the reed
  and kept **striking** him on the **head**.
And when they had **mocked** him,
  they stripped him of the **cloak**,
  dressed him in his **own** clothes,
  and led him off to **crucify** him.

Peter who "went out and began to weep" and Judas who "went off and hanged himself" should surface clearly from the narrative. Like a teacher illustrating an important point, you narrate how Scripture was fulfilled in the purchase of the potter's field.

(12) Jesus Before Pilate. A less sympathetic Pilate than we encounter in Luke and John interrogates a self-confident Jesus whose cryptic response confuses the governor. So Pilate poses a second, more urgent question. But Jesus's silence all the more confounds the pagan procurator.

(13) The Sentence of Death. Matthew papers this section with important contrasts. The *Gentile* governor and his wife recognize Jesus's innocence, but the *Jewish* leaders influence the crowd to seek the release of the *criminal* Barabbas (also known as *Jesus* Barabbas—which means "son of the *father*"), while the *innocent* Jesus, the Son of *God*, goes to his undeserved Death. In the comparison between Pilate and the religious leaders, the governor comes off much better. Though he eventually washes his hands of "this man's blood," he and his wife make efforts to release him, and Pilate is astute enough to recognize the poisonous "envy" that drives the leaders' conspiracy.

The mob's calling Jesus's blood upon themselves and their descendants causes worry that the passage could be misunderstood as laying responsibility for Jesus's Death on the shoulders of every Jew of every generation. Any effort to sanitize the Scriptures would be misguided for it could result in people approaching the Bible without questions or scrutiny. The better option is to read the narrative as given, but follow up with sound pastoral explanations that

Cyrenian = sī-REE-nee-un

(15) As they were going out, they met a **Cyrenian** named **Simon**;
  this man they **pressed** into service
  to carry his **cross**.

Golgotha = GAWL-guh-thuh

(16) And when they came to a place called **Golgotha**
  —which means Place of the **Skull**—,
  they gave Jesus **wine** to drink mixed with **gall**.

Jesus refuses the drugged wine that would dull his pain.

But when he had **tasted** it, he **refused** to drink.
After they had **crucified** him,
  they **divided** his garments by casting **lots**;
  then they sat down and kept **watch** over him there.
And they placed over his head the written **charge** against him:
  This is **Jesus**, the **King** of the **Jews**.

Speak the title with the mocking tones of the soldiers.

Crucifixion with "two revolutionaries" is yet another insult.

Two **revolutionaries** were crucified with him,
  one on his **right** and the other on his **left**.
Those passing by **reviled** him, **shaking** their heads and saying,
  "You who would **destroy** the temple and **rebuild** it in **three** days,
  save yourself, if you are the **Son** of **God**,
  and come **down** from the cross!"
Likewise the chief **priests** with the **scribes** and **elders** mocked
    him and said,

Both the bystanders and the priests feel vindicated. They think that Jesus is an obvious fraud, so their malice is unfettered.

  "He saved **others**; he **cannot** save **himself**.
So he is the **king** of **Israel**!
Let him come **down** from the cross now,
  and we will **believe** in him.
He trusted in **God**;
  let him **deliver** him now if he **wants** him.
For he said, 'I am the **Son** of God.'"

Share this final detail with sadness.

The **revolutionaries** who were crucified with him
  also kept abusing him in the **same** way.

(17) From **noon** onward, **darkness** came over the whole **land**
  until **three** in the afternoon.

Speak the Aramaic with emotion, but deliver the English translation in hushed, neutral tones.

Eli, Eli, lema sabachthani = Ay-LEE, ay-LEE, luh-MAH sah-bahk-tah-nee

And about three o'clock Jesus **cried** out in a loud voice,
  "Eli, Eli, lema sabachthani?"
  which means, "My **God**, my **God**, **why** have you **forsaken** me?"

can counter any possible misunderstanding. While that may concern you as homilist, as reader your goal is to render the characters: Pilate, who is eager to release the innocent Jesus; Pilate's wife who whispers her concerns about this "righteous" man; and the crowd that works itself into such a frenzy, intimidates Pilate, and gladly embraces responsibility for Jesus's Death.

(14) The Mockery of the Soldiers. The soldiers are astute at ridicule and each element is meant to mock—from the scarlet military cloak thrown over this defenseless man, to the crown of thorns that mimics

crowns worn by Greek kings, to the reed that imitates a kingly scepter. A passage like this illustrates the importance of the narrator's point of view. Here you can assume the persona of a first-century storyteller who has witnessed this cruel abuse. The soldiers' mockery conveys scorn not only for Jesus but for all the Jews whose "king" (Jesus) they laughingly hail.

(15) The Way of the Cross. With few words, Matthew describes one of the most significant journeys in history, and the only detail is that Simon was pressed to help Jesus complete the gruesome trek. Speak

slowly as if the weight of the Cross were pressing on your shoulders, all the while picturing Jesus and his pain.

(16) The Crucifixion. The narration here does not allow for much emotion. Relate the incidents with a reporter's objectivity. Reading slowly will help avoid a cold or uncaring tone. Speak "This is Jesus, the King of the Jews" in the dismissive voice of the soldiers who nailed the charge to the Cross. As there had been three prayers in the garden and three denials by Peter, so now there are three groups who taunt Jesus: the bystanders, the priests, and the

The bystanders are still derisive, though the one offering the sponge is likely sincere.

Elijah = ee-LĪ-juh

Pause before this line, then announce Jesus's Death with great reverence.

Suggest the deeper significance of the torn veil: Through Christ all people attain greater access to God.

Nature and the spirits of the dead react to Jesus's Death.

The centurion's declaration is sincere but understated.

centurion = sen-TOOR-ee-uhn; sen-TYOOR-ee-uhn

Speak of these women with familiarity and love.

Joseph, too, deserves a tone of deference and admiration. This act required courage.

Arimathea = ayr-ih-muh-THEE-uh

Some of the **bystanders** who heard it said,
   "This one is calling for **Elijah**."
Immediately one of them ran to get a **sponge**;
   he soaked it in **wine**, and putting it on a **reed**,
   gave it to him to **drink**.
But the rest said,
   "**Wait**, let us **see** if Elijah comes to save him."
But Jesus cried out **again** in a loud voice,
   and **gave** up his **spirit**.

[Here all kneel and pause for a short time.]

And **behold**, the **veil** of the **sanctuary**
   was torn in **two** from **top** to **bottom**.
The earth **quaked**, rocks were **split**, **tombs** were **opened**,
   and the bodies of many **saints** who had fallen **asleep**
      were **raised**.
And coming **forth** from their tombs after his **resurrection**,
   they entered the holy **city** and appeared to **many**.
The **centurion** and the men with him who were keeping **watch**
      over Jesus
   feared greatly when they saw the **earthquake**
   and all that was **happening**, and they said,
   "**Truly**, this **was** the Son of **God**!"
There were many **women** there, looking on from a **distance**,
   who had **followed** Jesus from Galilee, **ministering** to him.
Among them were Mary **Magdalene** and **Mary** the mother of
      James and **Joseph**,
   and the mother of the sons of **Zebedee**.

[18] When it was evening,
   there came a rich man from **Arimathea** named **Joseph**,
   who was himself a **disciple** of Jesus.
He went to **Pilate** and asked for the **body** of **Jesus**;
   then Pilate ordered it to be **handed** over.
Taking the body, Joseph **wrapped** it in clean **linen**
   and laid it in his **new tomb** that he had hewn in the **rock**.

revolutionaries. Note that there is no "good thief" in Matthew, and we're told that both "kept abusing him." Each group of scorners has its own motive for leveling abuse, so distinguish one group from the next.

(17) The Death of Jesus. The word "darkness" summarizes all the agony and rancor that preceded, while your tone suggests the awesome nature of the event you relate. Don't hold back on Jesus's cry of abandonment, but reserve the emotion for the Hebrew line, rendering the English translation in a whisper, as might a bystander who is moved by Jesus's anguish

and repeats the outcry to one nearby who could not hear it. Retain the whisper for the onlookers' remarks about "Elijah." The narration in between describes the efforts of one trying to be genuinely helpful by proffering wine. Matthew tells us Jesus "gave up his spirit," signaling that simultaneously Jesus was in control of his destiny but obedient to God's will in surrendering his life.

Suddenly, amazing, startling things begin to happen. The climactic upheaval that ensues legitimates Jesus's claims about himself. Mysteriously, but significantly, the Temple curtain is torn, the dead

rise from their tombs, and a pagan soldier makes a remarkable declaration of faith. As narrator, your tone suggests that each detail also justifies *your* faith in Jesus, so speak with excited energy. Name the brave "women," the only disciples to keep watch to the end, with special reverence, as if you know them and expect we do too.

(18) The Burial of Jesus. Joseph, a disciple described unapologetically as a "rich" man, receives the great privilege of conveying the body of Jesus to what will be but a temporary resting place. The mention of "linens" evokes a scene of tenderness, so

Allow the scene to linger for a moment.

Pharisees = FAYR-uh-seez

Their clamoring breaks the sacred mood.

They've managed to execute him; now they
can't allow him, in death, to thwart their plans.

Your tone should hint at hope
and Resurrection.

Then he rolled a huge **stone** across the **entrance** to the tomb
     and **departed**.
But Mary **Magdalene** and the **other** Mary
     remained **sitting** there, **facing** the tomb.

(19) The next **day**, the one following the day of **preparation**,
     the chief **priests** and the **Pharisees**
     gathered before **Pilate** and said,
     "**Sir**, we **remember** that this impostor while still alive said,
     'After **three** days I will be **raised** up.'
Give **orders**, then, that the grave be **secured** until the **third** day,
     lest his **disciples** come and **steal** him and say to the people,
     'He has been **raised** from the **dead**.'
This **last** imposture would be worse than the **first**."
Pilate said to them,
     "The guard is **yours**;
     go, **secure** it as best you can."
So they went and **secured** the tomb
     by fixing a **seal** to the stone and setting the **guard**.

[Shorter: Matthew 27:11–54]

TO KEEP IN MIND
Pray the Scriptures: Make reading these Scriptures a part of your
prayer life every week, and especially during the week prior to the
liturgy in which you will proclaim.

---

speak the words as if they were the linen
cloths wrapped around the body of the
Lord. The great grief of the two Marys
is starkly and powerfully conveyed by
the simple detail that they "remained . . .
facing the tomb."

(19) The Epilogue. Even his Death fails
to quell the controversy that swirled
around Jesus, and just when our hearts
want only to weep, we're forced to endure
more scheming from the Pharisees. Their
tone shatters the silence of the graveside
and their tone is clipped, businesslike, and

defensive. Seemingly annoyed, Pilate dismisses them curtly. Don't rush the details
regarding the effort to "secure" and "seal"
the tomb, for Matthew is thus asserting
that the Resurrection could in no way have
been faked. An anticlimactic ending, to be
sure, for we'd rather leave with the image
of the women's faithful vigil. But Matthew's
focus on the seal and the stone is a clever
hint that the real climax is yet to come.

HOLY THURSDAY: MASS OF THE LORD'S SUPPER

LECTIONARY #39

READING I   Exodus 12:1–8, 11–14

A reading from the Book of Exodus

The LORD said to **Moses** and **Aaron** in the land of **Egypt**,
  "This **month** shall stand at the **head** of your **calendar**;
  you shall reckon it the **first** month of the year.
Tell the whole **community** of Israel:
  On the **tenth** of this month every one of your **families**
  must procure for itself a **lamb**, one **apiece** for each **household**.
If a family is too **small** for a whole lamb,
  it shall **join** the **nearest** household in procuring one
  and shall **share** in the lamb
  in **proportion** to the number of **persons** who **partake** of it.
The lamb must be a year-old **male** and without **blemish**.
You may take it from either the **sheep** or the **goats**.
You shall keep it until the **fourteenth** day of this month,
  and **then**, with the whole assembly of Israel **present**,
  it shall be **slaughtered** during the evening **twilight**.
They shall take some of its **blood**
  and **apply** it to the two **doorposts** and the **lintel**
  of every **house** in which they **partake** of the lamb.
That same **night** they shall **eat** its roasted flesh
  with unleavened **bread** and bitter **herbs**.

Exodus = EK-suh-duhs

Israel is still in captivity when they receive these instructions. Let your tone convey the importance of this solemnity, for this night is like no other night, this meal like no other meal.

Moses = MOH-ziz; MOH-zis

Aaron = AYR-uhn

God is the speaker—a voice of both authority and compassion.

God's commands don't burden the needy; instead they make community.

Keep your pacing brisk; it's not the specifics that matter here, but the sense of God's providence and the people's obedience.

Slow your pacing for these important details that anticipate the blood of the messianic lamb.

READING I The three days of the Easter Triduum, from Holy Thursday till Easter Sunday, constitute but a single act of worship that celebrates Christ's single act of salvation—accomplished through the *totality* of his life, Death, and Resurrection. Salvation culminated on the Cross, but it neither began nor ended there. The Triduum's First Reading connects us to our roots as a community of faith. The last meal Jesus shared with his friends was celebrated because of the injunction laid down here and according to its prescriptions. The seemingly mundane details

about how, where, and when to eat a certain meal remind us that details *matter,* for *"God* is in the details." Still today, this ritual reminds Jews that this night is like no other night and this meal like no other meal. So adopt a lofty tone. Proclaiming the history of a royal family prior to the coronation of a new monarch would require the tone needed here. No matter the details, a dignified tone says: this is significant, listen!

Speak in the authoritative voice of God, but don't lack tenderness and compassion. Concerned for family needs and

wanting to avoid placing undue strain on any family, God orders smaller, poorer families to join those who are able to share. Tonight's readings all speak of communities gathered for a ritual meal. Communities gather for meals because meals make communities and this text understands that reality. Soon to leave their homes in Egypt, the Chosen People receive a ritual that not only will remind them of their origins but will forever draw them into a circle of *remembering*—the mechanism that better than any other binds groups together.

The sense of urgency and preparedness needs to be stressed. It describes the attitude with which we are to await the return of the Messiah. Pause, then make the second key announcement: "It is the Passover . . . ."

Don't shy from these hard words. The tone is one of divine authority and might, not vengeance.

Slow down for these references to "blood" and God's response to seeing it. Speak carefully and with compassion.

This is a direct command, kept by Jesus and the disciples. First pause and take a breath as you survey the assembly, then give the divine directive.

For meditation and context:

"This is **how** you are to eat it:
   with your loins **girt**, **sandals** on your **feet** and your **staff**
      in **hand**,
   you shall **eat** like those who are in **flight**.
It is the **Passover** of the LORD.
For on this **same** night I will go through **Egypt**,
   striking down every **firstborn** of the land, both **man** and **beast**,
   and executing **judgment** on all the **gods** of Egypt—**I**, the LORD!
But the **blood** will mark the **houses** where **you** are.
Seeing the blood, I will pass **over** you;
   thus, when I **strike** the land of **Egypt**,
   no destructive **blow** will come upon **you**.

"This day shall be a **memorial feast** for you,
   which all your **generations** shall celebrate
   with **pilgrimage** to the LORD, as a **perpetual** institution."

RESPONSORIAL PSALM   Psalm 116:12–13, 15–16bc, 17–18
(1 Corinthians 10:16)

R. **Our blessing-cup is a communion with the Blood of Christ.**

How shall I make a return to the LORD
   for all the good he has done for me?
The cup of salvation I will take up,
   and I will call upon the name of the LORD.

Precious in the eyes of the LORD
   is the death of his faithful ones.
I am your servant, the son of your handmaid;
   you have loosed my bonds.

To you will I offer sacrifice of thanksgiving,
   and I will call upon the name of the LORD.
My vows to the LORD I will pay
   in the presence of all his people.

TO KEEP IN MIND
Who really proclaims: "When the Sacred Scriptures are read in the Church, God himself speaks to his people, and Christ, present in his word, proclaims the gospel" (#29 GIRM).

Liturgy doesn't just recall what happened long ago. By remembering, we experience in the *present* those events of the past and the saving grace they made available. So speak these seemingly mundane details with anything but a mundane attitude, knowing your proclamation makes the historical moment present to the assembly.

Don't rush mention of unleavened bread and bitter herbs or shy from the graphic images of slaughtered lamb and blood-smeared doorposts, for these deepen the connection between this meal and Christ, our eternal lamb. "Loins girt," "san-

dals on your feet," and "staff in hand" lead to the declaration that Israel is to eat "like those . . . in flight," that is, in a state of constant anticipation, the way Israel was to await the Messiah and we are to await Christ's sure return. The complex God of the Old Testament threatens to strike "down every firstborn" but simultaneously assures the people, "no destructive blow will come upon you." Speak these alternately unsettling and comforting words like a judge who first addresses the perpetrator and then the victim of a terrible crime. Blood is the sign of life, but through the

shedding of blood death will be averted both once and forever.

READING II   You are privileged to proclaim and make present for your assembly a seminal moment in our faith story. Tonight's Gospel from John substitutes the washing of feet for the other Gospel tellings of the institution of the Eucharist. So it will be you who relates what is the New Testament's earliest account of the first Eucharist. Paul renders his telling in an emotional and personal way. Without having known Jesus, Paul

Corinthians = kohr-IN-thee-uhnz

Paul jumps right in, so start slowly and read with extra care, especially the reference to Christ's betrayal.

Pause after "handed on to you"; an implied "namely" precedes what follows.

Only here and in Luke's Gospel account do we find "do this . . . ." Speak with strength and love, but not sentimentality.

The words that convey Jesus's actions are important to stress: he "took," gave "thanks," and "broke" the bread.

Remember, Jesus also wants to speak these intimate words to his "friends" gathered in your church tonight.

The final sentence is Paul's great insight. He speaks with pride-filled hope ("For as often . . . ") and hope-filled gratitude ("until he comes.") First pause and make eye contact, then speak directly to the assembly.

Set the scene by stressing both Jesus's awareness and the lateness of the "hour."

There is striking juxtaposition between the stress on Jesus's love for "his own" and the mention of Judas's betrayal.

Iscariot = is-KAYR-ee-uht

Stress Jesus's fully conscious intentionality.

You might narrate from the perspective of the surprised disciples or with the loving intent in Jesus's heart; either way, pay attention to the details and use the verbs.

READING II   1 Corinthians 11:23–26

A reading from the first Letter of Saint Paul to the Corinthians

Brothers and sisters:
I **received** from the Lord what I also handed on to **you**,
   that the Lord **Jesus**, on the night he was handed **over**,
   took **bread**, and, after he had given **thanks**,
   broke it and said, "This is my **body** that is for **you**.
Do this in **remembrance** of me."
In the same way also the **cup**, after supper, saying,
   "This **cup** is the new **covenant** in my **blood**.
Do this, as often as you **drink** it, in **remembrance** of me."
For as often as you **eat** this bread and **drink** the cup,
   you proclaim the **death** of the **Lord** until he comes.

GOSPEL   John 13:1–15

A reading from the holy Gospel according to John

Before the feast of **Passover**, Jesus **knew** that his hour had **come**
   to pass from **this** world to the **Father**.
He loved his **own** in the world and he **loved** them to the **end**.
The **devil** had already induced **Judas**, son of Simon the **Iscariot**,
   to hand him **over**.
So, during **supper**,
   fully **aware** that the Father had put **everything** into his power
   and that he had come from God and was **returning** to God,
   he **rose** from supper and took **off** his outer garments.
He took a **towel** and **tied** it around his waist.
Then he poured **water** into a basin
   and began to **wash** the disciples' **feet**
   and dry them with the **towel** around his **waist**.

---

nonetheless asserts that he "received from the Lord what [he] also handed on," assurance that our ritual offers true and sure mediation of the Lord from whom it came.

   Though set in the context of a meal, Paul also stresses the sacrificial nature of the Eucharist. It was "on the night he was *handed over*" that Jesus made provision for all who would become disciples. We can almost hear nails pounding into the wood of the Cross, for Paul reminds us that what we celebrate is both meal and *sacrifice*. The Christian penchant for irony surfaces

again because for Jesus (and for us) it is death that brings new life.

   The words of institution are spoken not in Jesus's voice but Paul's. Despite Paul's brevity, we sense the emotion of Jesus's final moments with his closest friends knowing (though his friends do not) how and how soon his body and blood will be offered up. Only Luke and Paul record the words, "Do this in remembrance of me." This overly familiar phrase, spoken out of order in the Liturgy of the Word, may help us realize that this is exactly what we're doing here tonight. Uniting our past

and our future into the present act of worship, Paul reveals the Eucharist for what it is: wayfarers' food that sustains us until the day Christ returns.

GOSPEL   What an amazing event, made even more amazing by the fact that only John records it! John's unique perspective is evident here, for where the synoptic accounts (Matthew, Mark, and Luke) place the institution of the Eucharist, John talks of aprons, towels, and dirty feet. John's Jesus also wants to be remembered, but it's for rolling up his

Recall that in Luke, Peter once told Jesus, "Depart from me, Lord, for I am a sinful man." He seems to be speaking out of that same sensibility here. Peter's protests are as sincere as his later compliance.

Jesus is not rebuking him, but teaching.

His surrender to Jesus is total and unreserved.

Let Jesus's tone convey his love for Peter. There is a baptismal allusion here that suggests one who has received the cleansing of Baptism, like one returning from a bath, is clean and therefore doesn't need another bath, only the washing of feet, that is, cleansing of the grime of daily sin.

A new "beat" in the narrative. Don't rush the details. Jesus makes sure his disciples have learned the lesson. Do the same with your assembly.

The pronouns are the key to the meaning of this sentence.

They will need to follow him not only in service to one another but also in laying down their lives.

> He came to Simon **Peter**, who said to him,
>   "**Master**, are you going to **wash** my **feet**?"
> Jesus **answered** and said to him,
>   "What I am **doing**, you do not **understand now**,
>   but you **will** understand **later**."
> Peter **said** to him, "You will **never** wash my feet."
> Jesus answered him,
>   "Unless I **wash** you, you will have no **inheritance** with me."
> Simon Peter said to him,
>   "**Master**, then not only my **feet**, but my **hands** and **head**
>   as **well**."
> Jesus said to him,
>   "Whoever has **bathed** has no **need** except to have his
>   **feet** washed,
>   for he is **clean** all **over**;
>   so **you** are clean, but not **all**."
> For he **knew** who would **betray** him;
>   for this **reason**, he said, "Not **all** of you are clean."
>
> So when he had **washed** their feet
>   and put his **garments** back on and reclined at **table** again,
>   he **said** to them, "Do you **realize** what I have **done** for you?
> You call me '**teacher**' and '**master**,' and **rightly** so, for indeed I **am**.
> If **I**, therefore, the **master** and **teacher**, have washed **your** feet,
>   **you** ought to wash one **another's** feet.
> I have given you a **model** to follow,
>   so that as **I** have done for **you**, you should **also** do."

TO KEEP IN MIND
Careful preparation expresses your reverence for the Word.

sleeves—an enacted parable that manifests the essence of Jesus's ministry and even suggests participation in his Death.

Jesus's knowledge that his "hour" has come is key. As in John's Passion, Jesus here is fully aware and fully in charge of his destiny. John contrasts this consciousness with Peter and the Apostles' failure to "understand" what Jesus is doing. Realizing his time is short, Jesus strives to ensure that the followers who survive him will remember his style as well as his words. And he guarantees it, by pouring "water into a basin."

Jesus's desire to model humble service motivates his unsettling behavior. That Satan's work is done and Judas's heart lost brings urgency to Jesus's task and so he does willingly what even the lowliest slave could not be compelled to do. Peter thinks he's outdoing his friends in his unwillingness to let Jesus so demean himself. And when Jesus tells Peter he doesn't understand, Peter protests all the more and *proves* Jesus right. But Jesus insists that such humility typifies his life and ministry, and if Peter seeks to share that ministry then he must embrace this symbol. With characteristic overstatement, Peter invites

a fuller cleansing, demonstrating his understanding that belonging to Christ means holding nothing back. In a touching exchange between master and disciple Jesus tolerates Peter's naiveté and his zeal, assuring him "*you* are clean."

Direct Jesus's question to your listeners, for his command to imitate him is directed at all believers, not only those in leadership. Jesus's consummate integrity compelled him to ask of us only what he did first himself. And that is also his standard for remembrance: we remember the Lord not by recalling what he did but by doing it.

GOOD FRIDAY: PASSION OF THE LORD

LECTIONARY #40

READING I   Isaiah 52:13—53:12

Isaiah = ī-ZAY-uh

A reading from the Book of the Prophet Isaiah

God speaks of the servant with strength and pride. The word "See" calls us to attention!

> **See**, my **servant** shall **prosper**,
>   he shall be raised **high** and greatly **exalted**.

The mood suddenly shifts as the narration of the suffering of God's servant begins.

> Even as many were **amazed** at him—
>   so **marred** was his look beyond human semblance
>   and his **appearance** beyond that of the sons of man—
> so shall he **startle** many **nations**,
>   because of him **kings** shall stand **speechless**;

The sense of these verses is: In the same way that many were amazed at him—because he was so disfigured he didn't even look human—nations and kings will be startled and astonished by him.

> for those who have not been **told** shall **see**,
>   those who have not **heard** shall **ponder** it.

The voice shifts here to that of the foreign nations.

> Who would **believe** what we have heard?
>   To **whom** has the arm of the LORD been **revealed**?
> He grew up like a **sapling** before him,
>   like a **shoot** from the parched **earth**;
> there was in him no **stately** bearing to make us **look** at him,
>   nor appearance that would **attract** us to him.

The speakers marvel at their own blindness, yet in their defense, the servant did appear unremarkable and unattractive. However, they rue how they mistreated him.

> He was **spurned** and **avoided** by people,
>   a man of **suffering**, accustomed to **infirmity**,
> one of those from whom people **hide** their faces,
>   **spurned**, and we **held** him in no **esteem**.

READING I   Isaiah's song is about the reversals of lost and hopeless situations. He sings perhaps because he lived what it chronicles, or maybe just because God told him to. Isaiah took what he knew to be true and wrote it down so endless generations could redefine success and better understand that God's ways are not our ways. Our ways are often blind to the grace that's all around us.

Isaiah's Suffering Servant is hard to identify. Is he the prophet himself, the long awaited Messiah, or the nation of Israel? It doesn't really matter. The servant, however personified, works for God, does God's will, and dearly pays the price. The heart of the servant's message is this: we're being saved when we least expect it; God acts when we don't know it; hope is born when we're busy doing other things.

It's significant that the opening sentence is cast in the future tense, for "prospering" and being "raised high" are certainly no part of the servant's present experience, which is all rejection and misunderstanding. The suffering of the servant, the expiatory nature of his ministry, the willing embrace of condemnation despite total innocence, and his ultimate vindication through God's decisive intervention—for these reasons Christian faith identifies Jesus with the servant, drawn so presciently by Isaiah six centuries before.

Isaiah intricately weaves themes of contrasting colors. He begins proclaiming hope (the "servant shall prosper"), then immediately introduces a darker thread ("so marred was his look"). This interweaving continues throughout, for never is a dark detail mentioned without its brighter, hopeful consequence. The servant was "pierced" and "crushed," but it was for *our*

Contrast his innocence with *our* guilt.

Don't let this read like a list of injuries done to some stranger. Their sense of regret is heightened by the awareness of who it was who paid the price for them.

"Stripes" are the marks left behind from a whipping. Speak of them with gratitude.

Soften your tone here. "Lamb" and "sheep" are the same metaphor, so the pace can quicken on the second image. Your tone should reveal wonder at the servant's silent acceptance of his fate.

"Oppressed" and "condemned" are two distinct words; don't rush them together.

There is a deep sense of regret, perhaps even anger, over this indignity.

"Pleased" is a word that surprises, but it reveals that the servant's fate is within the will of God. Speak it with resignation.

The voice of God returns. Note the "if/then" clause that begins the sentence. Death alone is not what saves, but the intentionality of the one who gives his life.

Yet it was **our** infirmities that he bore,
　　our **sufferings** that he endured,
while we thought of him as **stricken**,
　　as one **smitten** by God and **afflicted**.
But he was **pierced** for our offenses,
　　crushed for our **sins**;
upon **him** was the chastisement that **makes** us **whole**,
　　by his **stripes** we were **healed**.
We had **all** gone astray like **sheep**,
　　each following his **own** way;
but the LORD laid upon **him**
　　the **guilt** of us **all**.

Though he was **harshly** treated, he **submitted**
　　and opened **not** his **mouth**;
like a **lamb** led to the **slaughter**
　　or a **sheep** before the **shearers**,
he was **silent** and opened not his **mouth**.
Oppressed and **condemned**, he was taken **away**,
　　and who would have thought any **more** of his destiny?
When he was **cut** off from the land of the **living**,
　　and **smitten** for the sin of his people,
a **grave** was assigned him among the **wicked**
　　and a **burial** place with **evildoers**,
though he had done no **wrong**
　　nor spoken any **falsehood**.
But the LORD was **pleased**
　　to **crush** him in **infirmity**.

If he gives his **life** as an offering for **sin**,
　　he shall see his **descendants** in a **long** life,
　　and the **will** of the LORD shall be **accomplished**
　　through him.

guilt. Unlike a dirge that speaks of *past* glory and *future* grief, this song promises a glory that flows *from* the abuse and affliction of God's Suffering Servant.

To communicate Isaiah's message, you must convey his *words* by the *sound* of your voice. Poetry is essentially aural, meant to be heard not read, because the sound of words communicates as forcefully as the words themselves. You'd need no interpreter to translate a plaintive song sung in a foreign language if the *sound* of words and music conveyed the deep emotions of the piece. Today, your voice must

be the music that communicates the meaning of Isaiah's hope-filled lament.

The future victory of God's sinless servant is assured from the start, so emphasize what the servant will do: "prosper," "be raised high," "startle," and make kings "speechless"! This initial note of triumph underlies all the later talk of sorrow from which that victory will spring. Though the servants' sorrow is past, it is described as graphically as if it were happening now.

"Who would believe" introduces a shocking acknowledgment. The Gentile nations speak ("Who would believe [it]"),

acknowledging the servant (Israel) as God's instrument and confessing their guilt for causing his unmerited suffering. A more tragic possibility has this startled question spoken by the prophet's own *disciples* in disbelief at their own thickheadedness as they look back with terrible regret at the great opportunity they missed: he grew among us, but we saw nothing special about him, so we gave him no respect. Theirs is a profoundly biblical insight: lacking God's vision, we judge by human standards and miss divinity in our midst.

Speak in a quieter, but persuasive tone.

Because of his **affliction**
  he shall see the **light** in **fullness** of days;
through his **suffering**, my servant shall justify **many**,
  and their **guilt** he shall **bear**.

The reading climaxes here. The servant is honored, but notice that it is because he suffered willingly!

Therefore I will give him his portion among the **great**,
  and he shall divide the **spoils** with the **mighty**,
because he **surrendered** himself to **death**
  and was counted among the **wicked**;
and he shall take away the **sins** of **many**,
  and win **pardon** for their **offenses**.

Slow your delivery as you read the final sentence, but notice the reading ends with good news, not sorrow.

For meditation and context:

RESPONSORIAL PSALM   Psalm 31:2, 6, 12–13, 15–16, 17, 25 (Luke 23:46)

R. Father, into your hands I commend my spirit.

In you, O LORD, I take refuge;
  let me never be put to shame.
In your justice rescue me.
Into your hands I commend my spirit;
  you will redeem me, O LORD,
    O faithful God.

For all my foes I am an object of reproach,
  a laughingstock to my neighbors,
    and a dread to my friends;
  they who see me abroad flee from me.
I am forgotten like the unremembered dead;
  I am like a dish that is broken.

But my trust is in you, O LORD;
  I say, "You are my God.
In your hands is my destiny; rescue me
  from the clutches of my enemies
    and my persecutors."

Let your face shine upon your servant;
  save me in your kindness.
Take courage and be stouthearted,
  all you who hope in the LORD.

TO KEEP IN MIND

Units of Thought: Running too many words together blurs meaning and fails to distinguish ideas. Punctuation does not always indicate clearly what words to group together or where to pause. Identify *units of thought* and use your voice to distinguish one from another.

READING II   Hebrews 4:14–16; 5:7–9

A reading from the Letter to the Hebrews

Brothers and sisters:
Since we have a **great** high **priest** who has passed through
    the **heavens**,
  Jesus, the Son of **God**,
  let us hold **fast** to our **confession**.

The opening sentence is an "if/then" construct: *If* (that is, *since*) "we have a great high priest," *then* "let us hold fast . . . ." Therefore you must read slowly so the if/then connection is heard. "Great high priest" = an assertion of Christ's superiority to the priests of the old Law.

Next, the people speak with stark candor: we stupidly thought he was "smitten" for his *own* failings; but "he was pierced for *our* offenses." *We* went "astray," but *he* paid the price! "Spurned," "suffering," and "hide their faces" are expressive words that communicate the contempt and ridicule he endured. "Smitten," "afflicted," "pierced," and "crushed" are also powerful, harsh-sounding words that convey the brutal injustice that God's servant endured.

In the next paragraph the servant resolutely embraces his fate without acrimony or protest. Like a sacrificial "lamb," a metaphor

closely identified with the innocent Christ, this man of sorrow accepts the final humiliation of being buried "with evildoers. . . though he had done no wrong." Speak with intensity of his pain and innocence, awed and grateful that this "lamb" went willingly "to the slaughter." The text never lapses into despair, so your resolute and hopeful tone must suggest that these events were within God's will, for God *allowed* him to be "crush[ed]" "in infirmity."

In the closing paragraphs, Isaiah asserts a radically new understanding of suffering that breaks with prior biblical tra-

dition. Instead of seeing it as punishment for sin, Isaiah declares a positive and expiatory value in suffering. The servant's affliction was not random or wasted, but so valuable that it brought reward for the servant and justification and healing for others. These positive affirmations undergird Catholicism's understanding, not just of Jesus's own suffering, but of the meaning and value of all human pain.

In the final paragraphs, God's voice returns with another oracle of future glory for the servant and of hope for the "many" for whom his voluntary suffering has won

Jesus was one of us. He understands our suffering and temptations.

Where he was *unlike* us is his total sinlessness!

Distinguish the words "mercy" and "grace."

"Tears and supplications" may allude to Gethsemane and perhaps elsewhere— weeping over Lazarus or mourning Judas's betrayal. His suffering was real. That's why he understands ours.

Take note: Jesus "learned" obedience through his suffering.

God's Son modeled obedience. We imitate him and find salvation. Make eye contact on "for all who obey him."

For we do not have a high priest
　who is **unable** to **sympathize** with our **weaknesses**,
　but one who has **similarly** been **tested** in every **way**,
　yet without **sin**.
So let us **confidently** approach the throne of **grace**
　to receive **mercy** and to find **grace** for timely **help**.

In the days when Christ was in the **flesh**,
　he offered **prayers** and **supplications** with loud **cries** and **tears**
　to the one who was able to **save** him from **death**,
　and he was **heard** because of his **reverence**.
Son though he **was**, he learned **obedience** from what he **suffered**;
　and when he was made **perfect**,
　he became the **source** of eternal **salvation** for all who **obey** him.

GOSPEL　John 18:1—19:42

The Passion of our Lord Jesus Christ according to John

Kidron = KID-ruhn

The garden is a peaceful, familiar place.

Judas = JOO-duhs

The shadow of Judas suddenly shifts mood.

(1) **Jesus** went out with his **disciples** across the Kidron **valley**
　to where there was a garden,
　into which he and his disciples **entered**.
Judas his **betrayer also** knew the place,
　because Jesus had **often** met there with his disciples.
(2) So Judas got a band of **soldiers** and **guards**
　from the chief **priests** and the **Pharisees**
　and went there with **lanterns**, **torches**, and **weapons**.

"Lanterns" = evoking the hour of darkness.

Jesus moves forward fully aware and in charge of his destiny.

Jesus, knowing **everything** that was going to happen to him,
　went out and said to them, "Whom are you **looking** for?"
They **answered** him, "**Jesus** the **Nazorean**."
He said to them, "**I AM**."
Judas his betrayer was **also** with them.
When he said to them, "**I AM**,"
　they turned **away** and fell to the **ground**.

Jesus's power overwhelms the guards. He'll be taken only when he permits it.

---

pardon. Ending on a note of sadness would counter the hope embedded in this text. Isaiah's new teaching is that suffering is often fertile ground in which new life takes root. This story does not end with death, but with hope of healing and salvation.

| READING II | In an earlier part of Isaiah's song, the Suffering Servant asserts, "I have not rebelled, have not turned back." Those words express the deeply biblical conviction that what God desires most is a humble, obedient heart. Simply put, obedience perfects the human

spirit. It was in obedience that Isaiah's servant suffered innocently, and Jesus exhibits the same exemplary obedience.

He's a "high priest" instead of a "servant," but a brother in suffering nonetheless, a mediator who willingly took on human flesh and embraced struggle and temptation, unique only in his total innocence and dedication (obedience) to God's will. *This* painting is rendered in brilliant tones, without Isaiah's darker hues. The text opens joyfully with an exhortation to trust in Christ's efficacious intercession. His *perfection* need not create a chasm

between him and us, for his innocence and obedience enable him to intercede for us.

"Let us hold fast" exhorts us to cling to hope for our "great high priest" (who is superior to the priests of the old Law), for he already knows our "weakness" and yet dispenses mercy. Isaiah anticipates the saving work of the Suffering Servant, but in Hebrews it is already realized. With a sacrifice that transcends the sacrifices of the old Law, Jesus has become our perfect representative before God.

"Loud cries and tears" alludes to Gethsemane where Jesus begged to be

Nazorean = naz-uh-REE-uhn

The theological significance of the "I AM" statements should not be ignored.

Shift your tone slightly to suggest the quoting of Scripture.

Violence expressed with "struck" and "cut off."

Malchus = MAL-kuhs

Jesus rebukes Peter.

Annas = AN-uhs
Caiaphas = KAY-uh-fuhs; KĪ-uh-fuhs

This is a significant quote attributed to Caiaphas.

Is Peter kept out or staying out from fear?

Peter doesn't want to be overheard denying Jesus.

So he **again** asked them,
  "**Whom** are you looking for?"
They said, "**Jesus** the **Nazorean**."
Jesus answered,
  "I **told** you that **I AM**.
So if you are looking for **me**, let **these** men **go**."
This was to **fulfill** what he had said,
  "I have not lost **any** of those you **gave** me."
Then Simon **Peter**, who had a **sword**, **drew** it,
  struck the high priest's slave, and **cut** off his right **ear**.
The slave's name was **Malchus**.
Jesus said to Peter,
  "Put your **sword** into its **scabbard**.
Shall I not **drink** the cup that the Father **gave** me?"

So the band of **soldiers**, the **tribune**, and the Jewish **guards**
    seized Jesus,
  bound him, and brought him to **Annas** first.
He was the **father-in-law** of **Caiaphas**,
  who was **high** priest that year.
It was **Caiaphas** who had **counseled** the Jews
  that it was better that **one** man should die rather than
    the **people**.

(3) Simon **Peter** and **another** disciple **followed** Jesus.
Now the **other** disciple was **known** to the high priest,
  and he entered the **courtyard** of the high priest with **Jesus**.
But **Peter** stood at the gate **outside**.
So the other **disciple**, the **acquaintance** of the high priest,
  went out and spoke to the **gatekeeper** and brought Peter in.
Then the **maid** who was the **gatekeeper** said to Peter,
  "You are not one of this man's **disciples**, **are** you?"
He said, "I am **not**."

---

spared the fate that awaited him. But those words are but a brushstroke on the canvas you are painting, not meant to reenact the agony of the garden. The point is "he was heard" not by being saved *from* death but by being delivered *through* it—the very theology for which Isaiah prepared us: suffering can take on salvific purpose and meaning. Even God's Son "*learned* obedience" and was "*made* perfect" by embracing suffering. He obeyed *freely* (not like some automaton), and fulfilled his mission, not despite but through struggle and temptation, and the result is "eternal salvation

for all." Hebrews holds out hope that "all who obey him" can likewise move through suffering to perfection. That suffering can yield perfection is counterintuitive, a mystery you are privileged to share with joy.

PASSION The gift of having four distinct Passion narratives is that each presents a different view of Jesus, of his antagonists, of the supporters who journey with him, and of the minor players whose presence adds texture to this tapestry of intrigue, betrayal, courtroom suspense, and brutal punishment. In

John's unique take on this solemn story, Jesus is a not a victim, but the shaper of his own destiny. Throughout John's version of the Good News, Jesus moves toward his "hour" of glory that culminates not in a palace but on Calvary's hill. John's understanding of Jesus won't permit episodes that compromise his portrait of a resolute Christ in full control of his destiny. The suffering remains, but the garden agony is gone, together with the mourning women, and the ridicule hurled at Jesus by venomous leaders and ignorant bystanders. Palm Sunday presents the synoptics' abandoned

Now the slaves and the **guards** were standing around
> a charcoal fire
> that they had made, because it was **cold**,
> and were **warming** themselves.
Peter was also standing there keeping **warm**.

This is a new scene, so renew your energy.

(4) The high priest **questioned** Jesus
> about his **disciples** and about his **doctrine**.
Jesus **answered** him,

Jesus is strong in his self-defense, showing the weakness of their "case."

> "I have spoken **publicly** to the world.
I have always taught in a **synagogue**
> or in the **temple** area where all the Jews **gather**,
> and in **secret** I have said **nothing**. Why ask me?
Ask those who **heard** me what I **said** to them.
They know what I said."
When he had **said** this,
> one of the temple **guards** standing there **struck** Jesus and said,
> "Is **this** the way you answer the high **priest**?"
Jesus answered him,

Deliver the line like a slap—fast and hard.

Jesus holds his ground.

> "If I have spoken **wrongly**, **testify** to the wrong;
> but if I have spoken **rightly**, why do you **strike** me?"
Then Annas sent him **bound** to **Caiaphas** the **high** priest.

Here begins another new scene.

(5) Now Simon **Peter** was **standing** there keeping **warm**.
And they **said** to him,
> "**You** are not one of his **disciples**, **are** you?"
He **denied** it and said,

Peter gets angry here.

> "I am **not**."
One of the **slaves** of the high priest,
> a **relative** of the one whose **ear** Peter had cut off, said,
> "Didn't I see you in the **garden** with him?"
Again Peter denied it.
And **immediately** the **cock** crowed.

The denials are brief, but with this line suggest the lasting impact on Peter.

(6, 7) Then they brought Jesus from **Caiaphas** to the **praetorium**.
It was **morning**.

---

martyr who reaches Golgotha only with the help of Simon, but each Good Friday John presents a self-possessed and purposeful Lord who moves knowingly toward Calvary where he mounts the Cross with the dignity of a king mounting his throne.

Though John omits the episode with Herod, it's clear throughout that the religious leaders are dependent on Roman authority to execute their designs against Jesus. In fact, John introduces Pilate to the narrative earlier than the synoptics. Pilate works harder here to find a way to set Jesus free and this detail, combined with

John's persistent use of the term "the Jews," suggests to some that John indicts only the Jews for the Death of Jesus. Much has been written to negate this notion and to dispel the false assumption that culpability for Jesus's Death has been inherited by every successive Jewish generation. The Church's clear teaching on this issue can be effectively addressed in the Homily.

Within one week we tell this story twice. Each time it is a ritual and sacramental moment, not simply a recounting of an important past event. Like the ritual repetition of the words of institution, the procla-

mation of the Passion affords each of us full *participation* in the most focused moment of salvation history. The proclamation of Scripture brings the saving events of the past into the present moment. Read with full awareness of this dynamic so that you can help your listeners experience the Passion as if for the first time. (Lack of preparation or overdramatization would compromise the mission.)

Consider using a single, excellent reader for the proclamation of this narrative. Though talent for solo delivery cannot be presumed, when it exists, it results in

This is a spat among political adversaries. Each is annoyed with the other.

And they **themselves** did not **enter** the praetorium,
    in order not to be **defiled** so that they could eat the **Passover**.
So **Pilate** came out to **them** and said,
    "What **charge** do you bring against this man?"
They **answered** and said to him,
    "If he were not a **criminal**,
    we would not have handed him **over** to you."
At **this**, Pilate said to them,
    "Take him **yourselves**, and **judge** him according to your **law**."
The Jews **answered** him,
    "We do not have the right to **execute** anyone,"
    in order that the word of **Jesus** might be **fulfilled**
    that he said indicating the kind of **death** he would die.

Pilate = Pī-luht

The scene shifts here. Pilate is "starting over" and is not presented as a villain.

So Pilate went **back** into the praetorium
    and **summoned** Jesus and said to him,
    "Are you the **King** of the **Jews**?"
Jesus answered,
    "Do you say this on your **own**
    or have **others** told you about me?"
Pilate answered,
    "I am not a **Jew**, **am** I?

Pilate is becoming impatient again.

Your own **nation** and the chief **priests** handed you over to me.
What have you **done**?"
Jesus answered,
    "My **kingdom** does not **belong** to **this** world.

Jesus is not passive, but engaged in debate.

If my kingdom **did** belong to this world,
    my attendants would be **fighting**
    to **keep** me from being handed over to the Jews.
But as it **is**, my kingdom is not **here**."
So Pilate said to him,
    "Then you **are** a king?"
Jesus answered,

Stress the verb "are," not the noun "king."

    "**You** say I am a king.

Jesus speaks with confidence.

For this I was **born** and for this I came into the **world**,
    to **testify** to the **truth**.

---

riveting proclamation. Typically, parishes assign the assembly the role of the crowd, a strategy that unfortunately requires them to read, rather than listen to, the entire Passion along with the readers. Most often, it's best for three fine readers to divide the lines and share the narration. The priest or deacon can portray Jesus while the other readers assume the remaining roles. But avoid the awkward situation of having someone read the dialogue of two characters who are speaking to each other. No matter the method, be sure your proclamation presents the Jesus of John's Gospel as

consummately aware of his *identity* as God's Son and so secure in his *relationship* with the Father that he remains the calm center of the storm that rages around him.

(1) Jesus's retreat to the familiar garden is cut short by Judas, who comes well-armed against his former teacher. With an insider's knowledge, Judas anticipates Jesus's movement and arrives with a noisy crowd of soldiers bearing "torches and weapons." A master of irony and symbolism, John has those who bring on the "hour of darkness" arrive as *light-bearers*, while the unarmed Jesus is made the target of an

enormous cohort. The synoptic Jesus is pitiable and depleted after the garden agony, but here Jesus bristles with authority and full knowledge of what will occur.

Jesus takes control, throwing down the gauntlet with his question to the mob. Their response is no match for his, for when he speaks the divine "I AM" the power of his confident presence knocks them to the ground. Jesus has not relinquished responsibility toward his own. "Let these men go" reveals his willingness to accept the crowd's designs against him, but not against his friends.

Everyone who **belongs** to the truth **listens** to my voice."
Pilate said to him, "What is **truth**?"

When he had **said** this,
   he **again** went out to the Jews and said to them,
   "I find no **guilt** in him.
(8) But you have a **custom** that I release one **prisoner** to you
     at **Passover**.
Do you want me to release to you the **King** of the **Jews**?"
They cried out **again**,
   "Not this one but **Barabbas**!"
Now Barabbas was a **revolutionary**.

Then Pilate took Jesus and had him **scourged**.
And the soldiers wove a **crown** out of **thorns** and placed it
    on his **head**,
   and clothed him in a **purple** cloak,
   and they came to him and said,
   "**Hail**, **King** of the **Jews**!"
And they **struck** him **repeatedly**.
(9) Once **more** Pilate went out and said to them,
   "**Look**, I am bringing him **out** to you,
   so that you may **know** that I find no **guilt** in him."
So Jesus came out,
   wearing the crown of **thorns** and the purple **cloak**.
And he said to them, "**Behold**, the man!"
When the chief priests and the guards **saw** him they **cried** out,
   "**Crucify** him, **crucify** him!"
Pilate said to them,
   "Take him **yourselves** and **crucify** him.
I find no **guilt** in him."
The Jews **answered**,
   "We have a **law**, and according to that **law** he ought to **die**,
   because he **made** himself the **Son** of **God**."

Pilate is seeking a quick resolution. Is he trying to put words in their mouths?

Barabbas = buh-RAB-uhs

This is a greatly understated scene, but the pain and shame are real.

Perhaps Pilate is saying: "Look at what you made me do!"

When a phrase is repeated, give greater stress to the second utterance.

The leaders' energy increases as they sense Pilate weakening.

Filled with rage, Peter wields a sword, harming both the slave and Jesus's cause. But his initiative is rebuffed; with equal energy, Jesus orders him to "put [his] sword into its scabbard," an echo, perhaps, of "Get behind me, Satan." Again, Jesus's willing embrace of "the cup" is clearly stressed.

(2) The Roman "soldiers, the tribune, and the Jewish guards" arrest Jesus, important details that demonstrate the complicity of the Romans. The memorable line "that it was better that one man die" should be spoken in the voice of Caiaphas.

(3) Peter has a companion who works hard to win him admittance to the high priest's courtyard and who'll soon witness his three denials. By underplaying the first denial you'll give yourself room to build. Peter's posturing at the Last Supper is already forgotten. At the moment, his sole aim is getting closer to the action. When "the other disciple" wins him entry to the courtyard, Peter tosses off a faint, over-the-shoulder response to the girl's question, possibly a futile effort to hide his cowardice from his friend.

(4) Consistent with John's Passion portrait, Jesus is remarkably composed before the high priest. But his candor is seen as disrespect and earns him a slap. The violent anger of the guard colors your tone when you narrate and when you speak his dialogue. Jesus is still recovering from the slap when he begins to reply, so give more intensity to his second clause than the first.

(5) The attack on Jesus got no response from Peter, but when he himself is attacked, he comes to life. "You are not one of this man's disciples?" stings harder than a slap, and Peter's response is quick.

The priests have pushed the right button in Pilate.

(10) Now when Pilate **heard** this statement,
    he became even **more** afraid,
    and went back into the **praetorium** and said to **Jesus**,
    "Where are you **from**?"
Jesus did not **answer** him.
So Pilate said to him,
    "Do you not speak to **me**?

Pilate's frustration turns on Jesus.

Do you not **know** that I have **power** to **release** you
    and I have power to **crucify** you?"
Jesus answered him,
    "You would have **no** power over me
    if it had not been **given** to you from **above**.

Jesus's tone is unapologetic.

For **this** reason the one who handed me **over** to you
    has the **greater** sin."
(11) **Consequently**, Pilate tried to **release** him;
    but the **Jews** cried out,
    "If you **release** him, you are not a **Friend** of Caesar.
Everyone who makes himself a **king** opposes **Caesar**."

Caesar = SEE-zer

"Friend of Caesar" is a title of honor bestowed by Rome on high-ranking officials, which Pilate might lose if he mishandles this situation.

Gabbatha = GAB-uh-thuh

When Pilate **heard** these words he brought Jesus out
    and **seated** him on the **judge's** bench
    in the place called **Stone Pavement**, in Hebrew, **Gabbatha**.
It was **preparation** day for **Passover**, and it was about **noon**.
And he said to the **Jews**,
    "**Behold**, your **king**!"
They **cried** out,
    "**Take** him away, **take** him away! **Crucify** him!"
Pilate said to them,
    "Shall I crucify your **king**?"

Pilate's words suggest his frustration with both Jesus and the priests.

This is a final effort to forestall.

The chief **priests** answered,
    "We have **no** king but **Caesar**."
Then he **handed** him over to them to be **crucified**.

Another new scene. Speak slowly.

Golgotha = GAWL-guh-thuh

(12) So they **took** Jesus, and, **carrying** the cross **himself**,
    he went out to what is called the **Place** of the **Skull**,
    in **Hebrew**, **Golgotha**.

The persistent "relative" of the victim of Peter's own violence tries (probably out of revenge) to force an admission. But once again, Peter fails to claim the one he swore never to abandon. Deliver "And again Peter denied it" as if speaking Peter's actual words of denial. Briefly, the stark crowing of the cock is mentioned. It was not predicted in this Gospel account, but narrate that painful moment with the regret that must have flooded Peter's heart.

(6) The politics of the scene that next unfolds are far from simple. Cast as a struggle between good and evil, the drama enacted before Pilate is not played with stereotypes. The Jewish authorities in John are not all cut from the same cloth; though some become chief instigators in the plot against Jesus, others, like Nicodemus and Joseph of Arimathea, are men of sincerity and deep integrity. In dealing with the characters John crafted, we can't ignore that the pagan governor is far more sympathetic than the Jewish leaders who deliver Jesus for judgment. Jesus has no advocate in Pilate's judgment hall, but the governor himself assumes that role, while simultaneously serving as the judge. John describes Pilate and Jesus interacting far longer than in the synoptics, adding details like their intriguing exchange about "truth"; Pilate emerges convinced of Jesus's innocence.

(7) The religious leaders who have come at early morning have roused Pilate from his bed but are unwilling to defile themselves by entering his preatorium. So he must go to them to hear their petty religious quarrel. Pilate questions Jesus and is annoyed at being questioned back by this Jew who disrupted his sleep. Gradually, though, Pilate seems drawn to Jesus and even jousts with him: "Then you *are* a

There they **crucified** him, and with him two **others**,
    one on either **side**, with Jesus in the **middle**.
Pilate also had an **inscription** written and put on the cross.
It read,

Proclaim the inscription slowly and with authority.

    "**Jesus** the **Nazorean**, the **King** of the **Jews**."
Now **many** of the Jews **read** this inscription,
    because the place where Jesus was **crucified** was near the **city**;
    and it was written in **Hebrew**, **Latin**, and **Greek**.
So the chief **priests** of the Jews said to **Pilate**,
    "Do not **write** 'The **King** of the Jews,'
    but that he **said**, 'I am the King of the Jews.'"
Pilate answered,
    "What I have **written**, I have written."

Speak the repetition deliberately: "What I have written, I / have / written!"

(13) When the soldiers had **crucified** Jesus,
    they took his **clothes** and **divided** them into four **shares**,
    a share for each **soldier**.
They also took his **tunic**, but the tunic was **seamless**,
    woven in one **piece** from the top **down**.
So they said to one another,

The cruel insensitivity of the Roman soldiers should be apparent.

    "Let's not **tear** it, but cast **lots** for it to see whose it will **be**,"
    in order that the passage of **Scripture** might be **fulfilled**
        that says:
    *They divided my **garments** among them,*
        *and for my **vesture** they cast **lots**.*

Use a tone shift when quoting Scripture.

(14) **This** is what the soldiers **did**.
Standing by the **cross** of Jesus were his **mother**
    and his mother's **sister**, **Mary** the wife of **Clopas**,
    and Mary of **Magdala**.
When Jesus **saw** his mother and the **disciple** there whom
        he **loved**
    he said to his mother, "**Woman**, behold, your **son**."
Then he said to the **disciple**,
    "Behold, your **mother**."
And from **that** hour the **disciple** took her into his **home**.

In this new scene the women are much grieved. Probably, *four* women are identified: "his mother's sister" is different from "Mary the wife of Clopas."

Clopas = KLOH-puhs
Magdala = MAG-duh-luh

king? . . . What is *truth*?" Genuinely taken with Jesus, Pilate appears to be pushed in a direction he's reluctant to go.

(8) A hopeful Pilate sees a possible solution in the "revolutionary" Barabbas. But when the tactic fails Pilate gives them blood as one more effort to stay the execution. By providing fewer details than the other Gospel writers, John softens the brutality and horror of the flogging and mockery of Jesus, but the brief narration should convey the soldiers' contempt as they crown Jesus with thorns and scourge him.

(9) Pilate's tone after the scourging suggests he thinks he's done enough to please these zealots. Their calls for Jesus's death clearly anger him, but even more, they frighten him. He realizes he's not done with this mess after all. For the Jewish leaders it's a clear-cut case: Jesus is *guilty*, a blasphemer deserving death.

(10) Pilate's mounting frustration with these leaders he now directs at Jesus: "Where are you from?" "Do you not speak?" "Do you not know?" Jesus's composure both troubles and impresses Pilate. Without exonerating Pilate, Jesus lays the brunt of

guilt for his execution on the leaders who falsely accused him.

(11) Sensing Pilate is weakening, the religious men pressure him more. Suspense heightens as the leaders resort to threats, telling Pilate he's not worthy of the title "Friend of Caesar." In response to threats to report him to Rome, Pilate sits Jesus on the judge's bench (for John, he's the one *true* judge) and taunts them, hailing Jesus as their "king." Rather than Jesus, the frenzied mob claims the pagan Caesar as their king. After a final effort to win pity for

In this new scene stress Jesus's awareness and control.

(15) **After** this, aware that **everything** was now **finished**,
in order that the **Scripture** might be **fulfilled**,
Jesus said, "I **thirst**."
There was a **vessel** filled with common **wine**.

hyssop = HIS-uhp

So they put a **sponge** soaked in wine on a sprig of **hyssop**
and put it up to his **mouth**.
When Jesus had **taken** the wine, he said,
"It is **finished**."

Jesus's "spirit" is the Holy Spirit, the spirit of the new creation. Jesus's Death is the giving of the Spirit.

And **bowing** his **head**, he handed **over** the **spirit**.

[Here all kneel and pause for a short time.]

(16) Now since it was **preparation** day,
in order that the **bodies** might not **remain**
on the cross on the **sabbath**,
for the sabbath day of **that** week was a **solemn** one,
the Jews asked **Pilate** that their legs be **broken**
and that they be taken **down**.

Breaking legs assured quicker death—by asphyxiation.

So the **soldiers** came and **broke** the legs of the **first**
and then of the **other** one who was crucified with Jesus.
But when they came to Jesus and saw that he was already **dead**,
they did **not** break his legs,

Blood and water are important theological symbols.

but one soldier thrust his **lance** into his **side**,
and immediately **blood** and **water** flowed out.
An **eyewitness** has **testified**, and his testimony is **true**;

Speak with conviction, stressing the "eyewitness."

he **knows** that he is speaking the **truth**,
so that you **also** may come to **believe**.
For this **happened** so that the **Scripture** passage might be **fulfilled**:
*Not a **bone** of it will be **broken**.*
And again **another** passage says:
*They will **look** upon him whom they have **pierced**.*

Arimathea = ayr-ih-muh-THEE-uh

(17) After **this**, **Joseph** of **Arimathea**,
secretly a **disciple** of Jesus for **fear** of the **Jews**,
asked **Pilate** if he could **remove** the body of Jesus.

With tender respect for Joseph and, later, Nicodemus.

Jesus—"Shall I crucify your king?"—darkness wins the battle and Pilate capitulates.

(12) John neither describes the Crucifixion nor provides details, save that Jesus hung between two unnamed criminals. In keeping with John's intent to paint a regal Christ who marches willingly toward his "hour of glory," take time with the brief narration that tells how Jesus carried the Cross "by himself." John offers no images of Jesus's brutal death, but focuses instead on Pilate's inscription that declares Jesus "King of the Jews." Proclaim it as a herald reading from a scroll. In the angry exchange

between Pilate and the priests, the governor has the final word and, knowingly or not, proclaims Jesus's true identity.

(13) The ruthless soldiers divide his clothes among them, but his valuable tunic they will not spoil, so they gamble to possess it. Your tone should suggest their blind self-interest and insensitivity. But the Scripture quotation, "they divided my garments" (Psalm 22:18), calls for sadness and resignation, as does the summary statement, "This is what the soldiers did."

(14) The tone shifts dramatically when you speak of "his mother." Unlike Matthew's

and Mark's accounts, Jesus is not abandoned here nor does he utter the cry of the forsaken, "My God, my God." The women whose presence offers hope and strength to the failing Jesus would be known and revered by the narrator, so speak reverently of them. He is *dying*, but Jesus is still ministering to others when he says "Woman, behold, your son," "Behold, your mother," tender words that express love.

(15) John shows Jesus mustering his last strength to fulfill Scripture: with full *awareness* and without anguish or despair he utters his final words, "I thirst." He's

Nicodemus = nik-uh-DEE-muhs

myrrh = mer

aloes = AL-ohs

Slow your pacing for these final lines.

Though the final line lacks drama, speak with solemn reverence of the burial of Jesus.

And Pilate **permitted** it.
So he came and **took** his body.
Nicodemus, the one who had first come to him at **night**,
    also came bringing a mixture of **myrrh** and **aloes**
    weighing about one hundred **pounds**.
They took the **body** of Jesus
    and bound it with **burial cloths** along with the **spices**,
    according to the Jewish **burial** custom.
Now in the **place** where he had been crucified there was a **garden**,
    and in the garden a **new tomb**, in which no one had yet
        been **buried**.
So they laid Jesus **there** because of the Jewish **preparation** day;
    for the **tomb** was close **by**.

TO KEEP IN MIND
Slow down: The larger the church, the larger the assembly, and the more complex the text, the slower you must read.

THE 4 STEPS OF *LECTIO DIVINA* OR PRAYERFUL READING

1. *Lectio:* Read a Scripture passage aloud slowly. Notice what phrase captures your attention and be attentive to its meaning. Silent pause.

2. *Meditatio:* Read the passage aloud slowly again, reflecting on the passage, allowing God to speak to you through it. Silent pause.

3. *Oratio:* Read it aloud slowly a third time, allowing it to be your prayer or response to God's gift of insight to you. Silent pause.

4. *Contemplatio:* Read it aloud slowly a fourth time, now resting in God's word.

---

given "sour" wine, not the narcotic beverage he rejected at the start of the Crucifixion in the Gospel account of Mark (15:23). Pause and imagine Jesus dropping his head in death; then, quietly, read the solemn narration. In handing over "the spirit," Jesus both surrenders his life and passes on the Holy Spirit. Take a substantial pause here for silence and prayer.

(16) Important details remain, for "preparation day" and "Sabbath" situate these events in time. We've passed the climax, but reporting how soldiers break the legs and thrust the lance requires some

intensity. The flow of "blood and water" both confirms Jesus's Death and provides a unique Johannine symbol, traditionally thought to represent Baptism and Eucharist. Speak reverently of it. John's reference to the "eyewitness" serves his mission to bolster the faith of his readers, so narrate with confidence. Remember, you aren't making a courtroom presentation, but presenting the faith of a believer.

(17) Speak of Joseph as a now revered member of the community, his secret discipleship made understandable by his "fear of the Jews." He asks a favor of Pilate who,

by granting it, is once again made sympathetic. Nicodemus, another secret disciple, now reveals his allegiance to Jesus by coming to care for his body and anointing it with oils and spices. Speak of the burial with tenderness, but with grief held in check. Imagine telling a friend about a funeral she was unable to attend: controlling your own sorrow, you would share the details with obvious love for the deceased. The "new tomb" becomes the temporary resting place of Jesus. But soon the world will know a newness that will change its face forever.

HOLY SATURDAY: EASTER VIGIL

LECTIONARY #41

READING I   Genesis 1:1—2:2

A reading from the Book of Genesis

(1) In the beginning, when God created the **heavens** and the **earth**,
    the earth was a formless **wasteland**, and **darkness** covered
        the **abyss**,
while a mighty **wind** swept over the **waters**.

(2) Then God **said**,
    "Let there be **light**," and there **was** light.
God saw how **good** the light was.
God then **separated** the light from the **darkness**.
God called the light "day," and the darkness he called "**night**."
Thus **evening** came, and **morning** followed—the **first** day.

(3) **Then** God said,
    "Let there be a **dome** in the **middle** of the waters,
    to **separate one** body of water from the **other**."
And so it **happened**:
    God **made** the dome,
    and it separated the water **above** the dome from the water
        below it.
God called the dome "the **sky**."
Evening came, and **morning** followed—the **second** day.

(4) **Then** God said,
    "Let the **water** under the sky be gathered into a single **basin**,
    so that the dry **land** may appear."

Genesis = JEN-uh-sis

Your first three words set the epic tone of what you relate. Be mindful of the five-part pattern of each day and use the repeated refrains to draw your listeners deeper into the pattern of God's creative work. The *repetitions* are intentional and meant to be apparent, so don't obscure them with novel readings on each day. The regularity, familiarity, and predictability give the passage much of its power, so don't rush.

The declaration that creation is "good" and the accomplishment of God's commands are stressed *each* time they recur.

Renew your energy (and make eye contact) with each "Then God said."

There are options for readings tonight. Ask your parish staff which ones will be used.

READING I The Vigil culminates our year of worship, for on this night we proclaim our best stories within our finest ritual. Lent (which means "spring") is a time of newness. Having cast off the sackcloth of repentance we begin where God began—when formless chaos became a world so good that God took a whole day just to enjoy it.

In contrast to other ancient creation stories, Genesis proclaims a God who creates out of love, not self-interest. The creatures of pagan myths were mere slaves made for the pleasure of the gods. But the God of Genesis creates a worthy world and then entrusts it to creatures made in his own image. This creator lives intimately with his creation. So speak with emotion that tells your listeners not just what was made when, but of the loving God who made it.

A pattern of refrains moves us through the days of creation. Each day contains 1) an *introduction*: "Then God said"; 2) God's spoken *command*: "Let there be"; 3) an announcement of the *accomplishment* of the command: "And so it happened"; 4) an *affirmation* of the goodness of each day's work: "God saw how *good* it was"; and 5) an *identification* of the day: "Evening came and morning followed the *first* day." The affirmations of goodness are not an artist's boast, but the awe of parents looking at the wonder they have

Identify each of God's creations—"the earth . . . the sea"—with tenderness.

There is much detail here: use the words marked for emphasis to guide you in placing your stress. But here it's the energy and enthusiasm that matter most, not the individual words.

Here, as before, emphasizing details is less important than conveying a sense of joy and wonder.

Speak the words "and he made the stars" quickly, with excitement, or slowly, with amazement. Note that the purpose of each of the lights is to serve humanity.

Each time it recurs, "Evening came, and morning followed" should convey the end of an epoch of time and creation. Speak with a sense of accomplishment, joy, and peace.

And so it **happened**:
  the water under the sky was **gathered** into its basin,
  and the dry **land** appeared.
God called the dry land "the **earth**,"
  and the basin of the **water** he called "the **sea**."
God saw how **good** it was.
Then God said,
  "Let the **earth** bring forth **vegetation**:
  every kind of **plant** that bears **seed**
  and every kind of **fruit tree** on earth
  that bears fruit with its **seed** in it."
And so it **happened**:
  the earth brought forth every **kind** of plant that bears **seed**
  and every kind of **fruit tree** on earth
  that bears fruit with its **seed** in it.
God saw how **good** it was.
Evening came, and morning **followed**—the **third** day.

(5) **Then** God said:
  "Let there be **lights** in the dome of the sky,
  to separate **day** from **night**.
Let them mark the fixed **times**, the **days** and the **years**,
  and serve as **luminaries** in the dome of the sky,
  to shed **light** upon the earth."
And so it **happened**:
  God made the **two** great lights,
  the **greater** one to govern the **day**,
  and the **lesser** one to govern the **night**;
  and he made the **stars**.
God set them in the dome of the **sky**,
  to shed **light** upon the earth,
  to **govern** the day and the night,
  and to separate the **light** from the **darkness**.
God saw how **good** it was.
Evening came, and **morning** followed—the **fourth** day.

made. Identify each day with joy and a sense of accomplishment. The refrains are part of the sacred poetry of the text, intentionally redundant because repetition draws us into the fabric of the story.

(1) God does not create from "nothing," but brings order to the "formless *wasteland*. The "mighty wind" is God's spirit transforming the terrifying chaos into ordered harmony.

(2) The energetic cadence that describes the creation of light reveals a God almost at play. God enjoys the effort, creating not with hands, but with the spoken word, a divine fiat! So speak with joyful power.

(3) "Then God said" moves us through the sequence of days, but each repetition requires fresh energy. Pause before each "And so it happened," and speak with delight and gratitude, the way you might describe watching a child take its first steps. After each "it happened" there is *elaboration* on what just occurred that requires a dose of fresh energy.

(4) Another command further distinguishes earth from sea, making dry land appear. The God who entrusted the earth to us designed its every detail, from the "plant that bears seed" (a pine or oak) to the "fruit tree . . . that bears fruit with its seed in it" (peaches and apples). The design and balance God established calls us to respect the earth and safeguard its God-given abundance. The refrain that names it "good" becomes an insistent reminder to prize and defend God's gift of creation.

(5) Recall the times you've gazed at a dewy sunrise, a radiant sunset, and the stars—many, magnificent, and mysterious

This "day" teems with life; there is much excitement and energy in these lines.

(6) **Then** God said,
  "Let the water **teem** with an **abundance** of living **creatures**,
  and on the **earth** let **birds** fly beneath the **dome** of the sky."
And so it **happened**:
  God created the great **sea** monsters
  and all kinds of **swimming** creatures with which the
      water **teems**,
  and all kinds of winged **birds**.
God saw how **good** it was, and God **blessed** them, saying,
  "Be **fertile**, **multiply**, and **fill** the water of the seas;
  and let the birds **multiply** on the earth."
Evening came, and morning **followed**—the **fifth** day.

Notice God "blesses" the creatures. End this section with calm satisfaction.

Renew energy once again with joy at the thrill of creating life.

(7) **Then** God said,
  "Let the **earth** bring forth all kinds of living **creatures**:
  cattle, **creeping** things, and wild **animals** of all **kinds**."
And so it **happened**:
  God made all **kinds** of wild **animals**, all kinds of **cattle**,
  and all kinds of **creeping** things of the earth.
God saw how **good** it was.

Reading reaches a sub-climax here. ALL creation is good!

(8) **Then** God said:
  "Let us make **man** in our **image**, after our **likeness**.
Let them have **dominion** over the **fish** of the sea,
  the **birds** of the air, and the **cattle**,
  and over all the wild **animals**
  and all the creatures that **crawl** on the **ground**."
God created **man** in his **image**;
  in the image of **God** he created him;
  male and **female** he created them.
God **blessed** them, saying:
  "Be **fertile** and **multiply**;
  fill the earth and **subdue** it.
Have **dominion** over the **fish** of the sea, the birds of the **air**,
  and all the **living** things that **move** on the earth."

Use a nobler, slower pacing here. Humans are made in God's own likeness! Take note of the plural pronouns. Use, don't rush, the repetitions, for they deepen our appreciation of these great truths.

Speak this as a blessing, not an order. All the beauty and good that God has created is entrusted to humanity.

dotting the night sky like glitter. Rejoice in these gifts: the sun that lends vigor to all living things, the moon that robs the night of its fearsome darkness—and speak of them with fresh vigor.

(6) There's no abatement of God's creativity. In vast numbers and varieties new creatures fill the seas and skies. An "abundance" of winged birds and swimming creatures, even "sea monsters" join the

chorus of praise that is God's bountiful creation. Ordering them to "be fertile, multiply," God grants the creatures license to *fill* the earth and seas.

(7) God's busiest day dawns. First, a vast array of living creatures springs to life from the now productive earth. "Wild" and "creeping" things of "all kinds" appear before a God as delighted as a child at her first circus. And, of course, this vast menagerie is pronounced "good."

(8) Superseding all that went before, comes a creature made "in our image, after our likeness," a creature who shares God's life! Slow your tempo and assume a tender, solemn quality. All the good that fills the world God now entrusts wholly to the woman and man. God gives "dominion" and commands them to "be fertile and multiply." God's giving is beyond human comprehension, for God gives *everything*. But, as

God **also** said:

"**See**, I give you every **seed**-bearing plant all over the **earth**
and every **tree** that has seed-bearing **fruit** on it to be your **food**;
and to all the **animals** of the land, all the **birds** of the air,
and all the living creatures that **crawl** on the **ground**,
I give all the **green** plants for **food**."
And so it **happened**.
God looked at **everything** he had made, and he found it
very good.
Evening came, and **morning** followed—the **sixth** day.

(9) Thus the **heavens** and the **earth** and all their array
were **completed**.
Since on the **seventh** day God was **finished**
with the work he had been doing,
he **rested** on the seventh day from all the **work** he
had **undertaken**.

[Shorter: Genesis 1:1, 26–31a]

This is a summary statement: God's creation is *very* good!

With a sense of accomplishment and pride, pause after "completed."

"Rested" suggests more than being idle; it means appreciating and delighting in the "work," that is, the beloved creation God has now completed.

For meditation and context:

RESPONSORIAL PSALM   Psalm 104:1–2, 5–6, 10, 12, 13–14, 24, 35 (30)

R. Lord, send out your Spirit, and renew the face of the earth.

Bless the LORD, O my soul!
  O LORD, my God, you are great indeed!
You are clothed with majesty and glory,
  robed in light as with a cloak.

You fixed the earth upon its foundation,
  not to be moved forever;
with the ocean, as with a garment, you
    covered it;
  above the mountains the waters stood.

You send forth springs into the watercourses
  that wind among the mountains.
Beside them the birds of heaven dwell;
  from among the branches they send forth
    their song.

You water the mountains from your palace;
  the earth is replete with the fruit
    of your works.
You raise grass for the cattle,
  and vegetation for man's use,
producing bread from the earth.

How manifold are your works, O LORD!
  In wisdom you have wrought them all—
the earth is full of your creatures.
  Bless the LORD, O my soul!

Or:

TO KEEP IN MIND
Always read Scriptures aloud, noting suggestions for stresses and pauses. After several readings, alter the stress markings to suit your style and interpretation.

---

anyone who inherits the family business knows, such giving is gift *and* responsibility. In granting dominion over plants and trees and every living creature, God does not speak with the authority of an overseer but with the tender love of a father blessing a newborn child. Finally, satisfied that long labor has yielded good results, God surveys all creation and calls it *very* good.

  (9) It would seem there's nothing left to tell. But Israel's cherished gift—the sacred Sabbath—is yet to come. People tend to think that work is never done. But

God says otherwise and becomes our role model for proper balance between work and holy rest.

READING II Until the coming of Christ this story remained a singular parable of God's unflinching demand that his people be willing to surrender everything. Popular culture prefers a gentle, indulgent God who looks the other way when we stumble. Israel never imagined such a deity. Their neighbors offered many "gods," but

Israel wasn't shopping for a god, because the one true God had chosen them. In the ancient world, human sacrifice was not unknown, so for Abraham to comply with God's brutal request is quite credible. But in the context of this liturgy, this story is not about a God who demands everything, but of a God who *gives* everything.

  As we celebrate the new covenant inaugurated in Christ's blood, we recognize in Isaac—innocent and willing to die, even to the point of carrying the wood for his own sacrifice—a type, or symbol, of the innocent Christ who carried the wood of

For meditation and context:

RESPONSORIAL PSALM   Psalm 33:4–5, 6–7, 12–13, 20, and 22 (5b)

R. The earth is full of the goodness of the Lord.

Upright is the word of the LORD,
  and all his works are trustworthy.
He loves justice and right;
  of the kindness of the LORD the earth
    is full.

By the word of the LORD the heavens
    were made;
  by the breath of his mouth all their host.
He gathers the waters of the sea as in a flask;
  in cellars he confines the deep.

Blessed the nation whose God is the LORD,
  the people he has chosen for his own
    inheritance.
From heaven the LORD looks down;
  he sees all mankind.

Our soul waits for the LORD,
  who is our help and our shield.
May your kindness, O LORD, be upon us
  who have put our hope in you.

TO KEEP IN MIND

Slow down: The larger the church, the larger the assembly, and the more complex the text, the slower you must read.

READING II   Genesis 22:1–18

A reading from the Book of Genesis

God put **Abraham** to the test.
He called to him, "**Abraham**!"
"**Here** I am," he replied.
Then God said:
  "Take your son **Isaac**, your **only** one, whom you **love**,
  and **go** to the land of **Moriah**.
There you shall **offer** him up as a **holocaust**
  on a **height** that I will point **out** to you."
Early the next **morning** Abraham saddled his **donkey**,
  took with him his son **Isaac** and two of his **servants** as well,
  and with the **wood** that he had cut for the holocaust,
  set out for the place of which God had **told** him.

On the **third** day Abraham got **sight** of the place from **afar**.
Then he **said** to his servants:
  "Both of you stay **here** with the **donkey**,
  while the **boy** and I go on over **yonder**.
We will **worship** and then come **back** to you."

Genesis = JEN-uh-sis

The opening line both introduces and states the point of the entire story. Pause slightly after "Abraham." His "Here I am" is spoken eagerly.

Isaac = Ī-zik

Moriah = moh-RĪ-uh

Don't give away what comes at the end of the sentence. God's voice is solemn, not stern. Emphasize the gravity of God's command by stressing "only" and "love."

Abraham works hard to hide his pain. Don't let this sound like an outing in the country.

Help us to sense the passage of time.

---

the Cross on which he died. But there's another dimension that mitigates the unthinkable aspects of this story. In Abraham, we find *another* "type," this time a symbol of the Father God who so loved the world that he sent his only Son to die for all. Given that, the answer to the question "What kind of God would put anyone through such a trial?" is this: a God who would go through it. For Christian readers, this is less a story about Abraham than it is

about God. It's a story that prepares the way for God's ultimate intervention in human history—sending his Son to freely die for us. By identifying with Abraham's turmoil as he prepares to carry out his gruesome task, we learn less about the man and more about the God who called him, for God never asks of us what he would not do first.

From the start, we know nothing awful will happen, but unlike us, Abraham does not know this is only a "test," so make his struggle stark and real. Abraham's naiveté ("Here I am!") in no way hints at the anguish that comes when God's authoritative voice orders Isaac's sacrifice. Don't signal the shocking directive by starting with too threatening a tone, and pay special attention to the words "your son Isaac, your *only* one, whom you *love*."

This image foreshadows Jesus's carrying his own Cross. Don't waste it.

This dialogue is poignant: Isaac is sincerely curious and unaware. Abraham speaks intentionally and his words are pained and weighty.

This is not a throwaway line when you consider what lies ahead.

Slowly: the scene grows tense and darker. Share one image at a time. Tying up the boy can't sound like he's buttoning Isaac's jacket.

Don't speak like you're describing a "close call," but as relating the actual slaughter. "But" breaks the mood; speak faster. The second "Abraham" is louder, stronger than the first.

"Here I am" has no sense of relief yet, just terror. The "Do not" commands can be spoken with calm and tender compassion. "I now know" is spoken solemnly. Pause after "beloved son."

This is a new beat; the pace is faster and the mood upbeat. The "ram" is replacement for Isaac. Don't rush.

Yahweh-yireh = YAH-way-YEER-ay means "The Lord will see (to it)."

Thereupon Abraham took the wood for the holocaust
and laid it on his son **Isaac's** shoulders,
while he **himself** carried the **fire** and the **knife**.
As the two walked on **together**, Isaac **spoke** to his father
Abraham:
"**Father**!" Isaac said.
"**Yes**, son," he replied.
Isaac continued, "Here are the **fire** and the **wood**,
but where is the **sheep** for the holocaust?"
"**Son**," Abraham answered,
"God **himself** will provide the sheep for the holocaust."
Then the two **continued** going forward.

When they **came** to the place of which God had **told** him,
Abraham built an **altar** there and arranged the **wood** on it.
Next he **tied** up his son Isaac,
and put him on **top** of the wood on the **altar**.
Then he **reached** out and took the **knife** to **slaughter** his son.
But the LORD's **messenger** called to him from **heaven**,
"**Abraham, Abraham**!"
"**Here** I am," he answered.
"Do not lay your **hand** on the boy," said the messenger.
"Do not do the least **thing** to him.
I know now how **devoted** you are to **God**,
since you did not **withhold** from me your own beloved **son**."
As Abraham looked **about**,
he spied a **ram** caught by its horns in the **thicket**.
So he went and **took** the ram
and offered **it** up as a holocaust in **place** of his son.
Abraham **named** the site **Yahweh-yireh**;
hence people now say, "On the **mountain** the LORD will **see**."

Without hinting to son or family the true nature of the mission he undertakes the very next morning, Abraham sets out. God promised to use Isaac to make Abraham's descendants numerous as the stars. Abraham's faith is so great that despite the impossibility of the situation, he continues to trust. Thus, Abraham becomes *another* "type"—the paragon of all believers who put their faith in God.

Use the unemotional tone of the narration to paint Abraham's stoic face as he saddles the donkey and assembles servants. His controlled dialogue, with the servants and with Isaac, reveals his determination to avoid alarming his son. Isaac is confused and says so. His question about the "sheep" requires Abraham to work even harder to maintain a calm exterior.

Covering his pain, he answers, ironically, that *God* will provide the sacrifice. While we know a *ram* waits in the brambles, Abraham thinks of *Isaac*.

Shocking details follow. Almost robotically, Abraham binds Isaac and places him on the altar. Your tone must suggest the immense (though unseen) effort it took to force himself to prepare the altar and the wood. Imagine Abraham's emotional strain as he places the boy "on top of the wood."

In a long passage like this, variety in pacing is urgent. Though it is "God" speaking, you must not adopt a monotone or an overly slow delivery. Speak like a parent giving good news to an anxious child—both reassuring and praising.

The fulfillment of these promises is what tonight's readings and tonight's liturgy are all about.

If you've given proper emphasis and not rushed the preceding, the final line will call us all to obedience.

For meditation and context:

Again the Lord's messenger **called** to Abraham from heaven
> and said:
"**I swear** by myself, declares the Lord,
that because you **acted** as you **did**
in not **withholding** from me your beloved **son**,
I will **bless** you **abundantly**
and make your **descendants** as **countless**
as the **stars** of the sky and the **sands** of the seashore;
your descendants shall take **possession**
of the **gates** of their **enemies**,
and in your **descendants** all the nations of the **earth** shall
> find **blessing**—
all **this** because you **obeyed** my **command**."

[Shorter: Genesis 22:1–2, 9a, 10–13, 15–18]

RESPONSORIAL PSALM   Psalm 16:5, 8, 9–10, 11 (1)

R. You are my inheritance, O Lord.

O Lord, my allotted portion and my cup,
> you it is who hold fast my lot.
I set the Lord ever before me;
> with him at my right hand I shall not
> be disturbed.

Therefore my heart is glad and my soul
> rejoices,
> my body, too, abides in confidence;
because you will not abandon my soul to the
> netherworld,
> nor will you suffer your faithful one to
> undergo corruption.

You will show me the path to life,
> fullness of joys in your presence,
> the delights at your right hand forever.

When you relate how he took the knife "to slaughter his son," remember Abraham believed he was really going to do it. Don't let that riveting moment end too soon; pause before God's voice intervenes and let the fearful image make its impact.

"But" is like a heavenly hand reaching out and catching Abraham's wrist just in time. At first urgent and authoritative, God's voice gradually mellows into tenderness and compassion. The incident with

the ram moves quickly, spoken with great relief, especially the comment that it was offered "in place of his son."

The true meaning of this story is found in the closing section: God does not desire the taking of human life, but the *giving* of one's whole self, as Abraham did. The Lord's messenger praises Abraham as a hero in faith and promises abundant blessings—blessings that will rain down not only on Abraham but on all who follow his example of steadfast trust.

READING III Certain stories are too important to forget, either because they define us, or because they remind us of who we are, or because of the significant characters they portray. This story is important for all three reasons. After gestating for three centuries in the womb of Egypt, Israel is delivered by God for new life in a new land. This is the foundational memory of the Jewish people. God

Exodus = EK-suh-duhs

Moses = MOH-ziz; MOH-zis

Pharaoh = FAYR-oh

Don't fear the repetitions in this text and trust the power of this story to move your listeners. Be confident that your listeners are eager to hear it again. Begin with the strong voice of God.

The sacred writer sees God behind all things, even Pharaoh's obstinacy.

"Pharaoh . . . army . . . chariots . . . charioteers": this will become a much repeated refrain. Use all the words each time it recurs.

"Column of cloud" and the "angel" are both manifestations of God's presence and protection. The action intensifies. Build suspense.

Slow your pace to suggest the passage of time over the long night. Pause after "all night long."

Speak with renewed vigor. Visualize what you describe.

Convey the wonder of this marvelous sight.

READING III   Exodus 14:15—15:1

A reading from the Book of Exodus

The LORD said to **Moses**, "**Why** are you crying **out** to me?
Tell the Israelites to go **forward**.
And **you**, **lift** up your **staff** and, with hand **outstretched**
        over the **sea**,
    split the sea in **two**,
    that the Israelites may pass **through** it on dry **land**.
But I will make the **Egyptians** so **obstinate**
    that they will go in **after** them.
Then I will receive **glory** through **Pharaoh** and all his **army**,
    his **chariots** and **charioteers**.
The Egyptians shall **know** that **I** am the **Lord**,
    when I receive **glory** through **Pharaoh**
    and his **chariots** and **charioteers**."

The **angel** of **God**, who had been **leading** Israel's camp,
    now **moved** and went around **behind** them.
The column of **cloud** also, leaving the **front**,
    took up its place **behind** them,
    so that it came **between** the camp of the **Egyptians**
    and that of **Israel**.
But the **cloud** now became **dark**, and thus the **night** passed
    without the rival **camps** coming any closer **together** all
        night long.
Then Moses **stretched** out his hand over the **sea**,
    and the LORD **swept** the sea
    with a **strong** east **wind** throughout the night
    and so **turned** it into **dry** land.
When the **water** was thus **divided**,
    the **Israelites** marched into the **midst** of the sea on **dry** land,
    with the water like a **wall** to their **right** and to their **left**.

acted directly and decisively in their history to save them from the oppression of Egypt's Pharaoh. And God's instrument was Moses.

The text presents a God who is *fully* in charge of all that occurs. Speaking in the first person, God asserts "*I* will make . . . *I* will receive . . . " Even when Moses acts, stretching arms over the sea, it is the *Lord* who turns it to dry land. God and Moses are the main players, God using Moses to

deliver Israel with mighty signs and wonders. Pharaoh and his army are not the pawns they might appear to be, used to bring God "glory." What's described here is the willful action of a king who had ten chances to get it right. Ten times he relented and reneged—agreeing after each plague to free the Israelites. But each time his obstinacy returned, till finally there was no turning back. God is not glorified by the destruction, but by proving that no worldly power can thwart God's will, for God keeps his promises.

God's glory is proven not only to the enemy, but to Israel herself. For when they saw Pharaoh's chariots in pursuit, they panicked and blamed Moses for endangering them. As Moses attempts to quell the people's fears, God takes charge again, ordering him to "go forward." The liturgical proclamation of this text narrates events that foreshadow our own deliverance in Christ's Passover from death to life, and symbolize our salvation in the waters of

Quicken your pace here. As narrator, shake your head (figuratively) at the foolishness of the Egyptians' tactics.

Aware that it was *God* who saved, speak slowly and quietly.

God's justice is uncompromising. Don't hold back in narrating the awful consequences for the Egyptians.

"Dawn" is the moment of liberation.

Narrate these lines without hint of vindictiveness.

Your voice fills with gratitude, relief, and not a little pride.

The Egyptians **followed** in **pursuit**;
     all Pharaoh's **horses** and **chariots** and **charioteers** went
          after them
     right into the **midst** of the sea.
In the **night** watch just before **dawn**
     the LORD **cast** through the column of the fiery cloud
     upon the Egyptian force a **glance** that threw it into a **panic**;
     and he so **clogged** their chariot wheels
     that they could hardly **drive**.
With **that** the Egyptians sounded the **retreat** before Israel,
     because the LORD was fighting for them **against** the Egyptians.

Then the LORD told **Moses**, "**Stretch** out your hand over the **sea**,
     that the water may flow **back** upon the Egyptians,
     upon their **chariots** and their **charioteers**."
So Moses **stretched** out his hand over the **sea**,
     and at **dawn** the sea flowed **back** to its normal **depth**.
The Egyptians were **fleeing** head **on** toward the sea,
     when the LORD **hurled** them into its midst.
As the water flowed **back**,
     it **covered** the **chariots** and the **charioteers** of Pharaoh's
          whole **army**
     which had **followed** the Israelites into the **sea**.
Not a single **one** of them escaped.
But the **Israelites** had marched on dry **land**
     through the **midst** of the sea,
     with the water like a **wall** to their **right** and to their **left**.
Thus the LORD **saved** Israel on that day
     from the **power** of the **Egyptians**.

Baptism. So you're not just proclaiming history, but describing our own movement from spiritual slavery to freedom.

Manifested as "angel" and "cloud," the Lord leads the people. But at night, when the shining cloud's light would have benefited the Egyptians, it becomes "dark," keeping the Egyptians at bay. Then, there is only darkness and waiting "all night long." Suddenly, Moses takes action. Note the strong rhythm of the lines that describe wind and sea and the recurring "s" sounds

that suggest both driving wind and raging storm. The force of the wind splits the sea. With utter conviction and a hint of vindication, marvel at the walls of water through which the people march on "*dry*" land."

Foolishly, Egypt follows right "into the midst of the sea," and your tone suggests the futility and arrogance of this misguided decision. Speak in hushed tones of the "night watch before dawn" but quickly build volume and intensity as the Egyptians "panic" and sound "the retreat."

Pharaoh's obstinacy sealed the fate of his army. We might wonder at the severity of their destruction, but Scripture never shies from linking actions with consequences. Divine justice is uncompromising: "not a single" Egyptian escaped. That sober truth is not spoken with rancor or vindictiveness. Don't gloat, but don't apologize either.

From destruction the story shifts focus to the wonder of Israel's deliverance through the miraculous corridor of water.

God's power inspires a reverential fear among the Israelites. Speak in hushed tones.

Miriam = MEER-ee-uhm

Aaron = AYR-uhn

Let the joy of this song ring in your voice and show on your face.

When Israel **saw** the Egyptians lying **dead** on the **seashore**
and beheld the great **power** that the LORD
had shown **against** the Egyptians,
they **feared** the LORD and **believed** in him and in his
servant Moses.

Then **Moses** and the **Israelites** sang this **song** to the LORD:
I will **sing** to the LORD, for he is **gloriously triumphant;**
horse and **chariot** he has **cast** into the **sea.**

For meditation and context:

RESPONSORIAL PSALM   Exodus 15:1–2, 3–4, 5–6, 17–18 (1b)

R. Let us sing to the Lord; he has covered himself in glory.

I will sing to the LORD, for he is gloriously
    triumphant;
    horse and chariot he has cast into the sea.
My strength and my courage is the LORD,
    and he has been my savior.
He is my God, I praise him;
    the God of my father, I extol him.

The LORD is a warrior,
    LORD is his name!
Pharaoh's chariots and army he hurled into
    the sea;
    the elite of his officers were submerged
    in the Red Sea.

The flood waters covered them,
    they sank into the depths like a stone.
Your right hand, O LORD, magnificent
    in power,
    your right hand, O LORD, has shattered
    the enemy.

You brought in the people you redeemed
    and planted them on the mountain of
    your inheritance—
the place where you made your seat,
    O LORD,
    the sanctuary, LORD, which your hands
    established.
The LORD shall reign forever and ever.

> **TO KEEP IN MIND**
>
> **Prophets**: In addition to troubling the comfortable, prophets comforted the troubled. With equal passion, the great seers spoke threat and consolation, indictment and forgiveness. You must do the same for the chosen people you call "parish."

Isaiah = Ī-ZAY-uh

"Husband" and "maker" are meant to express tenderness and compassion. Persuade us God can love us this much. The sense of the sentence is: the one who is now your husband is God, your Creator.

READING IV   Isaiah 54:5–14

A reading from the Book of the Prophet Isaiah

The One who has become your **husband** is your **Maker;**
    his name is the LORD of **hosts;**
your **redeemer** is the **Holy** One of **Israel,**
    called **God** of all the **earth.**

The repetition is intentional, reiterating the marvel of God's miraculous intervention. You'll need a tone of amazement, gratitude, and even pride to announce again how God granted such wonders! Finally, with reverential awe, tell how the people "feared . . . and believed." Hushed awe at witnessing God's great power suddenly turns to jubilant song. The joyous gratitude of those who sang becomes your joy, too, as you invite *all* to delight in God's saving power.

READING IV   Much of God's Word is about reversals, sometimes of expectations, other times of fortunes. God works differently than we humans, so our expectations are often thwarted by God's mysterious ways. The reality of sin often brings the reality of suffering into our lives. So we need God to reverse our situation by taking away consequences we've so often brought upon ourselves.

This reading deals with the severest consequence Israel had ever experienced—the exile and the related loss of nation, king, and Temple. The nation's devastation was complete and the loss of all her institutions robbed Israel of her identity. In this state, they questioned the validity of the covenant and their given role as God's Chosen People.

Isaiah now speaks to the forsaken city of Jerusalem using dramatic metaphors to announce Israel's deliverance from exile

Speak the line "like a wife forsaken . . ." briskly, and increase the intensity of "a wife married . . ."

Contrast the *regret* of "For a brief moment . . ." with the *joy* of "but with great tenderness . . ." The four lines that follow restate the same idea. Maintain the energy and conviction throughout.

"Redeemer" is a joyful title suggesting compassion, not authority.
Noah = NOH-uh
The exile is compared to Noah's flood. God is saying, "As I swore then, so I swear now never to punish you again."

These words represent the excess of divine love. Don't hold back.

Here, God speaks directly to Jerusalem. Speak lovingly, as if embracing one with whom you are reconciling.
carnelians = kahr-NEEL-yuhnz
Carnelians are reddish quartz and carbuncles are smooth, round, deep-red garnets.

God is making a promise. Speak with reassuring strength and conviction. Make sure it's clear when you finish this line that you've concluded the reading.

The LORD calls you **back**,
    like a wife **forsaken** and grieved in **spirit**,
    a wife married in **youth** and then cast **off**,
    says your God.
For a brief **moment** I **abandoned** you,
    but with great **tenderness** I will take you **back**.
In an outburst of **wrath**, for a **moment**
    I **hid** my **face** from you;
but with enduring **love** I take **pity** on you,
    says the LORD, your **redeemer**.
This is for me like the days of **Noah**,
    when I **swore** that the **waters** of Noah
    should never **again deluge** the earth;
so I have sworn not to be **angry** with you,
    or to **rebuke** you.
Though the **mountains** leave their **place**
    and the **hills** be **shaken**,
my **love** shall never **leave** you
    nor my covenant of **peace** be **shaken**,
    says the LORD, who has **mercy** on you.
O **afflicted** one, **storm-battered** and **unconsoled**,
    I lay your **pavements** in **carnelians**,
    and your **foundations** in **sapphires**;
I will make your **battlements** of **rubies**,
    your gates of **carbuncles**,
    and all your **walls** of precious **stones**.
All your **children** shall be taught by the LORD,
    and **great** shall be the **peace** of your children.
In **justice** shall you be **established**,
    far from the fear of **oppression**,
    where **destruction** cannot come **near** you.

and her restoration in the promised land. This is a *mood* reading that communicates through imagery and tone; your focus is not history but the depth of God's love. Isaiah portrays God as a husband and Israel as the estranged wife cast off for a time, but now called back. Emerging from a period of momentary anger and rejection, God takes "pity" on Israel. Pity is an important word. This is no worthy wife scorned in a self-indulgent fit of temper. God compares this time to that of Noah when God had to

start over since the stench of humanity's evil rose to the heavens. Now, as with Noah, God promises everlasting love, not momentary affection that changes with the wind, but permanent, committed love, bound in covenant relationship.

Such promises can't be delivered without feeling. Persuade us that God loves us, longs for us, like a husband loves a wife; that God forgives like some rare and special spouses forgive their partner's infidelity. If your listeners don't hear that, they won't have heard this reading. Your words must

be all the more persuasive since God uses *misfortune*—the exile—to win back unfaithful Israel.

The emotions here are varied: first the initial anger: "For a brief moment I abandoned you." Then overwhelming forgiveness: "but with great tenderness I will take you back." Ironically, expressing intense love requires controlled delivery; so don't exaggerate, but convey the depth of feeling expressed here.

TO KEEP IN MIND

Who really proclaims: "When the Sacred Scriptures are read in the Church, God himself speaks to his people, and Christ, present in his word, proclaims the gospel" (#29 GIRM).

RESPONSORIAL PSALM   Psalm 30:2, 4, 5–6, 11–12, 13 (2a)

R. I will praise you, Lord, for you have rescued me.

I will extol you, O LORD, for you drew
    me clear
    and did not let my enemies rejoice over me.
O LORD, you brought me up from the
    netherworld;
    you preserved me from among those
    going down into the pit.

Sing praise to the LORD, you his faithful ones,
    and give thanks to his holy name.
For his anger lasts but a moment;
    a lifetime, his good will.
At nightfall, weeping enters in,
    but with the dawn, rejoicing.

Hear, O LORD, and have pity on me;
    O LORD, be my helper.
You changed my mourning into dancing;
    O LORD, my God, forever will I give you
    thanks.

READING V   Isaiah 55:1–11

Isaiah = ī-ZAY-uh

Despite the imperatives, the tone is like inviting hungry, homeless children to a feast.

Ignore the comma after "come."

Ask the questions sincerely, as if expecting an answer.

To be nourished, it is necessary to *heed* and *listen* to the Lord; speak those words not as commands but as calls to conversion. "That you may have life" is the heart of God's promise. Speak slower here.

"Him" refers to David. The nation will be restored.

A reading from the Book of the Prophet Isaiah

Thus says the LORD:
All you who are **thirsty**,
    come to the **water**!
You who have no **money**,
    come, receive **grain** and **eat**;
come, without **paying** and without **cost**,
    drink **wine** and **milk**!
Why spend your **money** for what is not **bread**,
    your **wages** for what **fails** to **satisfy**?
Heed me, and you shall eat **well**,
    you shall **delight** in rich fare.
Come to me **heedfully**,
    listen, that you may have **life**.
I will **renew** with you the everlasting **covenant**,
    the **benefits** assured to **David**.

In the final section God speaks directly to Jerusalem in tender, consoling words, ("O afflicted one") assuring the city she will be restored to her original grandeur. Deliver the lines as if to someone who needs reassurance that they are truly pardoned. God promises to restore the people like a worker rebuilds a fallen city but, remarkably, using glowing sapphires and fiery rubies instead of bricks. Jerusalem's children will be comforted and all their fears relieved.

This Easter liturgy invites us to see in Israel's return from exile every Christian's deliverance from the bondage of sin through Christ's Death and Resurrection. All tonight's texts speak of hope, renewal, and salvation. Proclaim with a passion that characterizes a God who offers precious stones as signs of divine love, a love more enduring than the mountains from which they are mined.

READING V   Ours are lives of yearning, of constant desire for what truly satisfies. Wealth, power, prominence, and other worldly aspirations are often the objects of our hunger. But through the prophet Isaiah, God urges us not to waste our time on illusory pursuits, the junk food of the spiritual life. Food that fails to satisfy and drink that numbs the senses but fails to calm the soul can be found on every corner. Only the table of the Lord offers true sustenance, and it is set and ready to receive us.

God speaks urgently in these lines: "You who are thirsty, come!. . . Come, without paying . . . delight in rich fare!" The language is direct; God calls us personally and invites those who've exhausted their "wages" (and their lives!) on "what fails to satisfy."

As I made him a **witness** to the peoples,
       a **leader** and commander of **nations**,
so shall you **summon** a nation you knew **not**,
       and nations that knew you not shall **run** to you,
because of the LORD, your **God**,
       the **Holy** One of Israel, who has **glorified** you.

Seek the LORD while he may be **found**,
       call him while he is **near**.
Let the **scoundrel** forsake his **way**,
       and the **wicked** man his **thoughts**;
let him turn to the LORD for **mercy**;
       to our **God**, who is **generous** in **forgiving**.
For **my** thoughts are not **your** thoughts,
       nor are **your** ways **my** ways, says the LORD.
As high as the **heavens** are above the **earth**,
       so high are **my** ways above **your** ways
       and **my** thoughts above **your** thoughts.

For just as from the **heavens**
       the **rain** and **snow** come down
and do not **return** there
       till they have **watered** the earth,
       making it **fertile** and **fruitful**,
giving **seed** to the one who **sows**
       and **bread** to the one who **eats**,
so shall my **word** be
       that goes **forth** from my **mouth**;
my word shall not **return** to me **void**,
       but shall do my **will**,
       achieving the end for which I **sent** it.

Renew your energy. Imagine those you are trying to persuade getting up to leave. Your words must stop and hold them.

This is not a condemnation, but an earnest call for conversion.

This section explains why God can be so "generous in forgiving": God's plans are not our plans; God's methods not our methods. Speak slowly, with great dignity.

This is an important teaching about the efficacy of the Word of God: it accomplishes what it sets out to do! Go slowly. This is a long comparison: just as rain and snow don't evaporate and return to the sky till after they have watered the earth, helping seed to grow and yielding bread for the hungry, the word that goes forth from God's mouth does not return without having accomplished the purpose for which it was sent. Speak with conviction and authority.

End with confidence on a note of joy.

As Israel's time of exile draws to an end, Isaiah pens this message of hope and restoration. God *will* give new life and restore the "benefits assured to David." God had made a covenant with David, and even the infidelity that brought exile upon the people could not nullify it. Promise after promise, express God's commitment to renew the nation. But first the people must start over, leave their faithless ways behind in the land of exile, and adopt *God's* ways. Insistently, God pleads with the people to abandon wrongdoing. Without stridency, but with great urgency, God is saying, "Do it now; do it while there is time, before it's too late! No one will be excluded; no one will be turned away." God's mercy embraces even the "scoundrel" and the "wicked" for the "thoughts" and "ways" of our merciful Lord are as different from ours as the earth is from the heavens.

This final section calls for the childlike quality Jesus said qualifies us for the Kingdom of Heaven. Children know their neediness and trust their parents to satisfy it. God asks for that same trust. God's word is effective, and accomplishes what God intends. God says it and it is! (Remember tonight's First Reading?) Embracing that notion requires deep faith—a leap into the darkness, convinced a net of mercy waits below. Genuine faith necessitates that we hear these offers of renewal not as things *hoped for* but as things *assured*. So speak with confidence. In tonight's liturgy, as in every liturgy, God's promise of rich fare is fulfilled beyond all expectation at the table of the Eucharist.

For meditation and context:

RESPONSORIAL PSALM   Isaiah 12:2–3, 4, 5–6 (3)

R. You will draw water joyfully from the springs of salvation.

God indeed is my savior;
    I am confident and unafraid.
My strength and my courage is the LORD,
    and he has been my savior.
With joy you will draw water
    at the fountain of salvation.

Give thanks to the LORD, acclaim his name;
    among the nations make known his deeds,
    proclaim how exalted is his name.

Sing praise to the LORD for his glorious
        achievement;
    let this be known throughout all the earth.
Shout with exultation, O city of Zion,
    for great in your midst
    is the Holy One of Israel!

READING VI   Baruch 3:9–15, 32—4:4

Baruch = buh-ROOK

This is exhortation motivated by love.

The five lines following: "How is it . . . ?" ask the question: Do you know why? The answer comes in the eighth line.

Here is the answer. The tone is: I'll *tell* you why! But love is still the motive.

Here you announce the better way: follow it and find peace! You are cajoling, exhorting, wanting to spur a change in behavior. There is a lilting cadence in these lines. Don't rush them. "Days" and "peace" can be sustained.

A reading from the Book of the Prophet Baruch

Hear, O Israel, the **commandments** of **life**:
    listen, and know **prudence**!
How **is** it, Israel,
    that you are in the **land** of your **foes**,
    grown **old** in a **foreign** land,
defiled with the **dead**,
    accounted with those **destined** for the **netherworld**?
You have **forsaken** the fountain of **wisdom**!
    Had you **walked** in the way of **God**,
    you would have **dwelt** in enduring **peace**.
Learn where **prudence** is,
    where **strength**, where **understanding**;
that you may know **also**
    where are length of **days**, and **life**,
    where light of the **eyes**, and **peace**.
Who has **found** the place of **wisdom**,
    who has **entered** into her **treasuries**?

READING VI   For Baruch the "commandments" and wisdom are integrally linked. Wisdom, he asserts, is found only by embracing the Law of the Lord. So obedience, not intellectualism, leads to wisdom. Forsaking the Law extinguishes the light of truth and opens the door to death, which for Israel took the form of exile in Babylon, "the land of [her] foes." The path back to grace and life is wisdom herself. Wisdom is personified as a woman, but more significantly, wisdom is identified with the *Law*, "the book of the precepts of God," that is, the commandments given by God as a gift.

In Scripture, God's Law is not a burden, but a blessing that teaches us God's ways. Following the Law pleases God, but it also saves us from (self) destruction, a critical truth Israel repeatedly ignored. The result was the tragic loss of Temple, monarchy, and nation. In rich poetry that's filled with intentional repetition, Baruch implores Israel to return to the Lord by taking up the book of the commandments and enshrining it within their hearts. In Christian faith, Jesus is the embodiment of wisdom, the true teacher of what pleases God. He pointed to the commandments as the path to life, the gauge of true discipleship. Spoken in love, Baruch's powerful words are less reprimand and more expressions of God's parental care.

A dramatic shift in mood occurs here. This is a poetic song of praise to Wisdom.

"The One" refers to the omnipotent God. You are retelling the story of creation. Utilize a faster, joyous tempo.

Let your voice ring with joy at God's goodness on "Such is our God!"

A new beat begins here; speak in a more sober tone. In the phrase "Given her," "her" refers to "understanding." "Jacob" and "Israel" represent the whole people.

"She has appeared on earth" refers to Wisdom, now personified as the book of the Law.

Contrast those who "live" and those who "die." Pause before the next line.

"Glory" refers to the Law; "privileges" to knowing and observing the Law. You are saying, "Don't throw away the riches you've been given." End on a note of joy and gratitude.

The One who knows all **things** knows **her**;
    he has **probed** her by his **knowledge**—
the One who established the **earth** for all **time**,
    and **filled** it with four-footed **beasts**;
    he who **dismisses** the light, and it **departs**,
    calls it, and it **obeys** him **trembling**;
before whom the **stars** at their posts
    shine and **rejoice**;
when he **calls** them, they answer, "Here we **are**!"
    shining with **joy** for their **Maker**.
Such is our **God**;
    no **other** is to be **compared** to him:
he has traced out the whole way of **understanding**,
    and has given her to **Jacob**, his **servant**,
    to **Israel**, his beloved **son**.

Since then she has **appeared** on earth,
    and **moved** among people.
She is the **book** of the **precepts** of **God**,
    the **law** that endures **forever**;
all who **cling** to her will **live**,
    but those will **die** who **forsake** her.
Turn, O Jacob, and **receive** her:
    walk by her **light** toward **splendor**.
Give not your **glory** to **another**,
    your **privileges** to an **alien** race.
Blessed are we, O Israel;
    for what **pleases** God is **known** to us!

Consider how parents might confront an errant child. Motivated by love, they might ask, "How did you get into this mess, living 'in the land of your foes'?" Then they might answer their own question: "You have forsaken the fountain of wisdom!" That's why you've lost your way! After a reprimand, good parents also point out the advantages of right behavior, giving hope that one can find help and change. Baruch has the instincts of a good parent. Then he follows his exhortation to "learn," with a song of praise to the God who sustains the world and all that's in it.

The questions "Who has found?" and "Who has entered?" are really assertions that God is the answer to all our questions. Speak them with an energy that signals you can't wait to answer them yourself. With joy and a quickened tempo describe the God who "established the earth . . . and filled it," whom the sun and the stars gladly obey. The luminous stars model the quality of your proclamation, "shining with joy for [your] maker."

The final section personifies wisdom as the book of the Law that was given to Jacob (the Hebrew people) and still graces the earth. Baruch states that clinging to God's Law yields life, while forsaking her brings death. Urgently encourage us to "receive her (and) walk by her light." By teaching us what pleases God, the Law frees us to rejoice and to recognize how "blessed" we are!

For meditation and context:

RESPONSORIAL PSALM   Psalm 19:8, 9, 10, 11 (John 6:68c)

R. Lord, you have the words of everlasting life.

The law of the LORD is perfect,
   refreshing the soul;
the decree of the LORD is trustworthy,
   giving wisdom to the simple.

The precepts of the LORD are right,
   rejoicing the heart;
the command of the LORD is clear,
   enlightening the eye.

The fear of the LORD is pure,
   enduring forever;
the ordinances of the LORD are true,
   all of them just.

They are more precious than gold,
   than a heap of purest gold;
sweeter also than syrup
   or honey from the comb.

Ezekiel = ee-ZEE-kee-uhl

READING VII   Ezekiel 36:16–17a, 18–28

A reading from the Book of the Prophet Ezekiel

The **word** of the LORD came to me, saying:
   Son of **man**, when the house of **Israel** lived in their **land**,
   they **defiled** it by their **conduct** and **deeds**.
Therefore I poured out my **fury** upon them
   because of the **blood** that they poured out on the **ground**,
   and because they **defiled** it with **idols**.
I **scattered** them among the **nations**,
   dispersing them over **foreign** lands;
   according to their **conduct** and **deeds** I judged them.
But when they came among the nations **wherever** they came,
   they served to **profane** my holy name,
   because it was said of them: "**These** are the people of the LORD,
   yet they had to **leave** their **land**."
So I have **relented** because of my holy **name**
   which the house of Israel **profaned**
   among the **nations** where they **came**.
Therefore **say** to the house of Israel: **Thus** says the Lord GOD:
   Not for **your** sakes do I act, house of Israel,
   but for the sake of my holy **name**,
   which you **profaned** among the nations to which you **came**.

"Their land" is the land of Israel. Ezekiel's tone is blunt. Don't dilute the anger. "Fury," "scattered," "dispersing," "judged," "profane"—are strong words that convey God's wrath. Let them work.

"Because of the blood" refers to idol worship.

The exile is God's punishment for Israel's infidelity.

But the punishment "backfired" because it gave God a bad name.

Speak the taunt in the voice of the foreigners.

Pause at the start of this new beat. Frustrated, God reluctantly adopts a new approach. Note "profaned among the nations" is repeated three times.

God must restore his "holy name."

READING VII | A covenant grants privileges and imposes responsibilities on both parties. God's covenant with Israel was simple: they were to keep the Law and the Lord would be their God. But when Israel was unfaithful, offering blood sacrifices to idols, God allowed them to reap the consequences of their choices, and the people were scattered among the nations. This well-deserved consequence of their idolatry, however, cast God in a negative light among the very nations where the Jews dispersed. They taunt the Chosen People saying, "These are the people of the Lord, yet they had to *leave* their land."

God's response takes on remarkably human characteristics through a literary device called anthropomorphism that ascribes to God qualities more appropriate to human beings. The talk among the nations has sullied God's reputation, so God must take action to restore it. It should be the people who safeguard God's good name, but it falls to the Lord to do it himself. The foreign nations interpret Israel's plight as God's abandonment of the covenant with Israel. They don't see a caring parent using "tough love" to discipline a disobedient child; they see only punishment and rejection. So, for the sake "of my holy name," God decides to relent and start anew with these stubborn children.

Except for the first line, only God speaks throughout this text. But, unlike Reading V where God beckons tenderly,

God's anger slowly yields to mercy and love. Speak this as a promise.

I will prove the **holiness** of my great name, **profaned** among
 the **nations**,
  in whose **midst** you have profaned it.
Thus the nations shall **know** that I am the Lord, says the
 Lord **God**,
  when in their sight I prove my **holiness** through **you**.
For I will take you **away** from among the nations,
 gather you from all the foreign **lands**,
  and bring you **back** to your **own** land.

The tone becomes more reassuring and loving here.

I will sprinkle **clean water** upon you
 to **cleanse** you from all your **impurities**,
  and from all your **idols** I will cleanse you.

God will purify the people. This is an important image of Baptism for tonight's liturgy.

I will give you a **new** heart and place a new **spirit** within you,
 taking from your bodies your **stony** hearts
  and giving you **natural** hearts.

Make eye contact. This is a classic and memorable line. Speak slowly and sincerely.

I will put my **spirit** within you and make you live by my **statutes**,
 careful to observe my **decrees**.
You shall live in the land I gave your **fathers**;
 you shall be my **people**, and **I** will be your **God**.

Imagine saying this to a child you love to ensure the child's success and prosperity. "You shall be . . . I will be your God" should be spoken like a spouse vowing fidelity.

RESPONSORIAL PSALM Psalm 42:3, 5; 43:3, 4 (2)

For meditation and context:

R. Like a deer that longs for running streams, my soul longs for you, my God.

Athirst is my soul for God, the living God.
 When shall I go and behold the face
  of God?

I went with the throng
 and led them in procession to the house
  of God,
amid loud cries of joy and thanksgiving,
 with the multitude keeping festival.

Or:

Send forth your light and your fidelity;
 they shall lead me on
and bring me to your holy mountain,
 to your dwelling-place.

Then will I go in to the altar of God,
 the God of my gladness and joy;
then will I give you thanks upon the harp,
 O God, my God!

> **TO KEEP IN MIND**
> **Eye contact** is your means of connecting with those to whom you minister. You should look at the assembly during the middle and at the end of every thought or sentence.

here God is furious because the people have "defiled" the land through idol worship. This text adds an important piece to Scripture's mosaic image of God: God is capable of righteous anger, not just tender love. Making good use of words like "fury," "scattered," "dispersing," "judged," and "profane" will help you convey that truth.

 Halfway through the text, God orders the prophet to announce God's change of heart. But God must be clear on the reasons why. Three times God says the holy

name was "profaned among the nations." The repetitions betray concern that the people have not really learned their lesson and may soon forget the exile. So, God says, "Not for *your* sakes do I act," but to restore my reputation; though it looks like mercy, I do this to correct the false impression that I failed to be your God and your protector.

 But soon we sense that mercy will prevail and love will trump the call of justice. God will cleanse the people, change

them at their core, giving them new hearts—made of flesh, not stone. Mercy triumphs as we hoped. It always does—unless we just reject it. When finally we hear the tender "you will be my people and I will be your God" we know God has not only saved his "name" but also his people, who now will be empowered to keep God's statutes back home "in the land (of their) fathers."

For meditation and context:

RESPONSORIAL PSALM   Isaiah 12:2–3, 4bcd, 5–6 (3)

R. You will draw water joyfully from the springs of salvation.

God indeed is my savior;
    I am confident and unafraid.
My strength and my courage is the LORD,
    and he has been my savior.
With joy you will draw water
    at the fountain of salvation.

Give thanks to the LORD, acclaim his name;
    among the nations make known his deeds,
    proclaim how exalted is his name.

Sing praise to the LORD for his glorious
        achievement;
    let this be known throughout all the earth.
Shout with exultation, O city of Zion,
    for great in your midst
    is the Holy One of Israel!

Or:

For meditation and context:

RESPONSORIAL PSALM   Psalm 51:12–13, 14–15, 18–19 (12a)

R. Create a clean heart in me, O God.

A clean heart create for me, O God,
    and a steadfast spirit renew within me.
Cast me not out from your presence,
    and your Holy Spirit take not from me.

Give me back the joy of your salvation,
    and a willing spirit sustain in me.
I will teach transgressors your ways,
    and sinners shall return to you.

For you are not pleased with sacrifices;
    should I offer a holocaust, you would not
        accept it.
My sacrifice, O God, is a contrite spirit;
    a heart contrite and humbled, O God, you
        will not spurn.

TO KEEP IN MIND
Know the purpose of the letter: *It* dictates the tone. Often Paul is the writer. As teacher and spiritual leader, he is motivated by multiple concerns: to instruct, console, encourage, chastise, warn, settle disputes, and more. When reading from one of his letters, be aware of what he's trying to accomplish.

READING VIII   Romans 6:3–11

A reading from the Letter of Saint Paul to the Romans

Brothers and sisters:
Are you **unaware** that we who were **baptized** into Christ **Jesus**
    were baptized into his **death**?
We were indeed **buried** with him through baptism into **death**,
    so that, just as Christ was **raised** from the dead
    by the glory of the **Father**,
    we too might live in **newness** of **life**.

Paul's literary device is a rhetorical question. Let it sound like a question. Make eye contact with the assembly and speak as directly as Paul writes.

Work to make Paul's point explicit: what happened to Christ will happen to us. He died and was buried, then rose. We die and are buried in Baptism; we, too, will rise to new life.

READING VIII   The first seven readings carried us through salvation history; Paul now projects us into our future, reflecting on the implications of Christ's Death and Resurrection for all people and for all time. Paul's grand proclamation tonight is that our lives follow the pattern of the life of Jesus.

What happened to Christ happens to us; what's true of him is true of us—he died, we die; he rose, we rise. The life of the Christian is fully and inexorably connected to that of Christ.

Baptism is a once-in-a-lifetime initiation; but transformation into the likeness of Christ takes a lifetime. So Paul asks, "Are you not aware" that you are now living an entirely new life in Christ? Your old self died and was buried with him. His victory is our victory because through Baptism we experienced death and burial with Christ. But there's also an important difference: while our risen life has *begun* here on earth, it won't be *fully* realized till after death. In this life, we struggle with temptation and endure the consequences of sin. But though we sin, Paul reminds us we are no longer *slaves* of sin. There is no better day than this to claim the freedom (through forgiveness) that we received by dying with Christ in Baptism!

In a different text you'd want to contrast the words "death" and "buried" with "raised" and "new life," but not here. Here, death and burial don't carry a negative connotation because death is the *way* to life. Paul presents a series of balanced ideas that require careful contrast spoken in a tone that's hopeful and upbeat: "If we have grown into union with him through a *death*

Paul develops his idea: we were made one with Christ by sharing a death like his (Baptism); so we also will be made one with him by experiencing Resurrection.
Speak "We know" with conviction and good eye contact.

Don't let this sound redundant. Sustain your energy. Remember: "Died" and "live" are *both* spoken with a positive attitude.

"We know" means "we are *convinced*!"

"Dies no more . . . death no longer has power . . ." is the same idea stated twice: the greater stress goes to the second statement.

Balance the words "his death" and "his life."

Make eye contact with the assembly. We are *dead* to sin, but *alive* in Christ! Announce this joyfully!

For meditation and context:

For if we have grown into union with him through a **death** like his,
we shall also be **united** with him in the **resurrection**.
We know that our **old** self was **crucified** with him,
so that our **sinful** body might be done **away** with,
that we might no longer be in **slavery** to sin.
For a **dead** person has been **absolved** from sin.
If, then, we have **died** with Christ,
we believe that we shall also **live** with him.
We know that **Christ**, **raised** from the dead, dies no **more**;
death no longer has **power** over him.
As to his **death**, he died to sin **once** and for **all**;
as to his **life**, he lives for **God**.
Consequently, you **too** must think of yourselves as being **dead** to **sin**
and **living** for **God** in Christ **Jesus**.

RESPONSORIAL PSALM   Psalm 118:1–2, 16–17, 22–23

R. Alleluia, alleluia, alleluia.

Give thanks to the LORD, for he is good,
    for his mercy endures forever.
Let the house of Israel say,
    "His mercy endures forever."

The right hand of the LORD has struck
    with power;
    the right hand of the LORD is exalted.
I shall not die, but live,
    and declare the works of the LORD.

The stone which the builders rejected
    has become the cornerstone.
By the LORD has this been done;
    it is wonderful in our eyes.

TO KEEP IN MIND
Importance of the Narrator:
The narrator is often the pivotal role of a passage. Timbre, pitch, rate, and energy can make the same words convey very different moods or meaning. Sometimes the narrator is objective, but often the narrator has great interest in the events and characters of a story.

---

like his, we shall also be united with him in the *resurrection.*"

There's no lack of joy as Paul announces what "we *know*": that freedom and new life are available to all who believe. Paul uses strong, declarative sentences to present a series of important ideas in quick succession. "Christ . . . dies no more, . . . he died to sin once and for all . . . he lives for God!" Can you match his obvious enthusiasm in your oral delivery?

Paul melds instruction and exhortation into the final line. Proclaim your own faith and give thanks for the new life you've

received in Christ as you speak Paul's words. Today, we the Church celebrate Resurrection. And darkness flees the dawning of the light!

GOSPEL   A God like a mother birthing a world, a father willing to surrender an only son, a people in flight thrust into a new world by the labor pains of slavery and the hope of freedom, a God who is a lover wooing back his estranged "wife," God's love falling like rain on a thirsty earth, wisdom walking among us

wearing the robes of Law and justice, and stony hearts cleansed and melted into flesh: all this leads to an empty tomb, a tomb with slippery fingers that could not hold its occupant. What a bold, dramatic climax to a bold and climactic night!

Matthew's is the most spectacular Resurrection account. Unlike Mark's telling, this is not a tale of weary women looking for their Lord. God intervenes immediately, before the women see the empty tomb. The earth quakes, a huge stone rolls easily, an angel flashes like lightning, and soldiers freeze in fear. And the women's grief slowly

GOSPEL   Matthew 28:1–10

A reading from the holy Gospel according to Matthew

After the **sabbath**, as the first day of the week was **dawning**,
  Mary **Magdalene** and the **other** Mary came to see the **tomb**.
And **behold**, there was a great **earthquake**;
  for an **angel** of the Lord descended from **heaven**,
  approached, rolled back the **stone**, and **sat** upon it.
His appearance was like **lightning**
  and his clothing was white as **snow**.
The guards were **shaken** with fear of him
  and became like **dead** men.
Then the angel said to the **women** in reply,
  "Do not be **afraid**!
I know that you are seeking **Jesus** the **crucified**.
He is not **here**, for he has been **raised** just as he **said**.
Come and **see** the place where he lay.
Then go **quickly** and tell his **disciples**,
  'He has been **raised** from the dead,
  and he is going before you to **Galilee**;
  there you will **see** him.'
  Behold, I have **told** you."
Then they went away **quickly** from the tomb,
  fearful yet **overjoyed**,
  and ran to **announce** this to his disciples.
And behold, **Jesus** met them on their way and **greeted** them.
They **approached**, embraced his **feet**, and did him **homage**.
Then Jesus said to them, "Do not be **afraid**.
Go tell my **brothers** to go to **Galilee**,
  and there they will **see** me."

Take note of the proper observance of sabbath rest.

The opening mood is somber.

Suddenly, the mood shifts. These are grand events manifesting divine intervention.

Picture the women watching in awe. The image of the angel is striking.

The shock must have been great to knock out these soldiers.

Speak with calm assurance.

The angel invites them into the tomb that they might believe.

There is urgency in the angel's voice for this good news must be told!

Sustain the energy and urgency of the previous section.

Everything halts with the appearance of Jesus. Pause after "behold."

Speak with a tone that explains why Jesus chose these women to be the first witnesses of the Resurrection.

blooms into joy. The preparatory drama fits the dramatic development about to unfold.

You begin with the somber mood of the two Marys as they wend their way to the tomb. "Behold" shifts the mood and sparks excitement. A terrifying power grips the hill and the soldiers faint with fear. Though they don't run, the women need assurance from the angel who calms them, and then shares the amazing news they had not dared to hope. When he beckons them into the tomb, when he sends them to the disciples, the angel's voice is full of urgency that this Good News be quickly spread. So, joyfully, they run, though still shaken by the awesome presence of the angel and his wondrous news.

The women run head-on into an even greater shock: Jesus, alive and standing before them, and they, the first witnesses of the Resurrection. As you describe their instant response, your tone can suggest the unleashing of emotions that were welling up in them since the angel's appearance. "They approached, embraced his feet" sounds like a wave rushing down upon Jesus. "And did him homage" is slower and quieter, like the wave gently receding.

In his final sentences, Jesus calms and commissions, telling them to "go," but assuring them they will "see" him. His voice erases their fear and propels them down the hillside. Your voice rings with conviction that we, too, will see him.

EASTER SUNDAY OF THE RESURRECTION OF THE LORD

LECTIONARY #42

READING I   Acts of the Apostles 10:34a, 37–43

A reading from the Acts of the Apostles

Peter proceeded to **speak** and said:
   "You know what has **happened** all over **Judea**,
   beginning in **Galilee** after the **baptism**
   that **John** preached,
   how God **anointed** Jesus of **Nazareth**
   with the Holy **Spirit** and **power**.
He went about doing **good**
   and **healing** all those oppressed by the **devil**,
   for **God** was with him.
We are **witnesses** of all that he did
   both in the country of the **Jews** and in **Jerusalem**.
They put him to **death** by hanging him on a **tree**.
This man God **raised** on the **third** day and granted
    that he be **visible**,
   not to **all** the people, but to **us**,
   the witnesses **chosen** by God in **advance**,
   who **ate** and **drank** with him **after** he rose from the dead.
He **commissioned** us to **preach** to the people
   and **testify** that **he** is the one appointed by God
   as **judge** of the **living** and the **dead**.
To him all the **prophets** bear witness,
   that everyone who **believes** in him
   will receive **forgiveness** of **sins** through his **name**."

Except for the first six words, the entire reading is spoken in the voice of Peter. Rhetorical questions are a device meant to capture the listener's attention. Remember, Peter is making a public address.

Galilee = GAL-ih-lee; Nazareth = NAZ-uh-reth

"Spirit" and "power" are important characteristics of Jesus's ministry.

Jesus's healing ministry and exorcisms are important signs of who he is. Don't rush any of this first paragraph.

Pause to establish eye contact. "Peter is saying, "I was there!" There is a personal, intimate quality to this entire text.

Talk of Jesus's Crucifixion is followed immediately by talk of his Resurrection. Pause after "tree," then maintain an upbeat tone for the rest of the paragraph.

Speak "the witnesses chosen by God" in a humble tone. This emphasizes Peter's credibility.

"Preach" and "testify" will sound redundant unless you build energy from one to the other.

Employ ritardando (gradual slowing toward the end) on "through his name."

There are options for readings today. Ask your parish staff which ones will be used.

READING I   All creation is reborn with the new Adam who rises from the tomb. During the next fifty days as we move toward Pentecost, we will contemplate the post-Easter manifestations of Jesus, the meaning of his Death and Resurrection in our own lives, and our call to be Christ's body through which he continues to touch human pain and heal broken hearts.

A more confident and articulate Peter than we are used to weaves all these themes into the address he delivers to the household of the new convert Cornelius. Peter's confidence is rooted in what he later asserts: he has witnessed everything he describes. What he preaches is a basic catechism of early Christian faith that begins with a review of Jesus's earthly ministry. First, he recalls the baptism and Jesus's anointing with "the Holy Spirit and power." Second he clarifies why power was given to Jesus—not to lord it over anyone, but to concretely manifest God's love by doing good, by healing, and by driving out demons. Peter knows this is true. He saw it!

The fact that Peter and the Apostles "are witnesses" to the healing ministry of Jesus assures Luke's audience that what they hear proclaimed accurately reflects what Jesus himself preached. This is no minor issue for the infant Church (or for us who follow them), so work hard to bring these points to our attention.

Then Peter directly takes on the scandal of Jesus's ignominious Death, speaking without melancholy or embarrassment. And he can do that because he knows how

155

For meditation and context:

TO KEEP IN MIND

Always read Scriptures aloud, noting suggestions for stresses and pauses. After several readings, alter the stress markings to suit your style and interpretation.

Colossians = kuh-LOSH-uhnz

This short text requires slow reading.

"If then you were raised" means "*because* you were raised."

The tone is firm, yet encouraging.

Tell us two things: who will appear and what will happen.

TO KEEP IN MIND

Slow down: The larger the church, the larger the assembly, and the more complex the text, the slower you must read.

RESPONSORIAL PSALM   Psalm 118:1–2, 16–17, 22–23 (24)

R. This is the day the Lord has made; let us rejoice and be glad.
or
R. Alleluia.

Give thanks to the LORD, for he is good,
    for his mercy endures forever.
Let the house of Israel say,
    "His mercy endures forever."

"The right hand of the LORD has struck
        with power;
    the right hand of the LORD is exalted.
I shall not die, but live,
    and declare the works of the LORD.

The stone which the builders rejected
    has become the cornerstone.
By the LORD has this been done;
    it is wonderful in our eyes.

READING II   Colossians 3:1–4

A reading from the Letter of Saint Paul to the Colossians

Brothers and sisters:
If then you were **raised** with Christ, seek what is **above**,
    where Christ is **seated** at the right hand of **God**.
Think of what is **above**, not of what is on **earth**.
For you have **died**, and your life is **hidden** with Christ in **God**.
When Christ your life **appears**,
    then you too will appear with him in **glory**.

Or:

the story ends: God raised the man, Jesus from the dead! This, too, he knows from experience. Without pride, Peter asserts his credibility by claiming to be among the few privileged to see the risen Christ, a claim he concretizes by insisting they "*ate* and *drank* with him" after the Resurrection. Finally, Peter claims he and the others were commissioned by Jesus to "preach the gospel." Though he stresses future divine judgment (an important aspect of early preaching to pagans), Peter ends with his most hopeful message by recalling the words of the

prophets that promise forgiveness of sins to everyone "who believes in him."

READING II **COLOSSIANS 3.** Great spiritual and theological riches can be found in this brief passage! Short readings require more effort from the reader because every word counts. Jesus has not risen alone: we, who have died with him in Baptism, have also risen to new life! That is Easter's declaration. Besides celebrating a historical event, Easter announces the ever-present, mysterious reality that we "were raised *with* Christ."

But Easter also reminds us we must never take that reality for granted. Faith is not magic. It always requires that we respond to God's generous initiative. Paul insists there is something *we* must do and we must do it *now*: "seek what is above." In other words, put our sinful ways behind us and embrace the risen life we've begun to live, even if only partially, here in this life. Paul contrasts what "is on earth"—material things and passing concerns—with the spiritual values to which we aspire. "For you have died, and your life is hidden with Christ in God" tells a double truth: we

Corinthians = kohr-IN-thee-uhnz

This short text requires slow reading.

Listeners are expected to know the answer to the rhetorical question. Pause before giving the following command.

You will become a batch of "unleavened," that is, uncorrupted, dough.

Be more energetic on the second "yeast" clause. Use ritardando (gradual slowing toward the end) on the phrase "of sincerity and truth."

For meditation and context:

TO KEEP IN MIND

Units of Thought: Running too many words together blurs meaning and fails to distinguish ideas. Punctuation does not always indicate clearly what words to group together or where to pause. Identify *units of thought* and use your voice to distinguish one from another.

READING II   1 Corinthians 5:6b–8

A reading from the first Letter of Saint Paul to the Corinthians

Brothers and sisters:
Do you not **know** that a little **yeast** leavens **all** the dough?
Clear out the **old** yeast,
    so that you may become a **fresh** batch of dough,
    inasmuch as you are **unleavened**.
For our paschal **lamb**, **Christ**, has been **sacrificed**.
Therefore, let us **celebrate** the feast,
    not with the **old** yeast, the yeast of **malice** and **wickedness**,
    but with the **unleavened** bread of **sincerity** and **truth**.

SEQUENCE   Victimae paschali laudes

Christians, to the Paschal Victim
    Offer your thankful praises!
A Lamb the sheep redeems;
    Christ, who only is sinless,
    Reconciles sinners to the Father.
Death and life have contended in that
      combat stupendous:
    The Prince of life, who died, reigns
    immortal.

Speak, Mary, declaring
    What you saw, wayfaring.
"The tomb of Christ, who is living,
    The glory of Jesus' resurrection;
Bright angels attesting,
    The shroud and napkin resting.
Yes, Christ my hope is arisen;
    to Galilee he goes before you."
Christ indeed from death is risen, our new
      life obtaining.
    Have mercy, victor King, ever reigning!
    Amen. Alleluia.

already are living the risen life of the Kingdom, but not fully. There is joy but also moral imperative in those words—if we want to be ready when Christ comes!

Twice Paul uses the word "appears" to suggest coming glory and to pique our eagerness for it. Perhaps you can do the same if, instead of visualizing the "glory," you envision him whom Paul poignantly calls our "life."

I CORINTHIANS 5. This passage presents Eucharistic images. Because yeast causes fermentation, it serves as a natural symbol for anything that spreads, whether good or evil. Mindful that even those who have surrendered to Christ can succumb to corrupting influences, Paul uses yeast as a symbol to warn about the potential spread of wickedness within the human heart and even within the Christian community. Significantly, within the community of Christians at Corinth there was an individual who was spreading harmful errors.

For his imagery, Paul draws on Jewish custom that required that every crumb of leavened bread in the house be removed before the Passover so that no trace of the old could corrupt the new. Paul wants the Corinthians to be just as scrupulous about removing the old leaven of "malice and wickedness" from their hearts and calls on them to celebrate the feast with the unleavened bread (that is, bread that has *no* yeast) of "sincerity and truth." Here's his logic: even a pinch of old yeast pollutes the loaf, so celebrate with something new that's worthy of the feast! For us, Christ is the unleavened bread at this and at every celebration. By eating this bread we gain strength to resist the spread of evil within

GOSPEL   John 20:1–9

A reading from the holy Gospel according to John

On the **first** day of the **week**,
  Mary of **Magdala** came to the **tomb** early in the **morning**,
  while it was still **dark**,
  and saw the **stone removed** from the tomb.
So she **ran** and went to Simon **Peter**
  and to the **other** disciple whom Jesus **loved**, and told them,
  "They have taken the **Lord** from the **tomb**,
  and we don't know **where** they **put** him."
So **Peter** and the **other** disciple went **out** and came to the **tomb**.
They both **ran**, but the **other** disciple ran **faster** than Peter
  and arrived at the tomb **first**;
  he **bent** down and saw the **burial** cloths there, but did not go **in**.
When Simon **Peter** arrived **after** him,
  he went **into** the tomb and saw the **burial** cloths there,
  and the cloth that had covered his **head**,
  not with the **burial** cloths but rolled up in a **separate** place.
Then the **other** disciple **also** went in,
  the one who had arrived at the tomb **first**,
  and he **saw** and **believed**.
For they did not yet **understand** the Scripture
  that he had to **rise** from the **dead**.

The images are still of death and darkness. Speak of Mary in a way that conveys the mood with which she approached the tomb: weary and greatly saddened.

Magdala = MAG-duh-luh. Slowly; the mood is a bit melancholy.

Communicate Mary's obvious distress both as you narrate her seeking out Peter and in her dialogue.

Again, let your narration convey their frantic and impulsive response; but let Peter and John do the racing, not you.

Peter's arrival brings action back into the scene. He *enters*, *sees*, and *examines*.

John's entry into the tomb reintroduces mystery and awe. "He saw and believed" is John's climactic statement of faith. Pause before speaking, giving John a chance to be touched by the reality of the Resurrection.

This statement contains no trace of admonishment. It is understandable that they wouldn't yet fully "understand."

us. On this day of great rejoicing, no anger or judgment should color these words of exhortation, only sincere joy.

 GOSPEL   In John's telling, Mary Madgdalene experiences the shock of Easter alone, without the other women at her side. There is no angel heralding news of Resurrection, only an empty tomb that looks more like the work of conspirators than a miracle. In that early morning hour shadows of Good Friday still linger. The sober mood gives no hint of the dramatic reversal that will soon unfold. The

open-mouthed tomb and the massive stone beside it are sure evidence to Mary of foul play. So she does the only thing she can— she runs to the disciples. Signs of Peter's leadership surface twice in this brief text, and the first is Mary's choice to go to him and "the other disciple whom Jesus loved" (most likely John) to share her news.

The two react immediately and race to the tomb without alerting others. The younger John arrives sooner, but deferentially waits for Peter to go in first—another sign that Peter has already assumed a clear

preeminence within the apostolic brotherhood. John's peering into the tomb while waiting for the slower (older) Peter to arrive and enter deserves clear emphasis.

The details narrated after Peter's entrance in the tomb signal his dawning realization that the carefully "rolled up" cloth negates the possibility that grave robbers or even the authorities stole the body.

The other disciple (carefully identified as the one who "arrived at the tomb first") finally enters the tomb. John says simply that he "saw" and "believed," something not yet attested of Peter, the leader.

AFTERNOON GOSPEL   Luke 24:13–35

A reading from the holy Gospel according to Luke

That **very** day, the **first** day of the week,
    two of Jesus' **disciples** were going
    to a village seven **miles** from Jerusalem called **Emmaus**,
    and they were **conversing** about all the things that
        had **occurred**.
And it **happened** that while they were **conversing** and **debating**,
    Jesus **himself** drew near and **walked** with them,
    but their **eyes** were **prevented** from **recognizing** him.
He asked them,
    "What are you **discussing** as you walk along?"
They **stopped**, looking **downcast**.
One of them, named **Cleopas**, said to him in **reply**,
    "Are you the **only** visitor to Jerusalem
    who does not **know** of the things
    that have taken **place** there in these days?"
And he replied to them, "What **sort** of things?"
They **said** to him,
    "The things that happened to **Jesus** the **Nazarene**,
    who was a **prophet** mighty in **deed** and **word**
    before **God** and all the **people**,
    how our chief **priests** and **rulers** both handed him over
    to a sentence of **death** and **crucified** him.
But we were hoping that he would be the one to **redeem** Israel;
    and **besides** all this,
    it is now the **third** day since this took place.
Some **women** from our group, however, have **astounded** us:
    they were at the **tomb** early in the **morning**
    and did not find his **body**;
    they came back and reported
    that they had indeed seen a **vision** of **angels**
    who announced that he was **alive**.

The "day" of this occurrence is important. Emmaus = eh-MAY-uhs

Let your tone convey the irony of their failure to recognize the very one they're discussing.

Jesus is "playing dumb."

Cleopas = KLEE-oh-puhs. He responds with annoyance.

Jesus coaxes further. Initially their response might sound like: "How could you not know this?" But soon they are into the story.

We can't help but feel sorry for them and their sense of loss.

Are they dismissing the testimony because it came from women?

They just can't add two and two: the tomb was empty, angels announced his rising, this still does not add up to Resurrection.

Jesus's emotion is real: frustration and some sadness.

Whether it was the carefully folded cloths or something else that sparked his faith, we cannot say. But actually John believes without really seeing, for it will be Mary who first lays eyes on the risen Lord. But if John has just "believed," why does John say they did not yet understand "he had to rise from the dead"? Often, belief comes in stages. We witness the impossible, then later we wonder if what we saw was real. The truth of the Resurrection is not apprehended all at once. So the explanatory closing sentence is not judgmental because it speaks with present joyful faith about a previous (and reasonable) lack of understanding.

AFTERNOON GOSPEL This Gospel text is one of the truly paradigmatic Christian stories. It tells the tale of two disciples who meet the risen Jesus; but it's also the story of all of us who long to see the risen Lord and think we walk our road alone only to realize later that the Lord was walking by our side all along, and we failed to recognize him.

The hoped-for Messiah was betrayed by a trusted friend and executed in the most shameful way. So the two disciples make their way back home leaving behind the events of the Passion and all the hopes and dreams they had pinned on Jesus. They long for him and yet, when he approaches, they do not recognize him. Jesus plays dumb and coaxes them into telling him his own story, and then marvels at their lack of faith, their ignorance, and their inability to see in the very story they've just told the outlines of the One who stands before them.

New beat. Don't rush.

"Then some of those with us **went** to the tomb
　and found things **just** as the women had **described**,
　　but **him** they did not **see**."
And he said to them, "Oh, how **foolish** you are!
How **slow** of heart to believe all that the **prophets** spoke!
Was it not **necessary** that the Christ should **suffer** these things
　and enter into his **glory**?"

They plead with him to stay!

Then beginning with **Moses** and all the **prophets**,
　he **interpreted** to them what **referred** to him
　　in all the **Scriptures**.
As they approached the **village** to which they were **going**,
　he gave the impression that he was going on **farther**.
But they **urged** him, "**Stay** with us,
　for it is nearly **evening** and the day is almost **over**."
So he went in to **stay** with them.

Slowly narrate this Eucharistic scene. Pause after "gave it to them."

And it **happened** that, while he was with them at **table**,
　he took **bread**, said the **blessing**,
　　broke it, and **gave** it to them.

Try the line this way: "With that (pause) their eyes were open . . . ." Speak with energy and awe.

With **that** their eyes were **opened** and they **recognized** him,
　but he **vanished** from their **sight**.
Then they **said** to each other,
　"Were not our **hearts burning** within us
　while he **spoke** to us on the way and opened the **Scriptures**
　　to us?"

Use a quickened pace here, but keep it natural and realistic.

So they set out at **once** and returned to **Jerusalem**
　where they found gathered **together**
　the **eleven** and those with them who were saying,
　"The Lord has **truly** been **raised** and has appeared to **Simon**!"

Remember, this is a story. Tell it as if for the first time, with enthusiasm and suspense.

Then the **two** recounted
　what had taken **place** on the way
　and how he was made **known** to them in the **breaking** of **bread**.

Speak with great reverence and awareness of the significance of these lines. Use ritardando (slowing toward the end) when you speak "in the breaking of the bread."

They report everything—Jesus's powerful preaching, his arrest and Crucifixion, the women's report of the empty tomb and visions of angels, and the men's confirmation of what the women announced. And to all that Jesus says, "Oh, how foolish you are!" How could they have experienced and seen and heard so much and yet have so little faith?

　　Ever the teacher, Jesus again becomes the rabbi as he accompanies them to Emmaus, explaining the Scriptures all the while. They still don't know who he is, but they know they don't want to lose him, so when Jesus pretends he is going further, they coax him into staying. He gathers them at table, a familiar setting for him and his friends, where he *takes*, *blesses*, and *breaks*—unmistakable Eucharistic language. And suddenly their eyes are opened. And just as fast, he's gone. But they don't go looking for their elusive Lord. They are still so filled with his presence that they barely notice his departure. Their burning hearts convince them that their whole journey to Emmaus had been blessed with his presence. And they know they will never be without it again. That awareness propels them back to Jerusalem where they tell the disciples what they already know. In all of Scripture, there is no more important ecclesiological line than the one that ends this text: they knew him "in the breaking of the bread."

SECOND SUNDAY OF EASTER (OR SUNDAY OF DIVINE MERCY)

LECTIONARY #43

READING I Acts of the Apostles 2:42–47

A reading from the Acts of the Apostles

They **devoted** themselves
    to the **teaching** of the apostles and to the **communal** life,
    to the **breaking** of **bread** and to the **prayers**.
Awe came upon everyone,
    and many **wonders** and **signs** were done through the apostles.
All who believed were **together** and had all things in **common**;
    they would **sell** their property and possessions
    and **divide** them among all according to each one's **need**.
Every **day** they devoted themselves
    to **meeting** together in the **temple** area
    and to breaking **bread** in their **homes**.
They ate their meals with **exultation** and **sincerity** of heart,
    praising God and enjoying favor with all the people.
And every day the Lord **added** to their number those who were
    being **saved**.

The three most significant attributes of the community are named immediately. Be ready to give them proper stress.

Speak this with reverence for this blessed community.

Here is explanation of two of the three practices mentioned above.

Save your strongest emphasis for the reference to breaking bread.

Again, speak with humility and reverence about what God was accomplishing among them.

TO KEEP IN MIND
Careful preparation expresses your reverence for the Word.

READING I This text makes many today long for the harmonious lifestyle of the Christian community described here. Of course, this is not a complete picture of the early Christian community, but we tell one story at a time, and here it's a story of a very blessed period when extraordinary commitment and unity characterized the life of the infant Church. It's not uncommon that a special grace is given at the beginning of some grand movement, and clearly the power of the Spirit was evident among these believers, not only through the "many wonders and signs," but through this remarkable harmony that manifested God's presence.

Speaking of these early ancestors in faith is something like telling family here at home about relatives in a foreign country you visited for the first time. If the local family gathered to hear about the daily life and customs of their foreign cousins, you would eagerly share the warm memories that fill your mind and paint an ideal picture of those faraway relatives.

A similar warmth and enthusiasm should distinguish your description of the early Christian community. This orphaned Church, sorely missing their Lord, is thriving nonetheless. But while an observer would surely be impressed with them, they are far from impressed with themselves and don't view their lifestyle as the least bit heroic. The focus of their lives is threefold. First is the teaching of the Apostles—the bedrock foundation of their faith because the Apostles are a direct link to Jesus. Second is community living in common, that is, they share their material resources so that all are cared for and none is in need. And finally, they gather to break bread, the Eucharistic meal, shared in memory of

For meditation and context:

RESPONSORIAL PSALM   Psalm 118:2–4, 13–15, 22–24 (1)

R. Give thanks to the Lord for he is good, his love is everlasting.
or
R. Alleluia.

Let the house of Israel say,
  "His mercy endures forever."
Let the house of Aaron say,
  "His mercy endures forever."
Let those who fear the LORD say,
  "His mercy endures forever."

I was hard pressed and was falling,
  but the LORD helped me.
My strength and my courage is the LORD,
  and he has been my savior.
The joyful shout of victory
  in the tents of the just.

The stone which the builders rejected
  has become the cornerstone.
By the LORD has this been done;
  it is wonderful in our eyes.
This is the day the LORD has made;
  let us be glad and rejoice in it.

TO KEEP IN MIND
Posture speaks: Make sure it says what you want it to. Don't let your face or body contradict the good news you announce. Remember, readers are allowed to smile!

READING II   1 Peter 1:3–9

A reading from the first Letter of Saint Peter

Blessed be the **God** and **Father** of our Lord Jesus **Christ**,
    who in his great **mercy** gave us a new **birth** to a living **hope**
    through the **resurrection** of Jesus Christ from the **dead**,
    to an inheritance that is **imperishable**, **undefiled**, and **unfading**,
    kept in **heaven** for you
    who by the **power** of God are safeguarded through **faith**,
    to a **salvation** that is ready to be **revealed** in the final time.
In this you **rejoice**, although now for a **little** while
    you may have to **suffer** through various **trials**,
    so that the **genuineness** of your faith,
    more precious than **gold** that is **perishable** even though
        tested by **fire**,
    may prove to be for **praise**, **glory**, and **honor**
    at the revelation of Jesus **Christ**.
Although you have not **seen** him you **love** him;
    even though you do not see him **now** yet **believe** in him,
    you **rejoice** with an **indescribable** and **glorious** joy,
    as you attain the **goal** of your faith, the **salvation** of your **souls**.

This is the first of the six weeks we read from 1 Peter. Stress his name.

Don't rush this short reading. Begin with conviction and joy.

You're still speaking about the "new birth."

Though he speaks of rejoicing and suffering, the dominant theme is rejoicing.

This is the value of suffering; don't rush past it.

There is profound truth here. Be sure to fix a clear image of Jesus in your mind as you proclaim the lines.

Jesus. And because they are observant Jews, they also continue to frequent the Temple, faithfully observing Jewish prayer ritual.

Surely the warmth and peace within the community helped it to grow "every day." As you describe the life of our relatives in faith, make us long for that same oneness in spirit that increased the numbers of those "being saved."

READING II   We may not recognize the fine orator who speaks these lines as the same man who, in the

Gospel accounts, is more often a bumbling fisherman. For the next six weeks we'll be reading from Peter rather than Paul, so be sure to highlight Peter's name when announcing "A reading from . . . ." Peter's name evokes the image of an elder statesman, highly regarded because of his leadership role and his close personal association with Jesus.

The text begins with a very long and complex sentence that has a very poetic, almost song-like feel. Make the opening line your own prayer of praise and thanks to God, the God who has also given *you* "new

birth." What follows elaborates on the new birth—it came through the Resurrection of Jesus and it gives us access to "an inheritance" that won't perish or fade away. This birth is "kept in heaven" for us who are being protected by faith for our day of salvation. That's a lot of ideas to sustain and keep connected.

In a single breath, Peter speaks of rejoicing and suffering trials. There is no great dichotomy for him because suffering leads to a purified and genuine faith that leads to glory. So don't color those sentences in negative tones. The last sentence

GOSPEL   John 20:19–31

A reading from the holy Gospel according to John

On the evening of that **first** day of the week,
　　when the doors were **locked**, where the disciples were,
　　for **fear** of the Jews,
　　Jesus came and stood in their **midst**
　　and said to them, "**Peace** be with you."
When he had said this, he showed them his **hands** and his **side**.
The disciples **rejoiced** when they saw the Lord.
Jesus said to them again, "**Peace** be with you.
As the **Father** has sent **me**, so **I** send **you**."
And when he had **said** this, he **breathed** on them and said
　　　to them,
　　"**Receive** the Holy **Spirit**.
Whose **sins** you **forgive** are **forgiven** them,
　　and whose sins you **retain** are **retained**."

Thomas, called **Didymus**, one of the **Twelve**,
　　was **not** with them when Jesus came.
So the **other** disciples said to him, "We have seen the **Lord**."
But he said to them,
　　"Unless **I** **see** the mark of the **nails** in his hands
　　and put my **finger** into the nailmarks
　　and put my **hand** into his **side**, I will not **believe**."

The narrator is a believer; so are you.

Fear suddenly turns to joy. Stress "Jesus" whose entrance is surprising.

Perhaps they experience more relief than joy.

This familiar but critical line must not be rushed.

Pause before starting this paragraph to establish a mood shift.

Didymus = DID-uh-muhs

Let the disciples be as convinced as Thomas is skeptical.

He doesn't think he's being disrespectful because the scenario is so impossible!

TO KEEP IN MIND
Pauses are never "dead" moments. Something is always happening during a pause. Practice will teach you how often and how long to pause. Too many pauses make a reading choppy; too few cause ideas to run into one another.

---

is a classic, moving, and powerful statement of faith. Peter, whose love for Jesus flowed from his three years with the Lord, is deeply touched by these believers who love the Lord without the benefit of having known him. They are the people of whom Jesus speaks in today's Gospel; they are also the people who sit in the pews all around you.

GOSPEL   This is a rich and familiar Gospel story in which the narrator, as a concerned and proselytizing teacher, wants to build up the faith of his

readers by affirming the historical reality of the Resurrection. Work as hard as John does to share that central aspect of his message.

The story requires several rapid mood shifts and strong emotional involvement. In addition, you have Thomas to depict, not as a caricature, but as the somewhat too honest member of the fraternity who boldly expresses his doubts. We encounter two contrasting emotions in the opening sentence. First we learn the disciples are huddled behind locked doors for fear of the Jewish authorities. But immediately their

fear is overshadowed by the miraculous as Jesus suddenly appears in their midst.

Jesus immediately addresses the Apostles' anxiety and their eroded faith. He speaks "Peace" and shows "his hands and his side." But note that the disciples did not actually rejoice "when they saw the Lord," but only *after* he shows his wounds and proves his identity.

Repeat Jesus's greeting almost as if Jesus were insisting that they embrace the peace he offers. In the ensuing dialogue, Jesus does three things: he commissions them to go in his name; he imparts the Holy

A new scene begins. Start at a slightly faster pace.

Note the door is "locked."

"Then he said to Thomas" should suggest Jesus turning significantly in Thomas's direction.

"My Lord and my God" are two distinct declarations of faith.

Here is John's key point!

In John, Jesus's "signs" demonstrate his divine authority and represent the meeting of heaven and earth.

Now a week **later** his disciples were **again** inside
    and Thomas **was** with them.
Jesus came, although the doors were **locked**,
    and stood in their **midst** and said, "**Peace** be with you."
Then he said to **Thomas**, "Put your **finger** here and see my **hands**,
    and bring your **hand** and put it into my **side**,
    and do not be **un**believing, but **believe**."
Thomas answered and said to him, "My **Lord** and my **God!**"
Jesus said to him, "Have you come to **believe** because you have
        seen me?
Blessed are those who have **not** seen and **have** believed."

Now, Jesus did many **other** signs in the presence of his **disciples**
    that are not **written** in this book.
But **these** are written that you may come to **believe**
    that **Jesus** is the **Christ**, the Son of **God**,
    and that through this **belief** you may have **life** in his **name**.

> **TO KEEP IN MIND**
> **Endings**: Your inflection of the last line of the reading should always signal that the reading is about to end. Then pause (three beats!) and make eye contact before announcing (from memory) "The word [Gospel] of the Lord." Always pronounce "the" as "thuh" except before words beginning with a vowel.

Spirit; and he empowers them to forgive sins. Each action requires its own moment, and its own tone and coloring. The mood shifts dramatically at the mention of Thomas. We're back in the mundane as they argue about the Lord's appearance. Make the disciples as assured as Thomas is skeptical. As you narrate Jesus's second appearance, consider assuming the persona of one of the disciples who is glad to be vindicated before Thomas. Jesus's peace greeting takes less time here and the momentum progresses to the encounter between Thomas and Jesus. Truly contrite,

Thomas speaks from the deepest part of his being, for his eyes are suddenly opened and he recognizes Jesus without ever touching the wounds. Note that he addresses Jesus with two distinct titles, the second being the more significant. For Thomas and for us, Jesus's reply is the clear climax of the reading.

The denouement of the last paragraph allows you to express concern for the condition of our faith while confidently professing your own.

THIRD SUNDAY OF EASTER

LECTIONARY #46

READING I   Acts of the Apostles 2:14, 22–33

A reading from the Acts of the Apostles

Then **Peter** stood up with the **Eleven**,
   raised his voice, and **proclaimed**:
"You who are **Jews**, indeed **all** of you staying in Jerusalem.
Let this be **known** to you, and **listen** to my words.
You who are **Israelites**, **hear** these words.
Jesus the **Nazorean** was a man commended to you by **God**
   with mighty **deeds**, **wonders**, and **signs**,
   which **God** worked through him in your **midst**,
     as you yourselves **know**.
This man, delivered up by the set **plan** and **fore**knowledge of God,
   you **killed**, using **lawless** men to **crucify** him.
But God **raised** him up, **releasing** him from the throes of death,
   because it was **impossible** for him to be **held** by it.
For **David** says of him:
   *I saw the Lord ever **before** me,*
     *with him at my **right** hand I shall not be **disturbed**.*
   *Therefore my heart has been **glad** and my **tongue** has **exulted**;*
     *my flesh, **too**, will dwell in **hope**,*
   *because you will not **abandon** my soul to the **netherworld**,*
     *nor will you suffer your **holy** one to see **corruption**.*
   *You have made **known** to me the paths of **life**;*
     *you will fill me with **joy** in your **presence**.*

Peter has overcome fear. Speak with bold strength. Note: there are "Eleven" Apostles, not "Twelve."

Increase energy from "*Jews*" to "*all* of you."

Nazorean = naz-uh-REE-uhn
Speak with confidence and pride of "Jesus the Nazorean."

Note that he stresses that Jesus's Death was part of God's plan.

This is news that's unexpected and revolutionary.

Peter assigns David's words to Jesus, but they describe Peter's own new way of perceiving reality. Perhaps give this the quality of prayer.

Build your energy as you speak of "heart," "tongue," and "flesh."

There is a sense of deep gratitude in these lines.

READING I Here begins a series of proclamations heralding the Resurrection of Jesus and the salvation of the world. Of the five such proclamations in Acts, Peter is the unlikely source of four. Despite the fact that he's a fisherman, not a trained orator; that the religious authorities will frown on his public effort to win followers for Jesus; that the crowd thinks Peter and the disciples are drunk; and not least of all, that Peter stands up with no clear idea of what he is going to say—despite all this,

Peter validates Jesus's choice of him as leader. Emboldened by the Spirit, he utters an impassioned exhortation to the "Jews," and "*all* . . . staying in Jerusalem." "Listen to my words" is not the imperative of someone who's afraid or lacking confidence.

Why is this man who recently denied Jesus now emboldened? Because, like Jesus, he's been through his own Death and Resurrection. He quotes Psalm 16:8–11 attributing to Jesus what David says of the coming Messiah. But the psalm also speaks of Peter for whom Jesus is now "ever before [him]." When Jesus died, Peter thought all

was lost, but the Resurrection has convinced him that God does not abandon souls "to the netherworld"; *Jesus* has shown *Peter* "the paths of life" and filled him with joy.

Peter speaks bluntly to his audience, for Jesus was "commended to [them] by God" and yet they rejected him. Privileged with knowledge of God's Law, they turned Jesus over to "*lawless*" men." But Peter is not trying to indict his listeners for killing Jesus; he wants to convince them that Jesus overcame death. He cites Jesus's

Peter's tone is very direct and personal. He's telling them something "obvious."

"My brothers, one can **confidently** say to you
  about the patriarch David that he **died** and was **buried**,
  and his **tomb** is in our midst to this day.
But since he was a **prophet** and knew that God had sworn an
    oath to him
  that he would set one of his **descendants** upon his throne,
  he **foresaw** and **spoke** of the **resurrection** of the Christ,
  that neither was he **abandoned** to the **netherworld**
  nor did his **flesh** see **corruption**.
God **raised** this Jesus;
  of this we are all witnesses.
Exalted at the right hand of God,
  he received the promise of the Holy **Spirit** from the Father
  and **poured** him forth, as you **see** and **hear**."

"He" continues to refer to David. Peter ascribes to David a foreknowledge of the Resurrection of the Messiah.

The power of the Holy Spirit is being manifested in Peter's own impassioned preaching which they "see and hear."

For meditation and context:

RESPONSORIAL PSALM   Psalm 16:1–2, 5, 7–8, 9–10, 11 (11a)

R. Lord, you will show us the path of life.
or
R. Alleluia.

Keep me, O God, for in you I take refuge;
  I say to the LORD, "My Lord are you."
O LORD, my allotted portion and my cup,
  you it is who hold fast my lot.

I bless the LORD who counsels me;
  even in the night my heart exhorts me.
I set the LORD ever before me;
  with him at my right hand I shall not
    be disturbed.

Therefore my heart is glad and my
    soul rejoices,
  my body, too, abides in confidence;
because you will not abandon my soul
    to the netherworld,
  nor will you suffer your faithful one
    to undergo corruption.

You will show me the path to life,
  abounding joy in your presence,
  the delights at your right hand forever.

TO KEEP IN MIND

Read through all three readings and commentaries for your assigned Sunday. All three were chosen for this day, and each commentary has suggestions that can help you with your own passage.

credentials—"the mighty deeds, wonders, and signs." But the *greatest* sign is the Resurrection. David died and was buried, but Jesus was raised and now reigns at God's right hand. The energy with which you say "it was impossible for him to be held" (by death) should suggest the power with which Jesus conquered the grave.

Take Peter's declaration that "we are all witnesses" as a directive about how to proclaim: as a believer whose weak faith has grown strong because of Jesus's victory and his gift of joy.

READING II   With fatherly concern, Peter calls for behavior that's consistent with the new status we have received through the blood of Christ. He begins with an if/then clause that lacks but implies the "then." "If" you call on God, he says, *then* during your earthly "sojourning" you must "conduct yourselves with reverence." Though written during a time of persecution, this admonition is not restricted to a time of trial but is meant for all of life, for as Christians we live all of life like strangers in a strange land.

With parental warmth and care, Peter reminds us that we were "ransomed from [the] futile conduct" we inherited from our ancestors. He's referring to sin and saying we were freed from it, not through "perishable things like silver and gold," but through the "precious blood" of the eternal and spotless lamb, Jesus Christ.

There is careful reasoning in the lines of the final sentence where the author asserts that Jesus existed before the creation of the world but was "revealed" for

READING II   1 Peter 1:17–21

A reading from the first Letter of Saint Peter

Beloved:

If you invoke as **Father** him who judges **impartially**
according to each one's **works**,
conduct yourselves with **reverence** during the time
of your **sojourning**,
realizing that you were **ransomed** from your futile conduct,
handed on by your **ancestors**,
not with **perishable** things like silver or gold
but with the **precious** blood of **Christ**
as of a **spotless unblemished lamb**.

He was known before the **foundation** of the world
but revealed in the **final** time for **you**,
who through him believe in **God**
who raised him from the **dead** and gave him **glory**,
so that your **faith** and **hope** are in **God**.

This is the second of six consecutive weeks we read 1 Peter.
Note the intimate address.

Express the "then" of the if/then clause with your voice.

"Futile conduct" refers to sin. Let that be apparent.

Contrast the eternal worth of Christ's blood with the passing worth of precious metals.

You are speaking of Christ's preexistence.

Christ came in this final age for our benefit.

This is more than a statement of fact; it's an agenda.

TO KEEP IN MIND
"Ritardando" refers to the practice, common in music, of becoming gradually slower and expanding the words as you approach the end of a piece. Many readings end this way — with a decreased rate but increased intensity.

---

our benefit only in the "final time." Read slowly and deliberately to make the case that now our "faith and hope are in God."

By striving for a personal and intimate tone, using good eye contact, and caring about your listeners as Peter cared about his, you will achieve a sincerity that speaks powerfully of God's love—a love so great that, because of it, God allowed Jesus to die for us. If you can help your listeners to believe this, perhaps they will also believe that what God did for Jesus in raising him from the dead he'll also do for them.

GOSPEL Few Scripture passages are as beloved as this one. But it's not the story's narrative qualities that make it so appealing. There is comfort and reassurance here. There are answers to our deepest questions about faith and struggle, and about faith in the face of struggle. But most of all, there is much about us in this story, for we too often walk through life feeling afraid and alone; we too so often are unable to recognize the "stranger" who walks beside us and to cry "stay with us" to anyone who makes us feel safer or answers our questions.

The narration should immediately suggest the despondent mood of the two disciples. With a subtle coloring of the voice you can convey their dejection (most clearly heard on "all the things that had occurred.)" Without a somber opening, the exchange between Jesus and the two will feel abrupt and unexpected. Tell us they couldn't "recognize him," not with judgment, but with awareness that this is an all too common failing.

GOSPEL   Luke 24:13–35

A reading from the holy Gospel according to Luke

The disciples are downcast and somber.

Emmaus = eh-MAY-uhs

Speak with the full knowledge of an omniscient narrator.

Enjoy the little game.

Cleopas = KLEE-oh-puhs

His initial response betrays some irritation.

Jesus continues to "play dumb."

Don't rush. Let the narration revive and then dash the hope they placed in Jesus.

They relate the event, but clearly place no stock in the women's testimony.

That very **day**, the **first** day of the week,
      two of Jesus' **disciples** were going
      to a village seven **miles** from Jerusalem called **Emmaus**,
      and they were **conversing** about all the things that
            had **occurred**.
And it **happened** that while they were **conversing** and **debating**,
      Jesus **himself** drew near and **walked** with them,
      but their eyes were prevented from **recognizing** him.
He asked them,
      "What are you **discussing** as you walk along?"
They **stopped**, looking **downcast**.
One of them, named **Cleopas**, said to him in reply,
      "Are you the **only** visitor to Jerusalem
      who does not **know** of the things
      that have taken **place** there in these days?"
And he replied to them, "What **sort** of things?"
They **said** to him,
      "The things that happened to **Jesus** the **Nazarene**,
      who was a **prophet** mighty in **deed** and **word**
      before **God** and all the **people**,
      how our chief **priests** and **rulers** both handed him over
      to a sentence of **death** and **crucified** him.
But we were hoping that **he** would be the one to **redeem** Israel;
      and **besides** all this,
      it is now the **third** day since this took place.
Some **women** from our group, however, have **astounded** us:
      they were at the **tomb** early in the **morning**
      and did not find his **body**;
      they came back and reported
      that they had indeed seen a **vision** of **angels**
      who announced that he was **alive**.

Jesus's mood contrasts with the disciples'. He catches them off-guard and surprises (even annoys) them with his feigned ignorance and upbeat question. Though guilty of not knowing what *they* should know, the two are quick to challenge the stranger who seems to be the only person in the area unaware of what just happened there. They're so shaken by those events that they can't imagine someone so oblivious.

But Jesus intentionally plays dumb. "What sort of things?" he asks. Cleopas isn't in the mood and vents some anger. He's racked with disappointment at having seen the hoped-for Messiah strung up on a Cross. He needs to be angry with someone, and the stranger provides an easy target. But as soon as he focuses on Jesus, "a prophet, mighty in deed and word," he composes himself and temporarily retrieves his lost dream, before the memory of the Crucifixion dashes it once more. It's no surprise that Jesus responds to all this pouting with "how foolish you are!" for in their dejection, the disciples are obscuring their own vision. Like children who didn't get their promised birthday gifts, they release their hope like they'd release a party balloon that was no longer fun.

Their knowledge alone of the women's visit to the tomb should make them question their sour mood. How can they know these things and still persist in their dejection? Do they, perhaps, betray an unwillingness to rely on the testimony of "some women"? Your inflection there, as on the phrase "he was alive" (a slightly exaggerated "mimicking" of the angel), will suggest how absurd a claim they think this is.

This inability to believe wins no applause from Jesus and he names their

Even the men's testimony made little impression.

Speak more with sadness than indictment.

Jesus once again becomes the rabbi.

Jesus continues dissembling, perhaps to test their faith.

Though they can't name it yet, the disciples have established a connection.

Stress the words that highlight the Eucharistic character of the meal.

Share two important pieces of information: 1) they recognized him; 2) he vanished.

Don't rush this classic line. Speak with excitement and gratitude.

The pace quickens for this narration.

The joy of the Apostles matches that of the two disciples.

Employ ritardando (slowing toward the end) on "in the breaking of the bread."

Then some of those with us **went** to the tomb
  and found things **just** as the women had **described**,
  but **him** they did not **see**."
And he said to them, "Oh, how **foolish** you are!
How **slow** of heart to believe all that the **prophets spoke**!
Was it not **necessary** that the Christ should **suffer** these things
  and enter into his **glory**?"
Then beginning with **Moses** and all the **prophets**,
  he **interpreted** to them what **referred** to him
  in all the **Scriptures**.
As they approached the **village** to which they were going,
  he gave the impression that he was going on **farther**.
But they **urged** him, "**Stay** with us,
  for it is nearly **evening** and the day is almost **over**."
So he went in to **stay** with them.
And it happened that, while he was with them at **table**,
  he took **bread**, said the **blessing**,
  broke it, and **gave** it to them.
With **that** their eyes were **opened** and they **recognized** him,
  but he **vanished** from their sight.
Then they said to each other,
  "Were not our **hearts burning** within us
  while he **spoke** to us on the way and opened the **Scriptures**
    to us?"
So they set out at **once** and returned to **Jerusalem**
  where they found gathered together
  the **eleven** and those with them who were saying,
  "The Lord has **truly** been **raised** and has appeared to **Simon**!"
Then the **two** recounted
  what had taken **place** on the way
  and how he was made **known** to them in the **breaking** of **bread**.

lack of faith as an act of foolishness. They knew Jesus, they knew the Law, they heard the testimony of the women, and stand in the very presence of Jesus, and still don't understand. "Was it not necessary . . . " however, is more explanation than reproach. "Then beginning with Moses . . . " suggests a teacher rolling up his sleeves, preparing for a long task of instruction. Much time elapses between the start of the conversation and arriving at the village. Suggest that by pausing after "in all the Scriptures." Then highlight Jesus's pretense

of going further and their fervent request, "Stay with us."

Now you narrate the sacred moment that highlights the great truth of Christianity: the Christ we long for is already among us. In the Eucharist, under the guise of bread and wine, Christ comes to set our hearts on fire. The four actions: "took," "said," "broke," and "gave" are Jesus's gestures of unmasking himself. They are gestures of love that must be spoken in love. Their eyes open when Jesus gives them what they craved most—himself. Though he's suddenly gone, they spend no time looking for

him for now they know he'll never truly be gone. Throughout the afternoon they had enjoyed his sacred presence and they understand they'll never again be without it. With quickened tempo, narrate their return to Jerusalem where an equally enthused group of disciples greets them with their own miraculous news. Calmly conclude, recounting how they came to know him in the gesture that unites all believers, "the breaking of bread."

FOURTH SUNDAY OF EASTER

LECTIONARY #49

READING I   Acts of the Apostles 2:14a, 36–41

A reading from the Acts of the Apostles

Then **Peter** stood up with the **Eleven**,
    raised his **voice**, and proclaimed:
"Let the whole house of **Israel** know for **certain**
    that God has made both **Lord** and **Christ**,
    this **Jesus** whom you **crucified**."

Now when they **heard** this, they were cut to the **heart**,
    and they **asked** Peter and the **other** apostles,
    "What are we to **do**, my brothers?"
Peter said to them,
    "**Repent** and be **baptized**, every **one** of you,
    in the name of Jesus **Christ** for the forgiveness of your **sins**;
    and you will receive the gift of the Holy **Spirit**.
For the promise is made to **you** and to your **children**
    and to all those **far** off,
    whomever the Lord our God will **call**."
He testified with many other **arguments**, and was **exhorting** them,
    "**Save** yourselves from this corrupt generation."
Those who **accepted** his message were **baptized**,
    and about three **thousand** persons were added that day.

Peter delivers this oration on the day of Pentecost, in the company of "the Eleven."

He is bold from the start.

The crowd is instantly filled with guilt that leads to true contrition.

He's filled with concern for these lost sheep, but his tone is strong and commanding. Repentance means changed behavior that manifests a change of heart.

Blessing in one's life yields blessings for generations to come.

As narrator, speak with pride of Peter's evangelization.

Not *all* were baptized that day, but the number was still astounding.

READING I Two remarkable things occur in this episode. First is the amazing boldness of Peter who not long ago was unwilling to be identified with Jesus. Now he sets all fear aside and boldly declares his faith and wins three thousand souls for Christ. It's not uncommon that timid followers are suddenly emboldened after a great leader's death; they become imbued with the fallen leader's spirit and those who previously had scoffed begin to listen and reassess. Even in families, when a parent dies, survivors don the mantle of leadership the elder left behind. So we shouldn't be surprised that Peter rises to the occasion now that Jesus has ascended. These events occur on Pentecost, when the Spirit was poured out on the disciples. Thus emboldened, Peter is able to do what he has never done before: call the "whole house of Israel" to faith in Jesus, the crucified Messiah. Peter has survived a crisis and finds unexpected strength with which to deal with new challenges.

Second is the response of the Jewish audience. Immediately smitten by Peter's indictment, they seek his advice. It's one of those moments that's too good to be true, but only for people who have never experienced the power of God to do the impossible. Sustaining his energy and intensity, Peter tells them what's needed: "repent," "be baptized," "receive the gift of the Holy Spirit." Peter names these as essentials for salvation, so don't let them sound like options. Peter "testified" with "many other [obviously convincing] arguments." His hardest message is his last, where he calls his listeners to separate themselves from their "corrupt generation." You must plead as Peter did, for going against the crowd is difficult in any generation. Then marvel at

For meditation and context:

RESPONSORIAL PSALM   Psalm 23:1–3a, 3b–4, 5, 6 (1)

R. The Lord is my shepherd; there is nothing I shall want.
or
R. Alleluia.

The LORD is my shepherd; I shall not want.
    In verdant pastures he gives me repose;
beside restful waters he leads me;
    he refreshes my soul.

He guides me in right paths
    for his name's sake.
Even though I walk in the dark valley
    I fear no evil; for you are at my side,
with your rod and your staff
    that give me courage.

You spread the table before me
    in the sight of my foes;
you anoint my head with oil;
    my cup overflows.

Only goodness and kindness follow me
    all the days of my life;
and I shall dwell in the house of the LORD
    for years to come.

TO KEEP IN MIND

Openings: First, make eye contact with the assembly and announce, from memory, "A (pronounced "uh," not "ay") reading from . . ." Then pause (three full beats!) before starting the reading.

This is the third of six consecutive weeks we read from 1 Peter. Read the other commentaries for a fuller picture of this epistle.

Our patient suffering is compared to the suffering of Jesus. Don't rush. These words are meant to inspire.

In no way did Jesus deserve his suffering. He's citing Isaiah 53:9b.

Here he's alluding to Isaiah 53:4–12. The Servant/Jesus suffered without resistance.

Imagine Peter remembering his own failings as he says that, "free from sin," we now can "live for righteousness."
Imagine the pronouns are actually "we" and "our." Don't rush the gorgeous image "shepherd and guardian of your souls."

READING II   1 Peter 2:20b–25

A reading from the first Letter of Saint Peter

Beloved:
If you are **patient** when you suffer for doing what is **good**,
    this is a **grace** before God.
For to this you have been **called**,
    because **Christ** also suffered for **you**,
    leaving you an **example** that you should follow in his **footsteps.**
*He committed no **sin**, and no **deceit** was found in his mouth.*

When he was **insulted**, he returned **no** insult;
    when he **suffered**, he did not **threaten**;
    instead, he **handed** himself over to the one who judges **justly**.
He himself **bore** our sins in his **body** upon the **cross**,
    so that, **free** from sin, we might live for **righteousness**.
By his **wounds** you have been **healed**.
For you had gone **astray** like **sheep**,
    but you have now **returned** to the **shepherd** and **guardian** of
        your **souls**.

---

the number who heeded the call and pray that many might do the same today.

READING II   Peter calls his readers to recognize and follow the voice of the shepherd. Christ has set an example for us that we might "follow in his footsteps." But he walked a hard, painful road. His "example" was one of suffering innocence: he endured cruel punishment, which he did nothing to merit. And yet, says Peter, he returned no insults when insulted and made no threats when he was forced to suffer. Peter almost makes it

sound too easy. But perhaps Peter speaks this way because his mind is fixed on an image, not of the wounded "Suffering Servant" of the Isaiah text he paraphrases, but of the glorious, resurrected Lord who forgave the "insult" of Peter's own denials.

In the second paragraph, what was said of Isaiah's Suffering Servant (Isaiah 53) is now applied to Jesus. The Suffering Servant is the healing Savior who brings all stray sheep (Peter, you, your assembly) back to the fold. When we suffer, we do only what Jesus did first. Speak with gratitude as you help Peter convince us that out

of love, Jesus bore our sins "in his body." We "had gone astray like sheep" and through God's grace we have "returned to the shepherd and guardian of [our] souls."

GOSPEL   Today's Gospel pericope doesn't include Jesus's self-identification as "the Good Shepherd," but in the first half of the reading Jesus clearly contrasts himself with the false shepherds; that is, the Pharisees, who have just expelled from the Temple the man born blind whom Jesus cured. Jesus characterizes the false shepherds with stern disapproval; but

GOSPEL   John 10:1–10

A reading from the holy Gospel according to John

Jesus said:
"Amen, **amen**, I say to you,
whoever does not enter a sheepfold through the **gate**
but climbs over **elsewhere** is a **thief** and a **robber**.
But whoever enters through the **gate** is the **shepherd** of the sheep.
The gatekeeper **opens** it for him, and the sheep **hear** his voice,
as the shepherd calls his own sheep by **name** and **leads**
them out.
When he has driven out all his **own**,
he walks **ahead** of them, and the sheep **follow** him,
because they **recognize** his voice.
But they will not follow a **stranger**;
they will run **away** from him,
because they do not **recognize** the voice of strangers."
Although Jesus used this figure of **speech**,
the **Pharisees** did not realize what he was trying to **tell** them.

So Jesus said **again**, "**Amen, amen**, I say to you,
I am the **gate** for the sheep.
All who came **before** me are **thieves** and **robbers**,
but the sheep did not **listen** to them.
I am the **gate**.
Whoever enters through **me** will be **saved**,
and will come **in** and go **out** and find **pasture**.
A thief comes only to **steal** and **slaughter** and **destroy**;
I came so that they might have **life** and have it
more **abundantly**."

The double "Amen" signals an authoritative statement.

Jesus has in mind individuals who have deceived the people in this way.

Don't rush these details that are unfamiliar to modern ears.

A somber note is sounded here that signals danger.

There is both explanation and judgment in this statement.

Pharisees = FAYR-uh-seez

Again, he signals a significant teaching is about to be made.

The sheep were wise enough to ignore those who came to deceive them.

The focus is not on "me," but on those who "will be saved."

The "thief" comes to take life; Jesus comes to give it.

> **TO KEEP IN MIND**
> **Careful preparation** expresses your reverence for the Word.

warmth, reassurance, and tenderness color his voice as he speaks of the true shepherd. The warmth comes from the love he has for the sheep that are desperately in need of guidance.

In ancient Palestine, shepherds allowed flocks to commingle and form one communal sheepfold. To gather his own flock, a shepherd called his sheep. Only his sheep recognized his voice and followed him. Jesus compares this shepherd/sheep relationship to his intimate bond with his disciples; he contrasts it with the cruelty of the "thief" and "robber" who care nothing for the sheep. The Good Shepherd's sheep recognize, trust, and follow him because of his care and loving commitment. But "they will not follow a stranger" who has not spent himself in caring for them.

Despite Jesus's clear figure of speech, the Pharisees miss his point. Your tone asks, "How could they?!?" "Amen, amen" introduces Jesus's renewed (and intensified) effort to make his point. Not only is he the shepherd, Jesus is also the "gate" to the sheepfold through which every would-be shepherd must pass. Those who enter "through me" (his disciples, yourself), he names authentic shepherds who "come in and go out" and lead their sheep to green pasture. But he distinguishes again between the thieves who come only "to steal . . . and destroy" and those, like himself, who give access to fullness of life. Jesus disparages the false shepherds to warn both the Pharisees and his followers: the Pharisees he warns about arrogant self-deception; his followers he cautions about the danger of self-serving leaders. Most of all, he offers abundance of life and calls all to receive it.

FIFTH SUNDAY OF EASTER

LECTIONARY #52

READING I   Acts of the Apostles 6:1–7

A reading from the Acts of the Apostles

As the number of disciples continued to **grow**,
   the Hellenists **complained** against the Hebrews
   because their **widows**
   were being **neglected** in the daily distribution.
So the **Twelve** called together the **community** of the disciples
      and said,
   "It is not **right** for us to neglect the word of **God** to serve
      at **table**.
Brothers, **select** from among you seven **reputable** men,
   filled with the **Spirit** and **wisdom**,
   whom we shall **appoint** to this task,
   whereas **we** shall devote ourselves to **prayer**
   and to the ministry of the **word**."
The proposal was **acceptable** to the whole community,
   so they chose **Stephen**, a man **filled** with **faith** and the
      Holy Spirit,
   also **Philip**, **Prochorus**, **Nicanor**, **Timon**, **Parmenas**,
   and Nicholas of **Antioch**, a **convert** to Judaism.
They presented these men to the **apostles**
   who **prayed** and laid **hands** on them.

Margin notes:

Start with an upbeat tone, that is immediately broken by the word "complained."

Hellenists are Greek believers.

The Twelve immediately assume leadership and authoritatively address the problem in order to safeguard their ministry of evangelization.

Speak deliberately, as you imagine the instructions were given the first time.

Share this detail with joy, and then speak with pride of the seven men chosen for service.

Prochorus = PRAH-kuh-ruhs

Nicanor = nih-KAY-ner or ni-KAY-ner

Timon = TI-muhn

Parmenas = PAHR-muh-nuhs

Nicholas = NIK-oh-luhs; Antioch = AN-tee-ahk

Judaism = JOO-duh-iz-*m; JOO-dee-iz-*m

Recount the imposition of hands with great reverence.

READING I   Problems and challenges ride the same train as success. The opening sentence that heralds amazing growth in the number of disciples also signals the start of tension resulting from that success. After announcing the growth with joy and amazement, the word "complained" grabs our attention. Already dissension has crept in, factions have developed, and the Greek disciples complain that their widows are not being cared for "in the daily distribution" of food.

Recognizing the responsibilities of leadership, "the Twelve" immediately take action. Their response not only gives us insight into their problem-solving, but also into their priorities. To this day, we distinguish "Mary" and "Martha" spirituality: the first is more contemplative and inner-focused, the second more outward focused and service-oriented. The Apostles take the Mary approach and relegate the Martha ministry to seven men who will be ordained deacons and assigned the responsibility of caring for the physical needs of community members.

There is clear frustration in the reference to waiting on tables, yet, patiently, the Apostles suggest a solution. They ask for men who have a good reputation within the community and are filled with God's spirit, a marriage of practicality and idealism. Peace is restored, for the "whole community" embraces the proposal. When reading the seven names, imagine each man standing before the community and answering, "I am ready to serve." That will slow you down and help you read the names as if

This time the talk of exponential growth is only joyful. Be sure to suggest the unexpected nature of the conversion to the faith of "a large group of priests."

The word of God continued to **spread**,
    and the **number** of the disciples in Jerusalem
        increased **greatly**;
    even a large group of **priests** were becoming obedient
        to the faith.

For meditation and context:

RESPONSORIAL PSALM   Psalm 33:1–2, 4–5, 18–19 (22)

R. Lord, let your mercy be on us, as we place our trust in you.
or
R. Alleluia.

Exult, you just, in the LORD;
    praise from the upright is fitting.
Give thanks to the LORD on the harp;
    with the ten-stringed lyre chant his praises.

Upright is the word of the LORD,
    and all his works are trustworthy.
He loves justice and right;
    of the kindness of the LORD the earth is full.

See, the eyes of the LORD are upon those
        who fear him,
    upon those who hope for his kindness,
to deliver them from death
    and preserve them in spite of famine.

TO KEEP IN MIND
Practice pronunciation!

This is the fourth of six consecutive weeks we read from I Peter.

READING II   1 Peter 2:4–9

A reading from the first Letter of Saint Peter

Beloved:

You begin boldly, calling us to Christ.

Come to him, a **living** stone, **rejected** by human beings
    but **chosen** and **precious** in the sight of **God**,
    and, like **living** stones,
    let **yourselves** be built into a **spiritual** house
    to be a holy **priesthood** to offer **spiritual** sacrifices
    acceptable to God through Jesus **Christ**.
For it says in Scripture:

Render these lines with pride at the exalted role entrusted to us by Christ.

These words of Scripture are here confidently applied to Jesus.

Zion = Zī-ahn

    Behold, I am laying a **stone** in Zion,
    a **cornerstone**, **chosen** and **precious**,
    and whoever **believes** in it shall not be put to **shame**.

---

you knew the men. Then speak of the imposition of hands slowly and with reverence.

When you speak again of the growth, your voice fills with joy and confidence. Mention of the Jewish "priests" comes as a pleasant surprise: what a mighty God who can draw into the fold even those we least expect!

READING II Using a complex and well-developed image, Peter teaches us about the Church, her members, and their Lord. Christ is the "living stone," an image borrowed from Psalm

118:22. But because we are his followers we, too, are living stones that can be built into "a spiritual house," which is the Church. The development from "living stone" to "cornerstone, chosen and precious," to a stone that makes people stumble, shows a poet's hand at work, so as proclaimer, respect both the author's message and his method by highlighting the changing references to "stones" and helping us see each image as you speak it to life.

The text begins with a call, "Come to him." "Him" is Jesus the Lord, the "living

stone," rejected by people but "approved" by God, the same God who turns us into building blocks with which to erect the spiritual structure that is the Church. As such we are a "holy priesthood" called to offer "spiritual sacrifices" through Jesus. Your task is to help heighten your assembly's awareness of the significant role God has given to all who put their faith in Jesus, the cornerstone. Like him, we too can serve as priests offering worship to God in Christ.

But the very "stone" that claims our faith causes the non-believer to "stumble . . . and fall." Finally, you end with a barrage of

<table>
<tr>
<td>

Your tone shifts to one of regret over the fate of those who are "without faith."

</td>
<td>

Therefore, its value is for you who have **faith**, but for those
> **without** faith:
> > *The stone that the builders **rejected***
> > *has become the **cornerstone**,*
> and
> > *a stone that will make people **stumble**,*
> > *and a rock that will make them **fall**.*
> They stumble by **disobeying** the word, as is their **destiny**.

</td>
</tr>
</table>

This line explains the lines that preceded.

You are "a **chosen** race, a **royal** priesthood,
> a **holy** nation, a people of his **own**,
> so that you may announce the **praises**" of him
> who called you out of **darkness** into his wonderful **light**.

Don't rush these four images. Each has a distinctive meaning that should be underscored by your tone.

GOSPEL   John 14:1–12

A reading from the holy Gospel according to John

This is a central part of Jesus's farewell message. Speak it with authority and compassion.
In addition to comforting them, Jesus is also fortifying their faith.

Jesus said to his disciples:
> "Do not let your hearts be **troubled**.
You have faith in **God**; have faith also in **me**.
In my **Father's** house there are many **dwelling** places.
If there were **not**,
> would I have told you that I am going to prepare a **place**
> > for you?
And if I **go** and prepare a place for you,
> I will come **back** again and **take** you to myself,
> so that where **I** am you **also** may be.

There is an "if/then" relationship established that your tone should manifest.

Where I am going you **know** the way."
Thomas said to him,
> "**Master**, we do not know where you are **going**;
> how can we know the **way**?"

They "know" because Jesus *is* the "way."

Jesus said to him, "**I** am the **way** and the **truth** and the **life**.
No one comes to the **Father** except through **me**.
If you know **me**, then you will also know my **Father**.

In response to Thomas's frustration, Jesus makes a radical assertion about himself.

---

images borrowed from the Old Testament. Words and images that formerly were used to describe God's relationship with the Chosen People of Israel—"chosen race," "royal priesthood," "holy nation," and "a people of his own"—are now applied to Christian believers. By embracing this new identity and forsaking the darkness of their former paganism, the new Christians will "announce the praises" of the merciful God who freed them to live in "his wonderful light."

| GOSPEL | Shakespeare notwithstanding, parting is not always sweet sorrow. For Jesus and the disciples it is respectively frustrating and frightening. And this moment painfully illustrates (at least for Jesus) that a teacher rarely is granted certainty that his work is done and that students now know all they need to know. Much to the contrary, Jesus is confronted with a lack of understanding that seems to amaze and trouble him.

Jesus is aware of the disciples' mood, so he begins with (and twenty-seven verses later will repeat) the admonition "do not let your hearts be troubled." It's a familiar phrase that Jesus often used to remind his inner circle that only faith can cancel fear and heartsickness. Use the repetition in Jesus's ensuing dialogue as if he were working hard to ensure their understanding. "You know the way" that leads where I'm going, he claims. But Thomas tugs at his coat with childlike innocence. No we don't,

Don't rush these important lines that assert the oneness of Jesus and the Father.

Philip's tone is eager and naïve.

Avoid an angry tone, though Jesus is clearly frustrated.

Allow the parallels ("I/Father" and "Father/me") to slow your delivery.

The operative word here is "believe." Jesus commands faith, be it based on his assertion of oneness with God or upon his miraculous "works."
The double "Amen" signals a solemn pronouncement. Here it is a promise that Jesus's power will remain among them despite his going to the Father.

> TO KEEP IN MIND
> **Posture speaks**: Make sure it says what you want it to. Don't let your face or body contradict the good news you announce. Remember, readers are allowed to smile!

From now on you **do** know him and have **seen** him."
Philip said to him,
    "Master, **show** us the Father, and that will be **enough** for us."
Jesus said to him, "Have I been with you for so **long** a time
    and you **still** do not know me, Philip?
Whoever has seen **me** has seen the Father.
How can you say, '**Show** us the Father'?
Do you not **believe** that I am in the **Father** and the Father
    is in **me**?
The words that I **speak** to you I do not speak on my **own**.
The Father who **dwells** in me is doing his **works**.
Believe me that **I** am in the **Father** and the **Father** is in **me**,
    or else, believe because of the **works** themselves.
Amen, **amen**, I say to you,
    whoever **believes** in me will do the works that **I** do,
    and will do **greater** ones than these,
    because I am **going** to the **Father**."

he claims, so how can we find our way to you? Jesus's reply is slow, loving, and direct. Establish good eye contact as you proclaim Jesus's assertion that "I am the way . . . truth . . . life." Here Jesus makes remarkable and unique assertions about his identity. He has not come to show us a way, but to be the way. He did not come to teach the truth but to be truth. He does not just give life, he is life.

The exchange with Philip is deeply human, but more poignant than the dialogue with Thomas. "Show us the father," he asks in seeming earnestness, "and that will be enough for us." But this is no simple request because he's asking for a theophany, a divine manifestation akin to what was granted Moses in Exodus 24:9. Jesus responds not with reproach but with disappointment. "Philip," he says, don't you know me even after "so long a time?" Philip and the others clearly have much more to

learn. So, like a teacher reviewing the lesson for the fourth time, Jesus launches into his explanation: "I am in the Father and the Father is in me." He remains urgent to the end saying, "Believe me" and "Amen, amen, I say to you" to communicate his urgent message. The passage ends with a striking promise that those of us who believe will do even greater works than the ones that made these men his followers in the first place.

SIXTH SUNDAY OF EASTER

LECTIONARY #55

READING I   Acts of the Apostles 8:5–8, 14–17

A reading from the Acts of the Apostles

Philip went down to the city of **Samaria**
　　and proclaimed the **Christ** to them.
With one **accord**, the crowds paid **attention** to what was said
　　　by Philip
　　when they **heard** it and saw the **signs** he was doing.
For unclean **spirits**, crying out in a loud **voice**,
　　came out of many **possessed** people,
　　and many **paralyzed** or **crippled** people were **cured**.
There was great **joy** in that city.

Now when the **apostles** in **Jerusalem**
　　heard that Samaria had **accepted** the word of God,
　　they sent them **Peter** and **John**,
　　who went down and **prayed** for them,
　　that they might receive the Holy **Spirit**,
　　for it had not yet fallen upon **any** of them;
　　they had only been **baptized** in the name of the Lord **Jesus**.
Then they laid **hands** on them
　　and they **received** the Holy **Spirit**.

Suggest the remarkable nature of Philip traveling to Samaria.

Samaria = suh-MAYR-ee-uh

His ministry is immediately successful.

These are wonders worked not by Philip but by God.

Speak with great satisfaction of the "joy" in the city.

Suggest the too-good-to-believe quality of this news.

Use a prayerful tone here.

The physical gesture is important. You relate two separate moments: imposition of hands and the reception of the Holy Spirit.

READING I Despite the fact that the Church was undergoing severe persecution, Luke focuses us on successful evangelization carried out by zealous members of the community who, forced to scatter because of the persecution, bring the Good News even to the Samaritans. The text begins unobtrusively enough: Philip travels to Samaria, an outcast town, to proclaim "the Christ." But he apparently preached both in word and deed, for the people "heard" and "saw the signs he was doing."

Philip is not one of "the Twelve," but one of the men selected to help meet the needs of the Hellenist widows of whom we read in last Sunday's selection from Acts. He preaches to the Samaritans only because circumstances have brought him there, and yet he meets with remarkable success as an exorcist and healer. He casts out "unclean spirits" and cures paralytics and cripples! No wonder "great joy" fills the city.

Hearing what has happened, the Apostles dispatch Peter and John. Their response is immediate because the news seemed too good to be true—imbue your tone with that quality as you announce "that Samaria had accepted the word of God." Sometimes the gift of the Spirit was conferred simultaneously with Baptism, but that was not the case here. In the earnest voice of Peter pray that "they might *receive* the Holy Spirit." Then proclaim the final sentence with the joy of the community members who experienced the efficacious ministry of the two Apostles.

READING II In a hard and often hostile world, Christians must witness to their faith in Christ through patient

For meditation and context:

RESPONSORIAL PSALM   Psalm 66:1–3, 4–5, 6–7, 16, 20 (1)

R. Let all the earth cry out to God with joy.
or
R. Alleluia.

Shout joyfully to God, all the earth,
    sing praise to the glory of his name;
    proclaim his glorious praise.
Say to God, "How tremendous are
        your deeds!"

"Let all on earth worship and sing praise
        to you,
    sing praise to your name!"
Come and see the works of God,
    his tremendous deeds among the children
        of Adam.

He has changed the sea into dry land;
    through the river they passed on foot;
    therefore let us rejoice in him.
He rules by his might forever.

Hear now, all you who fear God,
        while I declare
    what he has done for me.
Blessed be God who refused me not
    my prayer or his kindness!

> **TO KEEP IN MIND**
> **Names** of characters are often the first word of a reading. Stress names so listeners don't miss who the subject is.

READING II   1 Peter 3:15–18

A reading from the first Letter of Saint Peter

The first word sets the tone.

The message is this: honor Christ in your life and be ready to explain why you can live with hope and joy even in the midst of trials.

Beloved:
Sanctify **Christ** as Lord in your hearts.
Always be ready to give an **explanation**
    to anyone who asks you for a **reason** for your hope,
    but do it with **gentleness** and **reverence**,
    keeping your conscience **clear**,
    so that, when you are **maligned**,
    those who **defame** your good conduct in Christ
    may **themselves** be put to shame.
For it is better to suffer for doing **good**,
    if that be the will of **God**, than for doing **evil**.
For **Christ** also suffered for sins once,
    the **righteous** for the sake of the **unrighteous**,
    that he might lead you to God.
Put to **death** in the **flesh**,
    he was brought to **life** in the **Spirit**.

maligned = muh-LĪN*D

Bringing shame on our detractors is God's business, not ours.

Suffering *will* come, but better to suffer for good than for evil.

Carefully balance the contrasting words to clarify the point. Don't rush.
End on a joyful note.

---

endurance of trial and opposition. Even more, Peter says, we are to be prepared to say *why* we can live with peace in the midst of turmoil. His instructions to speak "with gentleness and reverence" might double as advice for how to proclaim this passage. The text feels like one-on-one guidance passed from a wise teacher to a willing protégé. The mood is intimate and frank; the sharing easy and non-threatening. If your faith becomes evident from the joy in your life, Peter says, be ready to respectfully answer all inquiries about it. But don't let that opportunity became an

occasion of sin by answering out of anger or with judgment.

This wise teacher points out that following Christ inevitably leads to difficulties, such as being "maligned." But such abuse should not be feared. Constancy in faith will bring shame on those who defame us. We must find comfort in the knowledge that it is better "to suffer for doing good . . . than to suffer for doing evil." As Paul often does, Peter reminds us that Christ asks nothing of us that he did not first embrace. He, the "righteous" one, suffered for the sake of the "unrighteous." Now we can endure injustice and join it to the suffering

of Christ so that, just as *he* died "in the flesh" and was "brought to life in the Spirit," *wc* can undergo the same transition. Use the contrasts "righteous" and "unrighteous," "death" and "life," "flesh" and "Spirit" to emphasize the love Christ demonstrated by willingly dying for the unrighteous. But that death became life in the spirit; and that life is the hope you must awaken in us.

> **GOSPEL**   No matter how much we might wish it were otherwise, institutional order—and relationships

Jesus's disciples have now become your assembly.

This Advocate is not only comfort, but also challenge.
Advocate = AD-voh-k*t

Use these words to assure your listeners.

This is Jesus's promise of being with them *through* the Holy Spirit.

These words express intimacy between God and Jesus, and Jesus and the disciples.

Love is obedience that initiates a cycle of love.

TO KEEP IN MIND
Pray the Scriptures: Make reading these Scriptures a part of your prayer life every week, and especially during the week prior to the liturgy in which you will proclaim.

GOSPEL   John 14:15–21

A reading from the holy Gospel according to John

Jesus said to his disciples:
 "If you **love** me, you will keep my **commandments**.
And I will ask the **Father**,
 and he will give you another **Advocate** to be with you **always**,
 the Spirit of **truth**, whom the world cannot **accept**,
 because it neither **sees** nor **knows** him.
But **you** know him, because he **remains** with you,
 and will be **in** you.
I will not leave you **orphans**; I will **come** to you.
In a little while the world will no longer **see** me,
 but **you** will see me, because I **live** and **you** will live.
On that day you will realize that **I** am in my **Father**
 and **you** are in **me** and **I** in **you**.
Whoever has my commandments and **observes** them
 is the one who **loves** me.
And whoever **loves** me will be loved by my **Father**,
 and **I** will love him and **reveal** myself to him."

---

of any kind—requires obedience. "Keep my commandments" doesn't mean store the tablets safely, it means obey the commandments in every aspect of life. This is the Last Supper discourse, Jesus's love song for his disciples. But twice the lyrics speak of obedience.

The reason is found in the middle of the text: "I will not leave you orphaned," says Jesus. The opposite of being orphaned is living in family. So Jesus advises us about how to be a family characterized by love and hope. And he says it twice: "Keep my commandments." We won't have to do it

alone, Jesus assures us. He is our first advocate before the Father, but he will send "another Advocate" the world can't even "see." While the Greek word for advocate is a legal term that means "comforter" and "consoler," John's use of the word packs more punch. The Paraclete is a teacher, but in John the Paraclete is more *prosecutor* than *defense* attorney, giving witness to Christ and indicting the world for its lack of faith. Jesus manifests sincere affection for his disciples. When he promises "I will come to you," he does not mean

in the Parousia, but through the indwelling of the Holy Spirit.

How do we proclaim a text of extraordinary intimacy? Slowly, one image at a time, allowing the images to form in your mind as you read, then sharing them honestly. Imagine a situation that would call compassion and sincerity from you, a situation in which you would want to be a source of comfort and healing. These are not the empty words of a vacuous love song. Jesus's love is so great he can't help *expressing* it and *proving* it by gifting us with the Spirit.

THE ASCENSION OF THE LORD

LECTIONARY #58

READING I Acts of the Apostles 1:1–11

A reading from the Acts of the Apostles

In the **first** book, Theophilus,
　　I dealt with all that Jesus **did** and **taught**
　　until the day he was taken **up**,
　　after giving **instructions** through the Holy **Spirit**
　　to the **apostles** whom he had **chosen**.
He presented himself **alive** to them
　　by many **proofs** after he had suffered,
　　appearing to them during **forty days**
　　and speaking about the kingdom of **God**.
While **meeting** with them,
　　he enjoined them not to **depart** from Jerusalem,
　　but to wait for "the **promise** of the Father
　　about which you have heard me **speak**;
　　for **John** baptized with **water**,
　　but in a few days **you** will be baptized with the Holy **Spirit**."

When they had gathered **together** they asked him,
　　"**Lord**, are you at this time going to **restore** the kingdom
　　　　to Israel?"

You are communicating a faith story, not a history. Speak with great intentionality; Luke is trying to persuade.

Theophilus = thee-AWF-uh-luhs.

Stress the work of the Spirit.

"Forty" is a number that expresses an indeterminate, but sacred, period of time during which Jesus appeared to and instructed the disciples.

Speak these lines in the persona of Jesus.

Though they should know better, the question is sincere.

READING I The Book of Acts continues Luke's narration of God's saving action in history that began with the Chosen People, climaxed in Jesus, and now is made available to the Gentile nations. The Ascension marks a beginning, not a terminus. Here and in today's Gospel, Jesus *inaugurates* the Church's mission, placing on the disciples the work of advancing the Kingdom of God. When Acts was written, the Christian community was no longer awaiting Jesus's return within their lifetime. So they got busy evangelizing.

The language of Acts is full of action: "you will be baptized," "you will receive power," "you will be my witnesses," "why are you standing there looking at the sky?" There is no gloom or despondency in the lines, only confidence that this young community will carry on in Jesus's name until he *does* return in glory.

The refined writing of Acts is addressed to "Theophilus," perhaps a Roman official, or perhaps, as some commentators suggest, a symbolic name that refers to anyone who loves God. ("Theophilus" means "lover of God.") According to Luke, his story is primarily about how the *Holy Spirit* guides the new community to spread the Good News of Jesus. Thus, his two references to the Spirit in this text should be highlighted. Remarkably, the disciples still cling to the hope that Jesus will establish an earthly kingdom. So once again Jesus must play the patient teacher. Instead of the privileged knowledge they desire, Jesus promises the "power" of the Spirit, and then quickly disappears. In keeping with

This is what he gives in place of what they asked for. His words both reassure and inspire his friends. This prophecy continues being fulfilled to this day.

Judea = joo-DEE-uh; joo-DAY-uh
Samaria = suh-MAYR-ee-uh

Persuade your listeners that this promise applies to them as well.

Galilee = GAL-ih-lee

Slowly, and with a sense of awe. Obviously, this is not an ordinary occurrence. "As they were . . . " retains the mood of the previous line. Break the mood on "Suddenly two men."

The angels' tone is not berating, but "nudging." The words "will return" alert us of the need to be ready.

For meditation and context:

TO KEEP IN MIND
Importance of the Narrator:
The narrator is often the pivotal role of a passage. Timbre, pitch, rate, and energy can make the same words convey very different moods or meaning. Sometimes the narrator is objective, but often the narrator has great interest in the events and characters of a story.

He answered them, "It is not for you to know the **times** or **seasons**
that the **Father** has established by his own authority.
But you will receive **power** when the Holy **Spirit** comes upon you,
and you will be my **witnesses** in Jerusalem,
throughout **Judea** and **Samaria**,
and to the **ends** of the **earth**."
When he had **said** this, as they were **looking** on,
he was **lifted** up, and a **cloud** took him from their **sight**.
While they were looking intently at the sky as he was going,
suddenly two men dressed in white garments stood beside them.
They said, "Men of **Galilee**,
why are you standing there looking at the **sky**?
This **Jesus** who has been taken up from you into **heaven**
will **return** in the same way as you have seen him **going** into heaven."

RESPONSORIAL PSALM   Psalm 47:2–3, 6–7, 8–9 (6)

R. God mounts his throne to shouts of joy: a blare of trumpets for the Lord.
or
R. Alleluia.

All you peoples, clap your hands,
    shout to God with cries of gladness.
For the LORD, the Most High, the awesome,
    is the great king over all the earth.

God mounts his throne amid shouts of joy;
    the LORD, amid trumpet blasts.
Sing praise to God, sing praise;
    sing praise to our king, sing praise.

For king of all the earth is God;
    sing hymns of praise.
God reigns over the nations,
    God sits upon his holy throne.

the "There's important work to do!" feel of this text, the exhortation of the "two [angelic] men" reminds the disciples to "Get to it!" because neither they, nor we, know when Jesus "will return."

READING II   The three complex sentences of this text are essentially a prayer that asks God to grant the Ephesians gifts of "wisdom" and "revelation" with which to better understand him. The complexity of the words obscures

what is essentially a simple prayer that you must now make your own. You ask God to open "the eyes of [our] hearts," and enlighten us to perceive *three* things: "the hope" that results from God's call, "the riches of glory in his inheritance," and "the surpassing greatness of (God's) power."

God's mighty plan unfolded in the life of Jesus, who after dying and rising, now sits in power at the right hand of God. The "riches" of God's glory is the *salvation* Jesus won for

us. Now, from his heavenly throne Jesus reigns as *head* of his body, the Church, with "all things beneath his feet." The beautiful language and compelling imagery of the text lead to that climactic announcement, found in the closing lines. As members of his body, we share in the exaltation and lordship of Jesus, our head. What God did for Jesus by raising him from the dead and raising him above every creature in heaven and on earth, God did for all of "us who believe" in the mystery of Baptism.

READING II   Ephesians 1:17–23

A reading from the Letter of Saint Paul to the Ephesians

Brothers and sisters:
May the God of our Lord Jesus **Christ**, the Father of **glory**,
    give you a Spirit of **wisdom** and **revelation**
    resulting in **knowledge** of him.
May the eyes of your hearts be **enlightened**,
    that you may know what is the **hope** that belongs to his call,
    what are the **riches** of glory
    in his **inheritance** among the holy ones,
    and what is the surpassing **greatness** of his **power**
    for us who **believe**,
    in accord with the exercise of his great **might**,
    which he worked in **Christ**,
    raising him from the **dead**
    and seating him at his **right hand** in the heavens,
    far **above** every principality, authority, power, and dominion,
    and every **name** that is named
    not only in **this** age but also in the one to **come**.
And he put **all** things beneath his **feet**
    and gave him as **head** over all things to the **church**,
    which is his **body**,
    the **fullness** of the one who **fills** all things in **every** way.

Ephesians = ee-FEE-zhuhnz

Remember, you're proclaiming a prayer.

You want us to know three things (hope, riches, and the greatness of his power), so build your energy from the first to the last.

You are praising Christ with these words.

"Principality," "authority," "power," "dominion" refer to four distinct ranks of angelic powers. Don't speed through them.

"He" is the Father; "his" is Christ's. "Gave him as head" means that the Father made Christ head of the Church. Speak with joy and gratitude.

TO KEEP IN MIND
"Build" refers to increasing vocal *intensity* as you speak a certain word or sentence. It can be achieved by speaking *louder*, but a *quieter* voice might produce the same effect. Sometimes "build" is achieved by speaking *faster* and sometimes by speaking *slower*.

Don't let these complex sentences become a maze for you and your listeners. Once you know the main ideas in each sentence, share them one at a time using pauses and slow pacing, remembering, all the while, that you're speaking a prayer. The message of this text is quite beautiful, but it will take practice to make the sound of the words as beautiful as their meaning.

GOSPEL   Though this Gospel text proclaims Jesus as Lord with "all power in heaven and on earth" it begins with a reminder of failure for only "eleven" disciples make their way up the mountain of Ascension. This is a subtle cue that making "disciples of *all* nations" may be fraught with failure. If some who initially accepted Jesus's call abandoned him, surely some will rebuff future invitations. We're even told that though the Apostles "saw" and "worshipped" him, some "doubted" the Resurrection. But Matthew does not end his narrative on a sour note. The Ascension is Jesus's act of faith in his followers, delegating to them the work of the Kingdom he began. So the narration and Jesus's commissioning dialogue must be strong and authoritative. Jesus "ordered" the disciples to this mountain that evokes images not only of Moses's mountaintop encounter but also of Jesus's own mountaintop experiences—preaching the great sermon and his Transfiguration.

In his final address Jesus commands the disciples to *go*, *baptize*, *teach*, and *never forget* that he will be with them always. Zeal for the mission he entrusts to them

GOSPEL   Matthew 28:16–20

A reading from the holy Gospel according to Matthew

The eleven disciples went to **Galilee**,
  to the mountain to which Jesus had **ordered** them.
When they saw him, they **worshiped**, but they **doubted**.
Then Jesus **approached** and said to them,
  "All power in heaven and on earth has been **given** to me.
Go, therefore, and make disciples of **all nations**,
  baptizing them in the name of the **Father**,
  and of the **Son**, and of the **Holy Spirit**,
  teaching them to **observe** all that I have **commanded** you.
And behold, I am with you **always**, until the **end** of the **age**."

Their number is "eleven," not "twelve."

Galilee = GAL-ih-lee

Jesus "ordered" with authority.

Don't gloss over the significant phrase, "But they doubted."

Jesus is now Lord of the universe.

Keep Jesus's commands "Go . . . baptizing . . . teaching" distinct and be aware that he will ever be with them. That last admonition is a source of strength and courage both then and now.

TO KEEP IN MIND
Who really proclaims: "When the Sacred Scriptures are read in the Church, God himself speaks to his people, and Christ, present in his word, proclaims the gospel" (#29 GIRM).

THE **4** STEPS OF *LECTIO DIVINA* OR PRAYERFUL READING

1. *Lectio:* Read a Scripture passage aloud slowly. Notice what phrase captures your attention and be attentive to its meaning. Silent pause.

2. *Meditatio:* Read the passage aloud slowly again, reflecting on the passage, allowing God to speak to you through it. Silent pause.

3. *Oratio:* Read it aloud slowly a third time, allowing it to be your prayer or response to God's gift of insight to you. Silent pause.

4. *Contemplatio:* Read it aloud slowly a fourth time, now resting in God's word.

---

infuses his voice with strength. Matthew has no angels prod the men to "get on with it" because Jesus has filled them with hope and urgency for getting the job done. The authority Jesus has he gives his disciples, erasing any sense of failure from their minds. But where will the disciples find the courage to carry out their incredible mission? From the incredibly comforting assurance that the living presence of Jesus will be with his Church forever.

SEVENTH SUNDAY
OF EASTER

LECTIONARY #59

READING I   Acts of the Apostles 1:12–14

A reading from the Acts of the Apostles

After Jesus had been taken up to **heaven** the apostles
    returned to **Jerusalem**
    from the mount called **Olivet**, which is **near** Jerusalem,
    a **sabbath** day's journey away.

When they **entered** the city
    they went to the **upper room** where they were **staying**,
    Peter and **John** and **James** and **Andrew**,
    Philip and **Thomas**, **Bartholomew** and **Matthew**,
    James son of Alphaeus, Simon the **Zealot**,
    and **Judas** son of **James**.
All these devoted themselves with one accord to **prayer**,
    together with some **women**,
    and **Mary** the mother of **Jesus**, and his **brothers**.

Among the disciples there is a feeling of being lost and lonely.

Avoiding awkwardness, speak one thought at a time, so as not to rush this opening sentence.

Olivet = OL-ih-vet

The upper room is a familiar and comforting place.

Speak these names as you might if you were listing significant members of your own family.

Alphaeus = AL-fee-uhs

Zealot = ZEL-uht

Judas = JOO-duhs

Mary's presence is noteworthy. "Brothers" can mean "cousins" or "kin."

TO KEEP IN MIND

Units of Thought: Running too many words together blurs meaning and fails to distinguish ideas. Punctuation does not always indicate clearly what words to group together or where to pause. Identify *units of thought* and use your voice to distinguish one from another.

READING I   The Apostles have traveled "a sabbath day's journey," or a distance of a little over half a mile, from the top of Mount Olivet back to Jerusalem. They've witnessed Jesus's Ascension, but now they gather in the upper room focused entirely on prayer. We might expect an exciting development at this point, but nothing happens. And this week, that somehow feels appropriate. Prior to ascending, Jesus promised to send "another Advocate," so this is a time of waiting, perhaps a time of anxious anticipation for the eleven. In bridging the time between the ascent of Jesus and the descent of the Spirit, the men are not alone, for notably "some women" and "Mary the mother of Jesus" were among them. The mood is one of uncertainty, anxiety, and longing.

A short text like this calls for slow reading; but slow never means lacking energy or tension. Your main task is to render the Apostles' names as if they were people who matter to you and should matter to us, rather than as strangers in some story of long ago. Let your tone suggest their mood of prayerful but anxious waiting. Speak as if you "know" these men and the women in their company, which means you're sympathetic to their feelings and situation.

Stress the reference to "prayer" and don't rush the mention of the women and of Mary the Mother of Jesus. To these, too, the Spirit came, and together they fanned the flame of faith that became the Church.

READING II   Christianity has always presented a unique and countercultural view of suffering. Though often misunderstood and sometimes exaggerated,

For meditation and context:

RESPONSORIAL PSALM   Psalm 27:1, 4, 7–8 (13)

R. I believe that I shall see the good things of the Lord in the land of the living.
or
R. Alleluia.

The Lord is my light and my salvation;
   whom should I fear?
The Lord is my life's refuge;
   of whom should I be afraid?

One thing I ask of the Lord;
   this I seek:
to dwell in the house of the Lord
   all the days of my life,
that I may gaze on the loveliness
     of the Lord
   and contemplate his temple.

Hear, O Lord, the sound of my call;
   have pity on me, and answer me.
Of you my heart speaks; you my glance seeks.

TO KEEP IN MIND
Always read Scriptures aloud, noting suggestions for stresses and pauses. After several readings, alter the stress markings to suit your style and interpretation.

READING II   1 Peter 4:13–16

A reading from the first Letter of Saint Peter

Beloved:
Rejoice to the extent that you share in the **sufferings** of Christ,
   so that when his **glory** is revealed
   you may **also** rejoice **exultantly**.
If you are **insulted** for the name of Christ, **blessed** are you,
   for the Spirit of **glory** and of **God** rests upon you.
But let **no** one among you be made to suffer
   as a **murderer**, a **thief**, an **evildoer**, or as an **intriguer**.
But whoever is made to suffer as a **Christian** should not
    be **ashamed**
   but **glorify** God because of the **name**.

Imagine Peter in the Upper Room of the First Reading suddenly rising in the midst of the frightened disciples and proclaiming these words.

Convince us these assertions make sense. Imagine people you know who need this encouragement.

The tone shifts here. There is a strong, paternal quality to the teaching.

intriguer = in-TREEG-*r

End on a note of confident, deep joy.

Christianity finds goodness in suffering—when it results from our dedication to Christ. Peter speaks boldly about the near certainty that those who follow Christ will share in his suffering. But he assures his listeners that if we suffer *with* Christ we will share the "glory" that will be "revealed" in him. There is compelling power (and poetry) in his assertion that "If you are insulted for the name of Christ, blessed are you." And the blessing is God's Spirit dwelling within us!

Two aspects of Peter's words stand out. First, they paraphrase one of the Beatitudes spoken by Jesus. Secondly, they are words of contradiction: rejoice over *suffering*; be *happy* about being insulted. It's nonsense which, only if seen through eyes of faith, makes all the sense in the world. Consider your own experience of suffering and of the Gospel contradictions you've experienced: how being last made you first; how dying to self led to renewed life; how suffering gave birth to joy. Then, gently and lovingly, persuade us that this craziness actually makes sense.

Previously, Peter said it is better to suffer for "doing good . . . than for doing evil" (I Peter 3:17). He repeats himself here arguing that none should suffer for the evils of murder or stealing. But, when suffering comes because of our faith, we have reason to rejoice in being so favored. Surely there are "disciples" in your pews who long to hear that message.

GOSPEL It's a rare privilege, even in the Gospel accounts, to be able to listen in on Jesus's prayer. This sincere prayer, known as the "high priestly

GOSPEL   John 17:1–11a

A reading from the holy Gospel according to John

Jesus raised his eyes to **heaven** and said,
  "**Father**, the hour has **come**.
Give **glory** to your son, so that your son may glorify **you**,
  just as you gave him **authority** over all people,
  so that your son may give eternal **life** to all you gave him.
Now **this** is eternal life,
  that they should **know** you, the only **true** God,
  and the one whom you **sent**, Jesus **Christ**.
I glorified you on **earth**
  by accomplishing the **work** that you gave me to do.
Now glorify **me**, Father, with **you**,
  with the glory that I had with you before the world **began**.

"I revealed your **name** to those whom you gave me out
    of the world.
They **belonged** to you, and you **gave** them to me,
  and they have **kept** your word.
Now they know that everything you gave me is from **you**,
  because the words you gave to **me** I have given to **them**,
  and they **accepted** them and truly understood that I **came**
    from you,
  and they have **believed** that you sent me.
I **pray** for them.
I do not pray for the **world** but for the ones you have **given** me,
  because they are **yours**, and everything of **mine** is yours
  and everything of yours is **mine**,
  and I have been **glorified** in them.
And now I will no **longer** be in the world,
  but **they** are in the world, while **I** am coming to **you**."

First narrate, and then look to heaven as Jesus does.

Jesus is mindful of the suffering that will lead to "glory."

This statement is likely an editorial insertion for nowhere else does Jesus call himself "Jesus Christ."

Jesus glorified God by being wholly obedient to the divine will.

Let your tone convey Jesus's intimacy with God and his great concern for his disciples.

Despite times of frustration, Jesus now lauds his disciples' ability and willingness to embrace Jesus's teaching.

Pause before and after this line.

Again, we hear of Jesus's oneness with God.

The prayer ends abruptly, so slow your pace as you near the end. Focus on the assembly as you say, "they are in the world."

---

prayer," reveals two things: Jesus's intimacy with the Father and his candid love for his disciples. The prayer sums up Jesus's life of uncompromising dedication to God's will which, if it were to be summarized in one word, would be "obedience." Jesus's request to be glorified may feel awkward. But we must remember that in John, Jesus's glorification comes through his Death. Jesus knows his "hour" has arrived and that God will glorify him in the Resurrection and Ascension, but only after he has mounted the Cross and entered the tomb.

The Apostles are privileged to overhear Jesus's prayer that he addresses directly to the Father. You are privileged to pray his words, for your own ministry and the ministry of the Church. Take your cue from Jesus and look "up to heaven" as you pray the words. John's editorial aside, "Now this is eternal life," is a heartfelt assertion of who is the source of our hope. Though he is still with them, there is a clear sense that Jesus's earthly ministry is now concluded. Look at the assembly as you speak phrases like "I revealed your name," "the words you gave me I have given to them,"

and so forth. Strong eye contact may remind your listeners that, like the Apostles, they are *in* but not *of* the world.

Jesus anticipates his departure from "the world" realizing his followers cannot follow him. Concerns for their spiritual safety, reluctance to leave them, and desire to remain one with them imbue his words. By keeping in mind that Jesus's prophecy of glorification is now fulfilled in you and your assembly, you will understand the pride with which Jesus speaks of these he loves so tenderly.

PENTECOST SUNDAY: VIGIL

LECTIONARY #62

READING I   Genesis 11:1–9

A reading from the Book of Genesis

The whole world spoke the same **language**, using the same **words**.
While the people were **migrating** in the east,
    they came upon a valley in the land of **Shinar** and **settled** there.
They said to one another,
    "**Come**, let us mold **bricks** and harden them with **fire**."
They used bricks for **stone**, and **bitumen** for **mortar**.
Then they said, "Come, let us build ourselves a **city**
    and a **tower** with its top in the **sky**,
    and so make a **name** for ourselves;
    otherwise we shall be **scattered** all over the earth."

The LORD came down to **see** the city and the tower
    that the people had built.
Then the LORD said: "If **now**, while they are **one** people,
    all speaking the same **language**,
    they have started to do this,
    nothing will later **stop** them from doing whatever they **presume** to do.
Let us then go down there and **confuse** their language,
    so that one will not **understand** what another says."
Thus the LORD **scattered** them from there all over the earth,
    and they stopped **building** the city.

Genesis = JEN-uh-sis

As narrator, you know this innocent age is lost.

Shinar = SHĪ-nahr; SHEE-nahr

Speak with the arrogance that motivates their defiance.

bitumen = bih-TYOO-m*n; bih-TOO-m*n

"Tower" probably refers to a stepped pyramid-like structure.

Their plan is in direct defiance of God's order to "fill the earth." They plan to enhance their own reputation without any help from God.

This is a new scene. Immediately suggest the disapproval with which God views the city and tower.

God is not being vindictive, but protecting humanity from itself.

That God comes "down" signifies human smallness in contrast to God's might.

This might be the reply if a child at that time asked, "Why do people speak different languages?"

There are options for readings today. Ask your parish staff which ones will be used.

READING I   **GENESIS 11:1–9.** In the beginning, God's Spirit brought order out of chaos. But because of people's disobedience and pride, the same Spirit brought chaos to Babel. At Pentecost, the very same Spirit initiates the undoing of what we see beginning in this passage: the alienation of neighbor from neighbor and nation from nation, once again creating order from chaos.

Genesis chronicles the spread and consequences of sin through a series of stories that depict how sin alienates us from God (Adam and Eve are expelled from the garden), from one another (Cain kills his brother Abel), and even nation from nation (suddenly people speak different languages and can't communicate, leading to misunderstandings, conflicts, and war). Pentecost will miraculously reverse this situation by making diverse peoples able to understand one another. But tonight's the vigil, so we await that miracle.

To prepare for the Pentecost marvel, stress the human pride that wants to "make a name" for itself and the vanity that seeks to be like gods. That flawed and sinful motivation is what tears down the tower, not God's jealousy. To make that apparent, build tension between the narrator who reports this event of final alienation and the Babel builders who proudly undertake their project blind to the potential consequences. The narrator speaks nostalgically of "the good old days" when "the whole world spoke the same language." But lines like "a tower . . . in the

That is why it was called **Babel**,
    because there the Lord **confused** the speech of all the world.
It was from that place that he **scattered** them all over the **earth**.

Or:

READING I   Exodus 19:3–8a, 16–20b

A reading from the Book of Exodus

Moses went up the mountain to **God**.
Then the Lord **called** to him and said,
    "**Thus** shall you say to the house of **Jacob**;
    tell the **Israelites**:
    You have **seen** for yourselves how I treated the **Egyptians**
    and how I **bore** you up on **eagle** wings
    and brought you here to **myself**.
Therefore, if you **hearken** to my voice and keep my **covenant**,
    you shall be my special **possession**,
    dearer to me than all **other** people,
    though **all** the earth is mine.
You shall be to me a kingdom of **priests**, a **holy** nation.
That is what you must tell the Israelites."
So Moses went and summoned the **elders** of the people.
When he set before them
    all that the Lord had **ordered** him to tell them,
    the people all answered together,
    "**Everything** the Lord has said, we will **do**."

On the morning of the **third** day
    there were peals of **thunder** and **lightning**,
    and a heavy **cloud** over the mountain,
    and a very loud **trumpet** blast,
    so that all the people in the camp **trembled**.

Babel = BAB-*l; BAY-b*l

This might be the reply if a child asked, "Why do people speak differently?"

TO KEEP IN MIND
Practice pronunciation!

Exodus = EK-suh-duhs
Moses = MOH-ziz; MOH-zis

This is no ordinary climb up a mountain! Pause between "mountain" and "to God."

God's tone is awesome and proud, yet tender.

This is a conditional covenant. *God* will honor the covenant if the *people* honor it.

Note that God does not promise wealth or power, but holiness.

Let your voice ring with the excitement and fervor of the people.

Don't overdramatize these events. Capture, instead, the awe and dread of the assembled people.

---

sky" and "make a name for ourselves" reek of arrogance and reflect a desire to thwart God's will. God's response to this affront exhibits a familiar biblical anthropomorphism, that is, ascribing human reasoning and emotions to God. Avoid a vindictive tone, but don't be afraid to let God sound human. Like a parent who disciplines a presumptuous child, God rebukes for the good of humanity. Slowly and with regret, summarize what happened to the world as a result of pride: people were "scattered" and their tongues "confused." And only

God's Spirit will be able to untangle the mess human hands have made.

EXODUS 19:3–8a, 16–20b. This reading memorializes the inauguration of the Mosaic covenant at Mount Sinai. By the time of Jesus, the Jewish feast of Pentecost had become less a harvest festival and more a memorial of God giving the Law to Moses. This selection brings us to the edge of the covenant's ratification, though not to the dramatic event itself, which occurs five chapters later.

The way this passage is crafted results in suspense: God describes what will follow

if the covenant bond is established; Moses presents the conditions to the people who enthusiastically agree; impressive fireworks signal the approaching moment of commitment and then, as the people look on, Moses is summoned to the top of the mountain. And we're left wondering what will happen next.

As narrator, suggest that Moses's trip up the mountain will be no ordinary trek, but an encounter of supreme consequence. God's voice echoes with authority and pride in the way divine solicitude delivered Israel from slavery. God's offer of special

They set out with resolute courage.

"Smoke" and "fire" are manifestations of God.

"Trumpet" refers to a "shofar," an instrument made from the horn of a ram. Be mindful that this is not an everyday conversation.

This line goes back to the beginning, when God and Moses first began speaking. Take a long pause before announcing, "The word of the Lord."

Ezekiel = ee-ZEE-kee-uhl

To enhance rather than slight the unique features of this text (the refrain-like repetitions and the extraordinary visions) you will need extra preparation time. Practice until you are comfortable with and enjoying the rich imagery and the poetic flow of the language.

Ezekiel finds himself transported into the midst of this scene of devastation.

His despondency should be apparent in your tone.

prophesy = PROF-uh-sī

God *orders* Ezekiel to prophesy. Speak the words with authority.

But Moses led the people **out** of the camp to meet **God**,
    and they stationed themselves at the **foot** of the mountain.
Mount Sinai was all wrapped in **smoke**,
    for the Lord came down upon it in **fire**.
The smoke **rose** from it as though from a **furnace**,
    and the whole mountain trembled **violently**.
The **trumpet** blast grew louder and louder, while Moses
        was speaking,
    and God **answering** him with **thunder**.

When the Lord came **down** to the top of Mount Sinai,
    he summoned **Moses** to the **top** of the mountain.

Or:

READING I   Ezekiel 37:1–14

A reading from the Book of the Prophet Ezekiel

The hand of the **Lord** came upon me,
    and he led me out in the **spirit** of the Lord
    and set me in the center of the **plain**,
    which was now filled with **bones**.
He made me **walk** among the bones in every direction
    so that I saw how **many** they were on the surface of the plain.
How **dry** they were!
He asked me:
    Son of **man**, can these bones come to **life**?
I answered, "Lord God, you **alone** know that."
Then he said to me:
    Prophesy over these bones, and **say** to them:
    Dry bones, **hear** the word of the Lord!
Thus says the Lord God to these bones:
    See! I will bring **spirit** into you, that you may come to **life**.

status to Israel should sound more like a marriage proposal than a business proposition. Take time with the "kingdom of priests" and "holy nation" images, softening your volume without losing a sense of grandeur. The narration that precedes the people's response should create a sense of excitement and urgency. The people answer simply but with conviction: "Everything . . . we will do."

Night turns to day, and suddenly there are fireworks! Build your energy as you tell us that despite "peals of thunder and lightning" and "a very loud trumpet blast" (probably a metaphor for the howling wind),

Moses led the people up the mountain. Paint those images slowly, one brushstroke at a time, aware that you describe something none of us has ever experienced.

God and Moses are already dialoguing when the final sentence regresses to the time just prior to their face-to-face encounter. The sentence leaves us in suspense. Take a substantial pause before announcing "The word of the Lord," letting your voice suggest that the real excitement is yet to come. It is!

EZEKIEL 37:1–14. The most disorienting event in Israel's history was the exile. Nation, monarchy, and Temple all

were lost. Nothing was the same after that and hope languished with the debris of Jerusalem's walls. But in the midst of the exile, Ezekiel challenges the people's desperation by sharing this vision of the dry bones that promises mercy and offers striking images of restoration. Ezekiel himself, however, is slow to breathe the fresh air of hope. So God lets him linger among the bones to absorb the utter devastation they represent and then asks, "Can these bones come to life?" Ezekiel responds half-heartedly, "Lord God, you alone know that."

No human effort can remediate this situation, so God takes charge and orders

Don't overdramatize these events; they should have an air of reality. Achieve that with a lively rate; too slow a pace will make the lines burdensome. Throughout, tone and energy are more important than specific words.

prophesying = PROF-uh-sī-ing

These repetitions, like the repeated phrases of a song, add beauty to the text and etch its message in our memories. Don't treat them like redundancies to be gotten around as quickly as possible.
Only when they receive God's Spirit do the bones come alive.

This promise should arouse hope in the listener.

The fulfillment of the promise will prove God's sovereignty.

The covenant will not be abandoned!

Be sure you have given proper attention to the words "spirit," "life," "winds," and "breathe" that are so relevant to this solemnity. The final line contains two strong declarations: "I have promised," and "I will do it." Don't run them together.

I will put **sinews** upon you, make **flesh** grow over you,
    cover you with **skin**, and put **spirit** in you
    so that you may come to **life** and know that I am the Lord.
I, Ezekiel, prophesied as I had been told,
    and even as I was prophesying I heard a **noise**;
    it was a **rattling** as the bones came **together**, **bone** joining **bone**.
I saw the **sinews** and the **flesh** come upon them,
    and the **skin** cover them, but there was no **spirit** in them.
Then the Lord said to me:
    Prophesy to the spirit, **prophesy**, son of man,
    and **say** to the spirit: **Thus** says the Lord God:
    From the four winds **come**, O spirit,
    and **breathe** into these slain that they may come to **life**.
I **prophesied** as he told me, and the spirit **came** into them;
    they came **alive** and stood **upright**, a vast **army**.
Then he said to me:
    Son of man, these bones are the whole house of **Israel**.
They have been saying,
    "Our bones are **dried** up,
    our hope is **lost**, and we are **cut** off."
Therefore, prophesy and **say** to them: Thus says the Lord God:
    O my people, I will **open** your **graves**
    and have you **rise** from them,
    and bring you **back** to the land of **Israel**.
Then you shall **know** that I am the Lord,
    when I **open** your graves and have you **rise** from them,
    O my people!
I will put my **spirit** in you that you may **live**,
    and I will **settle** you upon your land;
    thus you shall know that I am the Lord.
I have **promised**, and I will **do** it, says the Lord.

Or:

Ezekiel to speak God's Spirit into the bones. A breathtaking scene unfolds. Amid the roar of wind and rattling bones, flesh, sinews, and skin appear on the skeletons. The restoration happens in stages: first come "sinews" and "flesh," then "breath" and "spirit." The powerful symbolism is a promise to Israel that the ordeal of exile *will* end: the nation will be restored and the Temple rebuilt, for God may chastise but never abandon the Chosen People.

You must bring these fantastical images to life, using the refrain-like repetitions to deepen our experience. You'll be

tempted to speak "I will *open* your graves and you shall *rise* from them" energetically and with conviction but then repeat that promise two lines later in a flat and lifeless way, as if the words were a nuisance to be gotten around as quickly as possible. The same is true of "I will bring *spirit* into you, that you may come to *life*." Treating these lines as redundancies is to miss the style and power of this literature. Achieve variety by stressing different words each time a phrase recurs. God's voice, urgent and strong, tells Ezekiel what to prophesy. He

obeys that insistent voice, then watches in wonder as the amazing events unfold. There is no narrator, only Ezekiel, speaking in this passage. Speak with his voice and emotional involvement. Doing less would be a disservice to the prophet, and to your assembly.

READING I | **JOEL 3:1–5.** The Bible sees God acting in the events of human history; so when Israel was beset by a devastating plague of locusts, the prophet Joel viewed it as God's judgment against the people's lukewarm faith. But

Joel = JOH-*l

This text forms the basis of much of Peter's Pentecost sermon (Acts 2:17–21).

This is a joyful promise of extraordinary grace.
Prophesy = PROF-uh-sī

Stress the variety of those who will receive the Spirit.

This is unexpected: "Even upon the servants." Give due stress to these words.

A more sober mood dominates here. The images are not terrifying, but awe-inspiring.

"Great" and "terrible" characterize the mood of the entire reading.

Only those who call on God need not fear the "terrible day" of the Lord.
Zion = Zī-ahn

"Zion" and "Jerusalem" are much beloved images that combine with "remnant" and "survivors" to create a sense of joyful hope.

> TO KEEP IN MIND
> **Prophets**: In addition to troubling the comfortable, prophets comforted the troubled. With equal passion, the great seers spoke threat and consolation, indictment and forgiveness. You must do the same for the chosen people you call "parish."

READING I   Joel 3:1–5

A reading from the Book of the Prophet Joel

Thus says the LORD:
I will pour out my **spirit** upon all **flesh**.
Your **sons** and **daughters** shall **prophesy**,
    your **old** men shall dream **dreams**,
    your **young** men shall see **visions**;
even upon the **servants** and the **handmaids**,
    in those days, I will **pour** out my spirit.
And I will work **wonders** in the heavens and on the earth,
    blood, **fire**, and columns of **smoke**;
the **sun** will be turned to **darkness**,
    and the **moon** to **blood**,
at the **coming** of the day of the LORD,
    the **great** and **terrible** day.
Then everyone shall be **rescued**
    who calls on the **name** of the LORD;
for on Mount Zion there shall be a **remnant**,
    as the LORD has said,
and in Jerusalem **survivors**
    whom the LORD shall **call**.

when Joel calls the nation to repentance, it responds with genuine contrition. God has already promised to restore the land, but now, with tremendous urgency as if the message must be shared before it's too late, God promises three more blessings, each announced by a divine declaration.

First will be an outpouring of God's Spirit. The Spirit will be given liberally, to a diversity of people: sons and daughters, old men and young, even servants and handmaids. Because Jewish tradition believed God's Spirit could be imparted only to great leaders like Moses, this promise is truly remarkable. The Spirit even makes servants the equals of their masters. An enthusiastic, generous energy pervades these lines. Speak them with joy.

Second will be awesome and sobering signs in the sky. But terrifying as they may be, the signs are actually blessings, for they help the believer prepare for the "great and terrible day" of the Lord, a day of new and unexpected wonders. "Terrible" captures the mood of these lines because it suggests not an awful but an *awesome* experience—like a tornado that's too enthralling

not to watch, but dangerous if you linger too long. Words like "fire," "smoke," and "the coming of the day" have special value today, so speak them with positive energy.

Third is the promise of deliverance. A significant pause after "terrible day" allows you to transition to the message of comfort that follows: "Everyone . . . who calls on the name of the Lord" will be rescued. They will be given a home in "Jerusalem" and "Mount Zion," beloved images of hope and comfort. But bittersweet news ends the passage, for only a "*remnant*" will hear the

For meditation and context:

TO KEEP IN MIND

Know the purpose of the letter: *It* dictates the tone. Often Paul is the writer. As teacher and spiritual leader, he is motivated by multiple concerns: to instruct, console, encourage, chastise, warn, settle disputes, and more. When reading from one of his letters, be aware of what he's trying to accomplish.

"Labor pains" is an unexpected image. Don't rush past it.

While we have already tasted life in the Spirit, we long for the fullness only the Kingdom will offer.

There is a lively, colloquial feel to Paul's logic. Recall your own longing for what you cannot see.

God provides for our inadequacy in prayer, letting the Spirit pray within us when we don't know how to pray.
Why do prayers often go unanswered? Paul helps us understand: "We do not know how to pray as we ought."
God, who searches hearts, understands our Spirit-led prayers better than we do. Confidently offer that assurance to your assembly and don't rush past this beautiful image.

RESPONSORIAL PSALM   Psalm 104:1–2a, 24, 35c, 27–28, 29bc–30 (30)

R. **Lord, send out your Spirit, and renew the face of the earth.**
or
R. **Alleluia.**

Bless the Lord, O my soul!
    O Lord, my God, you are great indeed!
You are clothed with majesty and glory,
    robed in light as with a cloak.

How manifold are your works, O Lord!
    In wisdom you have wrought them all—
the earth is full of your creatures;
    bless the Lord, O my soul! Alleluia.

Creatures all look to you
    to give them food in due time.
When you give it to them, they gather it;
    when you open your hand, they are filled
        with good things.

If you take away their breath, they perish
    and return to their dust.
When you send forth your spirit,
    they are created,
    and you renew the face of the earth.

READING II   Romans 8:22–27

A reading from the Letter of Saint Paul to the Romans

Brothers and sisters:
We know that all **creation** is groaning in **labor** pains even
        until **now**;
    and not **only** that, but we **ourselves**,
    who have the **firstfruits** of the Spirit,
    we also **groan** within ourselves
    as we wait for **adoption**, the **redemption** of our bodies.
For in hope we were **saved**.
Now hope that **sees** is not **hope**.
For who **hopes** for what one **sees**?
But if we hope for what we do **not** see, we wait with **endurance**.

In the **same** way, the Spirit **too** comes to the aid of our **weakness**;
    for we do not know **how** to pray as we ought,
    but the Spirit himself **intercedes** with inexpressible **groanings**.
And the one who **searches hearts**
    knows what is the **intention** of the Spirit,
    because he **intercedes** for the holy ones
    according to God's **will**.

Lord's call and find in God's arms a true place of refuge.

READING II Sometimes Paul theologizes, other times he teaches, chides, or argues. And there are times when he shares the words of life. For many, Romans, chapter eight, is such a time. Proclaim this passage from your own experience of patient endurance and expectant hope. You have known what it means to hope for what cannot be seen. Drawing on that experience will make com-

pelling your declaration that "hope that *sees* is not hope."

Paul focuses on the almost but-not-yet aspect of the Kingdom. The coming of the Holy Spirit inaugurated a new age that won't reach fulfillment till we reach the Kingdom. Now, we taste the "firstfruits of the Spirit," but we long for more. So with the rest of creation we "groan" as if in childbirth because our adoption as God's children isn't complete. "Hope" enables us to "wait with endurance." Paul defines hope as expecting what we cannot see because we can't hope for what's already

visible. We can hope only when what we desire is out of sight. Paul reasons like a believer, not a lawyer. Do the same, speaking from the depths of your own longing for what you cannot see—health of loved ones, a just society, inner peace.

If you have ever found your helplessness and speechlessness turned to prayer, then you can convincingly utter these words of encouragement. Speak the last sentence directly to the assembly. Like the searcher of hearts (what a splendid image!) speak comfort to individual faces who need to hear that the Spirit understands *their*

GOSPEL   John 7:37–39

A reading from the holy Gospel according to John

On the **last** and **greatest** day of the feast,
    Jesus stood up and **exclaimed**,
    "Let anyone who **thirsts** come to me and **drink**.
As Scripture says:
    *Rivers of **living** water will flow from within him* who
        believes *in me.*"

He said this in reference to the **Spirit**
    that those who came to believe in him were to **receive**.
There was, of course, no Spirit **yet**,
    because Jesus had not yet been **glorified**.

The last day of the feast was the eighth day, a full holiday, when only the high priest carried water. The water carried during the feast symbolized hope of Messianic deliverance.

Suggest that he rose and spoke boldly in order to be heard. Make eye contact as you speak, "Let anyone . . ."

"From within him" is one of those rare instances when you should stress the preposition.

Though this sounds parenthetical, sustain the energy. It's important.

Jesus was glorified through his ministry, Death, Resurrection, and Ascension.

inner pain and groaning and, unlike us, prays only according to God's perfect will.

GOSPEL   The Feast of Tabernacles commemorated Israel's wanderings in the desert and joyfully celebrated the harvest. Each day, water was carried into the city from the Pool of Siloam as a reminder of the miraculous water from the rock in the desert. On the eighth and final day, only the high priest brought water from Siloam to pour upon the Temple altar in prayer for plentiful rains. In the midst of the prayer and rejoicing, and aware the eyes of friend and foe were upon him, Jesus offered *himself* as the source of *living* water. Water will issue from him in the form of God's Spirit who will end our spiritual wanderings and our thirst by providing an inexhaustible abundance.

Scholars debate whether Christ or the believer is the *source* of "living water," but the grammar and this English translation favor the believer. The water represents wisdom that comes from the Spirit Jesus will impart to those who believe in him. Despite the desire of his enemies to find some word to use against him, Jesus daringly asserts, "Let anyone who thirsts come to *me.*" Read this short passage slowly to avoid finishing before your listeners have tuned in. The parenthetical statement that ends the text connects the coming of the Spirit with the glorification of Jesus through his Passion and Resurrection, so don't let it sound anticlimactic. Read as if you were taking the assembly into your confidence, sharing special information in a hushed but energized tone, all with the awareness that anticipating the "Spirit" is the purpose of this vigil.

PENTECOST SUNDAY: DAY

Read Exodus 19:1–15 and you'll find similarities between the Sinai covenant and the driving wind and flames of Pentecost.

The opening is subdued, void of any hint of the pending fireworks.

Note: the miracle will enable the nations to understand the Apostles, not each other. In Christ's Church, the common language will be the Spirit who draws all to oneness in Christ.

Distinguish the three distinct moments as the "tongues as of fire" appear, part, and rest on each one. Renew your energy on "And they were filled."

Drop your energy level for the narration about the devout Jews. Then raise it again on "At the sound."

"Astounded . . . amazement" suggest how to narrate this section.

The listing of nations adds to the overall animation if you vary the pacing and renew your energy at "Pontus" and "Egypt." Galileans = gal-ih-LEE-uhnz; Parthians = PAHR-thee-uhnz; Medes = meedz; Elamites = EE-luh-mīts; Mesopotamia = mes-uh-poh-TAY-mee-uh; Judea = joo-DEE-uh; Cappadocia = cap-uh-DOH-shee-uh; Pontus = PON-tuhs; Phrygia =FRIJ-ee-uh; Pamphylia = PAM-fil-ee-uh; Libya = LIB-ee-uh; Cyrene = sī-REE-nee

LECTIONARY #63

READING I   Acts of the Apostles 2:1–11

A reading from the Acts of the Apostles

When the time for **Pentecost** was **fulfilled**,
    they were all in one place **together**.
And **suddenly** there came from the **sky**
    a noise like a **strong** driving **wind**,
    and it **filled** the entire **house** in which they were.
Then there appeared to them **tongues** as of **fire**,
    which **parted** and came to **rest** on each **one** of them.
And they were all **filled** with the **Holy Spirit**
    and began to speak in different **tongues**,
    as the Spirit **enabled** them to **proclaim**.

Now there were **devout** Jews from every **nation** under heaven
    staying in Jerusalem.
At this **sound**, they gathered in a large **crowd**,
    but they were **confused**
    because **each** one heard them **speaking** in his own **language**.
They were **astounded**, and in **amazement** they asked,
    "Are not all these people who are speaking **Galileans**?
Then how does **each** of us hear them in his **native** language?
We are **Parthians**, **Medes**, and **Elamites**,
    inhabitants of **Mesopotamia**, **Judea** and **Cappadocia**,
    Pontus and **Asia**, **Phrygia** and **Pamphylia**,
    Egypt and the districts of **Libya** near **Cyrene**,
    as well as travelers from **Rome**,

READING I   The second paragraph describes a chaotic scene—huddled visitors to Jerusalem pulled into the streets by a fearful, thunderous phenomenon. The thunder occurs in the first paragraph where you'll need to create enough excitement to make the second paragraph plausible. The coming of the Spirit touches the assembled disciples *and* the whole city. Jews from many parts of the world are in Jerusalem to mark a festival that celebrates the grain harvest and the Sinai covenant (another fireworks-filled moment that inaugurated the original covenant the

way this moment inaugurates the *new* covenant, sealed in Christ's blood).

"Strong, driving wind" and "tongues as of fire" automatically signal Spirit, and summon rushing, compelling energy that manifests a new moment in salvation history. "They were all filled . . . " announces the dramatic power of God's Spirit. Speak slower here to stress the impact of God's intervention, then announce the results as manifested in the Apostles' sudden ability to speak in different languages.

"Jews from every nation" hear the Good News. Each proper name deserves

attention, not for its individual import, but because together they anticipate the universality of the Church. Picture each scene before you speak and you'll not just be reading words, but painting pictures.

The phenomenon of tongues creates puzzlement expressed in the words "confused," "astounded" and "amazement." Suggest those feelings, but don't overdramatize. Confusion turns to awe-filled joy in the last sentence as the speaker (and you) shifts from observer to believer and makes a statement of faith about the "*marvels* God has accomplished."

Cretans = KREE-tuhnz

The final line summarizes the amazement that builds throughout the listing. Distinguish the two ideas found here: "in our own tongues" and "the mighty acts of God."

For meditation and context:

TO KEEP IN MIND
Practice pronunciation!

---

both **Jews** and **converts** to Judaism, **Cretans** and **Arabs**, yet we hear them **speaking** in our own **tongues** of the mighty **acts** of **God**."

RESPONSORIAL PSALM   Psalm 104:1, 24, 29–30, 31, 34 (30)

R. Lord, send out your Spirit, and renew the face of the earth.
or
R. Alleluia.

Bless the LORD, O my soul!
    O LORD, my God, you are great indeed!
How manifold are your works, O LORD!
    the earth is full of your creatures.

If you take away their breath, they perish
    and return to their dust.
When you send forth your spirit,
        they are created,
    and you renew the face of the earth.

May the glory of the LORD endure forever;
    may the LORD be glad in his works!
Pleasing to him be my theme;
    I will be glad in the LORD.

Corinthians = kohr-IN-thee-uhnz

Only God's Spirit, not the false gods of pagan experience, enables us to profess Jesus as Lord.

Don't miss the passion in the writing. And keep in mind the need for harmony in your own world—whether local or global—to find a proper balance between Paul's logic and passion.

Don't stress the recurrences of "different"; instead, stress "service," "Lord," "workings," "God."

This line concludes and summarizes the first section.

Speak the body analogy carefully and slowly. Paul says much with few words. Stress the contrasts. Note the bolded suggestions for when to stress the word "one." The oneness of the body is maintained with the glue of the Spirit: "Jews or Greeks, slaves or free" reinforces that idea, saying no matter how large or diverse the community, it remains one body in the Spirit.

READING II   1 Corinthians 12:3b–7, 12–13

A reading from the first Letter of Saint Paul to the Corinthians

Brothers and sisters:
No one can say, "**Jesus** is **Lord**," except by the Holy **Spirit**.

There are different **kinds** of spiritual **gifts** but the same **Spirit**;
    there are different forms of **service** but the same **Lord**;
    there are different **workings** but the same **God**
    who produces **all** of them in **everyone**.
To **each** individual the **manifestation** of the Spirit
    is given for some **benefit**.

As a body is **one** though it has many **parts**,
    and **all** the parts of the body, though **many**, are **one** body,
    so also **Christ**.
For in **one** Spirit we were all **baptized** into **one body**,
    whether **Jews** or **Greeks**, **slaves** or **free** persons,
    and we were all given to **drink** of one **Spirit**.

READING II   Paul writes to a divided community splintered by the very reality that should be their source of unity, the Spirit. Today's reading from Acts paints a picture of Jew and Greek, slave and free brought together by the fearful noise of the Spirit. Crises cause differences to melt and oneness to deepen. But for Paul, what should open eyes to oneness and shut them to differences is not disaster but the fountain of the Spirit.

In Corinth, God's generosity had divided the community. All received gifts of the Spirit, but instead of rejoicing with each

other, they compared *their* gift to that of *others*, feeling blessed or shortchanged accordingly. The same Spirit, says Paul, who enables one to confess Jesus as Lord, created their community and distributed gifts among them. And knowing the assignment of charismatic gifts was the work of the Spirit should make it easier to deal with any disparities in the distribution.

Like parts of the body, gifts can't be ranked. The body, whether human or mystical, works only when all the parts labor in harmony. Each part has its own task and unless it is done well, the body suffers.

Gifts can bring out the best or worst in others—the worst is jealousy and rivalry, and that's what happened in Corinth. They forgot that gifts, though given to individuals, are to be exercised as "forms of *service*" for the benefit of all.

The opening proclamation is strong, and full of authority. With that authority call the community to oneness. This passage is so balanced and logical you might forget to give it emotional intensity. Remember that Paul cares passionately for the Corinthians and desires their harmony. Recall, too, the need for harmony among the factions that

For meditation and context:

TO KEEP IN MIND

Eye contact is your means of connecting with those to whom you minister. You should look at the assembly during the middle and at the end of every thought or sentence.

In John, Jesus's Resurrection, Ascension, and conferral of the Spirit all occur on one day.

Help your assembly hear each piece of information John has packed into this sentence.

Jesus is aware of their need for assurance.

This Gospel account says "his side" was pierced. Luke says "feet."

Stress "Lord" rather than "saw" because they rejoiced not at the sight but at the *certainty* that it was Jesus.

Now that they perceive, Jesus offers peace a second time.

"Breathed" sounds like it means. Today Jesus's formula points more to initiation through baptismal faith than to penance.

SEQUENCE   Veni, Sancte Spiritus

Come, Holy Spirit, come!
And from your celestial home
    Shed a ray of light divine!
Come, Father of the poor!
Come, source of all our store!
    Come, within our bosoms shine.
You, of comforters the best;
You, the soul's most welcome guest;
    Sweet refreshment here below;
In our labor, rest most sweet;
Grateful coolness in the heat;
    Solace in the midst of woe.
O most blessed Light divine,
Shine within these hearts of yours,
    And our inmost being fill!

Where you are not, we have naught,
Nothing good in deed or thought,
    Nothing free from taint of ill.
Heal our wounds, our strength renew;
On our dryness pour your dew;
    Wash the stains of guilt away:
Bend the stubborn heart and will;
Melt the frozen, warm the chill;
    Guide the steps that go astray.
On the faithful, who adore
And confess you, evermore
    In your sevenfold gift descend;
Give them virtue's sure reward;
Give them your salvation, Lord;
    Give them joys that never end. Amen.
    Alleluia.

GOSPEL   John 20:19–23

A reading from the holy Gospel according to John

On the evening of that **first** day of the week,
    when the doors were **locked**, where the **disciples** were,
    for fear of the **Jews**,
    Jesus came and **stood** in their midst
    and said to them, "**Peace** be with you."
When he had **said** this, he showed them his **hands** and his **side**.
The disciples **rejoiced** when they saw the Lord.
Jesus said to them **again**, "**Peace** be with you.
As the **Father** has sent **me**, so **I** send **you**."
And when he had said this, he **breathed** on them and said to them,
    "**Receive** the Holy **Spirit**.
Whose sins you **forgive** are **forgiven** them,
    and whose sins you **retain** are **retained**."

---

occasionally arise within your own parish. Keep in mind the Gospel's focus on forgiveness, and you'll communicate the logic *and* the passion of this important text.

 GOSPEL   It is the first day of the week (Resurrection day), and the disciples are hiding fearfully behind locked doors, when unexpectedly and miraculously, Jesus comes and offers "peace." That's a lot for a single sentence, so don't rush. The disciples will rejoice, but only once they're sure that the one before them is the same Lord who taught and prayed

and dined with them the past three years. It's not his face or familiar voice that persuades them but his pierced hands and side. Even on this joyful day the Gospel reminds us that it is a crucified Lord who leads us.

Once the disciples respond, Jesus repeats his peace greeting. He first greeted them before they understood it was really he, but perhaps he repeats it because peace is both hard to sustain and also the surest sign of the Spirit's presence.

"As the Father sent me" is meant as much to comfort as to commission. Jesus

makes them Apostles ("those sent"), but he also assures them that as the Father empowered *him* to do his work, so will he empower *them*. "Breathed" is John's version of Pentecost occurring on the day or of Resurrection; it reminds us of the imparting of life at creation: Jesus breathes *spiritual* life into his disciples and grants them the power to forgive—the surest way to sustain the life of the Spirit.

THE MOST HOLY TRINITY

LECTIONARY #164

READING I   Exodus 34:4b–6, 8–9

Exodus = EK-suh-duhs

Sinai = SĪ-nī

A reading from the Book of Exodus

Suggest Moses's reluctance to make the return trip.

Stress the word "commanded." These are blank tablets upon which God will once again inscribe the commandments.

God is the "Lord" of compassion, not terror.

Imagine God saying, "I am the Lord . . . merciful and gracious . . . ."

Moses expresses both awe and gratitude.

These words could as easily be on our lips today.

Early in the morning **Moses** went up Mount **Sinai**
    as the Lord had **commanded** him,
    taking along the two stone **tablets**.

Having come down in a **cloud**, the Lord **stood** with Moses there
    and proclaimed his **name**, "Lord."
Thus the Lord **passed** before him and **cried** out,
    "The Lord, the Lord, a **merciful** and **gracious** God,
    slow to **anger** and rich in **kindness** and **fidelity**."
Moses at once bowed down to the **ground** in **worship**.
Then he said, "If I find **favor** with you, O Lord,
    do come along in our **company**.
This is indeed a **stiff**-necked people; yet **pardon** our wickedness
        and sins,
    and **receive** us as your **own**."

TO KEEP IN MIND

Openings: First, make eye contact with the assembly and announce, from memory, "A (pronounced "uh," not "ay") reading from . . ." Then pause (three full beats!) before starting the reading.

READING I │ The mystery we call God is both near and distant; both frightening and familiar. Moses understands and reacts to both divine realities. In awed reverence he bows before the Lord; but he also asks forgiveness for his "stiff-necked people" the way a class president might petition the principal on behalf of classmates who pulled a harmful "senior prank" and still hope to graduate.

Keep in mind that Moses is making a return trip up the mountain with a *second* set of tablets that replaces the first pair he angrily smashed when he found the Israelites worshipping the golden calf. The restraint and patience God demonstrated at that time is the reason God claims to be "slow to anger and rich in kindness." Idolatry is the Old Testament's great sin, yet even such blatant sinfulness, God willingly forgives. Given the people's guilt, it's not easy for Moses to approach God again. But God has "commanded," so Moses returns. His bow is as much a sign of gratitude as of awe. So when you announce that the Lord "proclaimed his name" help us hear it, not as a show of power but as a pledge of fidelity. God gifts Moses and the people with his divine presence, so "The Lord, the Lord" should overpower with compassion, not might. Moses willingly concedes the people's sinfulness, but he doesn't hesitate to put a claim on God's mercy for he understands that God's presence blots out sin and makes them a holy people.

For meditation and context:

RESPONSORIAL PSALM   Daniel 3:52, 53, 54, 55 (52b)

R. Glory and praise for ever!

Blessed are you, O Lord, the God
    of our fathers,
    praiseworthy and exalted above all forever;
and blessed is your holy and glorious name,
    praiseworthy and exalted above all for
    all ages.

Blessed are you in the temple of your
    holy glory,
    praiseworthy and glorious above
    all forever.

Blessed are you on the throne
    of your kingdom,
    praiseworthy and exalted above all forever.

Blessed are you who look into the depths
    from your throne upon the cherubim,
    praiseworthy and exalted above all forever.

> **TO KEEP IN MIND**
> **Read through all three readings and commentaries** for your assigned Sunday. All three were chosen for this day, and each commentary has suggestions that can help you with your own passage.

Corinthians = kohr-IN-thee-uhnz

Short readings require *slow* reading.

Note that the word "rejoice" sets the tone for this brief reading.

Don't let this sequence of exhortations take on a scolding tone.

This is what we do at the "Kiss of Peace" during the Eucharist.

This is an important Trinitarian formula. Don't rush it. Place stress on the action ("grace," "love," "fellowship") rather than the person of the Trinity.

> **TO KEEP IN MIND**
> **Slow down**: The larger the church, the larger the assembly, and the more complex the text, the slower you must read.

READING II   2 Corinthians 13:11–13

A reading from second Letter of Saint Paul to the Corinthians

Brothers and sisters, **rejoice**.
Mend your ways, **encourage** one another,
    agree with one another, live in **peace**,
    and the **God** of love and peace will **be** with you.
Greet one another with a **holy** kiss.
All the **holy** ones greet you.

The **grace** of the Lord Jesus Christ
    and the **love** of God
    and the **fellowship** of the Holy Spirit be with **all** of you.

READING II These three verses end the Second Letter to the Corinthians. I like the parting words of a great pastoral leader, they appeal for right behavior and for peace within the community. Though four imperative verbs ("mend," "encourage," "agree," "live!") occur in short succession, the depth of feeling between Paul and the Corinthians allows what otherwise might sound harsh to be spoken and heard as gentle and loving advice.

Elsewhere, the letter contains strong emotions and admonitions, but this conclusion suggests the calm that follows a storm. Paul's words, wrapped in love, express concern for the welfare of his readers.

The final sentence, familiar to us as the celebrant's greeting at the start of Mass, is considered one of the New Testament's most unambiguous articulations of the Trinitarian formula. Paul renders it as a parting blessing to strengthen his readers for the kind of life he's just exhorted them

to live. Speak it as a tender blessing, and as you do think of ways God has blessed you: "The grace of . . . Jesus"—his saving love that brightened your dark moments; "the love of God"—that creative, life-giving love that sustained you through hard times; and "the fellowship of the Holy Spirit"—the Spirit's healing action in the community that resolved conflicts and brought together divergent points of view. This short passage can inspire hope that with God's help we can indeed "mend our ways."

GOSPEL   John 3:16–18

A reading from the holy Gospel according to John

God so **loved** the world that he gave his only **Son**,
    so that everyone who **believes** in him might not **perish**
    but might have eternal **life**.
For God did not send his Son into the world to **condemn**
        the world,
    but that the world might be **saved** through him.
Whoever **believes** in him will **not** be condemned,
    but whoever does **not** believe has **already** been condemned,
    because he has not believed in the name of the only **Son**
        of **God**.

Remember, Jesus is addressing Nicodemus.

Don't rush this beloved text. Take a substantial pause at the beginning to ensure all are ready and attentive.

Jesus's explanation reflects his great compassion.

Speak this affirmation with conviction.

Don't shy from the hard truth of this admonition. But speak with sorrow, not ill will.

TO KEEP IN MIND

Pauses are never "dead" moments. Something is always happening during a pause. Practice will teach you how often and how long to pause. Too many pauses make a reading choppy; too few cause ideas to run into one another.

GOSPEL This much beloved and oft quoted text also poses a hard question: "how could a loving God condemn someone to hell?" Whether it comes from a skeptic or a seeker who is baffled by this seeming contradiction in God's character, it's a question that requires great pastoral care. Of course, God's love is unconditional, but love proffered can be rejected. "Condemnation" is not God's choice, but ours. By the choices we make, we begin living our eternal destiny right here on earth. Here, Jesus speaks to Nicodemus, as sincere a seeker as there ever was, and affirms the generosity of God's love as manifested in God's willingness to give "his only Son." Jesus spoke with deep conviction flowing from his intimate knowledge of the Father and his awareness that he is the Son who will be given up for the world.

Lest Nicodemus misunderstand, Jesus explains further. "God did not send his Son . . . to condemn" but to save the world. "Whoever believes . . . " does not refer to accidents of history or opportunity, but a personal decision to accept Christ as Savior. "Whoever does not believe . . . " speaks of those who have encountered Christ and rejected his light. Therefore, speak with the regret of the Shepherd who would gladly abandon the ninety-nine to seek out the lost sheep. There is no righteousness here, only heartfelt sadness that some will incur judgment for rejecting love itself.

THE MOST HOLY BODY AND BLOOD OF CHRIST (CORPUS CHRISTI)

LECTIONARY #167

Deuteronomy = d<u>oo</u>-ter-AH-nuh-mee; dy<u>oo</u>-ter-AH-nuh-mee

READING I   Deuteronomy 8:2–3, 14b–16a

A reading from the Book of Deuteronomy

"Remember" is a key concept of this passage.

Moses said to the **people**:
"Remember how for forty **years** now the Lord, your God,
   has **directed** all your journeying in the desert,
   so as to **test** you by **affliction**

Avoid a scolding tone; instead, strive for a tone of encouragement.

   and **find** out whether or not it was your intention
   to **keep** his commandments.
He therefore let you be afflicted with **hunger**,
   and then fed you with **manna**,
   a food **unknown** to you and your fathers,

Moses is stressing the miraculous nature of the manna.

   in order to show you that not by bread **alone** does one live,
   but by every **word** that comes forth from the mouth
     of the Lord.

These, of course, are the words Jesus famously quotes to Satan during the temptations in the desert.

Renew your energy here, calling for strong memories of God's goodness.

"Do not **forget** the Lord, your God,
   who brought you **out** of the land of **Egypt**,
   that place of **slavery**;
   who **guided** you through the vast and terrible **desert**
   with its saraph **serpents** and **scorpions**,

The energy builds on each successive phrase that names the merciful works of God.

   its parched and **waterless** ground;
   who brought forth **water** for you from the flinty **rock**
   and **fed** you in the desert with **manna**,

This is an intentional repetition. Give it even more energy than at its first iteration.

   a food **unknown** to your fathers."

| READING I | Every Eucharist is an invitation to do what Moses asks here: "Remember." At Mass we remember that, in Christ, God changed the world forever and we profess faith in truths that we can never prove. Moses is asking something much easier—that the people remember how God saved them from slavery in Egypt, led them through the desert, and provided for all their needs. Given that these are the very people who lived through the

exodus, Moses's call to remember shouldn't be necessary. But human frailty knows few limits. Memory is fragile and quickly fades and sometimes we even question very powerful experiences of God's intervention in our lives.

Moses alludes to two great miracles that demonstrated God's care of the Israelites as they wandered the desert. Beset by scorpions and serpents and suffering hunger and thirst, the people longed for deliverance. God did not disappoint and

provided miraculous manna to nourish the people, a food "unknown to you and your fathers." When thirst was the problem, God ordered Moses to strike a rock and water gushed forth. But these events seem distant now and God's direct involvement is no longer assumed. Was it God or was it just good luck and natural phenomena that saved them? Because of such fragile faith Moses reminds the people of the miracles,

For meditation and context:

RESPONSORIAL PSALM   Psalm 147:12–13, 14–15, 19–20 (12)

R. **Praise the Lord, Jerusalem.**
or
R. **Alleluia.**

Glorify the LORD, O Jerusalem;
  praise your God, O Zion.
For he has strengthened the bars
    of your gates;
  he has blessed your children within you.

He has granted peace in your borders;
  with the best of wheat he fills you.
He sends forth his command to the earth;
  swiftly runs his word!

He has proclaimed his word to Jacob,
  his statutes and his ordinances to Israel.
He has not done thus for any other nation;
  his ordinances he has not made known
    to them. Alleluia.

Corinthians = kohr-IN-thee-uhnz

A short reading requires slow reading.

With strong, sustained eye contact you can help communicate the text's ecclesiological subtext.

Note Paul reverses the bread/cup sequence to sustain his focus on the "body."

The obvious answer to these rhetorical questions is an enthusiastic yes.

We are "one body," and that body is the body of Christ.

READING II   1 Corinthians 10:16–17

A reading from the first Letter of Saint Paul to the Corinthians

Brothers and sisters:
The cup of **blessing** that we bless,
  is it not a participation in the **blood** of Christ?
The **bread** that we break,
  is it not a participation in the **body** of Christ?
Because the loaf of bread is **one**,
  we, though many, are one **body**,
  for we all partake of the **one loaf**.

insisting God alone sustained them through the hardest time in their lives.

The second paragraph reiterates the command to "not forget." Here Moses clearly identifies *who* ought to be remembered: the God "who brought you out," the God "who guided you through," the God "who brought forth water," and "fed you." St. Paul, as does Jesus in today's Gospel, finds in the miracle of the manna a foreshadowing of the Eucharist. So cast a spotlight on that reference.

READING II Paul's questions are not what they seem. They appear to call for faith in the real presence of Christ in the Eucharistic elements. However, Paul is not focusing us on the elements themselves, but on the totality of Christ who is present in the elements. It is the person of Christ—his life, Death, and Resurrection—that we encounter and confess when we receive the Eucharist.

But Paul goes a step further. It is not only the "bread," but also "we," many though we are, who are now Christ's body. As Christ's body, we are placed on the Eucharistic table right along with the Lord, broken and shared right along with him. The consequence is that Eucharist is not just a way of becoming one with Jesus, but a way of entering more deeply into community, embracing an ecclesial spirituality of communion with one another. We cannot

For meditation and context:

TO KEEP IN MIND
Always read Scriptures aloud, noting suggestions for stresses and pauses. After several readings, alter the stress markings to suit your style and interpretation.

SEQUENCE   Lauda, Sion, Salvatorem

Laud, O Zion, your salvation,
Laud with hymns of exultation,
    Christ, your king and shepherd true:

Bring him all the praise you know,
He is more than you bestow.
    Never can you reach his due.

Special theme for glad thanksgiving
Is the quick'ning and the living
    Bread today before you set:

From his hands of old partaken,
As we know, by faith unshaken,
    Where the Twelve at supper met.

Full and clear ring out your chanting,
Joy nor sweetest grace be wanting,
    From your heart let praises burst:

For today the feast is holden,
When the institution olden
    Of that supper was rehearsed.

Here the new law's new oblation,
By the new king's revelation,
    Ends the form of ancient rite:

Now the new the old effaces,
Truth away the shadow chases,
    Light dispels the gloom of night.

What he did at supper seated,
Christ ordained to be repeated,
    His memorial ne'er to cease:

And his rule for guidance taking,
Bread and wine we hallow, making
    Thus our sacrifice of peace.

This the truth each Christian learns,
Bread into his flesh he turns,
    To his precious blood the wine:

Sight has fail'd, nor thought conceives,
But a dauntless faith believes,
    Resting on a pow'r divine.

Here beneath these signs are hidden
Priceless things to sense forbidden;
    Signs, not things are all we see:

Blood is poured and flesh is broken,
Yet in either wondrous token
    Christ entire we know to be.

Whoso of this food partakes,
Does not rend the Lord nor breaks;
    Christ is whole to all that taste:

Thousands are, as one, receivers,
One, as thousands of believers,
    Eats of him who cannot waste.

Bad and good the feast are sharing,
Of what divers dooms preparing,
    Endless death, or endless life.

Life to these, to those damnation,
See how like participation
    Is with unlike issues rife.

When the sacrament is broken,
Doubt not, but believe 'tis spoken,
    That each sever'd outward token
        doth the very whole contain.

Nought the precious gift divides,
Breaking but the sign betides
    Jesus still the same abides,
        still unbroken does remain.

Lo! the angel's food is given
To the pilgrim who has striven;
    See the children's bread from heaven,
        which on dogs may not be spent.

Truth the ancient types fulfilling,
Isaac bound, a victim willing,
    Paschal lamb, its lifeblood spilling,
        manna to the fathers sent.

Very bread, good shepherd, tend us,
Jesu, of your love befriend us,
    You refresh us, you defend us,
    Your eternal goodness send us
In the land of life to see.

You who all things can and know,
Who on earth such food bestow,
    Grant us with your saints, though lowest,
    Where the heav'nly feast you show,
Fellow heirs and guests to be. Amen. Alleluia.

---

encounter Christ without encountering his whole body, the Church.

So ask Paul's sublime questions with your own inner voice answering yes; ask them earnestly, communicating your own absolute faith in these mysteries; ask them with a joy that says how amazingly wonderful it is to be sharers in the mysteries of Christ. Read slowly and utilize the appropriate pauses. Use eye contact to connect with your listeners. Convey Paul's message

with a direct and unadorned delivery, with care in your voice, and a smile on your face as you marvel at the diversity of the "many" who miraculously become "one body."

GOSPEL   It's nearly impossible to imagine a reaction to Jesus's startling announcement different from that of "the crowds." Surely Jesus had to know he'd meet with unparalleled skepticism. Yet there is no hint of apology or explanation in his words. He is earnest and

persuasive, uttering words of self-offering, not self-aggrandizement.

The quarrelers appear both angry and confused. They must decide whether this man is a blasphemer, a lunatic, or possibly a prophet. Though Jesus responds with "Amen, amen," a formula that suggests solemn assurance, his words are of little help to anyone who's mad at him or anyone who thinks him mad. As he addresses the cynical and the confused, we hear no trace of

GOSPEL   John 6:51–58

A reading from the holy Gospel according to John

Jesus said to the Jewish **crowds**:
  "I am the living **bread** that came down from **heaven**;
  whoever **eats** this bread will live **forever**;
  and the **bread** that I will give
  is my **flesh** for the life of the **world**."

The Jews **quarreled** among themselves, saying,
  "How can this man give us his **flesh** to eat?"
Jesus said to them,
  "**Amen, amen,** I say to you,
  unless you **eat** the flesh of the Son of Man and **drink** his **blood**,
  you do not have **life** within you.
Whoever **eats** my flesh and **drinks** my blood
  has **eternal** life,
  and I will **raise** him on the last day.
For my flesh is **true food**,
  and my blood is **true drink**.
Whoever eats my flesh and **drinks** my blood
  remains in **me** and I in **him**.
Just as the living Father sent **me**
  and I have life because of the **Father**,
  so also the one who **feeds** on me
  will have life **because** of me.
This is the bread that came down from **heaven**.
Unlike your **ancestors** who ate and still **died**,
  whoever eats **this** bread will live **forever**."

As narrator, you've already dealt with the disturbing nature of these words and speak now as a believer.

Jesus came to be our bread and to willingly surrender his life that it might become our source of nourishment.

The crowd's tone betrays both doubt and anger.

Speak this solemn pronouncement with great conviction.

Participation in the Body and Blood of Christ is participation in the whole life of Christ and in his saving activity.

This is Good News proclaimed with conviction and joy.

There is great intensity here; great love and urgency.

An allusion to the desert manna.

Draw a sharp contrast between the "ancestors who ate and still died," and those who are given the opportunity to live forever.

anger or judgment in his words. Instead, Jesus offers himself as the (*only*) hope for eternal life, urging the crowd to let him who is "true food" and "true drink" be their source of nourishment.

In the contours of this text we find an outline of the life and ministry of Jesus—from his coming as the bread from heaven, through his willing self-sacrifice for the salvation of the world, to his ongoing presence among believers as the bread that gathers them around the table of Communion. "I am the living bread that came down from heaven," suggests the Incarnation; "my flesh for the life of the world" alludes to his sacrificial Death; and "Whoever eats my flesh and drinks my blood" suggests the Eucharistic sacrament that makes Christ's Death and Resurrection constantly present and available within the believing community. The words are unusual, but you must deliver them with conviction and love.

SAINTS PETER AND PAUL, APOSTLES: VIGIL

LECTIONARY #590

READING I   Acts of the Apostles 3:1–10

A reading from the Acts of the Apostles

These details show the disciples maintained the Jewish prayer customs. Don't rush.

Peter and **John** were going up to the **temple** area
    for the three o'clock hour of **prayer**.
And a man crippled from **birth** was **carried**
    and placed at the **gate** of the temple called "the **Beautiful** Gate"

Apparently the man has solicitous friends or family.

    every **day** to beg for **alms** from the people who entered
        the temple.

Quicken the pace a bit to suggest his recognition of an opportunity to ask for alms.

When he saw **Peter** and **John** about to go into the **temple**,
    he **asked** for **alms**.
But Peter looked **intently** at him, as did John,

Peter's voice, whether soft or bold, rings with confidence and authority.

    and said, "**Look** at us."
He paid **attention** to them, expecting to **receive** something
        from them.
Peter said, "I have neither **silver** nor **gold**,

The words Peter speaks take the place of a healing touch. They carry power and grace.

Nazareth = NAZ-uh-reth

    but what I **do** have I **give** you:
    in the name of Jesus **Christ** the Nazorean, **rise** and **walk**."

Stress the moment of human contact between Peter and the beggar.

Then Peter **took** him by the right hand and **raised** him up,
    and **immediately** his **feet** and **ankles** grew **strong**.
He leaped up, stood, and **walked** around,

Don't overplay the joy. Speak not as the man but as an observer touched by the dramatic healing.

    and went into the **temple** with them,
    walking and **jumping** and **praising** God.

READING I This powerful and compelling story affords a glimpse into the life of the early Christian community and two of its pillar personalities. This episode will end with Peter and John under arrest for testifying to Jesus. The courage of these early leaders is manifested in their willingness to frequent and preach in the public arena of the Temple, disregarding their personal safety.

The lame beggar has no knowledge of Peter and John and seeks from them no more than coins for his bodily sustenance.

But Peter and John see beyond what's sensible. Their intent look suggests a sudden prompting of the Spirit, to which they yield, sensing God has more than a temporary gesture in mind for this man. Peter's words have captured the Christian imagination. They are enshrined in song and have echoed throughout centuries of Christian ministry as countless followers of Jesus reached out, without silver or gold but with the love and the power of Christ, to touch and transform human lives.

The intervention in the lame beggar's life is quite dramatic. Peter speaks the name of Jesus and in that kerygmatic moment the man is literally healed of his disability. Powerful signs continue to manifest the healing power of Christ that now has been transferred to his disciples. Surely such signs had much to do with winning converts to the new way proposed by Jesus and his followers. But equally important as the man's healing is his joyous response. After Peter helps him rise, he does not run to family or friends or to show himself to

When all the people **saw** the man walking and praising God,
   they **recognized** him as the one who used to sit begging
   at the Beautiful Gate of the **temple**,
   and they were filled with **amazement** and **astonishment**
   at what had **happened** to him.

Let your tone suggest that with the "wonder" belief began to creep into the hearts of the observers.

RESPONSORIAL PSALM   Psalm 19:2–3, 4–5 (5)

For meditation and context:

R. Their message goes out through all the earth.

The heavens declare the glory of God,
   and the firmament proclaims
      his handiwork.
Day pours out the word to day;
   and night to night imparts knowledge.

Not a word nor a discourse
   whose voice is not heard;
through all the earth their voice resounds,
   and to the ends of the world,
      their message.

> **TO KEEP IN MIND**
> **Openings:** First, make eye contact with the assembly and announce, from memory, "A (pronounced "uh," not "ay") reading from . . ." Then pause (three full beats!) before starting the reading.

READING II   Galatians 1:11–20

A reading from the Letter of Saint Paul to the Galatians

Galatians = guh-LAY-shuhnz

Paul's assertive opening sets the tone for the reading.

I want you to **know**, brothers and sisters,
that the **Gospel** preached by me is not of **human** origin.
For I did not **receive** it from a human being, nor was I **taught** it,
   but it came through a revelation of Jesus **Christ**.

For Paul, these are important details that assert his legitimacy as an Apostle.

For you heard of my former way of life in **Judaism**,
   how I **persecuted** the Church of God beyond measure
   and tried to **destroy** it, and **progressed** in Judaism
   beyond **many** of my **contemporaries** among my race,
   since I was even more a **zealot** for my ancestral traditions.
But when **God**, who from my mother's **womb** had set me apart
   and **called** me through his **grace**,
   was pleased to reveal his **Son** to me,
   so that I might **proclaim** him to the **Gentiles**,

Shift to a more subdued tone as Paul confesses his prior persecution of the Church.

Paul never shies from asserting his qualifications. But here he stresses his deep commitment to Judaism to demonstrate the power of God in transforming his life. Your tone becomes more intense as Paul describes God's initiative in his life. Help us hear his gratitude.

---

the awed crowd. Instead, he immediately enters the Temple with the disciples, joyously walking and even leaping, but more importantly, *praising* God whose power touched him through the authoritative words of Peter and the Lord whom Peter served and proclaimed.

READING II | Paul's authority as an Apostle was sometimes challenged and such was the case in Galatia. The text chosen for this solemnity that honors him presents Paul's own

defense of his ministry and his frank admission of a former life that accounted for the fear and suspicion that often trailed him.

Paul first claims that he was called to his ministry directly by Christ, not by fellow believers or by any of the Twelve. His insight, he asserts, is God-given; it is a revelation, a direct infusion of divine wisdom, and not the result of tutelage from any "human being." Stellar credentials, indeed!

Next comes his confession of crimes against the very community he now purports to lead. His language is graphic and brutally blunt as he admits he "persecuted

the Church" and "tried to destroy it." He doesn't apologize for this behavior but explains that his zeal flowed from his commitment to Judaism in which he "progressed beyond many . . . among [his] race." It was God's direct intervention, not a gradual conversion, that changed Paul's life and commitments. Through revelation he came to know Christ, and through revelation he was commissioned to preach the Good News "to the Gentiles," information revealed here though not in a similar passage in the Book of Acts.

These are important details to Paul, but you can read them briskly. Their overall import is to say Paul is a true Apostle called by God.

Arabia = uh-RAY-bee-uh
Damascus = duh-MAS-kuhs
Cephas = SEE-fuhs

Paul's contact with Cephas (Peter) is significant.

Don't overdramatize this assertion. Instead, let us hear confident gratitude in Paul's declaration.

I did not immediately consult **flesh** and **blood**,
nor did I go up to **Jerusalem**
to those who were **Apostles** before me;
rather, I went into **Arabia** and then returned to **Damascus**.

Then after **three years** I went up to Jerusalem
to confer with **Cephas** and **remained** with him for fifteen **days**.
But I did not see any **other** of the Apostles,
only **James** the brother of the Lord.
—As to what I am **writing** to you, behold,
before **God**, I am not **lying**.

GOSPEL   John 21:15–19

A reading from the holy Gospel according to John

Jesus had **revealed** himself to his **disciples**
and, when they had finished breakfast, said to **Simon Peter**,
"**Simon**, son of **John**, do you **love** me more than **these**?"
Simon Peter answered him, "**Yes**, Lord, you **know** that
I love you."
Jesus said to him, "**Feed** my **lambs**."
He then said to Simon Peter a **second** time,
"**Simon**, son of **John**, do you **love** me?"
Simon Peter answered him, "**Yes**, Lord, you **know** that
I love you."
He said to him, "**Tend** my **sheep**."
He said to him the **third** time,
"Simon, son of John, do you **love** me?"
Peter was **distressed** that Jesus had said to him a **third** time,
"Do you love me?" and he said to him,
"Lord, you know **everything**; you **know** that I **love** you."

Read this slowly to help set up the scene.

Peter's three responses should exhibit decreasing self-absorption and growing commitment.

Each time, it becomes easier for Peter to respond.

The repetitions wound Peter. So now he abandons all defenses and speaks unguardedly to the Lord.

In the last section, Paul states his credentials once again. His reference to going "up to Jerusalem" not only asserts that he had consulted none of the Apostles previously, but it simultaneously claims the title of Apostle for himself. After his blinding encounter with Christ on the road to Damascus, Paul retreated to the desert of Arabia and only after three more years did he finally consult with Peter, a claim he solemnly asserts. Paul was an unlikely Apostle who entered, by his own admission, through the back door. But the one who opened the door was Christ the Lord!

GOSPEL   Jesus is risen and appears a third time to the disciples, this time in the early morning along the beach. Remarkably, though not uncharacteristically, Jesus calls the disciples to gather for a meal, which this time he has apparently prepared himself. All these significant details are shared nondescriptly in a matter of a few lines. The "daybreak" setting is important for it suggests a time apart, a time for Jesus to be alone with the disciples when dawn signals fresh possibilities and the dim light hides the full potential that awaits.

Breakfast is quickly disposed of and the text launches into what was perhaps Jesus's most significant dialogue with Peter, his handpicked leader of the band of disciples he also had chosen. Much speculation surrounds Jesus's triple inquiry, and the most consistent opinion posits that Jesus is granting Peter an unspoken opportunity to undo his triple denials that must have left him terribly scarred. As motivation for Jesus's interrogation, we might speculate that Jesus is confronting Peter with his failure. After all, Peter bragged that though the others might abandon Jesus, *he*

"Feed my lambs . . . sheep" constitutes a profound invitation to share not only in Christ's ministry, but also in his Passion and Death.

Adapted from a contemporaneous proverb about old age, this statement looks presciently to Peter's own death.

Speak the closing injunction with full awareness of all that it will cost Peter.

Jesus said to him, "**Feed** my sheep.
Amen, **amen**, I say to you, when you were **younger**,
  you used to **dress** yourself and go where you **wanted**;
  but when you grow **old**, you will **stretch** out your hands,
  and someone **else** will **dress** you
  and **lead** you where you do not **want** to go."
He said this signifying by what kind of **death** he would
    glorify **God**.
  And when he had said this, he said to him, "**Follow** me."

TO KEEP IN MIND

Endings: Your inflection of the last line of the reading should always signal that the reading is about to end. Then pause (three beats!) and make eye contact before announcing (from memory) "The word [Gospel] of the Lord." Always pronounce "the" as "thuh" except before words beginning with a vowel.

---

never would. Such bravado could easily merit a subtle "I told you so."

But Jesus does none of that. His dialogue has deeper purpose. If Peter is indeed to lead the soon-to-be-orphaned assembly of believers, he will need confidence and assurance that Jesus has not abandoned him the way he abandoned the Lord, even if only briefly. So Jesus gives him the opportunity to make a clear and firm decision about where his loyalties lie. Are they with himself and his preoccupation with self-protection or are they with the Lord who requires risk and the abandonment of all that was previously held sacred, even self-preservation?

Each time he repeats, "Yes, Lord, you know that I love you," Peter must deepen his commitment, because each time he's told to tend or feed the "lambs" and "sheep" he grows in his awareness of the demands this call will place on him. When at last he confesses, "You know *everything*," Peter is not only acknowledging Jesus's knowledge of his denials but also his own desire to give everything to this man who has become more important to

him than his own life. His final "you know that I love you" expresses his commitment to feed Christ's lambs with his own blood, if necessary.

Jesus's response, which is but a thinly veiled reference to Peter's future death, confirms that "love" of Christ demands everything of the believer. Nothing can be held back. At every moment, the faithful disciple hears Christ's call to "follow me."

SAINTS PETER AND PAUL, APOSTLES: DAY

LECTIONARY #591

READING I   Acts of the Apostles 12:1–11

A reading from the Acts of the Apostles

In those days, King **Herod** laid **hands** upon some members of the
    Church to **harm** them.
He had **James**, the brother of **John**, **killed** by the sword,
    and when he saw that this was **pleasing** to the Jews
    he proceeded to arrest **Peter** also.
—It was the feast of Unleavened Bread.—
He had him taken into custody and put in **prison**
    under the guard of four **squads** of four soldiers **each**.
He intended to bring him before the **people** after **Passover**.
Peter thus was being kept in prison,
    but **prayer** by the church was **fervently** being made
    to God on his **behalf**.

On the very **night** before Herod was to bring him to **trial**,
    Peter, secured by **double** chains,
    was sleeping between two soldiers,
    while outside the **door** guards kept **watch** on the prison.
Suddenly the **angel** of the **Lord** stood by him,
    and a **light** shone in the cell.
He tapped Peter on the side and **awakened** him, saying,
    "Get up **quickly**."
The chains **fell** from his wrists.
The angel said to him, "Put on your **belt** and your **sandals**."

A dark tone pervades the opening lines.

Herod = HAYR-uhd

There is a sadistic quality to Herod's behavior.

All these details are relevant; they are about the community's chief leader and they will demonstrate God's awesome power.

The prayers of the "Church" are efficacious, so stress them.

In Scripture, angels elicit great awe and fear.

Your pace can quicken to suggest the energy the angel tries to summon from Peter.

READING I The blood of martyrs has already begun to flow. James, the brother of John and the son of Zebedee, was beheaded by Herod Agrippa around the year AD 44. Now Peter's life is threatened. Of course, the leaders drew the attention and the ire of Jewish and Roman authorities, but the threat of punishment for fidelity to Christ was a constant possibility for all believers. By this time, the esteem of the people of Jerusalem for this new sect had waned, and growing suspicion surrounded the early Church community.

Several Gospel events and dialogues with the Lord establish Peter's primacy among the Apostles. This incident certainly serves to confirm his status as Christ's chosen leader. While James was martyred, Peter's life is spared. But, as with all of Jesus's miracles, we must view this circumstance not as evidence of God playing favorites but of God's power to intervene in human events to demonstrate his love and sovereignty. Peter, after all, will eventually die a martyr's death. This is but a temporary reprieve that allows Peter to do the

important work of establishing and strengthening the fledgling community.

The story of Peter's deliverance from prison is quite dramatic and calls for lively storytelling. Peter himself cannot believe God is taking direct action on his behalf; he thinks he is only dreaming or experiencing a vision. But we're told the "church" prayed fervently for him. And the prayers are answered in the form of an awe-inspiring angel. The details of how closely Peter was guarded and of the number of chains and guards around him are important for establishing this as a truly divine intervention.

He **did** so.
Then he said to him, "Put on your **cloak** and **follow** me."
So he followed him out,
    not **realizing** that what was happening through the angel
        was **real**;
    he thought he was seeing a **vision**.
They passed the **first** guard, then the **second**,
    and came to the iron **gate** leading out to the city,
    which **opened** for them by itself.
They **emerged** and made their way down an **alley**,
    and **suddenly** the angel **left** him.
Then Peter recovered his **senses** and said,
    "Now I **know** for certain
    that the **Lord** sent his **angel**
    and **rescued** me from the hand of **Herod**
    and from all that the Jewish people had been **expecting**."

Your pace can quicken to suggest the energy the angel tries to summon from Peter.

Don't rush these details.

For meditation and context:

RESPONSORIAL PSALM   Psalm 34:2–3, 4–5, 6–7, 8–9 (5b)

R. The angel of the Lord will rescue those who fear him.

I will bless the LORD at all times;
    his praise shall be ever in my mouth.
Let my soul glory in the LORD;
    the lowly will hear me and be glad.

Glorify the LORD with me,
    let us together extol his name.
I sought the LORD, and he answered me
    and delivered me from all my fears.

Look to him that you may be radiant with joy,
    and your faces may not blush with shame.
When the poor one called out, the
        LORD heard,
    and from all his distress he saved him.

The angel of the LORD encamps
    around those who fear him, and
        delivers them.
Taste and see how good the LORD is;
    blessed the man who takes refuge in him.

TO KEEP IN MIND
Read through all three readings and commentaries for your assigned Sunday. All three were chosen for this day, and each commentary has suggestions that can help you with your own passage.

The chains fall away and the angel gives prosaic orders to dress, obviously in anticipation of a sudden departure.

Details of more guards and self-opening gates deepen our sense that Peter is indeed in the grip of a powerful God who has full control of all of life's details. Only when the angel disappears does Peter fully realize he was not dreaming. Peter declares that God was his advocate rescuing him from the designs of the king and the sinister expectations of the people.

READING II   The Second Letter to Timothy is a sincere and direct communication from a veteran leader to a young protégé offering words of advice and encouragement. Clearly, this portion contains what might be construed as a last will and testament. Paul is facing death and speaks of it unreservedly and in poetic terms. He is being "poured out" and his "departure has come," says Paul. What follows are phrases that have entered modern parlance, for it is commonplace to speak of one "fighting the good fight," "finishing the race," and "keeping the faith."

For Paul these are assertions of his own fidelity to Christ. Despite frequent opposition from within the body of believers and especially from without, and despite much travail, including multiple shipwrecks, Paul has endured and has never compromised. This earthly life presented him no accolades, but he's confident that a "crown of righteousness" awaits him in the Kingdom.

Not only was Timothy Paul's protégé, he was also a frequent companion on missionary journeys and someone on whom Paul relied to carry out special tasks and

Don't let these lines lapse into indulgent self-pity. Paul is strong in his faith and speaks with confidence and pride.

Paul attributes his success as well as his reward to the Lord.

Paul continues to rely on Christ's constant support.

Gentiles = JEN-tils

This is a reference to his first trial where his friends failed to stand by him.

End on a note of joyful praise. This is not a perfunctory salutary close.

TO KEEP IN MIND

Units of Thought: Running too many words together blurs meaning and fails to distinguish ideas. Punctuation does not always indicate clearly what words to group together or where to pause. Identify *units of thought* and use your voice to distinguish one from another.

READING II   2 Timothy 4:6–8, 17–18

A reading from the second Letter of Saint Paul to Timothy

I, **Paul**, am already being poured out like a **libation**,
　　and the time of my **departure** is at hand.
I have competed **well**; I have **finished** the race;
　　I have kept the **faith**.
From now on the crown of **righteousness** awaits me,
　　which the **Lord**, the just **judge**,
　　will **award** to me on that day, and not only to **me**,
　　but to all who have **longed** for his appearance.

The Lord stood by me and gave me **strength**,
　　so that through me the proclamation might be **completed**
　　and all the **Gentiles** might **hear** it.
And I was **rescued** from the lion's mouth.
The **Lord** will rescue me from **every** evil threat
　　and will bring me **safe** to his heavenly kingdom.
To him be **glory forever** and **ever**. **Amen**.

---

serve as his emissary. The relationship between them was both personal and strong, so it is not surprising that Paul would write in such personal terms to his younger colleague. In reviewing his life and ministry, Paul not only claims a merited crown for himself but for "all who have longed for [Christ's] appearing."

Paul acknowledges that his strength and perseverance came from Christ, but that grace was granted so that he might accomplish his mission to preach the Gospel to the Gentiles. His allusion to being "rescued from the lion's mouth" refers to his first trial in Asia where all his friends abandoned him. Despite this, the Lord proved faithful and delivered him. Buoyed by this memory, Paul can confidently proclaim his trust in the Lord whose kingdom, at least for him, draws ever nearer.

GOSPEL   This solemnity honors Peter for the incomparable role he was given by Jesus and which he faithfully played till his death as a martyr. Many significant moments could be chosen to highlight his singular status, but none would be more significant than the one that comprises this Gospel reading. Jesus's inquiry regarding the opinion of the crowd is merely a prelude to posing the same question to the disciples. It is their opinion, not the crowd's, that Jesus wants articulated.

As usual, Peter takes the lead. But this time he does not embarrass himself, and instead he earns high praise from the Lord. Peter declares something he could not possibly know. And neither, of course, could the crowds. In Matthew, Peter embellishes the response given in Mark's Gospel account

Establish the scene, and then pause before posing the question.

Caesarea = sez-uh-REE-uh; see-zuh-REE-uh
Philippi = fih-LIP-ī

Let the replies suggest the animation of the responding disciples.

Elijah = ee-Lī-juh
Jeremiah = jayr-uh-Mī-uh

Ask the question more significantly this second time.

There are two parts to Peter's reply. Don't rush them together.

Jesus's response is singularly effusive.

Jonah = JOH-nuh

Imagine Jesus looking directly at Peter as he speaks his name.

With full knowledge of all that he is asking of Peter (and of the consequences that will befall him) Jesus makes these solemn promises.

In the last two lines, try stressing the words: "earth," "heaven," "loose," "heaven."

> **TO KEEP IN MIND**
> **Importance of the Narrator**:
> The narrator is often the pivotal role of a passage. Timbre, pitch, rate, and energy can make the same words convey very different moods or meaning. Sometimes the narrator is objective, but often the narrator has great interest in the events and characters of a story.

GOSPEL   Matthew 16:13–19

A reading from the holy Gospel according to Matthew

When **Jesus** went into the region of Caesarea **Philippi**
  he asked his **disciples**,
  "**Who** do people say that the Son of **Man** is?"
They replied, "Some say John the **Baptist**, others **Elijah**,
  still others **Jeremiah** or one of the **prophets**."
He said to them, "But who do **you** say that I am?"
Simon **Peter** said in reply,
  "You are the **Christ**, the **Son** of the living **God**."
Jesus said to him in reply, "**Blessed** are you, Simon son of Jonah.
For **flesh** and **blood** has not revealed this to you, but my
    heavenly **Father**.
And so I say to **you**, you are **Peter**,
  and upon this **rock** I will build my **Church**,
  and the gates of the netherworld shall not **prevail** against it.
I will give you the **keys** to the Kingdom of **heaven**.
Whatever you **bind** on **earth** shall be **bound** in **heaven**;
  and whatever you **loose** on earth shall be **loosed** in heaven."

where Peter only names Jesus "the messiah." Though Matthew may have combined the confession in Mark with a profession of faith that gained currency only after the Resurrection, the combination of declarations wins him a singular distinction. "Blessed are you . . . " Jesus declares, for "flesh and blood has not revealed this to you."

This is a God-given insight, neither merited nor earned. But this unique privilege, granted to Peter and not to the other Apostles, qualifies him to be the foundation upon which Jesus will build his Church.

Significantly, it is not Peter's gift of leadership or oratory, not his courage, or his distinctive goodness that sets him apart as "rock" (or in Greek, *Cephas*, the name by which he is known in Paul's letters). This insight he is granted, this central insight that calls him to embrace the role of witness to Jesus as the Messiah of Israel, is what marks Peter in so distinctive a manner. His knowledge and devotion to Jesus make him the keeper of the "keys of the kingdom" and the wielder of the authority to "bind" and to "loose."

The Church will remain secure, Jesus assures him, for the powers of death, symbolized by "Hades," the abode of the dead, will not prevail against her. Death will never overcome the Church of Christ.

FOURTEENTH SUNDAY IN ORDINARY TIME

LECTIONARY #100

READING I   Zechariah 9:9–10

A reading from the Book of the Prophet Zechariah

Thus says the LORD:
Rejoice **heartily**, O daughter **Zion**,
    shout for **joy**, O daughter Jerusalem!
See, your **king** shall come to you;
    a just **savior** is he,
meek, and riding on an **ass**,
    on a **colt**, the **foal** of an ass.
He shall banish the **chariot** from Ephraim,
    and the **horse** from Jerusalem;
the **warrior's** bow shall be banished,
    and he shall proclaim **peace** to the nations.
His **dominion** shall be from **sea** to **sea**,
    and from the **River** to the **ends** of the **earth**.

Zechariah = zek-uh-Rī-uh

The voice of God will speak the balance of the text.

Zion = Zī-ahn

There is much energy and joy in these lines fueled by a vision of a world transformed.

This is an ironic image of a powerful yet humble ruler.

Ephraim = EE-fray-im; EF-r*m

The messianic king will destroy the implements of war. Your tone says, "Yes, this can happen!"

bow = boh (*not* bow that rhymes with plow)

Again, let your tone and demeanor persuade us that God *can* accomplish this mighty work.

TO KEEP IN MIND

Prophets: In addition to troubling the comfortable, prophets comforted the troubled. With equal passion, the great seers spoke threat and consolation, indictment and forgiveness. You must do the same for the chosen people you call "parish."

READING I The prophet Zechariah (responsible for chapters one through eight) had begun his work at the end of the exile, around the time of the rebuilding of the Temple, when hopes were high that the kingdom would be restored to the greatness it had known under King David. But the verses from chapter 9 that we read today comes from a much later time—likely more than one hundred years later—when those carrying on Zechariah's work were beginning to think the Kingdom would not be restored at that time. Instead they imagined an "eschatological" restoration. The Kingdom and the Messiah would come at the end of time. When that Messianic king came, they thought, he would be riding the appropriate animal: the foal of an ass. The kings of Israel rode horses during war, but rode young donkeys when they came in peace. Jesus was remarkable in his culture for his humility, but his choice of the colt of an ass for his entrance into Jerusalem was not simply a gesture of humility. Rather it was the sign of a great king of Israel coming in peace.

Jesus's kingship was fraught with irony: he never led an army, never lived in a palace, never sat upon a throne. But today, during a prelude to his Passion, he represents the noble kings of Israel. Let some real life experience of serene dignity inspire you, so that like Zechariah, you too can burn with enthusiasm for the messianic joy that will one day engulf the earth.

The opening lines explode with the joy of a promise long deferred finally fulfilled. The energy and joy in those lines is born of the realization that our "king shall come." Sustain the joy as you announce that the king, who is a "just savior," will be "meek and riding on an ass"—a symbol of peace.

For meditation and context:

RESPONSORIAL PSALM   Psalm 145:1–2, 8–9, 10–11, 13–14 (1)

R. I will praise your name for ever, my king and my God.
or
R. Alleluia.

I will extol you, O my God and King,
   and I will bless your name for ever
     and ever.
Every day will I bless you,
   and I will praise your name for ever
     and ever.

The LORD is gracious and merciful,
   slow to anger and of great kindness.
The LORD is good to all
   and compassionate toward all his works.

Let all your works give you thanks, O LORD,
   and let your faithful ones bless you.
Let them discourse of the glory of your
    kingdom
   and speak of your might.

The LORD is faithful in all his words
   and holy in all his works.
The LORD lifts up all who are falling
   and raises up all who are bowed down.

TO KEEP IN MIND

Eye contact is your means of connecting with those to whom you minister. You should look at the assembly during the middle and at the end of every thought or sentence.

READING II   Romans 8:9, 11–13

A reading from the Letter of Saint Paul to the Romans

Brothers and sisters:
You are not in the **flesh**;
   on the **contrary**, you are in the **spirit**,
   if only the Spirit of God **dwells** in you.
Whoever does not have the **Spirit** of Christ does not **belong**
    to him.
If the Spirit of the one who **raised** Jesus from the dead **dwells**
    in you,
   the one who raised **Christ** from the dead
   will give life to **your** mortal bodies also,
   through his **Spirit** that dwells in you.
Consequently, brothers and sisters,
   we are not **debtors** to the flesh,
   to live **according** to the flesh.
For if you live according to the **flesh**, you will **die**,
   but if by the **Spirit** you put to **death** the deeds of the body,
   you will **live**.

Establish eye contact and speak directly to the assembly mindful that "flesh" and "spirit" mean "saved" and "unsaved."

Embracing the "Spirit" has serious consequences.

Make this sound like the good news it is.

Through Baptism, we live a wholly new life.

Utilize contrasting tones for the warning of death and the promise of life.

He will destroy the implements of war: "chariot," "horse," and "bow." (But imagine your own implements of war—bickering, jealousy, anger—that also need banishing.) Help us believe God can and will do this, and not only to the "ends of the earth," but within our own hearts.

READING II   Paul is masterful at drawing contrasts, and here his dichotomy is between "flesh" and "spirit." In Paul's worldview, flesh and spirit don't distinguish the physical body from the soul. Instead, "flesh" refers to the human person

in its entirety—body *and* soul, but in an *unredeemed* state. So living in the flesh means failing to claim the grace and salvation won for us by Christ. "Spirit," on the other hand, refers to the Christian who, though still living in the flesh, has started living a new life of grace, guided by the Holy Spirit. Baptized Christians who possess the Holy Spirit live "*in* the spirit" and enter into a new relationship with God

As you pray over this passage, sense the Spirit who "dwells in you" and recall your own failings and successes in trying to live the life of the Spirit. Then, as a fellow

believer, warn and encourage your listeners in a tone that expresses deep concern for them. Contrasting vocal tones will help differentiate between not *having* the "Spirit of Christ" and having that Spirit "*dwelling* in you." Paul says the Spirit is from God who raised Jesus from the dead. If that Spirit is in us, then God will do for us what he did for Christ. Deliver that hopeful message slowly and gently.

As you read the lines following "Consequently," recall your own indebtedness to God. The contrast between living by "the flesh" or by "the spirit" is one of

GOSPEL   Matthew 11:25–30

A reading from the holy Gospel according to Matthew

At that time **Jesus** exclaimed:
  "I give **praise** to you, Father, Lord of heaven and earth,
  for although you have **hidden** these things
    from the **wise** and the **learned**
  you have **revealed** them to **little** ones.
Yes, Father, such has been your gracious **will**.
All things have been handed over to **me** by my **Father**.
No one knows the **Son** except the **Father**,
  and no one knows the **Father** except the **Son**
  and **anyone** to whom the Son wishes to **reveal** him.

"**Come** to me, all you who labor and are **burdened**,
  and I will give you **rest**.
Take my **yoke** upon you and **learn** from me,
  for I am **meek** and **humble** of heart;
  and you will find **rest** for yourselves.
For my yoke is **easy**, and my burden **light**."

Margin notes:

Jesus is at prayer praising the Father.

Contrast "the wise and learned" with "little ones."

Here Jesus addresses the crowd.
Jesus is articulating the profound truth of his oneness with the Father.

Take a short pause to shift to the more tender tone of the following verses.

These lines call for a very direct, personal, and loving tone.

This is a counterintuitive declaration. Let your tone hint at its deep meaning

---

TO KEEP IN MIND
Pray the Scriptures: Make reading these Scriptures a part of your prayer life every week, and especially during the week prior to the liturgy in which you will proclaim.

"sadness" versus "joy," for the former leads to death and the latter to life. Insist on the truth of the last sentence and smile the announcement that we "will live."

 GOSPEL   Jesus, concerned about those who do not believe, praises God for giving the childlike what is beyond the grasp of the so-called wise of the world. So the theme of reversal and counterintuitive wisdom is immediately introduced.

Then Jesus continues by articulating his unique relationship with the Father.

Jesus is the eternal God, one with the Father, possessing full knowledge of God as God has full knowledge of him. Out of these two premises—the ability of the childlike to grasp deeper truths than the learned and Jesus's oneness with the Father—Jesus speaks the unique and gentle call that comprises one of the New Testament's most tender texts.

In the context of this passage from Matthew, Jesus's words refer to the oppressive and legalistic system imposed upon the people by the scribes and Pharisees. These laws were focused on themselves and required exacting observance that became a labor and burden rather than the experience of freedom one finds when truly centered in the will of God. So Jesus offers *his* "yoke" in place of the Law with all its burdensome scribal accretions.

Jesus's yoke does not offer license in place of Law; rather, he offers obedience to his teaching and to the deeper Law of love. His burden is easy and his yoke light because they lead to truth and to love and are infinitely lighter than those we impose upon ourselves when we rebel and turn to sin.

FIFTEENTH SUNDAY IN ORDINARY TIME

LECTIONARY #103

Isaiah = ī-ZAY-uh

READING I   Isaiah 55:10–11

A reading from the Book of the Prophet Isaiah

Note that God's voice speaks throughout. Immediately, you're into the simile. Work hard to make its meaning explicit.

Thus says the LORD:
Just as from the heavens
   the **rain** and **snow** come down
and do not **return** there
   till they have **watered** the earth,
   making it **fertile** and **fruitful**,

Renew your energy on this parenthetical phrase.

giving **seed** to the one who sows
   and **bread** to the one who eats,
so shall my **word** be
   that goes forth from my **mouth**;
my word shall not return to me **void**,

The last three lines restate what was just stated in the preceding lines, so renew your energy here as well.

   but shall do my **will**,
   achieving the end for which I **sent** it.

> **TO KEEP IN MIND**
> "**Blessed is the one who reads aloud** and blessed are those who listen to this prophetic message and heed what is written in it, for the appointed time is near" (Revelation 1:3).

READING I The Bible views God's Word as a force, an active agent that effects what it sets out to do. God's Word never "goes in one ear and out the other." Such ineffectiveness is not within the nature of the Word of God. God's Word is efficacious, active, and living; in St. Paul's words, "sharper than a two-edged sword." These brief verses are taken from a longer passage in which God's voice summons all the thirsty, the poor, and the hungry to "come to the water!" (55:1). And, of course, God invites in order to transform. Those who answer God's call won't walk away thirsty, hungry, and poor. They will be filled and satisfied, for such is the bounty of God.

This short, one-sentence reading makes a single point: "my word" achieves "the end for which I sent it." But it will take conscious effort—speaking slowly, with adequate energy and conviction, and balancing parenthetical phrases—to make the prophet's point by means of a complex simile. So first, fix the meaning of the simile in your mind: Rain and snow fall to the ground and don't return to heaven without watering and softening the ground into fertility. As it melts, snow saturates the earth making possible the transition of seed to bread. Rain and snow are vehicles of God's care, turning parched land into baskets of bread and fruit.

For meditation and context:

TO KEEP IN MIND
Eye contact is your means of connecting with those to whom you minister. You should look at the assembly during the middle and at the end of every thought or sentence.

RESPONSORIAL PSALM   Psalm 65:10, 11, 12–13, 14 (Luke 8:8)

R. The seed that falls on good ground will yield a fruitful harvest.

You have visited the land and watered it;
    greatly have you enriched it.
God's watercourses are filled;
    you have prepared the grain.

Thus have you prepared the land: drenching
        its furrows,
    breaking up its clods,
softening it with showers,
    blessing its yield.

You have crowned the year with your bounty,
    and your paths overflow with a rich
        harvest;
the untilled meadows overflow with it,
    and rejoicing clothes the hills.

The fields are garmented with flocks
    and the valleys blanketed with grain.
    They shout and sing for joy.

READING II   Romans 8:18–23

A reading from the Letter of Saint Paul to the Romans

Make eye contact and slowly begin contrasting "present time" with "the glory to be revealed."

Brothers and sisters:
I consider that the **sufferings** of this present time are as **nothing**
    compared with the **glory** to be revealed for us.

Immediately, the vision expands to include all of creation. Let your tone also become expansive.

For **creation** awaits with eager **expectation**
    the **revelation** of the children of God;
    for creation was made subject to **futility**,
    not of its own **accord** but because of the one who **subjected** it,
    in hope that creation itself
    would be set **free** from **slavery** to corruption

Creation, too, endures the consequences of human sin.

    and share in the glorious **freedom** of the children of God.
We know that all creation is groaning in **labor** pains even
        until **now**;

With all creation, we groan in anticipation of the glory that will be revealed when we claim our full status as the adopted children of God.

    and not only that, but we **ourselves**,
    who have the **firstfruits** of the Spirit,
    we **also** groan within ourselves

Sustain eye contact till the end.

    as we wait for **adoption**, the **redemption** of our bodies.

Inevitably, unavoidably (though in God's timing, not ours) God's Word achieves the end for which God sends it: to soften the arid land of human hearts and make them fertile places where God's will can germinate and bear fruit. Since today this sentence stands alone (unlike the last time we saw it in Reading V of the Easter Vigil), read it extra slowly, like the lyrics of a song, paying special attention to the poetic imagery.

READING II If you brought to mind the worst things happening in your life and in the larger world right now

and then imagined the most consoling news possible—whatever it would be that would make you happiest—would the second set of images overshadow the first? For Paul they did. For him "the sufferings of this present time" were as *nothing* compared with "the glory" that would come his way because of Christ. Without being blind to the realities around him, Paul imagined the invisible realities God destined us to share with Christ. Your task is to express his excitement and hope and make it real for your listeners.

A fascinating feature of Paul's teaching is that while "creation" endures the "futility" and "corruption" that are the wage of sin, creation, too, will reap and enjoy the blessings and glorious freedom of "the children of God." Christ's saving act brings salvation to all creation, so nature will also share in the glory of Christ's redemption. That is good news that needs to sound like good news.

Paul concludes with a powerful image of a woman giving birth. "All creation is groaning" as if in labor. In all of life there is a sense of a "more" that awaits fulfillment.

GOSPEL   Matthew 13:1–23

A reading from the holy Gospel according to Matthew

A serene scene, but the crowds immediately change the mood.

On that day, **Jesus** went out of the house and sat down by the **sea**.
Such large **crowds** gathered around him
   that he got into a **boat** and sat down,
   and the whole crowd stood along the **shore**.
And he spoke to them at length in **parables**, saying:

Tell the story colorfully, remembering you are speaking metaphorically of people and the situations that prevent them from embracing the Kingdom.

   "A **sower** went out to sow.
And as he sowed, some seed fell on the **path**,
   and **birds** came and **ate** it up.
Some fell on **rocky** ground, where it had little **soil**.

Show regret over this lost opportunity.

It sprang up at **once** because the soil was not **deep**,
   and when the **sun** rose it was **scorched**, and it **withered** for
     lack of **roots**.
Some seed fell among **thorns**, and the thorns grew up and
   choked it.

These lines reveal the power of God to overcome all obstacles.

But **some** seed fell on **rich** soil, and produced **fruit**,
   a **hundred** or **sixty** or **thirtyfold**.

Proclaim this line as a solemn conclusion.

Whoever has **ears** ought to **hear**."

The disciples approached him and said,
   "Why do you speak to them in **parables**?"

The tone of the question suggests a request for insider knowledge.

He said to them in reply,
   "Because **knowledge** of the mysteries of the kingdom of
     heaven
   has been granted to **you**, but to **them** it has **not** been granted.

Jesus first answers forthrightly, then, ironically, speaks another parable.

To anyone who **has**, **more** will be given and he will grow **rich**;
   from anyone who has **not**, even what he **has** will be
     taken away.

That same awareness is in us, for though we have "the firstfruits of the Spirit" we await the liberation of our bodies from our old and sinful self. Though saved, we live in an in-between place in which the power of sin still calls us, and where we, on occasion, fail. But the love of God has claimed us and so ultimately, we are his, though we must patiently await our full "adoption" and the "redemption of our bodies." Aware of your own personal longing, speak of "groaning" as a mother-cry—pain and joy combined to birth the new creation.

GOSPEL Among Jesus's parables, this one probably generates the most debate. The parable is simple enough, for it speaks of the miraculous power of God present in the ministry of Jesus. The astonishing success represented by seed that yields "a hundredfold" (an impossible amount) suggests that divine intervention will overcome opposition to the Gospel and ensure the dramatic growth of the Kingdom. It's the allegorical interpretation that follows the parable that fuels controversy. Once rejected by many scholars, allegorical interpretation has regained some currency, at least to the point that most scholars would not rule out allegorical elements in many of the parables.

There are three distinct movements in this pericope. First is the parable itself. Second is Jesus's response to the question of why he teaches in this cryptic manner. Third is the allegorical interpretation, placed on the lips of Jesus, of the various elements of his story.

Jesus's tone becomes more intense and his frustration shows as he speaks of those who will not listen or understand.

Don't rush the reference to Isaiah, nor the quote from his prophecy.

This is **why** I speak to them in parables, because
> they **look** but do not **see**, and **hear** but do not **listen**
> > or **understand**.

Isaiah's prophecy is **fulfilled** in them, which says:
> *You shall indeed **hear** but not **understand**,*
> > *you shall indeed **look** but never **see**.*
> ***Gross** is the heart of this people,*
> > *they will hardly **hear** with their ears,*
> > *they have **closed** their eyes,*
> > *lest they **see** with their eyes*
> > *and **hear** with their ears*
> *and **understand** with their hearts and be **converted**,*
> > *and I **heal** them.*

Jesus's tone is warm as he commends them for their perception.

"Amen, I say to you" signals a solemn pronouncement. What follows should be directed at your assembly, for they, too, have seen what prophets longed for but never saw.

"But **blessed** are your eyes, because they **see**,
> and your **ears**, because they **hear**.

Amen, I say to you, many **prophets** and **righteous** people
> **longed** to see what you see but did **not** see it,
> and to **hear** what you hear but did **not** hear it.

Sustain a lively pace and an upbeat, conversational tone.

"**Hear** then the parable of the sower.
The seed sown on the **path** is the one
> who **hears** the word of the kingdom without **understanding** it,
> and the **evil** one comes and **steals** away
> what was sown in his **heart**.

The seed sown on **rocky** ground
> is the one who hears the word and receives it at **once** with **joy**.

But he has no **root** and lasts only for a **time**.

With each "seed" contrast the initial attitude and response of the believer with the eventual loss of faith that results from the specific circumstances.

By their nature, parables—and any form of metaphorical speech—require effort to understand and apply. Therefore, such constructs will be more accessible to seekers, those disposed to explore a story's meaning, than to listeners at large. Reflecting Semitic thought, the Gospel presents understanding as a special gift that God bestowed upon true disciples but withheld from the crowds. However, individuals are held responsible for failing to understand because they "look but do not see and hear but do not listen."

In Matthew, Jesus's explanation of why he speaks in parables is less scandalous than in Mark, for here Jesus says he uses parables "*because*" not "*so that*" the crowds will fail to understand. At the start of the parable the seed seems to represent God's Word and the hearers are the soil into which it falls. But in Jesus's interpretation, we realize the seed represents believers and their various levels of appropriating the Word.

Tell the parable slowly to allow the significance of each image to settle before moving on to the next. For Jesus and his audience this is familiar imagery, but as the disciples' question reveals, the point is elusive. Remember throughout that Jesus desires that no one be lost. His emotions are a mix of regret, warning, and uneasy hope. Eye members of the assembly when you say "good soil," incorporating different sections of the church on "a hundred," "sixty," and "thirtyfold."

Jesus's tone should reveal regret that genuine zeal was so soon lost.

Speak with affection and joy of the ones who yield abundance.

When some **tribulation** or **persecution** comes because of the word,
he immediately **falls** away.
The seed sown among **thorns** is the one who hears the word,
but then worldly **anxiety** and the lure of **riches** choke the word
and it bears no **fruit**.
But the seed sown on **rich** soil
is the one who hears the word and **understands** it,
who indeed **bears** fruit and yields a **hundred** or **sixty**
or **thirtyfold**."

[Shorter: Matthew 13:1–9]

TO KEEP IN MIND
Importance of the Narrator:
The narrator is often the pivotal role of a passage. Timbre, pitch, rate, and energy can make the same words convey very different moods or meaning. Sometimes the narrator is objective, but often the narrator has great interest in the events and characters of a story.

THE 4 STEPS OF *LECTIO DIVINA* OR PRAYERFUL READING

1. *Lectio:* Read a Scripture passage aloud slowly. Notice what phrase captures your attention and be attentive to its meaning. Silent pause.

2. *Meditatio:* Read the passage aloud slowly again, reflecting on the passage, allowing God to speak to you through it. Silent pause.

3. *Oratio:* Read it aloud slowly a third time, allowing it to be your prayer or response to God's gift of insight to you. Silent pause.

4. *Contemplatio:* Read it aloud slowly a fourth time, now resting in God's word.

"Whoever has ears" tells your listeners not only to think about what was said, but to work hard at penetrating its meaning. When explaining the parable, reflect the confusion of the one who does not understand the reign, the joy of the one who eagerly "hears the word" but quickly loses it, and the waning interest of the one worn away by anxiety and seduced by "the lure of riches." With renewed energy and joy look at the assembly and call them the "good soil" who yield abundance.

SIXTEENTH SUNDAY IN ORDINARY TIME

LECTIONARY #106

READING I   Wisdom 12:13, 16–19

A reading from the Book of Wisdom

You are addressing God, extolling his power and mercy.

Might makes justice possible.

"Temerity" = audacity, an insolence unacceptable to God.

Freely, God chooses to treat us with mercy. Let your tone suggest God's mildness and leniency.

Speak with gratitude of how God's example has taught us how to act and given us reason to hope for mercy.

There is no god besides **you** who have the **care** of all,
    that you need **show** you have not **unjustly** condemned.
For your **might** is the source of **justice**;
    your **mastery** over all things makes you **lenient** to all.
For you **show** your might when the perfection of your power
      is **disbelieved**;
    and in those who **know** you, you rebuke **temerity**.
But though you are **master** of might, you judge with **clemency**,
    and with much **lenience** you govern us;
    for **power**, whenever you **will**, **attends** you.
And you taught your people, by these deeds,
    that those who are **just** must be **kind**;
and you gave your children good ground for **hope**
    that you would permit **repentance** for their **sins**.

TO KEEP IN MIND

Openings: First, make eye contact with the assembly and announce, from memory, "A (pronounced "uh," not "ay") reading from . . ." Then pause (three full beats!) before starting the reading.

READING I Only when one possesses the opposite attribute can exercise of a virtue be truly free. Consequently, only the powerful can be truly gentle; only the mighty can be truly just; and only the one who has *mastery* over all" can be "*lenient* to all." This is an irony we find throughout Scripture and in everyday life. When we lack full power, self-serving motives can easily creep in. Fear, rather than generosity, can become the real—even if unconscious—motive of our good works. "I'll be good to you, so you'll be good to me" can be the unspoken motivation. And concern over how we might be perceived by others might be the driving motive of "just" behavior. Only when we don't *have* to do something—when we have nothing to *lose*—can we say we're truly free to do it.

The author of Wisdom understands that truth. No one, he says, no god and no person, can challenge the actions of our God—even when God condemns—for our God has the "care of all," is "the source of justice" (understood as goodness and holiness) and is "lenient to all."

God doesn't sit back when his sovereign power is questioned, the writer adds, and God rebukes any audacity among those who know him and his might. Having boldly defended God's strength, the author then links God's power to God's mercy. Earlier we read, "Your mastery . . . makes you lenient." Now the author claims, "You judge with clemency, and with much lenience

For meditation and context:

RESPONSORIAL PSALM   Psalm 86:5–6, 9–10, 15–16 (5a)

R. Lord, you are good and forgiving.

You, O LORD, are good and forgiving,
  abounding in kindness to all who call
    upon you.
Hearken, O LORD, to my prayer
  and attend to the sound of my pleading.

All the nations you have made shall come
  and worship you, O LORD,
  and glorify your name.
For you are great, and you do wondrous
    deeds;
  you alone are God.

You, O LORD, are a God merciful and
    gracious,
  slow to anger, abounding in kindness
    and fidelity.
Turn toward me, and have pity on me;
  give your strength to your servant.

TO KEEP IN MIND
Slow down: The larger the church, the larger the assembly, and the more complex the text, the slower you must read.

This is the third consecutive week we read from Romans.
Establish eye contact and be sure all are attentive before you begin.

The Spirit prays when we cannot.

Be the searcher of hearts speaking comfort.

The Spirit knows God's perfect will for us and intercedes for us accordingly.

READING II   Romans 8:26–27

A reading from the Letter of Saint Paul to the Romans

Brothers and sisters:
The **Spirit** comes to the aid of our **weakness**;
  for we do not **know** how to pray as we **ought**,
    but the Spirit **himself** intercedes with inexpressible **groanings**.
And the one who **searches hearts**
  knows what is the **intention** of the Spirit,
  because he **intercedes** for the holy ones
  according to God's **will**.

TO KEEP IN MIND
Posture speaks: Make sure it says what you want it to. Don't let your face or body contradict the good news you announce. Remember, readers are allowed to smile!

[because] power . . . attends you" whenever you want it. Use the contrasts in those lines, juxtaposing divine power with the divine inclination to forgive. Gratitude characterizes the final sentences. Thank you, says the author to God, for teaching us by your kind example; thank you for giving us, your children, reason to hope that we will be allowed to repent for our sins. This passage is a perfect preparation for the parable of the wheat and the weeds in today's Gospel.

READING II | (See also commentary for the Second Reading of the Vigil of Pentecost.)
  We stare at the mystery of death and recognize the inadequacy of speech. Yet we often stand before a person who has lost a loved one and try to express feelings that will not be squeezed into words. It's a hard lesson to learn that there are times when we simply will not know how to speak as we ought, just as there are times when "we do not know how to *pray* as we ought." And such times, Paul tells us, ought not to be feared or resisted.

Instead, they can be viewed as one of those ironic Kingdom moments when our "weakness" becomes God's strength. At such times, if our hearts are open, the Spirit comes to the rescue teaching us with a look or a touch, or with patient and wordless endurance what cannot be expressed in speech. In our prayer, too, the Spirit provides what we lack, interceding for us "with inexpressible groaning."
  Recall a time when words you didn't have suddenly issued from your lips, and tap that memory before trying to proclaim this brief passage. Reading slowly won't be

GOSPEL   Matthew 13:24–43

A reading from the holy Gospel according to Matthew

Jesus proposed another **parable** to the crowds, saying:
"The kingdom of **heaven** may be likened to a man
  who sowed **good** seed in his field.
While everyone was **asleep** his **enemy** came
  and sowed **weeds** all through the wheat, and then went off.
When the crop **grew** and bore **fruit**, the weeds appeared as **well**.
The slaves of the householder **came** to him and said,
  '**Master**, did you not sow **good** seed in your field?
Where have the **weeds** come from?'
He answered, 'An **enemy** has done this.'
His slaves said to him,
  'Do you want us to go and **pull** them up?'
He replied, '**No**, if you pull up the **weeds**
  you might uproot the **wheat** along with them.
Let them grow together until **harvest**;
  then at harvest time I will say to the harvesters,
  "First collect the **weeds** and tie them in bundles for **burning**;
  but gather the **wheat** into my **barn**."'"

He proposed **another** parable to them.
"The kingdom of heaven is like a **mustard** seed
  that a person took and **sowed** in a field.
It is the **smallest** of all the seeds,
  yet when full-**grown** it is the **largest** of plants.
It becomes a large **bush**,
  and the '**birds** of the sky come and **dwell** in its branches.'"

He spoke to them **another** parable.
"The kingdom of heaven is like **yeast**
  that a woman took and mixed with three measures
   of wheat flour
  until the whole **batch** was **leavened**."

Storytelling should never be rushed.

Be aware of the recurring contrasts between joy and malice in this parable.

First, the "slaves" are confused and frustrated.

But here they grow angry.

The master's cautious forbearance has both an obvious and deeper motive.

Renew your energy for the start of a new parable.

Stress the contrast between the size of the seed and the plant it produces.

Here is an image of comfort and protection.

Once again, renew your energy to sustain the attention of your assembly.

Well-placed stress will help indicate why this parable is being shared.

---

enough to do Paul justice this week. This is a life-giving passage that has pulled many a sinking spirit out of the quicksand of despair. You will need your own memory of a time when you ran out of words to say to God, yet found your communication intensified rather than terminated, and let that memory power your proclamation.

    Imagine the last sentence addressed to someone ready to leap from depression's roof-top and urgently assure them that the one "who searches hearts" (that's one of Paul's best lines, inspired by Psalm 139:1) *knows* their turmoil and *hears* the "groanings" the Spirit has turned into prayer.

GOSPEL   Jesus the storyteller is concocting images that reveal aspects of the mystery of the Kingdom. Most of the pericope is spoken by Jesus, whom we can picture walking among the crowd, energized by the creative flow of his poetic images, working hard to hold and instruct his listeners. For the sequence of parables to be most effective, establish a sense of extemporaneous sharing designed specifically to meet the needs of the crowd and your assembly.

    Transition slowly from one parable to the next by pausing, as if trying to conjure a new image, then shift focus and share the

image with a new part of the assembly. The wheat and weeds story shifts between moods of joy and malice. Each reference to the "good seed" is upbeat, but a threatening tone introduces "the enemy" and "the weeds." The slaves are confused and then angry. The owner is philosophical, his concern for the wheat obvious. He is neither naïve nor unaware. His forbearance has purpose; not to indulge the "weeds" but to safeguard the "wheat" that might be destroyed along with the weeds if action is taken too soon.

    But there is also another motive. Jesus's enemies criticized him for associating with

Now the narrator speaks and offers an explanation, quoting Psalm 78:2, for the use of cryptic parables.

All these things Jesus spoke to the crowds in **parables**.
He spoke to them **only** in parables,
   to **fulfill** what had been said through the **prophet**:
     *I will open my mouth in **parables**,*
      *I will **announce** what has lain **hidden** from the*
     foundation *of the world.*

As the scene shifts, so does the tone that now becomes more intimate.

Then, **dismissing** the crowds, he went into the **house**.
His **disciples** approached him and said,
   "Explain to us the parable of the weeds in the field."

This allegorical explanation can move along at a good pace.

He said in reply, "He who sows good seed is the Son of **Man**,
   the field is the **world**, the **good** seed the **children**
     of the kingdom.
The **weeds** are the children of the **evil** one,
   and the **enemy** who sows them is the **devil**.
The **harvest** is the **end** of the age, and the harvesters are **angels**.
Just as **weeds** are collected and burned up with **fire**,
   so will it be at the **end** of the age.
The Son of Man will send his **angels**,
   and they will collect out of his kingdom
     all who cause others to **sin** and all **evildoers**.

The judgment announced here serves as a warning for anyone with "ears."

They will throw them into the fiery **furnace**,
   where there will be wailing and grinding of **teeth**.

The promise of glory for the righteous sparks hope and joy.

Then the **righteous** will shine like the **sun**
   in the **kingdom** of their Father.
Whoever has **ears** ought to **hear**."

[Shorter: Matthew 13:24–30]

TO KEEP IN MIND
Careful preparation expresses your reverence for the Word.

---

sinners. Jesus counters that only God can separate good from the bad, and only at the end when true identities will be revealed—and when some in one camp surely will be revealed as belonging in the other! In telling the parable, contrast the master's attitude toward the "weeds" that are to be bundled and burned, with his affection for the "wheat" that is to be gathered, lovingly, into his barn.

The parable of the "mustard seed" speaks of the improbable but inevitable growth of God's Kingdom that starts small and grows large. Your vocal delivery can suggest that gradual growth: speak slowly and quietly about "the smallest of all the seeds," then stand back beholding before you "the largest of plants." Kneading is hard work, which you can suggest by the way you say "into *three /measures /of flour*," accenting each word as if pushing palms into the dough. Speak the quote cited from the Book of Psalms (78:2) with dignity and authority.

The allegorical explanation Jesus provides at the disciples' request operates on three levels. In the ministry of Jesus the wheat represents the outcasts, and weeds are the hypocritical religious leaders; for the Evangelist Matthew, wheat is the Church community, and weeds symbolize the nation of Israel that has turned a deaf ear to the Messiah; and for the burgeoning Christian community the wheat are good and holy members while the weeds are those of weak faith and moral discipline. Jesus explains the parable carefully, detailing each analogy. The last line (see Daniel 12:3) carries Jesus's urgent appeal that all strive to be among those who "will shine like the sun" in God's Kingdom.

SEVENTEENTH SUNDAY IN ORDINARY TIME

LECTIONARY #109

READING I 1 Kings 3:5, 7–12

A reading from the first Book of Kings

The LORD appeared to **Solomon** in a **dream** at night.
God said, "**Ask** something of me and I will **give** it to you."
Solomon answered:
"O LORD, my **God**, you have made me, your servant, **king**
    to succeed my father **David**;
    but I am a mere **youth**, not knowing at all how to **act**.
I serve you in the midst of the people whom you have **chosen**,
    a people so **vast** that it cannot be **numbered** or **counted**.
Give your servant, therefore, an **understanding** heart
    to **judge** your people and to distinguish **right** from **wrong**.
For who is able to **govern** this vast people of yours?"

The LORD was **pleased** that Solomon made this request.
So God said to him:
    "Because you have asked for **this**—
    not for a **long** life for yourself,
    nor for **riches**,
    nor for the life of your **enemies**,
    but for **understanding** so that you may know what is **right**—
    I **do** as you requested.
I give you a heart so **wise** and **understanding**
    that there has never been **anyone** like you up to now,
    and **after** you there will come no one to **equal** you."

Solomon = SOL-uh-muhn

Set the mood for the mysterious nocturnal theophany that will alter Solomon's life.

Solomon readily confesses his inadequacies.

His responsibilities loom larger and larger.

Clearly, he doesn't feel up to the task.

The narrator and God speak approvingly of Solomon's choice.

"This" contrasts with what most might have asked.

This is a singular promise, never abandoned. Let it sound as remarkable as it is.

READING I   It would be just as remarkable in our day for one to choose "wisdom" over riches and power. But Solomon is presented as making that choice in this seminal scene that lays the foundation for the wisdom he later demonstrates in multiple arenas of life, both practical and philosophical. That Solomon would make this choice suggests the ultimate value of wisdom. No other value ranks above it.

Within our culture, faith in "dreams" has long since waned, so you must introduce this story with a certainty that says

substantial things *can* happen even in insubstantial dreams. God's voice must not seem threatening or stern; instead, it soothes the young man's fears as it encourages him to "ask something." Solomon is a "mere youth" who is overwhelmed by his responsibilities, and keenly aware of his deficiencies. Yet he desires nothing more than to serve well. He is sincere and unassuming in his deprecating assessment of himself and in his request for "an understanding heart." When he asks, who can "govern this vast people?" he knows one answer is, "Not me."

The narrator, like an avuncular observer, expresses pride in the young man. God is equally proud. Slowly and gently God commends and instructs Solomon. "You could have asked for futile and empty treasures," God says, in other words, "but instead you've requested the ability to do what is right!" God's final announcement is a solemn *promise* spoken with emphasis and great love.

READING II   In times of trial, on the darkest days, few words of Scripture offer comfort and healing like

RESPONSORIAL PSALM   Psalm 119:57, 72, 76–77, 127–128, 129–130 (97a)

R. Lord, I love your commands.

I have said, O LORD, that my part
   is to keep your words.
The law of your mouth is to me more precious
   than thousands of gold and silver pieces.

Let your kindness comfort me
   according to your promise to your
      servants.
Let your compassion come to me that
   I may live,
   for your law is my delight.

For I love your commands
   more than gold, however fine.
For in all your precepts I go forward;
   every false way I hate.

Wonderful are your decrees;
   therefore I observe them.
The revelation of your words sheds light,
   giving understanding to the simple.

TO KEEP IN MIND

"**Build**" refers to increasing vocal *intensity* as you speak a certain word or sentence. It can be achieved by speaking *louder*, but a *quieter* voice might produce the same effect. Sometimes "build" is achieved by speaking *faster* and sometimes by speaking *slower*.

READING II   Romans 8:28–30

A reading from the Letter of Saint Paul to the Romans

Brothers and sisters:
We know that all things work for **good** for those who love **God**,
   who are called according to his **purpose**.
For those he **foreknew** he also **predestined**
   to be conformed to the **image** of his **Son**,
   so that he might be the **firstborn**
   among **many** brothers and sisters.
And those he predestined he also **called**;
   and those he called he also **justified**;
   and those he justified he also **glorified**.

This is the fourth consecutive week we read from Romans.

You begin with a dramatically counterintuitive declaration. Don't rush, and speak with conviction.

What remains should not take on the feel of courtroom argument, but of a loving teacher explaining a profound life-truth.

Take pleasure in the build as it continues to rise and leads to the joyful announcement of glorification.

these words of Paul's. His message is counterintuitive, meaningful only to ears of faith and those who have taken the long view and seen pain, sorrow, disappointment, and disillusion gradually yield new life and grace.

Paul's words are taken from a longer discourse in which he discusses the challenges of human life and the pain that so often invades it. This brief passage comprises the heart of his fervent meditation, but there's so little flesh around it that it might mistakenly be proclaimed without the emotional momentum it would have if Paul's text were read from the beginning.

Well-balanced and scholarly, these lines appear void of emotion. To understand them fully, read the passages that precede and follow this one in your Bible (or from last and next week's Second Readings in this volume) and sense the intensity you would have reached had you begun at verse one instead of twenty-eight. Despite its brevity, you must help us hear in this brief excerpt the emotional peak Paul intends to reach.

The second and third sentences *assure* like a kind grandparent, not *prove* like a courtroom lawyer, that with God

nothing is useless and nothing happens in vain. Build from one verb to the next, stressing both the repeated verb and each *new* verb: "Those he *foreknew* he also *predestined* . . . those he *predestined* he also *called*," and so forth. Persuade anyone who doubts it that they, too, can be "*glorified*."

GOSPEL   In Jesus's stories, the Kingdom is a seeker, looking for and finding *us* rather than the other way around. The "treasure" seems to reach up through the ground to grab the man's attention. God's initiative, repeated in each story,

GOSPEL   Matthew 13:44–52

A reading from the holy Gospel according to Matthew

Jesus said to his disciples:
   "The kingdom of **heaven** is like a **treasure** buried in a **field**,
     which a person **finds** and **hides** again,
     and out of **joy** goes and sells all that he **has** and **buys** that field.
Again, the kingdom of heaven is like a **merchant**
     searching for fine **pearls**.
When he finds a pearl of great **price**,
     he goes and **sells** all that he has and **buys** it.
Again, the kingdom of heaven is like a **net** thrown into the **sea**,
     which collects **fish** of every kind.
When it is **full** they haul it **ashore**
     and sit down to put what is **good** into buckets.
What is **bad** they throw **away**.
Thus it will be at the **end** of the age.
The **angels** will go out and separate the **wicked**
     from the **righteous**
     and throw them into the fiery **furnace**,
     where there will be **wailing** and grinding of **teeth**.

"Do you **understand** all these things?"
They answered, "**Yes**."
And he replied,
   "Then every **scribe** who has been **instructed** in the kingdom
     of heaven
   is like the **head** of a household
     who brings from his storeroom both the **new** and the **old**."

[Shorter: Matthew 13:44–46]

Imagine the three images Jesus offers with excitement and surprise.

The pacing is crisp, creating impact from the accumulation of one image atop another.

The feel of this third image differs from the two preceding, so shift to a more serious tone.

This is an image of ultimate judgment. Speak it with appropriate weightiness.

Jesus is clearly teacher of his eager disciples.

This activity of bringing into play both the "new" and the "old" relates to your ministry of situating the old truths of our faith into the new realities of our time.

---

is non-exclusive; all are given equal opportunity to possess a treasure beyond price.

But there is also a role for the seeker. Having encountered a valuable treasure, one must employ all available means to secure it, even to the point of hiding the treasure from its rightful owners in order to purchase it without their knowledge. Jesus is not endorsing spurious tactics. But, as in other parables, he creates a character who employs questionable behavior to make his point that acquiring the Kingdom of God is worth resorting to whatever means are necessary.

So each parable issues a call and stresses the *rewards* of sacrificing everything for God's reign. Lend urgency to your storytelling by employing a faster than usual rate because you're suggesting the breathless excitement of worker and merchant who must run off quickly to negotiate purchases without attracting attention. Therefore, each character mutes his excitement until the two instances of "and buys" that announce completion of their commerce.

The dragnet story reminds us of the Kingdom's all-encompassing reach. The net collects things of "every kind," not just what

is good and worthy. Good and evil coexist in the Kingdom; only at the end will evil be excluded. Judgment rings through the lines, though not without a sense of loss. The message is that to be counted among the "righteous," as with the acquisition of the treasures, no sacrifice will be too great.

Finally, Jesus teaches that the true disciple finds treasure in both the "old" Law of the prophets and the "new" Law of Jesus.

EIGHTEENTH SUNDAY IN ORDINARY TIME

LECTIONARY #112

Isaiah = ī-ZAY-uh

Make eye contact and entreat joyfully.

Stress the verbs each time they recur. They are not commands but earnest pleading to do the right thing!

You are speaking poetry: "wine and milk" should conjure the deepest longings of our hearts.

The earnest pleading continues to build. Don't lose your energy.

Speak this solemn promise slowly, with full awareness of its implications.

READING I   Isaiah 55:1–3

A reading from the Book of the Prophet Isaiah

Thus says the LORD:
All you who are **thirsty**,
   come to the **water**!
You who have no **money**,
   come, receive **grain** and **eat**;
come, without **paying** and without **cost**,
   drink **wine** and **milk**!
Why spend your money for what is not **bread**;
   your **wages** for what fails to **satisfy**?
Heed me, and you shall eat **well**,
   you shall delight in rich **fare**.
Come to me **heedfully**,
   listen, that you may have **life**.
I will **renew** with you the everlasting **covenant**,
   the **benefits** assured to **David**.

TO KEEP IN MIND

Openings: First, make eye contact with the assembly and announce, from memory, "A (pronounced "uh," not "ay") reading from . . ." Then pause (three full beats!) before starting the reading.

READING I Familiar to us from their annual proclamation at the Easter Vigil, these verses from Isaiah possess a unique power. And their energy and passion rival anything in the Song of Songs. During Israel's darkest period, the exile, the most profound words of consolation sprang from the prophets of the Lord, particularly the two whom scholars believe wrote in the name of their mentor, Isaiah. Writing near the end of the exile, the words of this passage from Second Isaiah express a lover's pleading call to "come," "eat," "drink," "heed," "listen," "COME!" God's arms are outstretched, ready to comfort, God's table is set with the richest fare. And God holds nothing back in requesting our response. Who offers such magnanimity: a parent entreating a runaway child, a humanitarian facing near-starved refugees? Remember your pews abound with "hungry," "thirsty" people who mistake junk food that "fails to satisfy" for the bread of life God offers. Speak directly, meeting listeners' eyes as you say "come to the water!" Address other faces with "receive grain and eat " and still others with "come without paying," then offer "wine and milk" to everyone.

"Why spend your money?" conveys the futility of wasted effort and wasted lives that run in circles. Instead, God offers to renew the promise of everlasting relationship he made to King David. God will watch over us, correct us when necessary, and love us forever. Sustain an urgent tone until the final joyous promise of this "everlasting" relationship and "benefits" derived from David, our ancestor in faith.

READING II Paul's profound awareness of the consequences of Christ's Death and Resurrection spill over

For meditation and context:

TO KEEP IN MIND

Units of Thought: Running too many words together blurs meaning and fails to distinguish ideas. Punctuation does not always indicate clearly what words to group together or where to pause. Identify *units of thought* and use your voice to distinguish one from another.

This is the fifth consecutive week we read from Romans.

Though you ask them as sincere questions, you already know the answers! Speak with an undercurrent of joy.

Don't rush the list, but let each potential obstacle have its moment.

Answer decisively!

Speak out of your own faith conviction.

Your listeners won't be able to apprehend the astrological references in this listing, but strive to communicate a message that says, "Nothing, nothing in your life or in the cosmos will separate you from God's love!"

Take a substantial pause before announcing, "The word of the Lord."

TO KEEP IN MIND

Practice pronunciation!

RESPONSORIAL PSALM   Psalm 145:8–9, 15–16, 17–18 (16)

R. The hand of the Lord feeds us; he answers all our needs.

The LORD is gracious and merciful,
    slow to anger and of great kindness.
The LORD is good to all
    and compassionate toward all his works.

The eyes of all look hopefully to you,
    and you give them their food in due season;
you open your hand
    and satisfy the desire of every living thing.

The LORD is just in all his ways
    and holy in all his works.
The LORD is near to all who call upon him,
    to all who call upon him in truth.

READING II   Romans 8:35, 37–39

A reading from the Letter of Saint Paul to the Romans

Brothers and sisters:
What will **separate** us from the love of **Christ**?
Will **anguish**, or **distress**, or **persecution**, or **famine**,
    or **nakedness**, or **peril**, or the **sword**?
No, in all these things we conquer overwhelmingly
    through him who **loved** us.
For I am **convinced** that neither **death**, nor **life**,
    nor **angels**, nor **principalities**,
    nor **present** things, nor **future** things,
    nor **powers**, nor **height**, nor **depth**,
    nor any **other** creature will be able to **separate** us
    from the **love** of God in Christ **Jesus** our **Lord**.

into lavish and extravagant oratory that proclaims how God has removed every obstacle to our oneness with him and shattered every power that would separate us from his love. By dint of repetition and the cumulative effect of seemingly endless elements Paul convinces! Others might ask, *"Who* will separate us from Christ?" and answer, "No one." *"What* will separate us from Christ? Nothing." But Paul's exhaustive listing becomes a poetic device that builds impact, letting his point sink in.

Christ's saving action has changed reality forever. Now, through the grace he

won for us, we can overcome all worldly hardships and suffering. Even otherworldly powers ("angels . . . principalities") will have no sway. We are freed from all outside forces, especially astrological forces suggested by "present things . . . future things" (the discernment of astrologers) and "powers," "height," "depth" (references to forces exerted by the planets).

Achieve a proper pace by looking at a different face as you name each potential obstacle. Will "anguish" do it? Imagine a "no" before continuing. Will "distress?" Another "no." They *cannot* separate us

because through Christ "who loved us" we now have the power to conquer all these.

"I am *convinced*" (find a substitute reader if you're not!) asks that, rooted in your own faith, you name all the things in life that have tried and failed to separate you from God's love. Your conviction and desire to persuade turns this text into a hymn of praise to "Jesus, our Lord."

| GOSPEL | Matthew only hints at Jesus's reaction to John's death: "He withdrew . . . to a deserted place." Narrate John's death with grief that

GOSPEL   Matthew 14:13–21

A reading from the holy Gospel according to Matthew

When Jesus heard of the **death** of John the **Baptist**,
  he **withdrew** in a boat to a deserted place by **himself**.
The crowds **heard** of this and **followed** him on foot from
    their towns.
When he **disembarked** and saw the vast **crowd**,
  his heart was moved with **pity** for them, and he cured
    their **sick**.
When it was evening, the **disciples** approached him and said,
  "This is a **deserted** place and it is already **late**;
  dismiss the crowds so that they can go to the villages
  and buy **food** for themselves."
Jesus said to them, "There is no **need** for them to go away;
  give them some food **yourselves**."
But they said to him,
  "Five **loaves** and two **fish** are all we **have** here."
Then he said, "Bring them **here** to me,"
  and he ordered the crowds to **sit** down on the grass.
Taking the five loaves and the two fish, and looking up
    to **heaven**,
  he said the **blessing**, **broke** the loaves,
  and gave them to the **disciples**,
  who in turn gave them to the **crowds**.
They all **ate** and were **satisfied**,
  and they picked up the fragments left **over**—
  twelve wicker **baskets** full.
Those who ate were about five **thousand** men,
  not counting **women** and **children**.

A classic story like this requires thoughtful preparation.

Herod = HAYR-uhd

The narrative starts with a jolt. Jesus seeks isolation.

Their needs call Jesus out of his retreat.

"Moved with pity" and "cured their sick" are two separate moments. Don't rush them together.

"Evening" suggests the passage of time and a quiet, weary mood.

Are the disciples anticipating the crowd's needs or seeking to avoid responsibility for feeding the crowd?

Jesus is being intentionally obscure.

Jesus takes charge, giving orders and evoking confidence.

Pay special attention to the Eucharistic language here.

God's providence meets need with abundance.

Citing the numbers reinforces the notion of God's abundance and the significance of the miracle.

---

surfaces again when Jesus responds with "pity" and cures "their sick." John's death was surely a blow for Jesus; his need for solitude may reflect his grief and his need to ponder the fate that awaited him.

The throng shifts Jesus's focus from his needs to theirs. His ministry to them spills into "evening" and the disciples worry that the crowd will look to them for sustenance. Watching for their reaction, Jesus suggests coyly that they feed the crowd. With more truth than they realize, the disciples confess, "We have nothing." That may be the heart of the message here.

What follows is clear Eucharistic language that suggests this story is not an instance of God unlocking human generosity. That would be a story about what *we* can do (recall, it's the disciples, not the crowd, who are ordered to produce food). Especially because of the Eucharistic analogy, it is imperative this be seen as a story about *God's* action. Only God can take our paltry offerings and transform them into the bread of life, into food for the world.

When the disciples mention "five loaves and two fish," you almost see their shoulders shrug in resignation. But Jesus takes charge, instructing them and ordering the crowds. Narrate the sacramental moment slowly, highlighting the Eucharistic actions of taking, blessing, and breaking. Here is the embodiment of Isaiah's promise, "Heed me, and you shall eat well." Let your tone fill in for Matthew who comments on the amazing miracle with few words and less emotion. In this Eucharistic setting, even details about scraps suggest that with God all hungers can be satisfied.

NINETEENTH SUNDAY IN ORDINARY TIME

LECTIONARY #115

READING I   1 Kings 19:9a, 11–13a

A reading from the first Book of Kings

At the mountain of God, **Horeb**,
  Elijah came to a **cave** where he took shelter.
Then the LORD said to him,
  "**Go** outside and stand on the **mountain** before the LORD;
  the LORD will be **passing** by."
A strong and heavy **wind** was rending the mountains
  and crushing **rocks** before the LORD—
  but the LORD was not in the **wind**.
After the wind there was an **earthquake**—
  but the LORD was not in the earthquake.
After the earthquake there was **fire**—
  but the LORD was not in the **fire**.
After the fire there was a tiny **whispering** sound.
When he **heard** this,
  Elijah **hid** his face in his cloak
  and went and stood at the **entrance** of the cave.

See the parallels with Moses in Exodus 33:21–23.

Horeb = HOHR-eb

Elijah = ee-LĪ-juh

Elijah took shelter here from his enemies and death threats.

Here is the authoritative voice of God.

As narrator, suggest the fearsome aspects of these phenomena.

Slow your pace considerably. God is fully revealed not in nature's fury but in the revealed word, spoken softly in the heart.

He hides his face because, as God warned Moses, "No one can see me and live" (Exodus 33:20).

TO KEEP IN MIND
Careful preparation expresses your reverence for the Word.

READING I   After forty days fleeing the wrath of his angry monarchs, Elijah reaches Mount Horeb (another name for Mount Sinai where Moses also met the Lord). Exhausted and praying for death, Elijah was eager to drop the mantle of his office. But God had sent an angel to minister to the burnt-out prophet and, thus refreshed, Elijah journeyed to the mountaintop. Here, God calls him to stand at the mouth of the cave where he's hiding and await the appearance of the Lord. God wants to show Elijah that his fears are unfounded and that God has abandoned neither prophet nor nation. Here Elijah will learn that God is master of the unexpected.

Your tone should suggest Elijah's fear and exhaustion when you speak of the "cave" where he "took shelter." Then, God's strong voice orders him out of hiding, saying: Watch for me on the mountain (the traditional place of encounter with God). The grand natural phenomena *ought* to be divine manifestations. But they're not. Nonetheless, describe each one as if it *were* the theophany Elijah expects. Each is terrifying: the "wind" shaking rocks loose from the mountain, the "earthquake" loosening the ground beneath his feet, the "fire" threatening to engulf him. Then, the "the tiny whispering sound." Give that a different read and pause after "sound," as if listening and *recognizing* God in the hushed whisper. Suddenly, Elijah hides his face, a clear sign—though it's never stated—that he has sensed divinity in that surpassing calm. Aware he has stood in the presence of almighty God, Elijah returns to the cave knowing this God who appears in surprising ways has more surprises in store.

For meditation and context:

RESPONSORIAL PSALM   Psalm 85:9, 10, 11–12, 13–14 (8)

R. Lord, let us see your kindness, and grant us your salvation.

I will hear what God proclaims;
    the LORD—for he proclaims peace.
Near indeed is his salvation to those who
        fear him,
    glory dwelling in our land.

Kindness and truth shall meet;
    justice and peace shall kiss.
Truth shall spring out of the earth,
    and justice shall look down from heaven.

The LORD himself will give his benefits;
    our land shall yield its increase.
Justice shall walk before him,
    and prepare the way of his steps.

TO KEEP IN MIND

Openings: First, make eye contact with the assembly and announce, from memory, "A (pronounced "uh," not "ay") reading from . . ." Then pause (three full beats!) before starting the reading.

READING II   Romans 9:1–5

A reading from the Letter of Saint Paul to the Romans

Brothers and sisters:
I speak the **truth** in Christ, I do not **lie**;
    my conscience joins with the Holy **Spirit** in bearing
        me witness
    that I have great **sorrow** and constant **anguish** in my heart.
For I could wish that I myself were **accursed** and cut **off**
        from Christ
    for the **sake** of my own people,
    my **kindred** according to the flesh.
They are **Israelites**;
    theirs the **adoption**, the **glory**, the **covenants**,
    the giving of the **law**, the **worship**, and the **promises**;
    theirs the **patriarchs**, and from them,
    according to the flesh, is the **Christ**,
    who is **over** all, God **blessed** forever. **Amen.**

Pause after introducing the reading so you can prepare to begin boldly.

The tone shifts here, making it clear he's being bold about his sorrow, not condemnation. "Sorrow" and "anguish" are *two* expressions of grief, not one.

For emphasis, he says the same thing twice: "my own people, my kindred . . . ." Think of those you love as you speak these words.

Don't speed through this list; each item names a divine favor bestowed on Israel.

You end on a joyous note of praise and thanks to God.

READING II Few passages in Paul begin as bluntly as this one. He voices deep grief over the unwillingness of many Israelites to embrace faith in Jesus. Early Christians struggled with the scandal of Israel's rejection of Jesus, the Messiah God first sent to the Jews. Paul's pain is so great that he would even consider sacrificing his own salvation and be "cut off from Christ" if it would help his people to embrace him. There is no hint of condemnation here, only genuine concern for his people. The mystery pondered is God's elective mercy, not Israel's sinfulness. A giant "why" hovers over this passage.

When you begin, speak the first sentence from memory. Then punctuate "I, do, not, lie," word by word, maintaining direct eye contact. Don't assume Paul's "great sorrow and constant anguish" are hyperbole. Paul loved his heritage and wanted nothing more than to see his people recognize the Messiah as he did. That's why he can make the almost unthinkable assertion that he would trade his salvation for theirs.

Paul then lists the privileges God entrusted to Israel, making Israel the doorway that ushered Christ into the world. The use of the present tense ("theirs [that is, "theirs *is*," not "theirs *was*"] the adoption, the glory . . . the patriarchs") asserts Paul's conviction that Israel continues to enjoy these benefits. Read the list slowly, each item another reason why Paul so deeply loves his people. The reading ends with a doxology, a word of honest praise for the God who reigns "over all."

GOSPEL   Matthew 14:22–33

A reading from the holy Gospel according to Matthew

After he had **fed** the people, Jesus made the disciples get
   into a **boat**
   and **precede** him to the other side,
   while he **dismissed** the crowds.
After doing so, he went up on the mountain by **himself** to **pray**.
When it was **evening** he was there **alone**.
Meanwhile the **boat**, already a few miles **offshore**,
   was being **tossed** about by the waves, for the **wind** was
      against it.
During the **fourth** watch of the night,
   he came **toward** them walking on the **sea**.
When the disciples **saw** him walking on the sea they
      were **terrified**.
"It is a **ghost**, " they said, and they cried out in **fear**.
At once Jesus spoke to them, "Take **courage**, it is **I**; do not
   be **afraid**."
Peter said to him in reply,
   "**Lord**, if it is **you**, command me to **come** to you on the water."
He said, "**Come**."
Peter **got** out of the boat and began to **walk** on the water
      toward Jesus.
But when he saw how **strong** the wind was he became
   frightened;
   and, beginning to **sink**, he cried out, "Lord, **save** me!"
Immediately Jesus stretched out his **hand** and **caught** Peter,
   and said to him, "O you of **little** faith, why did you **doubt**?"
After they got into the **boat**, the wind **died** down.
Those who were in the boat did him **homage**, saying,
   "Truly, you are the **Son** of **God**."

The opening scene is a denouement, with Jesus needing time alone after the intense day of preaching and the miraculous feeding of the crowd.

"Meanwhile" signals a change in mood that signals the distress of the disciples.

"Fourth watch" = the hours between 3 AM and 6 AM. Narrate his movement on the water as if you could see it happening.

Of course, this incredible sight would strike fear in the disciples' hearts.

Don't match the distress of the disciples. Instead, Jesus's tone can be authoritative but calm.

Peter is a mix of daring and trembling excitement.

Speak in a way that suggests his tentative steps upon the water.

Quicken the pace and increase your volume.

Jesus's question is more resignation than reproach.

Pause after "died down" to suggest the sudden silence and to motivate their declaration of faith.

GOSPEL   In Matthew, this story, which immediately follows the multiplication of loaves and fishes, serves a different purpose than in Mark. There, despite this great miracle, the disciples remain unaware of Jesus's identity, Mark telling us their hearts "were hardened," and they'd not yet understood "the incident of the loaves." But in Matthew, the episode reveals a deepening sense of discipleship and a growing understanding among Jesus's closest followers, especially Peter, of Jesus's true identity. Thus, anticipating the words of the centurion at the Cross, they are able to proclaim Jesus the "Son of God." Ultimately, the incident says to us what it said to the disciples: in Jesus we find a divine person who transcends human categories and before whom we have little choice but to do "him homage."

To tell the story well, be attentive to Matthew's nuances. The prelude to the miracle story is full of clues about tone and purpose. Jesus "*made*" the disciples depart and then "he went up on the mountain," so often a place of encounter with God. And he went there "by himself to *pray*," a rare occurrence in Matthew. While he is praying the disciples get in trouble. You're given few words with which to create the storm and the disciples' fear.

Jesus' first comment, "It is I," echoes with the divine self-revelation it implies. Then he speaks his oft repeated, "do not be afraid." Peter's faith surges, then falters—the beginning of a pattern. But Jesus's presence in the boat helps them all to see and to proclaim who it is who multiplies loaves and walks upon the sea.

THE ASSUMPTION OF THE BLESSED VIRGIN MARY: VIGIL

LECTIONARY #621

READING I   1 Chronicles 15:3–4, 15–16; 16:1–2

A reading from the first Book of Chronicles

David assembled all **Israel** in **Jerusalem** to bring the **ark**
    of the Lord
  to the place that he had **prepared** for it.
David also called together the sons of **Aaron** and the **Levites.**

The **Levites** bore the ark of God on their **shoulders** with **poles**,
  as **Moses** had ordained according to the word of the Lord.

David commanded the **chiefs** of the Levites
    to appoint their kinsmen as **chanters**,
      to play on musical **instruments**, **harps**, **lyres**, and **cymbals**,
    to make a loud **sound** of **rejoicing**.

They brought in the **ark** of God and set it within the **tent**
  which David had **pitched** for it.
Then they offered up **burnt** offerings and **peace** offerings to God.
When David had **finished** offering up the burnt offerings and
    peace offerings,
  he **blessed** the people in the name of the Lord.

Chronicles = KRAH-nih-k*ls

The reading begins with a sense of expectancy, like the excitement before the start of a parade or a major championship.

Aaron = AYR-uhn

Levites = LEE-vīts

The "poles" were both a means of transport and a way of preventing the ark from being touched.

Moses = MOH-ziz; MOH-zis

Let your tone echo the "rejoicing" commanded by David.

lyres = līrz

cymbals = SIM-buhlz

Prior to the building of the Temple, the ark was housed in a traveling tent or tabernacle.

The final moment is grand and solemn. David blesses the people in God's name, confident, because of the Ark, of God's presence among them. Today it is Mary who fills us with confident hope.

| READING I | Because God is invisible, concrete objects become important conveyors of the divine mystery. Within Judaism, which permitted no graven images, the ark of the covenant was one of its most important and sacred objects for it contained the tablets of the Law given to Moses on Mount Sinai and some of the manna that fed the Israelites during their long desert sojourn. Built according to God's instructions to Moses (Exodus 25:10–16), the ark was entirely covered with gold and crowned with two golden cherubim, from between which God was said to speak to Moses. Precious and sacred, the ark was not to be touched, and when transported was veiled with skins and a blue cloth so even the priests who carried it could not see it.

Why do we read of this sacred object today? Because Mary is considered the ark of the *new* covenant. Moses's ark contained the tablets of the old Law and the ark itself represented God's presence among the Jewish people. The ark of Moses gave the people hope, marched before them into battle, and was enshrined first in a tent and eventually in the holy of holies of Solomon's temple. The Church sees in Mary a new ark of the covenant. Within her body she carried the new hope of Israel and of all humankind. As the ark traveled from place to place with the divine presence within it, so Mary traveled carrying the precious child within her womb and was greeted with joy by Elizabeth and the child of *her* womb, John. The ark of the covenant, then, is a type or foreshadowing of Mary, the bearer of Emmanuel, God with us.

For meditation and context:

TO KEEP IN MIND
Tell the story: The reading of Scripture is a storytelling moment. Storytellers are people of imagination. They help us to see, hear, feel, and smell the elements of the story because they themselves experience these sensory aspects of a story.

Corinthians = kohr-IN-thee-uhnz

Speak this opening sentence slowly and carefully with special attention to the word "immortality" (*not* "immorality!").

This is grand rhetoric; don't cheapen it with an overly dramatic delivery or with lifeless expression.

Logical reasoning bursts into sudden praise.

Take a brief pause after "victory" before announcing its source: "our Lord Jesus Christ."

TO KEEP IN MIND
Slow down: The larger the church, the larger the assembly, and the more complex the text, the slower you must read.

RESPONSORIAL PSALM   Psalm 132:6–7, 9–10, 13–14 (8)

R. Lord, go up to the place of your rest, you and the ark of your holiness.

Behold, we heard of it in Ephrathah;
　we found it in the fields of Jaar.
Let us enter into his dwelling,
　let us worship at his footstool.

May your priests be clothed with justice;
　let your faithful ones shout merrily for joy.
For the sake of David your servant,
　reject not the plea of your anointed.

For the LORD has chosen Zion;
　he prefers her for his dwelling.
"Zion is my resting place forever;
　in her will I dwell, for I prefer her."

READING II   1 Corinthians 15:54b–57

A reading from the first Letter of Saint Paul to the Corinthians

Brothers and sisters:
When that which is **mortal** clothes itself with **immortality**,
　then the word that is **written** shall come **about**:

　　*Death is swallowed up in **victory**.*
　　***Where**, O death, is your **victory**!*
　　***Where**, O death, is your **sting**!*

The sting of death is **sin**,
　and the **power** of sin is the **law**.
But thanks be to **God** who gives us the **victory**
　through our **Lord** Jesus **Christ**.

READING II   St. Paul was privileged with great theological insight and prophetic vision. In this chapter of Corinthians he has been arguing for the reality of bodily resurrection against skeptics in the community who could not conceive how there could be any corporeal life after death. They insisted that the afterlife was a purely spiritual existence, for the soul not the body. Some of them argued that this purely spiritual resurrection was *already* bestowed upon the Christian believer, and not the *future* reality Paul so assiduously taught.

Paul argues against these misunderstandings by reasserting the fact of Jesus's own bodily Resurrection, demonstrating the foolishness of *denying* the Resurrection, and then presenting his insights into what resurrected life in a resurrected body might be like. It is during his discussion of that last point that our reading picks up today. Possibly borrowing an image from Hosea (13:14), Paul utilizes a remarkable rhetorical device to challenge death itself. Where are your "victory" and your "sting?" he asks. Like a scorpion, death possesses a sting, which is sin, and with that sting it injects its deadly venom. But "sin" gets its power from the "law" and Christ has transcended the Law so that now we are saved not by the Law's works but by grace. And for that Paul gives abundant and joyful thanks. And in Mary, who alone with Jesus enjoys full bodily Resurrection, we find added reason for rejoicing.

Let your tone suggest Jesus's effort to communicate to a large crowd.

Raise your volume slightly to suggest the cry emanating from the crowd.

Don't let Jesus's reply suggest any trace of reproach against Mary. What Jesus offers are the true reasons Mary was blessed—not for carrying and nursing but for hearing and observing.

TO KEEP IN MIND

Importance of the Narrator: The narrator is often the pivotal role of a passage. Timbre, pitch, rate, and energy can make the same words convey very different moods or meaning. Sometimes the narrator is objective, but often the narrator has great interest in the events and characters of a story.

GOSPEL   Luke 11:27–28

A reading from the holy Gospel according to Luke

While **Jesus** was speaking,
    a **woman** from the crowd called out and **said** to him,
    "**Blessed** is the womb that carried you
    and the **breasts** at which you nursed."
He replied,
    "**Rather**, blessed are those
    who **hear** the word of God and **observe** it."

GOSPEL   The role of Mary before, during, and after the life of Jesus was and is to point to her Son. Her significant function within Catholic piety is never to draw attention to herself, but like the moon, to reflect the blazing radiance of the source of all light, her divine Son. And so this text is eminently appropriate today. Though we celebrate a solemnity of Mary, the Scripture text seems unwilling to echo the praise the woman in the crowd lavishes on Mary. Overtly, what it says is that praise should fall upon those, *all* of those, who "hear" and "observe" the Word of God. It would seem Jesus is slighting his own Mother.

But, of course, what Jesus calls for is exactly what Mary did in her own life. Elizabeth proclaims that truth about her younger cousin when she says, "Blessed are you who believed that what was spoken to you by the Lord would be fulfilled" (Luke 1:45). Mary is the first of those believers extolled by Jesus. She not only heard God's Word, she carried it within her womb. So Jesus's reply is no slight against Mary, his Mother. Instead, it invites everyone to be like her, by *hearing* and *observing*.

THE ASSUMPTION OF THE BLESSED VIRGIN MARY: DAY

LECTIONARY #622

READING I   Revelation 11:19a; 12:1–6a, 10ab

A reading from the Book of Revelation

God's **temple** in heaven was **opened**,
  and the **ark** of his covenant could be **seen** in the temple.

A great **sign** appeared in the sky, a **woman** clothed with the **sun**,
  with the **moon** under her **feet**,
  and on her **head** a **crown** of twelve **stars**.
She was with **child** and wailed aloud in **pain** as she **labored** to
    give birth.
Then **another** sign appeared in the sky;
  it was a huge red **dragon**, with seven **heads** and ten **horns**,
  and on its heads were seven **diadems**.
Its **tail** swept away a third of the **stars** in the sky
  and **hurled** them down to the **earth**.
Then the dragon **stood** before the woman about to give birth,
  to **devour** her child when she gave birth.
She gave birth to a **son**, a **male** child,
  destined to **rule** all the nations with an iron **rod**.
Her child was caught up to **God** and his **throne**.
The woman herself **fled** into the **desert**
  where she had a place prepared by **God**.

READING I   John's grand, apocalyptic vision presents a "woman" who symbolizes Israel, the Church, and in the context of this liturgy, Mary, the Mother of Jesus. Within this cosmic vision, we discern the outlines of Mary the Mother and of the divine child who will become the Messiah who brings "salvation." In Mary, Old and New Testaments meet. For Israel, the ark of the covenant that housed the commandments *represented* God's presence. But in the New Testament, Mary actually *bears* divine presence within her.

She conceives Jesus, God's incarnate Son, and becomes the ark of the *new* covenant.

This vision evokes another woman and mother, Eve, the primordial mother of humankind. Mary is the *new* Eve through whom a new creation is initiated in Christ, who, in turn, becomes the new Adam. This reading underscores the many ways in which the threads of God's plan of salvation intersect in the person of Mary. As you proclaim this scene of clashing cosmic forces, give prominence to the woman at the center of the drama by stressing her dignity,

the overpowering threat that menaces her, and God's ultimate intervention.

Tell the story in a clear, compelling way that arouses imaginations and opens hearts to what God is saying through these odd, portentous images. The tone of the opening lines suggests the grand scope of what follows. (The deleted half of the opening verse describes the Temple opening amid roaring thunder and lightning!)

The grand image of the woman crowned with stars suddenly yields to a sobering image of a mother wailing in childbirth. As we honor Mary, we see her fate

Pause, and then begin the narration.

This declaration should resound with power and hope for the destiny of the "male child" encompasses all nations and brings "salvation" under the "authority" of God's Anointed.

For meditation and context:

TO KEEP IN MIND

Posture speaks: Make sure it says what you want it to. Don't let your face or body contradict the good news you announce. Remember, readers are allowed to smile!

Corinthians = kohr-IN-thee-uhnz

Take a slight pause after the salutation, and then boldly declare the great truth of Christ's Resurrection—that presages our own.

Though Paul's tone is logical and well reasoned, let the good news of what he says also shine through: yes, a *man* caused death, but a man also brought *life*; in Adam we all *die*, but in Christ we *live*!

Besides balancing Paul's ideas, be sure you also provide contrast by giving negative and positive values to the death-life images.

Here, too, there is an undercurrent of hope and joy. Although there is a proper order, we will get our turn.

"Those who belong to Christ" believed in him and lived so as to resemble him.

Don't get thrown by the double "when;" imagine the second "when" as "after." Distinguish the three ranks of spiritual being he names.

End on a note of regal power. Christ will reign forever and over all things, including the great enemy—death.

Then I heard a loud voice in **heaven** say:
   "Now have **salvation** and **power** come,
       and the **Kingdom** of our **God**
       and the **authority** of his **Anointed** One."

RESPONSORIAL PSALM   Psalm 45:10, 11, 12, 16 (10bc)

R. The queen stands at your right hand, arrayed in gold.

The queen takes her place at your right hand
   in gold of Ophir.

Hear, O daughter, and see; turn your ear,
   forget your people and your father's house.

So shall the king desire your beauty;
   for he is your lord.

They are borne in with gladness and joy;
   they enter the palace of the king.

READING II   1 Corinthians 15:20–27

A reading from the first Letter of Saint Paul to the Corinthians

Brothers and sisters:
Christ has been **raised** from the **dead**,
   the **firstfruits** of those who have fallen **asleep**.
For since **death** came through **man**,
   the **resurrection** of the dead came **also** through man.
For just as in **Adam** all **die**,
   so too in **Christ** shall all be brought to **life**,
   but each one in proper **order**:
   Christ the **first**fruits;
   then, at his **coming**, those who **belong** to Christ;
   then comes the **end**,
   when he hands over the **Kingdom** to his God and **Father**,
   when he has **destroyed** every **sovereignty**
   and every **authority** and **power**.
For he must **reign** until he has put all his enemies under his **feet**.
The **last** enemy to be destroyed is **death**,
   for "he subjected **everything** under his feet."

---

mirror that of her Son. Great privilege brought great trial into her life. Such suffering, so common in the lives of saints, purifies human hearts and makes Mary one with all human suffering and struggle.

The red dragon symbolizes the devil and all forces that oppose God's will. The "seven heads" suggest the seven hills on which pagan Rome was built. Great danger threatens the mother's child who is destined to "shepherd" (a gentle word) but, ironically, with a rod of "*iron*." Heaven has the final word, for mother and child are delivered from the monstrous menace.

Announce with joy that the child was swept up into heaven; then, without anxiety, speak of the woman fleeing to the safe place prepared for her by God.

| READING II | Paul's bedrock conviction is that Jesus's Resurrection |

changed everything. So he boldly heralds that truth at the start of this reading. God did something unique in Christ. But what God did in Jesus was to be a template for what would happen to all who believe in him. What God began in Christ is now the norm. Christ is the "firstfruits" of those who

have died because the singular privilege granted to him will be granted to *all* who die in him. Unflinchingly, Paul heralds that all can share Christ's victory over death.

Paul contrasts Adam whose sin brought "*death*" into the world with Christ whose self-sacrifice brings "*life*." Through the new Adam, Christ, God undid the damage done by the first Adam. With masterful balance and elegant simplicity, Paul applies his persuasive logic. Those who are "in Adam" are destined to die, those who are "in Christ" (of whom Mary ranks first) "shall be brought to life." The Church's conviction

Mary's faith in the angel's message impels her haste.

Don't rush the naming of the location and key players.

Judean = <u>joo</u>-DEE-uhn; <u>joo</u>-DAY-uhn

That the "infant leaped" and that Elizabeth was "filled with the Holy Spirit" are both significant details.

Pause before announcing Elizabeth's greeting. She sees more than her young cousin standing before her. Suggest this with a tone of reverence and admiration.

Don't recite the blessing as in the Hail Mary, but as a spontaneous exclamation.

Don't ignore Elizabeth's naming Jesus "Lord."

What is said of Mary can be said of all believers who hear this Gospel today.

GOSPEL   Luke 1:39–56

A reading from the holy Gospel according to Luke

Mary set out
   and traveled to the **hill** country in **haste**
   to a town of **Judah**,
   where she entered the house of **Zechariah**
   and greeted **Elizabeth**.
When Elizabeth **heard** Mary's greeting,
   the infant **leaped** in her womb,
   and Elizabeth, **filled** with the Holy **Spirit**,
   cried out in a loud **voice** and said,
   "**Blessed** are you among women,
   and blessed is the **fruit** of your **womb**.
And how does this happen to **me**,
   that the mother of my **Lord** should come to me?
For at the moment the **sound** of your greeting reached my **ears**,
   the **infant** in my womb leaped for **joy**.
Blessed are you who **believed**
   that what was spoken to you by the **Lord**
   would be **fulfilled**."

TO KEEP IN MIND
Names of characters are often the first word of a reading. Stress names so listeners don't miss who the subject is.

---

that Mary has already experienced the fullness of Resurrection and dwells with Jesus in the heavenly Kingdom is the reason this text is read today.

But this great mystery unfolds in proper order. The first to experience Resurrection is Christ himself. But later, at the "end," *all* who "belong to Christ" will experience Resurrection. The vanquishing of the forces that resist God's Kingdom also follows a sequence. Christ will hand over the Kingdom to the Father only after he has destroyed all those foes: the lesser enemies ("every sovereignty . . . authority and power") will be overcome first; then the greatest enemy will be vanquished—death itself. And death will be defeated in the place where it has reigned since the dawn of humanity—our human bodies.

Christ promised to prepare for us a place where our bodies will be free from the destruction that results from sin. Mary stands as his pledge that this promise will be fulfilled in *us* because it has already been fulfilled in *her*. Taken into heaven in body and in soul, Mary now lives the resurrected life Jesus first experienced, and that we will experience if we trust in him.

GOSPEL Scripture constantly presents figures whose lives are interrupted and upended by God; Mary and Elizabeth are but two in a long and illustrious line. After the shock of her encounter with Gabriel, Mary hastens to the side of her cousin whose unexpected pregnancy is the sign that confirms the angel's promise. These women, bound by more than blood, are vessels of grace and

The canticle stands apart from the rest of the text. Pause before beginning and sustain a fairly brisk and joyful tempo.

Though called "blessed," Mary identifies herself as a lowly "servant."

Note the shift to third-person plural.

"Fear" of the Lord is a venerable biblical notion that should be highlighted.

The God of the Bible, even the New Testament, is not unidimensional: besides mercy and love there is also strength and justice.

These reversals are typical of the Kingdom of God. Give them proper stress.

The song ends on a note of enduring gratitude.

Pause before reading this coda that tells us Mary stayed till the birth of John.

TO KEEP IN MIND

Who really proclaims: "When the Sacred Scriptures are read in the Church, God himself speaks to his people, and Christ, present in his word, proclaims the gospel" (#29 GIRM).

And **Mary** said:

"My soul proclaims the **greatness** of the Lord;
    my spirit **rejoices** in God my **Savior**
    for he has with **favor** on his lowly servant.
From this day all **generations** will call me **blessed**:
    the Almighty has done **great** things for me
    and **holy** is his Name.
He has **mercy** on those who **fear** him
    in every generation.
He has shown the **strength** of his arm,
    and has scattered the **proud** in their conceit.
He has cast down the **mighty** from their **thrones**,
    and has lifted up the lowly.
He has filled the **hungry** with **good** things,
    and the **rich** he has sent away **empty**.
He has come to the **help** of his servant Israel
    for he has remembered his promise of **mercy**,
    the promise he made to our **fathers**,
    to **Abraham** and his children for **ever**."

Mary **remained** with her about three **months**
    and then **returned** to her **home**.

---

conduits of love. In her Spirit-led greeting Elizabeth not only names Mary and the child she bears as "blessed" but also becomes the first to identify Jesus as "Lord."

Zechariah doubted the angel, but Mary comes in expectant faith to assist her aged cousin in her pregnancy. Rejoicing in the grace God has bestowed on her, Mary knows that "generations" will follow Elizabeth's lead and call her "blessed." For that faith Elizabeth and Luke both praise her. Holding nothing back, Mary has trusted and surrendered and become the first and most ideal disciple. In her canticle, she expresses the longings of generations of faithful Israelites. She sings of God's goodness, acknowledges God's favor upon the lowly, and names the amazing reversals that characterize the kingdom—the mighty are cast down and the lowly lifted up, the rich go away empty while the hungry are fed. Midway through, the song shifts from first to third person plural. Mary, no longer speaking only of herself, becomes spokesperson for all the "poor ones" who rejoice in their neediness and their dependence on God.

Narrate the visitation story with Elizabeth's joy, suggesting the strength the women derived from each other's company. While briskly proclaimed, Mary's canticle contains powerful and important images that should not be rushed. In this song we find our own spiritual communion with these two women, and we are reminded that Mary was destined for the unique distinction we celebrate today.

TWENTIETH SUNDAY
IN ORDINARY TIME

Isaiah = ī-ZAY-uh

It is God's voice that speaks throughout. Begin slowly and with authority.

These are the joyful consequences of heeding God's commands.

Be sure to bring attention to the fact God is speaking now of "foreigners."

Don't let these criteria sound like harsh requirements. They are joyful duties that bring peace.

profanation = prah-fuh-NAY-shuhn

Jerusalem is built on the same "holy mountain" that accommodates God's "house of prayer." Name both places with reverence and love.

Speak as if before an audience that would discourage such divine generosity.

TO KEEP IN MIND
Careful preparation expresses your reverence for the Word.

LECTIONARY #118

READING I   Isaiah 56:1, 6–7

A reading from the Book of the Prophet Isaiah

Thus says the LORD:
Observe what is **right**, do what is **just**;
　for my **salvation** is about to come,
　my **justice**, about to be **revealed**.

The **foreigners** who join themselves to the LORD,
　ministering to him,
loving the name of the LORD,
　and becoming his **servants**—
all who keep the sabbath free from **profanation**
　and hold to my **covenant**,
them I will bring to my holy **mountain**
　and make **joyful** in my house of prayer;
their burnt **offerings** and **sacrifices**
　will be **acceptable** on my altar,
for my **house** shall be called
　a house of **prayer** for all **peoples**.

 READING I A rare and wonderful harmony unites all of today's readings, which focus on the universality of God's mercy. Israel's identity flowed from its conviction that its people were unique as God's Chosen People. The awareness that God does offer salvation, not based on ethnicity, but on fidelity to God's Law and the Sabbath dawned slowly upon Israel. The opening imperatives to "observe . . . do what is just/right" are directed to all who desire mercy. Deliver those imperatives

boldly. Then, announce the grace they bring into one's life: "salvation" and "justice."

During the postexilic time when these chapters of Isaiah were written, the people were perhaps better prepared to hear a message of God's universal love. After all, it was the pagan King Cyrus who ended the exile and permitted them to return to Israel. But extending membership in the community of the Lord to foreigners reversed long-entrenched chauvinistic attitudes. But the prophet lists certain behaviors ("ministering," "loving," "becoming his servants") that

are required responses to God's offer of love. Distinguish the criteria one from another and avoid an "if/then" quality, (that is, "If you do these things, then you'll belong to me") and strive instead for a "since/then" tone (that is, "Since many foreigners join themselves to the Lord, becoming his servants, then . . . "). Even today narrow prejudice seeks to exclude some from God's Kingdom. Fix such people in your mind as you announce that God's mercy is extended to all.

For meditation and context:

RESPONSORIAL PSALM   Psalm 67:2–3, 5, 6, 8 (4)

R. O God, let all the nations praise you!

May God have pity on us and bless us;
    may he let his face shine upon us.
So may your way be known upon earth;
    among all nations, your salvation.

May the nations be glad and exult
    because you rule the peoples in equity;
    the nations on the earth you guide.

May the peoples praise you, O God;
    may all the peoples praise you!
May God bless us,
    and may all the ends of the earth fear him!

READING II   Romans 11:13–15, 29–32

A reading from the Letter of Saint Paul to the Romans

Brothers and sisters:
I am speaking to you **Gentiles**.
Inasmuch as I am the **apostle** to the Gentiles,
    I **glory** in my ministry in order to make my race **jealous**
    and thus **save** some of them.
For if their **rejection** is the **reconciliation** of the world,
    what will their **acceptance** be but **life** from the **dead**?

For the **gifts** and the **call** of God are **irrevocable**.
Just as you once **disobeyed** God
    but have now received **mercy** because of **their** disobedience,
    so they have now **disobeyed** in order that,
    by virtue of the mercy shown to **you**,
    they **too** may now receive mercy.
For God delivered **all** to disobedience,
    that he might have **mercy** upon all.

Gentiles = JEN-tils

Establish clear eye contact.

You'll need a deliberate and slow delivery to ensure Paul's benevolent motive is clear.

Paul is expressing his sincere hope for the salvation of all his people.

irrevocable = ih-REV-uh-kuh-b*l

Paul is clear: God called Israel and that call is not revoked!

Paul's logic is a bit convoluted here, so read carefully.

The sin in which we are all immersed manifests God's bountiful mercy.

READING II   It was a profound and enduring sorrow for Paul that his own people, whom he loved, had rejected Jesus. He sees his ministry to the Gentiles as an opportunity to arouse "jealousy" in his own people and thus, perhaps, draw them to Christ. Put plainly, the Apostles are now free to expand their preaching from Jews only to all Gentiles. Paul hopes those efforts will be so successful that Jews will become envious of Gentiles and want to repossess what they thoughtlessly rejected. Ever the optimist, Paul reasons that just as their rejection of Jesus bore good fruit for the Gentiles, their acceptance of Jesus would result in nothing less than "life from the dead!"

Then Paul asserts a truth that the Second Vatican Council strongly reaffirmed in *Nostra Aetate (Declaration on the Relation of the Church to Non-Christian Religions), 4:* "The gifts and the call of God are irrevocable." God's covenant with Israel still stands. In verses deleted from our portion, Paul speaks of the Jews as the root and we Gentiles as branches grafted onto the root. Paul reasons that just as God used the Jew's disobedience to show mercy to us Gentiles, so God can use their disobedience to show mercy to the Chosen People themselves. Paul's point is clear: "*all*" people are imprisoned in their own disobedience and are equally dependent on God's generous mercy. Use the balances and contrasts in Paul's writing to teach with conviction that God's love is free and, echoing Isaiah, given to "all."

GOSPEL   Hostility between Israelites and Canaanites was well established, and Jesus is keenly aware that this woman is no daughter of Israel. First he

Tyre = tīr

Sidon = Sī-duhn

Let your tone indicate these are not natural destinations for Jesus.

Canaanite = KAY-nuh-nīt

Again, your tone suggests disapproval of a "Canaanite."

Her earnest plea should make Jesus's silence unexpected and confusing.

They're embarrassed by her public display.

Her plea is urgent but dignified.

Does Jesus know this retort won't deter her?

Her reply is remarkable not for its cleverness but for the faith it expresses.

His admiration for her is abundantly evident.

Matthew gives only a terse report of the healing. But be sure it's heard and understood.

GOSPEL   Matthew 15:21–28

A reading from the holy Gospel according to Matthew

At that time, **Jesus** withdrew to the region of **Tyre** and **Sidon**.
And behold, a **Canaanite** woman of that district came
    and called out,
  "Have **pity** on me, Lord, Son of **David**!
My **daughter** is tormented by a **demon**."
But Jesus did not say a **word** in answer to her.
Jesus' **disciples** came and asked him,
  "Send her **away**, for she keeps **calling** out after us."
He said in reply,
  "I was sent only to the lost sheep of the house of **Israel**."
But the woman came and did Jesus **homage**, saying,
    "**Lord**, **help** me."
He said in reply,
  "It is not right to take the food of the **children**
  and throw it to the **dogs**."
She said, "**Please**, Lord, for even the **dogs** eat the scraps
  that fall from the table of their **masters**."
Then Jesus said to her in reply,
  "O **woman**, **great** is your faith!
Let it be done for you as you **wish**."
And the woman's daughter was **healed** from that **hour**.

TO KEEP IN MIND

Tell the story: The reading of Scripture is a storytelling moment. Storytellers are people of imagination. They help us to see, hear, feel, and smell the elements of the story because they themselves experience these sensory aspects of a story.

---

ignores her, and then announces his ministry is for his own people, not hers. Finally, at least in Matthew, her faith evokes a compliment and a miracle. Or perhaps Jesus risks appearing harsh and annoying to play devil's advocate to make the point we've already encountered in today's other readings: God welcomes all people into the Kingdom. Would there be a better way to confront jingoistic attitudes than to seemingly endorse them and in the process make them appear uncharitable and ungodly?

Stress "Tyre," "Sidon," and "Canaanite" to signal Jesus is in Gentile territory. The woman is self-confident (or perhaps desperate) as she calls on Jesus. Give her plea the urgency that would drive a mother to approach a stranger on the street. Demonic possession was no less terrifying than leukemia or cyanide poisoning would be today. As narrator, remain objective about Jesus's uncharacteristic lack of response. Pause there to imagine eyes darting quickly from Jesus to the woman, wondering what will happen.

The disciples rush to fill the silence and whisper instructions to Jesus. Jesus answers calmly, like a politician who's just received the reply he needed from a canny aid. Undeterred, and perhaps listening to her heart instead of his words, the woman steps forward and quietly commands his help. Jesus pushes farther, comparing Gentiles to "dogs," a word the disciples might have used. Undaunted, the woman brilliantly turns his argument against him. So Jesus, before all and with love and admiration, extols the "great faith" that coaxed a miracle.

TWENTY-FIRST SUNDAY IN ORDINARY TIME

LECTIONARY #121

Isaiah = ī-ZAY-uh

READING I   Isaiah 22:19–23

A reading from the Book of the Prophet Isaiah

The voice we hear is the Lord's. Speak with power and authority.

Shebna = SHEB-nah

Eliakim = ee-LĪ-uh-kim

Hilkiah = hil-KĪ-uh

Let your tone soften as you speak of Eliakim.

These lines are not just about shaming one official, but about elevating a more worthy officeholder.

Speak with pride of "the key" that will be placed on his shoulders.

Don't rush these lines: we need to recognize their echoes in today's Gospel.

The reference to "peg" is an allusion to the set-up of a tent.

Thus says the Lᴏʀᴅ to **Shebna**, master of the **palace**:
"I will **thrust** you from your office
    and pull you down from your **station**.
On that day I will summon my **servant**
    Eliakim, son of **Hilkiah**;
I will clothe **him** with your **robe**,
    and **gird** him with your **sash**,
    and give **over** to him your **authority**.
He shall be a **father** to the inhabitants of Jerusalem,
    and to the house of **Judah**.
I will place the **key** of the House of **David** on **Eliakim's**
    shoulder;
    when he **opens**, no one shall **shut**,
    when he **shuts**, no one shall **open**.
I will **fix** him like a peg in a **sure** spot,
    to be a place of **honor** for his family."

TO KEEP IN MIND
Practice pronunciation!

READING I   Arrogance and opposition to Isaiah's inspired advice to King Hezekiah, one of Israel's few good kings, has caused Shebna, the "master of the palace," to fall from favor and lose his privileged position to Eliakim. Prophets speak for God; to oppose them is to oppose the divine will, and such impudence is always treated harshly in the Scriptures. Isaiah warned Hezekiah not to join a rebellion against the Assyrians, but Hezekiah refused to listen, expecting support from Egypt that never materialized. So he *bought* his safety by looting gold from the Temple and offering it as tribute.

But king and people earn Isaiah's bitter condemnation when, after this narrow escape, they fail to repent or pray for the dead and choose instead to feast and rejoice. For trusting in political alliances rather than the Lord, the people and Shebna incur the Lord's wrath.

Don't overdramatize the announcement of God's harsh judgment, but don't soften it, either. You are naming the consequences of infidelity and pride. God's anger continues in the subsequent lines. We can almost visualize a court-martial where an officer's stripes and buttons are ripped from his uniform as we hear of Shebna's fate.

The mood softens when God refers to Eliakim becoming "father to the inhabitants of Jerusalem." "The key" that God will place on Eliakim's shoulders is a sign of authority and a clear point of connection with today's Gospel. The reference to "opening" and "shutting" also anticipates Jesus's words to Peter. Give them regal dignity that culminates in the promise that Eliakim will become a source of honor for all his ancestors.

For meditation and context:

This is the eighth consecutive week we read from Romans.

Beginning with an exclamation is not easy. Don't stretch or overdramatize the word, but stress "depth," "riches," "wisdom," and "knowledge" instead.

These are not real questions, but rhetorical devices that acclaim God's wisdom.

Proclaim this familiar formula as if for the first time.

Take a brief pause, and then speak this brief prayer of praise.

RESPONSORIAL PSALM   Psalm 138:1–2, 2–3, 6, 8 (8bc)

R. Lord, your love is eternal; do not forsake the work of your hands.

I will give thanks to you, O LORD, with all
   my heart,
  for you have heard the words of my mouth;
in the presence of the angels I will sing
   your praise;
  I will worship at your holy temple.

I will give thanks to your name,
   because of your kindness and your truth:
when I called, you answered me;
  you built up strength within me.

The LORD is exalted, yet the lowly he sees,
  and the proud he knows from afar.
Your kindness, O LORD, endures forever;
  forsake not the work of your hands.

READING II   Romans 11:33–36

A reading from the Letter of Saint Paul to the Romans

Oh, the **depth** of the **riches** and **wisdom** and **knowledge** of God!
How **inscrutable** are his judgments and how **unsearchable**
   his ways!
  *For who has **known** the mind of the Lord*
   *or who has been his **counselor**?*
  *Or who has given the Lord **anything***
   that he may be repaid?
For **from** him and **through** him and **for** him are all things.
To him be glory **forever**. **Amen**.

READING II The past two weeks we've seen Paul struggling with a bittersweet reality: while his own people have rejected Christ, pagans have embraced him. Paul finds much to mourn and much to celebrate in that reality. As a learned Pharisee well versed in the Law and in the ways of God, Paul is inclined to seek logic and reason for the circumstances he encounters. He has an explanation: the Jews' rejection of Christ has pushed Paul outward toward the Gentiles for whom he now recognizes his special missionary responsibility—bad news for his own people, but good news for Gentiles.

But Paul realizes that he must leave the realm of logic and stop trying to "understand" what God is doing. His only real choice is to marvel at God's wisdom. Privileged as he was with mystical revelations, Paul cannot penetrate the "inscrutable . . . judgments" and "unsearchable . . . ways" of the Lord. Paul borrows phrases from Isaiah and Job (not cited in the text) to express his wonder at humanity's inability to contribute anything to the wisdom and judgment of God.

God is more than anyone can fathom, he acknowledges. This irony of Jewish rejection and pagan acceptance results from God's impenetrable judgments, and who are we to question a God whose "riches" and "wisdom" and "knowledge" are so deep? So Paul rejoices in God's mysterious goodness, and allows his pain over the unbelief of his people to be displaced by gratitude for a God "*from*" and "*through*" and "*for*" whom all things exist. Enjoy the rare opportunity to stress prepositions and then make the final declaration a joyous prayer of praise.

GOSPEL   Matthew 16:13–20

A reading from the holy Gospel according to Matthew

Jesus went into the region of Caesarea **Philippi** and
   he asked his disciples,
  "Who do people say that the Son of **Man** is?"
They replied, "Some say John the **Baptist**, others **Elijah**,
   still others **Jeremiah** or one of the **prophets**."
He said to them, "But who do **you** say that I am?"
Simon **Peter** said in reply,
  "You are the **Christ**, the **Son** of the living **God**."
Jesus said to him in reply,
"**Blessed** are you, Simon son of **Jonah**.
For flesh and **blood** has not revealed this to you, but my
      heavenly **Father**.
And so I **say** to you, you are **Peter**,
  and upon this **rock** I will build my **church**,
  and the gates of the **netherworld** shall not **prevail** against it.
I will give you the **keys** to the kingdom of **heaven**.
Whatever you bind on **earth** shall be bound in **heaven**;
  and whatever you **loose** on earth shall be **loosed** in heaven."
Then he strictly **ordered** his disciples
  to tell **no** one that he was the **Christ**.

Caesarea Philippi = sez-uh-REE-uh fih-LIP-ī

Here, Jesus refers to himself in the third person. Ask the question as a teacher might.

Elijah = ee-Lī-juh

Now, Jesus shifts to the first person and puts the question directly to them.

Make sure to highlight that it is Peter speaking.

The ecclesiological implications of this moment are significant, as will be the reference to binding and loosing.

Jesus builds his Church not on the *faith* but on the *person* of Peter.

For the Apostles these would surely be mysterious words. Note the suggestions for placement of stress.

Pause after Jesus's pronouncement. Then announce his order to keep silent.

TO KEEP IN MIND
Pray the Scriptures: Make reading these Scriptures a part of your prayer life every week, and especially during the week prior to the liturgy in which you will proclaim.

GOSPEL | Whatever Jesus's reason for posing his question to the disciples—is he simply inviting them to focus on him and better recognize who it is who walks among them, or is he sensing in Peter the dawning of a realization that could come only by divine revelation?—the significant moment occurs when Peter makes *his* response. The comments regarding the crowd's speculation are interesting for what they reveal about how Jesus has captured the popular imagination. His presence is so strong and enigmatic that people have been forced to wonder "who is this,

really?" What they see doesn't add up, so they speculate on the "more" they strongly sense in Jesus.

The other Apostles offer only the opinions of the crowd, each trying to trump the others with his report of the latest speculation. But none offers his own opinion. None, that is, till Peter speaks. Jesus immediately lauds him for his insight. But the praise is not for human wisdom born within Peter, but for an open mind and heart that could receive divine wisdom only the Father could impart. Like Paul after him, Peter was privileged with a revelation that

enabled him to recognize Jesus's true and full identity.

Jesus lavishes praise and promises extravagant reward. His tone must assure not only *Peter* that these promises will be fulfilled but also the other disciples who may be wondering if Jesus has chosen the worthiest candidate for the singular honor and unique role he confers on Peter. The closing narration can be spoken in Jesus's voice, as if he were giving the order not to reveal to others what no mere human has revealed to them.

TWENTY-SECOND SUNDAY IN ORDINARY TIME

LECTIONARY #124

READING I   Jeremiah 20:7–9

A reading from the Book of the Prophet Jeremiah

You **duped** me, O Lord, and I **let** myself be duped;
    you were too **strong** for me, and you **triumphed**.
All the day I am an object of **laughter**;
    everyone **mocks** me.

Whenever I **speak**, I must **cry** out,
    violence and **outrage** is my message;
the word of the Lord has brought me
    derision and **reproach** all the day.

I say to myself, I will not **mention** him,
    I will speak in his name no **more**.
But then it becomes like **fire** burning in my heart,
    imprisoned in my bones;
I grow **weary** holding it in, I cannot **endure** it.

Jeremiah = jayr-uh-Mī-uh

This is a familiar, classic text. Focus more on the feeling than the words, mindful that Jeremiah is warring not with God but within himself.

All his complaints are literally true.

He does not want to proclaim such an unpopular and easily derided message.

In vain he resolves to abandon his ministry.

But it wells up within him and he cannot resist!

And yet he does endure and finds the strength to go on.

TO KEEP IN MIND
Always read Scriptures aloud, noting suggestions for stresses and pauses. After several readings, alter the stress markings to suit your style and interpretation.

READING I Anyone too eager to play the prophet is likely no prophet at all. Prophets most often reminded people they were failing in their responsibilities to God and the covenant. If you trouble those who have grown too comfortable, you can count on plenty of trouble yourself. Jeremiah got more than his share.

Serving in the kingdom of Judah starting during the reign of Josiah, a reformer king, Jeremiah was called to chastise the people for frequent lapses into idolatry and faithlessness. For this Jeremiah was attacked, beaten, and put into stocks. His life was threatened several times, he was imprisoned, and even thrown into a cistern. It's no wonder he's sometimes called the "crying prophet."

After the humiliation of being put in stocks Jeremiah openly laments the consequences of his faithful service to God. But Jeremiah is so keen on doing God's will, so attuned to God's designs that, like it or not, he cannot help but remain a mouthpiece for God's unsettling word. Reluctance and compulsion are at war in Jeremiah, causing great tension. He was "duped," he complains, and naive youth that he was when first called, he *let* himself be duped. Now, regretting his gullibility, he rails against a "too strong" God who "triumphed" over him. His efforts have earned him "derision and reproach," so he will stop his mouth to stop the "laughter" that greets his prophecy. While some prophets comfort the disturbed, he only disturbs the comfortable, and he's tired of speaking only "violence and outrage." But as soon as he resolves to speak no more the "word" sears his heart and he wearies with "holding it in." More

For meditation and context:

> **TO KEEP IN MIND**
> **Units of Thought**: Running too many words together blurs meaning and fails to distinguish ideas. Punctuation does not always indicate clearly what words to group together or where to pause. Identify *units of thought* and use your voice to distinguish one from another.

This is the ninth consecutive week we read from Romans.

Let the word "urge" set your tone.

It's ourselves, not our things, that God desires from us.

Juxtapose the words "conform" and "transformed."

Don't elide these words; keep their meanings separate and distinct.

> **TO KEEP IN MIND**
> **Careful preparation** expresses your reverence for the Word.

RESPONSORIAL PSALM Psalm 63:2, 3–4, 5–6, 8–9 (2b)

R. My soul is thirsting for you, O Lord my God.

O God, you are my God whom I seek;
  for you my flesh pines and my soul thirsts
  like the earth, parched, lifeless and
    without water.

Thus have I gazed toward you in the
    sanctuary
  to see your power and your glory,
for your kindness is a greater good than life;
  my lips shall glorify you.

Thus will I bless you while I live;
  lifting up my hands, I will call upon
    your name.
As with the riches of a banquet shall my soul
    be satisfied,
  and with exultant lips my mouth shall
    praise you.

You are my help,
  and in the shadow of your wings I shout
    for joy.
My soul clings fast to you;
  your right hand upholds me.

READING II Romans 12:1–2

A reading from the Letter of Saint Paul to the Romans

I **urge** you, brothers and sisters, by the **mercies** of God,
  to offer your bodies as a **living** sacrifice,
  holy and **pleasing** to God, your spiritual **worship**.
Do not **conform** yourselves to this age
  but be **transformed** by the renewal of your **mind**,
  that you may discern what is the **will** of God,
  what is **good** and **pleasing** and **perfect**.

weary from resisting than from doing, he yields again to God's irresistible call.

READING II This brief passage delivers a powerful message. Note the word "urge" and let it set the tone for your reading. Make your whole life a worthy sacrifice, Paul urges us. We no longer offer as sacrifice to God the bodies of dead animals; instead, we offer our living selves that are "holy and acceptable." And that offering becomes our "spiritual worship."

Many generations think theirs is a godless age and sometimes they're right. But whatever the current condition of the world, Christians must remember they are *in* but not *of* the world. Paul urgently reminds us of this, asking that we "not conform" ourselves to this age. He sustains the hope of constant renewal urging us to "be transformed" so we might use our gift of reason to choose what is "good, and pleasing and perfect" rather than the distractions and poisons offered by "this age." It may help to think of someone you love who has been seduced by those empty distractions and make these words of Paul your prayer for them.

GOSPEL Like the "word" that burns in Jeremiah, Jesus's mission burns within him. To deny it is to deny his very self. Yet Jesus understands the price of fidelity to the divine will. Because the world is dark and sinful, it will come against the light and innocence of Christ. So he knows he must steel himself for what lies ahead and seeks the strength of his close comrades to bolster his courage if it should waver.

Jesus's motivation is a significant part of this narration. He must make his coming Passion convincing and startling to elicit Peter's forceful response.

At least Peter has the sense to take Jesus aside before he begins to bluster.

Jesus seems genuinely concerned about Peter's impact on his resolve.

Jesus is fully back into teaching mode here.

But the teaching is as challenging as his words to Peter.

We can hear regret in his voice over those who will make this deadly choice.

Maintain good eye contact with various parts of the assembly as you ask the questions.

Let the final sentence ring with noble authority.

GOSPEL   Matthew 16:21–27

A reading from the holy Gospel according to Matthew

Jesus began to show his **disciples**
    that he must go to **Jerusalem** and **suffer** greatly
    from the elders, the chief priests, and the scribes,
    and be **killed** and on the **third** day be **raised**.
Then **Peter** took Jesus aside and began to **rebuke** him,
    "God **forbid**, Lord! No such thing shall **ever** happen to you."
He turned and said to Peter,
    "Get **behind** me, Satan! You are an **obstacle** to me.
You are thinking not as **God** does, but as human **beings** do."

Then Jesus said to his **disciples**,
    "Whoever wishes to come **after** me must **deny** himself,
    take up his **cross**, and **follow** me.
For whoever wishes to **save** his life will **lose** it,
    but whoever **loses** his life for **my** sake will **find** it.
What **profit** would there be for one to gain the whole **world**
    and forfeit his **life**?
Or what can one give in **exchange** for his life?
For the Son of **Man** will come with his **angels** in his
        Father's **glory**,
    and then he will **repay** all according to his **conduct**."

TO KEEP IN MIND

Tell the story: The reading of Scripture is a storytelling moment. Storytellers are people of imagination. They help us to see, hear, feel, and smell the elements of the story because they themselves experience these sensory aspects of a story.

But Peter fails to see that. His divinely granted recognition of Jesus as Messiah is not matched by intuition regarding the fate that awaits Jesus. So Peter plays Satan and wins Jesus's sharp rebuke for becoming an "obstacle" to his resolve. It's not hard to feel for Peter. Clearly, Jesus's words shock him. When Peter pronounced Jesus "Messiah" he likely pictured the traditional hero riding into battle, not trudging to his death under the weight of a cross. He wants to erase such images from Jesus's mind, and his own. Apparently, resignation to his fate was no easy task even for Jesus. He doesn't need Peter to dilute his resolve and slaps him with a stinging reprimand. But immediately the criticism turns into a teaching moment as he observes that human and divine thought are worlds apart.

Then Jesus enunciates the demanding nature of discipleship. His standards are uncompromising, and the tone he took with Peter provides a clue about the directness needed to speak these lines. Anything but total surrender to God's Kingdom is futile wheel-spinning. *Lose* your life, if you would find it, he says; deny yourselves, to avoid destroying yourselves. Ask the questions bluntly, then use the last sentences to assure your listeners that their rewards will far exceed any necessary sacrifices.

TWENTY-THIRD SUNDAY IN ORDINARY TIME

LECTIONARY #127

Ezekiel = ee-ZEE-kee-uhl

READING I   Ezekiel 33:7–9

A reading from the Book of the Prophet Ezekiel

The voice of God will be speaking throughout.

God confers on Ezekiel both an honor and a grave responsibility.

You must communicate two things: the seriousness of God's message, and the importance of conveying the message to the people.

Perhaps a slower pace will help communicate God's regret that some will hear but not heed the prophet's warning.

TO KEEP IN MIND

Prophets: In addition to troubling the comfortable, prophets comforted the troubled. With equal passion, the great seers spoke threat and consolation, indictment and forgiveness. You must do the same for the chosen people you call "parish."

Thus says the LORD:
   You, son of man, I have appointed **watchman** for the house
      of **Israel**;
   when you **hear** me say anything, you shall **warn** them for me.
If I tell the wicked, "O **wicked** one, you shall surely **die**,"
   and you do not **speak** out to **dissuade** the wicked from his way,
   the wicked shall **die** for his guilt,
   but I will hold you **responsible** for his death.
But if you **warn** the wicked,
   trying to **turn** him from his way,
   and he **refuses** to turn from his way,
   he shall **die** for his guilt,
   but **you** shall **save** yourself.

READING I This is a serious and sobering message, especially for anyone who exercises the care of souls. It points to the gravity of undertaking ministry in the name of the Lord. Last week we heard Jeremiah bemoan the weightiness of God's service. Likely, he realized that the special understanding imparted to the prophet constitutes a grave burden because at stake are life and death, both for the minister and for those entrusted to his care.

Here, Ezekiel proclaims a message that echoes throughout the Hebrew Scriptures: with election comes responsibility; what applies to a people, applies also to the individual. Ezekiel conveys this message with the image of a "watchman" whose task it was to stand on the hilltop watching for approaching danger and give warning when aggressors approached. In like manner, the prophet must recognize and warn of the dangers that lurk in the hearts and actions of the people of Israel. Because of the exile,

Ezekiel directs his words to individuals rather than the nation as a whole. His role is as important as the military sentinel, God says, because negligence on the part of watchman or prophet could be fatal for all.

Divine warnings must be delivered undiluted, God says, no matter how unpopular they are. Speak what must be spoken and you will live. Those who ignore you are responsible for their own fate; but *fail* to carry out your charge, and the lives of

For meditation and context:

RESPONSORIAL PSALM   Psalm 95:1–2, 6–7, 8–9 (8)

R. If today you hear his voice, harden not your hearts.

Come, let us sing joyfully to the LORD;
  let us acclaim the rock of our salvation.
Let us come into his presence with
    thanksgiving;
  let us joyfully sing psalms to him.

Come, let us bow down in worship;
  let us kneel before the LORD who made us.
For he is our God,
  and we are the people he shepherds,
    the flock he guides.

Oh, that today you would hear his voice:
  "Harden not your hearts as at Meribah,
    as in the day of Massah in the desert,
  where your fathers tempted me;
    they tested me though they had seen
      my works."

TO KEEP IN MIND

Pauses are never "dead" moments. Something is always happening during a pause. Practice will teach you how often and how long to pause. Too many pauses make a reading choppy; too few cause ideas to run into one another.

READING II   Romans 13:8–10

A reading from the Letter of Saint Paul to the Romans

Brothers and sisters:
Owe **nothing** to **anyone**, except to **love** one another;
  for the one who loves another has fulfilled the **law**.
The commandments, "You shall not commit **adultery**;
  you shall not **kill**; you shall not **steal**; you shall not **covet**,"
  and whatever other commandment there may be,
  are summed up in this saying, **namely**,
  "You shall love your **neighbor** as **yourself**."
Love does no **evil** to the neighbor;
  hence, love is the **fulfillment** of the law.

Pause briefly in the middle of this sentence, and then surprise us with the focus on "love."

The list of commandments is a parenthetical construct; list them quickly to get to the point that sums them up: "love your neighbor."

Reflect on this truth in your preparation. Love never seeks to harm the other. When you proclaim, do so from your own deep conviction.

---

those who are lost are on *your* head. As lectors we share the responsibility of making sure God's Word is heard with the clarity and impact God intends.

READING II   As we continue to wend our way through the Letter to the Romans, recognize the immensely pastoral approach Paul adopts in his teaching. His instruction here is practical and clear, direct and unadorned. Though Paul wrote before the Gospel accounts were composed, he is obviously aware of the teaching of Jesus and here summarizes it elegantly by defining the "law" as a command to love one's neighbor, a command derived by both Jesus and Paul from Leviticus 19:18.

If the essence of the Law is love, then the commandments serve primarily as illustrations of *how* to love. And the demands of love are simple: do "no evil to the neighbor." In such economical writing no word is wasted. Establish eye contact before you speak and look from face to face as you announce the "love" that fulfills the "law." The listing of the commandments is parenthetical and *not* the main point; that point is found in the command to "love your neighbor as yourself." The last sentence restates what was said in the first, a clear sign that this is the heart of Paul's message. Abandon any kind of didactic tone here and speak, instead, in a gentle, slow, and earnest manner, again catching the eyes of the assembly as you share this great truth.

GOSPEL   Matthew 18:15–20

A reading from the holy Gospel according to Matthew

Jesus said to his disciples:
 "If your brother **sins** against you,
  go and **tell** him his fault between you and him **alone**.
If he **listens** to you, you have **won** over your brother.
If he does **not** listen,
  take one or two **others** along with you,
  so that 'every **fact** may be established
  on the testimony of two or three **witnesses**.'
If he refuses to **listen** to them, tell the **church**.
If he refuses to listen even to the **church**,
  then treat him as you would a **Gentile** or a **tax** collector.
Amen, I say to you,
  whatever you **bind** on **earth** shall be bound in **heaven**,
  and whatever you **loose** on earth shall be **loosed** in heaven.
Again, amen, I say to you,
  if **two** of you agree on earth
  about anything for which they are to **pray**,
  it shall be **granted** to them by my heavenly Father.
For where **two** or **three** are gathered together in my **name**,
  there am I in the **midst** of them."

Jesus is giving instruction, so assume the tone of a benevolent teacher.

We hear stress in the phrase "If he does not listen," but it lessens as you speak of the strategy of including "witnesses."

This sentence stands alone as a clear, direct, blunt statement.

Regret colors the tone as you describe the fate of the obstinate community member.

Gentile = JEN-tĭl

"Amen" signals a significant teaching. "Amen, amen" doubles the focus on the statement that follows.

The loosing/binding saying is more juridical. This one about prayer has a more pastoral and comforting quality.

TO KEEP IN MIND

Names of characters are often the first word of a reading. Stress names so listeners don't miss who the subject is.

THE 4 STEPS OF *LECTIO DIVINA* OR PRAYERFUL READING

1. *Lectio:* Read a Scripture passage aloud slowly. Notice what phrase captures your attention and be attentive to its meaning. Silent pause.

2. *Meditatio:* Read the passage aloud slowly again, reflecting on the passage, allowing God to speak to you through it. Silent pause.

3. *Oratio:* Read it aloud slowly a third time, allowing it to be your prayer or response to God's gift of insight to you. Silent pause.

4. *Contemplatio:* Read it aloud slowly a fourth time, now resting in God's word.

GOSPEL Just two weeks ago, in an earlier chapter of Matthew (16:13–20), we heard the same injunction regarding binding and loosing. At that time it was addressed only to Peter; now it is extended to the entire community. As the Christian assembly grows, the need for discipline becomes more apparent. So Jesus's mandate no longer applies only to nonbelievers to whom the Gospel is preached and who may or may not have embraced it, but also to those already *within* the community who fail to live the Gospel's precepts.

As in the First Reading, clear directions are given for handling correction among the community of believers, but these words of Jesus evoke a very different mood. Rather than warning of dire consequences, Jesus endorses repeated efforts to win over a recalcitrant sister or brother. The approach is immensely practical as well as inspired: try to work it out, and if that fails, get help. When that, too, is unsuccessful, take it to a higher authority. Each step is intended to resolve the problem with the least amount of effort and disruption to the community.

The tone changes when "even the church" is ignored. Now the believer is categorized with those who are least acceptable within the Jewish community—the "Gentile" and "tax collector." For such cases the power to bind and loose is conferred upon the entire Church community. The importance of the community is restated in the final sentence where, in no uncertain terms, Jesus guarantees God's answer to our prayers. Why is community prayer so efficacious? Because even where only "two or three" are gathered, Christ is fully present.

THE EXALTATION
OF THE HOLY CROSS

LECTIONARY #638

READING I   Numbers 21:4b–9

A reading from the Book of Numbers

With their **patience** worn out by the **journey**,
  the people complained against **God** and **Moses**,
  "**Why** have you brought us up from Egypt to die in this desert,
  where there is no **food** or **water**?
We are **disgusted** with this wretched food!"

In **punishment** the LORD sent among the people saraph **serpents**,
  which **bit** the people so that many of them **died**.
Then the people came to Moses and said,
  "We have **sinned** in complaining against the LORD and you.
Pray the LORD to **take** the serpents from us."
So Moses **prayed** for the people, and the LORD said to Moses,
  "**Make** a saraph and mount it on a **pole**,
  and if any who have been bitten **look** at it, they will **live**."
Moses accordingly made a **bronze** serpent and mounted it
    on a **pole**,
  and whenever anyone who had been bitten by a serpent
  looked at the bronze serpent, he **lived**.

Start slowly so your listeners don't miss the details.

Moses = MOH-ziz; MOH-zis
Their tone is unattractive and whiny.

Their disrespect and lack of gratitude are palpable here. It's a deliberately provocative line.
The Bible often sees cause/effect connections between human behavior and natural phenomena; here God's wrath is understood as causing the snakes' appearance.
Now the pleading is sincere and less whiny.
Two moments here: Moses prays; God responds.
saraph = SAYR-uhf; type of venomous snake

Narrate these lines slowly as a manifestation of God's indulgent mercy.

TO KEEP IN MIND
Always read Scriptures aloud, noting suggestions for stresses and pauses. After several readings, alter the stress markings to suit your style and interpretation.

READING I Often depicted as coiled around a cross-shaped rod, the saraph serpent of Moses is viewed in Christianity as a type of the Cross of Jesus. Clearly, that is the reason this text is chosen for today's First Reading.

The events related in this Scripture portion dramatize one of the frequent moments of vacillation that characterized the Israelites, especially during the desert years. Though delivered from Egyptian slavery through wonderful manifestations of God's power and protection, years of wandering in the desert have wearied the people and eroded their faith. So once again they complain against God and Moses. They wonder aloud why they left the comforts of Egypt for a pipedream of freedom in a foreign land. And they accuse Moses of leading them to their death. They even denigrate the miraculous manna God sent to feed them in the wilderness calling it "*wretched*" food." The Lord acts decisively and punishes the people for their lack of faith and ingratitude by sending a seeming plague of poisonous serpents.

Coming to their senses, the people repent and plead for mercy. God graciously responds and orders Moses to construct the bronze serpent promising that it will be a source of healing. Persons bitten by poisonous snakes need only look upon the bronze serpent and they will live.

For meditation and context:

TO KEEP IN MIND

Openings: First, make eye contact with the assembly and announce, from memory, "A (pronounced "uh," not "ay") reading from . . ." Then pause (three full beats!) before starting the reading.

RESPONSORIAL PSALM   Psalm 78:1bc–2, 34–35, 36–37, 38 (7b)

R. Do not forget the works of the Lord!

Hearken, my people, to my teaching;
  incline your ears to the words
    of my mouth.
I will open my mouth in a parable,
  I will utter mysteries from of old.

While he slew them they sought him
  and inquired after God again,
Remembering that God was their rock
  and the Most High God, their redeemer.

But they flattered him with their mouths
  and lied to him with their tongues,
Though their hearts were not steadfast
    toward him,
  nor were they faithful to his covenant.

Yet he, being merciful, forgave their sin
  and destroyed them not;
Often he turned back his anger
  and let none of his wrath be roused.

Philippians = fih-LIP-ee-uhnz

READING II   Philippians 2:6–11

A reading from the Letter of Saint Paul to the Philippians

Command the attention of your listeners.

Begin slowly, but with solid energy and speak the Lord's name with reverence.

"Rather" signals a shift. As important for our salvation as what he rejected was what Christ humbly embraced.

Christ endured great pain to become one of us. Speak with gratitude.

Another significant shift: tempo quickens. You can get louder or softer, but more intense.

Slowly—stress "heaven," "earth," and "under the earth." The hymn is citing Isaiah 45:23.

Your greatest energy goes to the acclamation of Christ, followed by a slightly lower-key delivery of the final line.

Brothers and sisters:
  Christ **Jesus**, though he was in the form of **God**,
    did not regard **equality** with God something to be **grasped**.
  Rather, he **emptied** himself,
  taking the form of a **slave**,
  coming in **human** likeness;
  and found human in **appearance**,
  he **humbled** himself,
  becoming **obedient** to **death**,
    even death on a **cross**.
Because of this, God greatly **exalted** him
  and bestowed on him the **name**
  which is above **every** name,
  that at the name of **Jesus**
  every knee should **bend**,
  of those in **heaven** and on **earth** and **under** the earth,
  and every tongue **confess** that
  Jesus Christ is **Lord**,
  to the **glory** of God the **Father**.

READING II This text from Philippians is proclaimed every year on Palm Sunday of the Lord's Passion. Its theological significance is great because it traces the trajectory of Christ's eternal existence from before the Incarnation when he enjoyed equality with God; through his Incarnation when he willingly surrendered that status to become human in all things but sin and accepted even Death on a Cross; to his exaltation by God and his establishment as eternal Lord over heaven and earth.

Probably a hymn that predates Paul, the text was appropriated by the Apostle to expound this lofty theology of Christ's pre-existence, his humility and willingness to be subjected to all the consequences of sin that characterize mortal life, and his embrace of the Cross—a phrase likely added by Paul—that led both to our salvation and to Jesus's being highly exalted by God and made eternal Lord.

The first half of the hymn (up to "death on a cross") refers exclusively to Christ, telling us who he is—equal with God, born as a man, humble, obedient. But God is the

subject of the second half and there we learn what God has done for Christ: exalted him and given him the name above every other. Though the hymn first lauds Christ for humbling himself to become human, it is Paul's mention of the Cross that is especially important today.

The text reminds us that the pattern of the life of Christ must also be ours: the path to exaltation runs through the Cross because God's Kingdom is a place of reversals where emptying leads to filling and humility to glorification. The hymn stresses

Name the characters clearly.

Nicodemus = nik-uh-DEE-muhs

Lift your voice and raise your volume as you begin the analogy.

Moses = MOH-ziz; MOH-zis

The tone of this declaration changes from the more didactic beginning. This is an assertion of God's profound and unconditional love of humankind.

Slow down as you conclude and speak with deep gratitude.

TO KEEP IN MIND
Read through all three readings and commentaries for your assigned Sunday. All three were chosen for this day, and each commentary has suggestions that can help you with your own passage.

GOSPEL   John 3:13–17

A reading from the holy Gospel according to John

Jesus said to **Nicodemus**:
"No one has gone up to **heaven**
    except the one who has come **down** from heaven, the Son
        of **Man**.
And just as Moses lifted up the serpent in the **desert**,
    so must the Son of **Man** be lifted up,
    so that everyone who **believes** in him may have eternal **life**."

For God so **loved** the world that he gave his only **Son**,
    so that everyone who **believes** in him might not **perish**
        but might have eternal **life**.
For God did not send his Son into the world to **condemn**
        the world,
    but that the world might be **saved** through him.

Christ's oneness with humanity, but "death on a cross" asserts what makes him unique.

 GOSPEL In this brief exchange with Nicodemus, Jesus has already expounded a profound truth in the enigmatic statement that to enter the Kingdom of God one has to be reborn of water and the Spirit. The dialogue with Nicodemus, a Pharisee and member of the Sanhedrin, serves Jesus's purpose to contrast human obduracy with God's overwhelming generosity. Jesus chastises Nicodemus for his failure to understand

and then makes another enigmatic statement when he alludes to the episode of Moses and the bronze serpent.

Though Nicodemus could not possibly understand the reference to the Son of Man needing to be lifted up in order to become the source of eternal life, he is certainly aware that the serpent "lifted up" in the desert by Moses became a source of divine healing. The great signs of healing that Jesus performed convinced Nicodemus that only one who has God "with him" could do such things. So Nicodemus might well have understood that in the reference

to the saraph serpent Jesus was making a significant and dramatic assertion about himself and his role in God's plan for Israel.

The final part of the exchange between Jesus and the older scholar of the Law focuses on the divine motive for the Incarnation: extravagant love. God did not become human for the purpose of judgment and condemnation—though we can condemn ourselves when we refuse the gift of ultimate love God offers—but God sent his Son for only one reason: "that the world might be saved through him."

TWENTY-FIFTH SUNDAY IN ORDINARY TIME

LECTIONARY #133

READING I   Isaiah 55:6–9

A reading from the Book of the Prophet Isaiah

> **Seek** the LORD while he may be **found**,
>   **call** him while he is **near**.
> Let the scoundrel **forsake** his way,
>   and the wicked his **thoughts**;
> let him turn to the LORD for **mercy**;
>   to our **God**, who is generous in **forgiving**.
> For **my** thoughts are not **your** thoughts,
>   nor are your **ways my** ways, says the LORD.
> As high as the **heavens** are above the **earth**,
>   so high are **my** ways above **your** ways
>   and **my** thoughts above **your** thoughts.

Isaiah = ī-ZAY-uh

Speak the lines not with fear but hope.

Even among believers there are "scoundrels" and "wicked" who need the exhortation to abandon the ways of death.

Recall God's merciful forgiveness to you as you speak these earnest lines.

Be attentive to the words that need to be balanced: "my," "your," "heavens," "earth."

TO KEEP IN MIND

Prophets: In addition to troubling the comfortable, prophets comforted the troubled. With equal passion, the great seers spoke threat and consolation, indictment and forgiveness. You must do the same for the chosen people you call "parish."

READING I   This is the third time that portions of the Isaiah passage read at the Easter Vigil are reprised during this liturgical year. See that commentary for a fuller discussion of this Scripture. The reason for its selection today is its obvious connection to the Gospel parable that graphically illustrates how different God's ways are from our own. The magnanimous landowner of the Gospel parable is Isaiah's God who is "generous in forgiving." And the same God who says, "My thoughts are not your thoughts" also asks, "Am I not free to do as I please with my money?"

Isaiah's message declares that God is not only willing but ever ready to seek out and heal the sinner. One has only to heed God's urgent call. But today, the urgency of the first lines is motivated not by impending doom but by prospects of rich mercy.

"Wake up and be forgiven," the prophet says. "More than you could *hope* for, far more than *you* would give, is the generosity of our God. Repent *now*, *today*, while there is still time."

But beyond God's mercy we hear also a declaration of God's transcendent ways. "For my thoughts . . . " explains God's extravagant behavior. God's goodness overwhelms us because it surpasses all our

For meditation and context:

TO KEEP IN MIND
Slow down: The larger the church, the larger the assembly, and the more complex the text, the slower you must read.

RESPONSORIAL PSALM   Psalm 145:2–3, 8–9, 17–18 (18a)

R. The Lord is near to all who call upon him.

Every day will I bless you,
    and I will praise your name forever
      and ever.
Great is the LORD and highly to be praised;
    his greatness is unsearchable.

The LORD is gracious and merciful,
    slow to anger and of great kindness.
The LORD is good to all
    and compassionate toward all his works.

The LORD is just in all his ways
    and holy in all his works.
The LORD is near to all who call upon him,
    to all who call upon him in truth.

Philippians = fih-LIP-ee-uhnz

The reading is short, so read slowly. The meaning of this first sentence is not readily apparent—another reason to go slowly.

In few words Paul makes huge statements, so don't rush the lines. Give them the gravitas they require.

If he lives, he can continue to do good.

He already knows life with Christ will be better than this life.

But he's willing to postpone eternity for their sake.

He's asking them to make worthwhile his sacrifice to go on living.

READING II   Philippians 1:20c–24, 27a

A reading from the Letter of Saint Paul to the Philippians

Brothers and sisters:
Christ will be **magnified** in my body, whether by **life** or by **death**.
For to me life is **Christ**, and death is **gain**.
If I go on living in the **flesh**,
    that means fruitful **labor** for me.
And I do not know which I shall **choose**.
I am caught between the **two**.
I long to **depart** this life and be with **Christ**,
    for that is far **better**.
Yet that I **remain** in the flesh
    is more necessary for **your** benefit.

Only, conduct yourselves in a way **worthy** of the gospel of **Christ**.

---

expectations. God's ways are not our ways! In making that point, stress the pronouns "your" and "my" that contrast human with divine ways and wisdom. In comparison, God's mercy sails through space while human mercy rides the subway.

READING II   Called "the letter of joy," Philippians presents an imprisoned Paul who, though facing death, rejoices equally over the possibilities of living or dying, and relishes the opportunities

each provides. The great truth for Paul is that Christ will be glorified both in Paul's dying and his living; therefore, life holds little more attraction for him than death.

    Paul's declaration that "life is Christ" reveals the depth of his faith and his privileged insight into spiritual truth. How do you deliver his assertion convincingly, neither undermining nor overplaying his sincerity? How do you make "death is *gain*"

sound genuine? The best way is to mean it yourself and to speak from a conviction that eternity with Christ is something we all ought strongly to desire.

    Paul is torn, for while he prefers to "depart" this life and be with Christ, he also desires to go on living for the sake of those he has brought to Christ. He would honestly welcome either option. But in the end, his love for his spiritual children tips the scales in favor of living for their sakes, which for Paul is both joy and *sacrifice*.

GOSPEL   Matthew 20:1–16a

A reading from the holy Gospel according to Matthew

Jesus told his disciples this **parable**:
   "The kingdom of **heaven** is like a **landowner**
   who went out at dawn to hire **laborers** for his vineyard.
After **agreeing** with them for the usual **daily** wage,
   he sent them into his **vineyard**.
Going out about **nine** o'clock,
   the landowner saw others standing **idle** in the marketplace,
   and he said to them, 'You **too** go into my vineyard,
   and I will give you what is **just**.'
So they **went** off.
And he went out again around **noon**,
   and around **three** o'clock, and did **likewise**.
Going out about **five** o'clock,
   the landowner found **others** standing around, and said to them,
   'Why do you stand here **idle** all day?'
They answered, 'Because no one has **hired** us.'
He said to them, 'You **too** go into my vineyard.'
When it was **evening** the owner of the vineyard said
      to his foreman,
   '**Summon** the laborers and give them their **pay**,
   beginning with the **last** and ending with the **first**.'
When those who had started about **five** o'clock came,
   each received the usual **daily** wage.
So when the **first** came, they thought that they would
      receive **more**,
   but each of them **also** got the usual wage.

The parable as a whole, not its individual parts, teaches about God's Kingdom.

Stress the fact that owner and laborers have reached a mutual "agreement."

His tone is benevolent as he tells them to "go into my vineyard." Use the time references to suggest the passage of time and his sustained concern for the laborers.

The owner's return visits to the marketplace suggest his concern for the workers who had not yet found employment.

There is no judgment in his inquiry, "Why do you stand here idle?"

There is poignancy in their simple reply that no one has hired them.

Hold briefly after ordering the foreman to "give them their pay," and slowly finish with the instruction to begin "with the last . . . ."

As the laborers come for their pay, communicate each one's attitude as he approaches the foreman: the last hired are surprised; the first, anticipating a higher wage, quickly move from disappointment to manifest anger.

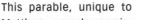

GOSPEL   This parable, unique to Matthew, sounds surprisingly contemporary in its description of the plight of day laborers in the ancient world. It is a story about the nature of the Kingdom of God in which the main character is an enigmatic "owner" whose behavior, at least in the eyes of his workers, is eccentric at best.

Reading I told us that God's ways and ours are not alike. The owner's behavior here could not be less like the expected behavior of even the fairest contemporary employer. Our expectations are a fair day's pay for a fair day's work. Parity is the guide. Often, especially in sports, a salary suddenly seems inadequate or unfair because another player's salary has set a new benchmark for compensation.

But Jesus is not offering guidelines for labor arbitration. He is making a point about the abundance of the Kingdom. "Fair" has a wholly different meaning here, determined not by our small and petty notions but by God's inscrutable wisdom. Largesse is the standard of the Kingdom. Everyone can get a full day's pay because payment is not earned but awarded in the Kingdom, and God can be as generous as he wants.

The owner is composed as he makes his response. He's resolute, but not alienating; he wants to teach more than scold.

Without an accusatory tone, the owner asserts freedom to use his money as he pleases. He is encouraging them to avoid envy, not accusing them of that sin.

Jesus delights over God's impartial mercy.

TO KEEP IN MIND
Importance of the Narrator:
The narrator is often the pivotal role of a passage. Timbre, pitch, rate, and energy can make the same words convey very different moods or meaning. Sometimes the narrator is objective, but often the narrator has great interest in the events and characters of a story.

And on receiving it they **grumbled** against the landowner, saying,
　'These last ones worked only one **hour**,
　and you have made them **equal** to us,
　who bore the day's **burden** and the **heat**.'
He said to one of them in reply,
　'My **friend**, I am not **cheating** you.
Did you not **agree** with me for the usual daily wage?
Take what is yours and **go**.
What if I wish to give this **last** one the same as **you**?
Or am I not free to do as I **wish** with my own money?
Are you **envious** because I am **generous**?'
Thus, the **last** will be **first**, and the **first** will be **last**."

　　While living in the world, in the "not yet" of the Kingdom, adopting Kingdom values will make us "first" in the eyes of God but may put us "last" in human rankings. Success and reward cannot be the motivation for serving Christ. In the reordered value system of the Kingdom, the "first" who serve Christ shall be "last" in the eyes of the world. But in the end, the first who became last will be the last who become first. For it will be God who distributes rewards and God is sovereign Lord, lavishing gifts on whomever he wills.

TWENTY-SIXTH SUNDAY IN ORDINARY TIME

LECTIONARY #136

READING I   Ezekiel 18:25–28

Ezekiel = ee-ZEE-kee-uhl

First it is the prophet and then the Lord who speaks.

Quote the people's complaint in a dismissive tone.

God is given a very human attitude. Use it.

This is well laid-out reasoning delivered like a fine teacher.

Convey God's enthusiasm for just such conversion from sin.

With these two very similar expressions, the second receives the greater stress.

For meditation and context:

A reading from the Book of the Prophet Ezekiel

Thus says the LORD:
You say, "The LORD's way is not **fair**!"
Hear now, house of Israel:
    Is it **my** way that is unfair, or rather, are not **your** ways unfair?
When someone virtuous turns **away** from virtue to commit
        iniquity, and **dies**,
    it is because of the **iniquity** he committed that he must die.
But if he **turns** from the wickedness he has committed,
    and does what is right and **just**,
    he shall **preserve** his life;
    since he has turned **away** from all the sins that he
        has committed,
    he shall surely **live**, he shall **not** die.

RESPONSORIAL PSALM   Psalm 25:4–5, 6–7, 8–9 (6a)

R. Remember your mercies, O Lord.

Your ways, O LORD, make known to me;
    teach me your paths,
guide me in your truth and teach me,
    for you are God my savior.

Remember that your compassion, O LORD,
    and your love are from of old.
The sins of my youth and my frailties
        remember not;
    in your kindness remember me,
because of your goodness, O LORD.

Good and upright is the LORD;
    thus he shows sinners the way.
He guides the humble to justice,
    and teaches the humble his way.

TO KEEP IN MIND

Read through all three readings and commentaries for your assigned Sunday. All three were chosen for this day, and each commentary has suggestions that can help you with your own passage.

READING I "Parents eat sour grapes, but the children's teeth are set on edge." So went a contemporaneous proverb, cited earlier in this chapter of Ezekiel (18:2), which makes children accountable for the sins of their parents. In this ancient culture, individual identity developed very slowly, subsumed for centuries within the identity of the community. But Ezekiel champions the notion of individual responsibility. The trauma of the exile contributed to the emergence of a maturing sense of personal accountability.

Speaking for the Lord, Ezekiel calls on the Israelites to take responsibility for their own decisions and realize they have the power to turn from bad to good and from good to bad, as we will see in today's Gospel.

In response to a childlike whine that God's ways are "not fair!" God asks for an honest assessment of just whose ways are not fair, God's or the people's? God explains how divine judgment is meted out: each one is judged on his or her own behavior. But God is not reversing the notion of corporate responsibility, only providing a corrective that brings understanding into proper balance. As with so much in the matters of faith, this is a both/and not an either/or situation. Both truths are held in tension.

And it's a lesson we all must learn at some time or other. Present hope to the "wicked" that by turning from their wickedness they can "preserve [their] life." The last line states twice that conversion leads to life because God, like a loving parent, frustrated or not, always goes the extra mile when it comes to forgiving any wrong.

Philippians = fih-LIP-ee-uhnz

Employ a consistent pattern of stress on the "any" clauses, peaking your energy on "complete my joy."

His tone grows more urgent.

Let your tone suggest the *joy* one can find in this radical humility.

The exalted hymn that follows demonstrates the selflessness Paul called for above.

Your energy is high as you speak of "Christ Jesus, who . . . was in the form of God," then gradually fades to a softer "death on a cross."

A cymbal clash begins the last section: "God greatly exalted him . . . ." Sustain the intensity through the final proclamation of Christ's lordship.

READING II   Philippians 2:1–11

A reading from the Letter of Saint Paul to the Philippians

Brothers and sisters:
If there is any encouragement in **Christ**,
    any solace in **love**,
    any participation in the **Spirit**,
    any **compassion** and **mercy**,
    complete my joy by being of the **same** mind, with the
        same **love**,
    united in heart, thinking **one** thing.
Do nothing out of **selfishness** or out of **vainglory**;
    rather, humbly regard others as more **important**
        than yourselves,
    each looking out not for his **own** interests,
    but also for those of **others**.

Have in you the same **attitude**
    that is also in Christ **Jesus**,
        who, though he was in the form of **God**,
            did not regard **equality** with God
            something to be **grasped**.
        Rather, he **emptied** himself,
            taking the form of a **slave**,
            coming in **human** likeness;
            and found human in **appearance**,
            he **humbled** himself,
            becoming **obedient** to the point of **death**,
            even death on a **cross**.
    Because of this, God greatly **exalted** him
        and bestowed on him the **name**
        which is above **every** name,
        that at the name of **Jesus**
        every knee should **bend**,

READING II This text was also proclaimed last week. See that commentary for additional reflection on this passage.

So important to Paul is oneness among the believers that he spares no effort in pleading the cause of unified love. His energy builds from the first line as he lists all those things in whose name he compels their response; then he asks unabashedly, "*complete* my joy" by being "of the *same* mind." Only someone who cares deeply can scold, nag, prod, love, and teach all at once. "Do nothing out of . . . " echoes with

the urgency of a dying parent or a departing leader who wants to ensure that structures and relationships will remain intact. Paul also calls for heroic selflessness, urging that they think of others as superior to themselves. Sounding neither condescending nor overly pious, share this advice as a God-given formula for sanctity.

Next begins a glorious hymn proclaimed every Palm Sunday. This mystical, musical passage revels in the paradox of Christ's grandeur and his remarkable humility. Having laid the foundation with his call to humility, Paul now offers its ultimate

paradigm: Jesus. In effect, Paul says, "If thinking of others as superior seems like asking a lot, just look at Christ! He was God, yet became human like us and even endured the most humiliating of deaths— all for love of us!" By offering Jesus as a model, Paul implies that what happened to him can happen to us: he humbled himself, but was exalted by God; he embraced the lonely Cross but now receives praise from "heaven," "earth," and all things "under." In our lives, too, humility can lead to glory.

of those in **heaven** and on **earth** and **under** the earth,
and every tongue **confess** that
Jesus Christ is **Lord**,
to the **glory** of God the **Father**.

[Shorter: Philippians 2:1–5]

GOSPEL   Matthew 21:28–32

A reading from the holy Gospel according to Matthew

Jesus said to the chief **priests** and **elders** of the people:
    "What is your **opinion**?
A man had two **sons**.
He came to the **first** and said,
    'Son, go out and work in the **vineyard** today.'
He said in reply, 'I will **not**,'
    but **afterwards** changed his **mind** and **went**.
The man came to the **other** son and gave the **same** order.
He said in reply, '**Yes**, sir,' but did not **go**.
Which of the two did his father's **will**?"
They answered, "The **first**."
Jesus said to them, "**Amen**, I say to you,
    tax collectors and **prostitutes**
    are entering the kingdom of God before **you**.
When **John** came to you in the way of **righteousness**,
    you did not **believe** him;
    but tax collectors and prostitutes **did**.
Yet even when you saw **that**,
    you did not later **change** your minds and **believe** him."

Don't let the last line sound like an after-thought, but make it part of the prayer that extols Christ's glory.

Your opening tone can signal that there is already an adversarial exchange in progress.

Keep the mood of the parable lively and colloquial.

Don't get overly serious about the change of heart.

Don't give away that this constitutes a "gotcha" question.

Their response is flippant. They haven't made any connections.

Jesus bares his anger here; no need to try to soften it.

Here is his sharpest criticism and therefore his warning of judgment.

> **TO KEEP IN MIND**
> **Careful preparation** expresses your reverence for the Word.

GOSPEL   Jesus draws an ever clearer line in the sand between himself and the Pharisees as his tolerance of hypocrisy and spiritual barrenness grows thin. This passage follows the cleansing of the Temple and the cursing of the fig tree—an enacted parable that speaks of judgment coming upon those who feign goodness but fail to bear the fruit of righteousness.

In addition, the elders have questioned his authority to teach and refused to answer his questions regarding John's baptism. So he makes them the target of his pointed parable. Since you won't offer an opinion about John, says Jesus, consider *this* case. The leaders saw his question about John as a trap and spinelessly backed away. But this question seems safe, so they take the bait.

Jesus points to the primacy of deeds over words. The greatest crime of the leaders is not their hypocrisy but their failure to teach, their unwillingness to understand that physicians heal the sick, not those who are well. Instead, they turn their backs on the sick, even after seeing John call the most reviled to genuine conversion. This intentional blindness is what Jesus repudiates here.

With the question "Which of the two . . . ?" he pushes the leaders to the wall, but gets a defensive response. They won't add two and two and see that many sinners have already done exactly as the son in Jesus's parable. Using similar language about the son who *"changed his mind* and went" while "you [the leaders] *did not later change your minds* and believe," the text contrasts the second son's change of heart with the priests' failure to respond to the conversion of tax collectors and prostitutes.

TWENTY-SEVENTH SUNDAY IN ORDINARY TIME

LECTIONARY #139

Isaiah = ī-ZAY-uh

Even in this introduction we hear tones of joy and hope.

These lines speak of joyous industriousness and loving care of the vineyard.

Pause after "wine press" to suggest the passage of time.

Joyful expectancy turns to bitter disappointment.
After a pause, begin with a clear shift to a more severe tone.

While the vineyard owner is defending himself, he is not defensive. The argument is reasoned and calm.

Here, reason gives way to disappointment and anger.

READING I   Isaiah 5:1–7

A reading from the Book of the Prophet Isaiah

Let me now sing of my **friend**,
    my friend's **song** concerning his **vineyard**.
My friend had a vineyard
    on a fertile **hillside**;
he **spaded** it, cleared it of **stones**,
    and planted the **choicest** vines;
within it he built a **watchtower**,
    and hewed out a **wine** press.
Then he looked for the crop of **grapes**,
    but what it yielded was **wild** grapes.

Now, inhabitants of **Jerusalem** and people of **Judah**,
    judge between me and my vineyard:
What **more** was there to do for my vineyard
    that I had not **done**?
Why, when I looked for the crop of grapes,
    did it bring forth **wild** grapes?
Now, I will let you know
    what I mean to **do** with my vineyard:
take away its **hedge**, give it to **grazing**,
    break through its **wall**, let it be **trampled**!

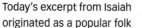 Today's excerpt from Isaiah originated as a popular folk ballad that Isaiah may have sung himself at local harvest festivals and which he turns into a prophetic allegory about the people's infidelity and God's condemnation. We don't learn of Isaiah's allegorical intent until the final stanza where the vineyard is identified as "the house of Israel" and the vine-dresser, by implication, as the Lord.

In this last verse where "the people of Judah" are called God's "cherished plant," we also find a clue to the proclamation of this text. Without that phrase, we might think God had entirely given up on Israel and left her to tend for herself. But that phrase reminds us that God never really abandons his people. If he allows judgment, it is only as a way of breaking open and tilling the soil so it can receive anew the seed of God's love.

Throughout the text we're reminded that the owner of the vineyard has done all he could to ensure a good harvest. But the vineyard produced bitter grapes nonetheless. Eventually, even the hardworking, vigilant owner gives up and allows the vineyard to be overrun with weeds. Thus, there are two themes playing throughout—attentive care and concern, and exasperation and anger.

The first verse begins with an upbeat and pleasant tone. Describe the "fertile hillside" and the busy work of spading, clearing, and planting with the enthusiasm of a new landowner preparing his first crop. Pride and love build the "watchtower" and "wine press." After spring rains and summer sun have done their work the landowner "looked for the crop of grapes."

The exasperation continues to grow.

By now, we sense it must be the Lord who is speaking.

Make clear, direct eye contact and speak these lines slowly and deliberately.

Yes, I will make it a **ruin**:
   it shall not be **pruned** or **hoed**,
   but overgrown with **thorns** and **briers**;
I will command the clouds
   not to send **rain** upon it.
The vineyard of the Lord of hosts is the house of **Israel**,
   and the people of **Judah** are his cherished **plant**;
he looked for **judgment**, but see, **bloodshed**!
   for **justice**, but hark, the **outcry**!

For meditation and context:

RESPONSORIAL PSALM   Psalm 80:9, 12, 13–14, 15–16, 19–20 (Isaiah 5:7a)

R. The vineyard of the Lord is the house of Israel.

A vine from Egypt you transplanted;
   you drove away the nations and planted it.
It put forth its foliage to the Sea,
   its shoots as far as the River.

Why have you broken down its walls,
   so that every passer-by plucks its fruit,
the boar from the forest lays it waste,
   and the beasts of the field feed upon it?

Once again, O Lord of hosts,
   look down from heaven, and see;
take care of this vine,
   and protect what your right hand
      has planted,
   the son of man whom you yourself
      made strong.

Then we will no more withdraw from you;
   give us new life, and we will call upon
      your name.
O Lord, God of hosts, restore us;
   if your face shine upon us, then we shall
      be saved.

TO KEEP IN MIND

Eye contact is your means of connecting with those to whom you minister. You should look at the assembly during the middle and at the end of every thought or sentence.

A substantial pause here allows you to register the shock and disappointment of finding only "*wild* grapes."

The owner responds with anger, like an employer dealing with a subordinate who has disappointed time and again despite much effort and training. "Now" signals the consequences. Anger and judgment build in the next sentence where the owner's identity is suggested. Only divine power can "command the clouds," so the tone becomes authoritative and powerful. But the final lines convey the pained disappointment of a God whose love is scorned and unrequited.

READING II   Just as we turn to busy people when we need something done, it would seem we should turn to those in greatest need when we need our faith bolstered. Paul proves that irony by telling the Philippians to "have no anxiety" while he himself faces the possibility of imminent death. His deep faith, fostered over many years and through many trials, has convinced him that God is an ally we can trust in all situations, someone we approach not desperately but "with thanksgiving." That within his jail cell he could well up with peace and gratefulness proves to Paul that a power that "surpasses all understanding" stood guard over his heart and mind.

Perhaps at a time when you faced incredible odds or an impossible situation, you found yourself buoyed up by a strength and serenity you didn't know you had. Remember that graced moment as you read and let it color how you communicate Paul's experience of grace.

READING II Philippians 4:6–9

Philippians = fih-LIP-ee-uhnz

A reading from the Letter of Saint Paul to the Philippians

This line obviously requires direct eye contact and sincere delivery.

Speak with conviction born of your own experience of God's love.

Brothers and sisters:
Have no **anxiety** at all, but in **everything**,
  by **prayer** and **petition**, with **thanksgiving**,
  make your requests **known** to God.
Then the **peace** of God that surpasses all understanding
  will guard your **hearts** and **minds** in Christ **Jesus**.

Don't let the word "finally" cause you to rush. You can use the same intonation on each item as you move through the list. Each is different and requires its own emphasis.

Finally, brothers and sisters,
  whatever is **true**, whatever is **honorable**,
  whatever is **just**, whatever is **pure**,
  whatever is **lovely**, whatever is **gracious**,
  if there is any **excellence**
  and if there is anything worthy of **praise**,
  think about **these** things.

Keeping all the items you've just enumerated in mind, speak this command to stay focused on the good.

Take a long pause before announcing, "The word of the Lord."

Keep on **doing** what you have learned and received
  and heard and seen in me.
Then the God of **peace** will be with you.

GOSPEL Matthew 21:33–43

This section of Matthew consists of several polemical confrontations with the Jewish elders. Your introductory tone can establish that context.

Suggest the same enthused activity we saw in the First Reading as the property owner plants and digs and builds. Confident in his "tenants," he embarks on his journey.

"When vintage time . . . " should suggest the passage of much time since grape vines don't yield for several years.

A reading from the holy Gospel according to Matthew

Jesus said to the chief **priests** and the **elders** of the people:
  "Hear another **parable**.
There was a landowner who planted a **vineyard**,
  put a **hedge** around it, dug a **wine** press in it, and built
    a **tower**.
Then he leased it to **tenants** and went on a **journey**.
When **vintage** time drew near,
  he sent his **servants** to the tenants to obtain his **produce**.

Paul expects the Parousia—Christ's return in glory—at any time; and if Jesus doesn't come soon, surely his own death *will*. The twin convictions inspire his instructions to be wholly focused on what is "true," " honorable," " just," "pure," "lovely," and "gracious." If ever we needed support for telling children, spouses, friends, or ourselves that spending time with mindless pursuits that don't uplift the spirit is not worthy of us, here we have it. In good times or bad, as we endure trouble or await success, our minds and hearts should focus only on those things that beat in rhythm with the heart of God.

Paul urges his readers to follow his example if they want peace. And that's as true for us as for the Philippians. Especially regarding the end, we know neither when Christ will return nor when our individual lives will end. So remind us through this reading that we must never let down our guard nor turn away from the life we "have [already] learned and received." Paul dares to hold himself up as an example. Now you must dare to speak with his strength and loving assurance.

GOSPEL | Jesus's story opens like Isaiah's song: upbeat and without hint of the gloom to follow. The level of allegory in the parable is debated, but no one questions the clear correlation between the details of the story and the situation it points to. Throughout Israel's history, God sent messengers whose ministry was most often resisted and rejected. In Mark's telling, these prophets came to claim "*some* of the produce" expected of the tenants. Matthew forgoes the qualifier, and its absence indicates that God's claim

Your tone shifts to characterize the violent ambush that surprised the "servants."

"Again he sent" conveys the attitude of the property owner who expects a better reception but is sorely disappointed that they were treated "the same way."

Finally, willing to try once more, he dispatches his son with a tone that says, "If they know what's good for them, 'They will respect my son.'"

The conspiratorial tenants whisper words like daggers. "Seized," "threw," and "killed" are separate actions that build in intensity and violence.

Pause before asking the question of the elders.

Their reply might be showy, as if demonstrating their righteousness for the listening crowds.

Jesus's rejoinder reveals his frustration; we can imagine his head shaking as he says "Did you never read . . . ?"

This is a severe punishment that can apply to us as readily as to our ancestors in faith.

But the tenants **seized** the servants and one they **beat**,
  another they **killed**, and a third they **stoned**.
Again he sent **other** servants, more **numerous** than the first ones,
  but they treated them in the **same** way.
Finally, he sent his **son** to them, thinking,
  'They will **respect** my son.'
But when the tenants **saw** the son, they said to one another,
  'This is the **heir**.
Come, let us **kill** him and acquire his **inheritance**.'
They **seized** him, threw him out of the **vineyard**, and **killed** him.
What will the **owner** of the vineyard do to those tenants when
    he **comes**?"
They answered him,
  "He will put those wretched men to a wretched **death**
  and lease his vineyard to **other** tenants
  who will **give** him the produce at the proper **times**."
Jesus said to them, "Did you never read in the Scriptures:
  The **stone** *that the builders* **rejected**
    has become the **cornerstone***;*
  by the **Lord** *has this been done,*
    and it is **wonderful** *in our eyes?*
Therefore, I say to you,
  the kingdom of God will be taken **away** from you
  and given to a people that will **produce** its fruit."

TO KEEP IN MIND
Who really proclaims: "When the Sacred Scriptures are read in the Church, God himself speaks to his people, and Christ, present in his word, proclaims the gospel" (#29 GIRM).

---

on the "produce," that is, the good works of the people, was absolute.

In addition to messengers, the landowner also sends his son in the apparently naïve belief that surely he would win the respect of the tenants. Instead, the evil tenants conspire to kill him to acquire his inheritance. Matthew's reversal of Mark's wording has the "son" *first* thrown out of the vineyard and *then* killed. This was probably an effort on Matthew's part to suggest Jesus being taken out of Jerusalem for his execution.

Rather than answering his own question as he does in Mark, here Jesus puts the question of what ought to be the fate of the villainous tenants directly to the chief priests and elders. They respond insightfully that the tenants should be put to death and their land turned over to more worthy tenants who will give the landowner his proper due at the "proper times." But by recognizing the seriousness of the tenants' treachery and understanding the proper judgment for such behavior, the religious leaders, in effect, pronounce judgment on themselves. After quoting Psalm 118:22,

which anticipates Jesus's ultimate victory at the hands of God, Jesus announces a dire fate for the blind leaders who have impeded the work of God's Kingdom rather than furthering its growth: "the kingdom . . . will be taken away from you and given to a people that will produce its fruit." That revelation need not be delivered with anger, but it is the solemn judgment of one whose love has been rebuffed and who must now seek another with whom to share it.

TWENTY-EIGHTH SUNDAY IN ORDINARY TIME

LECTIONARY #142

READING I   Isaiah 25:6–10a

Isaiah = ī-ZAY-uh

A reading from the Book of the Prophet Isaiah

On this **mountain** the LORD of hosts
    will provide for all **peoples**
a feast of rich **food** and choice **wines**,
    juicy, **rich** food and **pure**, choice wines.
On this mountain he will destroy
    the **veil** that veils all peoples,
the **web** that is woven over all nations;
    he will destroy **death** forever.
The Lord GOD will wipe away
    the **tears** from every face;
the reproach of his people he will **remove**
    from the whole earth; for the LORD has **spoken**.
    On that **day** it will be said:
"Behold our **God**, to whom we looked to **save** us!
    This is the LORD for whom we looked;
    let us rejoice and be **glad** that he has saved us!"
For the hand of the LORD will **rest** on this mountain.

This opening phrase will be repeated below. Stress it each time.

The specifics are less important than the joyous energy created by this imagery. Your pacing can be brisk since it's the tone that matters most.

These are images of liberation and hope.

The destruction of death climaxes the passage.

Build in intensity, beginning softly and rising as you go.

Speak with authority, for you speak for the Lord.

Make eye contact to ensure your assembly knows this applies equally to them.

Try a slower reading of this final line.

TO KEEP IN MIND
Careful preparation expresses your reverence for the Word.

READING I   The connection with today's Gospel might escape you until you realize that, like the king in the parable, the "Lord of hosts" is preparing a rich feast to which "all peoples" are invited. The image of the great banquet as the ultimate symbol of salvation, of the time when God's rule will be fully established, has a long history that predates even Isaiah. Isaiah speaks of a future time when all the darkness and sorrow that claim us will be banished, when death will be destroyed and all tears wiped away.

Isaiah does more than write poetry. He feeds the religious imagination of his people and paints the picture of a time that is not yet, but *will* be. Such writing is important because words create reality. Imagination "sees" what is not yet, and then goes out and makes it happen. By drawing these powerful images Isaiah is changing reality—he dreams a dream and the act of dreaming helps it come true.

Let the rich imagery draw you in. Imagine the banquet hall where a sumptuous repast is readied; see the "veil" that separates us from knowledge of God being lifted and the spider's "web" that imprisons us in our ignorance and isolation being brushed away. You describe a moment of supreme triumph when you announce "he will destroy death *forever*!" Rejoice that tears will be wiped away and guilt and shame erased, "for the Lord has spoken" a new world into existence.

For meditation and context:

Philippians = fih-LIP-ee-uhnz

The reading begins on a down stroke ("humble circumstances") and immediately bounces up ("with abundance").

A sustained hopeful tone will reinforce his point of coping equally with "every circumstance."

This sentence states what he has learned. Give it emphasis.

His gratitude is sincere.

Paul has learned to go to the table of God's bounty before approaching any human table, so he can speak confidently of God's goodness.

Remember, this is a prayer.

RESPONSORIAL PSALM   Psalm 23:1–3a, 3b–4, 5, 6 (6cd)

R. I shall live in the house of the Lord all the days of my life.

The LORD is my shepherd; I shall not want.
  In verdant pastures he gives me repose;
beside restful waters he leads me;
  he refreshes my soul.

He guides me in right paths
  for his name's sake.
Even though I walk in the dark valley
  I fear no evil; for you are at my side
with your rod and your staff
  that give me courage.

You spread the table before me
  in the sight of my foes;
you anoint my head with oil;
  my cup overflows.

Only goodness and kindness follow me
  all the days of my life;
and I shall dwell in the house of the LORD
  for years to come.

READING II   Philippians 4:12–14, 19–20

A reading from the Letter of Saint Paul to the Philippians

Brothers and sisters:
I know how to live in **humble** circumstances;
  I know also how to live with **abundance**.
In **every** circumstance and in all **things**
  I have learned the **secret** of being well fed and of going hungry,
  of living in **abundance** and of being in **need**.
I can **do** all things in him who **strengthens** me.
Still, it was kind of you to **share** in my distress.

My God will fully supply whatever you **need**,
  in accord with his glorious **riches** in Christ **Jesus**.
To our **God** and **Father**, glory **forever** and **ever**. **Amen**.

Joy crescendos in the closing lines that announce the coming of "our God." The prophet sees what we cannot and announces with certainty—despite appearances to the contrary—that God moves inexorably toward us dispensing salvation.

 Paul has learned a secret from living in scarcity and in abundance. All things are doable and all is tolerable, he says, because of Christ who

provides the strength to embrace abundance without pride and endure want without resentment. At the time of this writing, Paul languishes in prison facing death. Yet his spirit is undaunted and he proves the sincerity of his words by being able to express gratitude, speaking words of encouragement, and ending in prayer. Paul was not a victim of circumstances. His secret is that in Christ he found a way to hover above life's circumstances so that when abundance gives way to need and

comfort yields to bare necessity, the faith path he walks remains stable and unshaken.

We almost sense regret that the Philippians have been so generous in sending money not just once but multiple times. Paul has learned to rely solely on God; in this instance at least, the Philippians' generosity has made that unnecessary. Nonetheless, he thanks them sincerely for wanting to relieve his "distress."

GOSPEL   Matthew 22:1–14

A reading from the holy Gospel according to Matthew

Jesus again in reply spoke to the chief priests and **elders**
   of the people
  in **parables**, saying,
  "The kingdom of **heaven** may be likened to a **king**
  who gave a **wedding** feast for his son.
He dispatched his servants
   to **summon** the invited guests to the feast,
  but they **refused** to come.
A **second** time he sent **other** servants, saying,
  'Tell those invited: "**Behold**, I have **prepared** my banquet,
  my calves and fattened cattle are **killed**,
  and everything is **ready**; **come** to the feast."'
Some **ignored** the invitation and went **away**,
  one to his **farm**, another to his **business**.
The rest laid **hold** of his servants,
  mistreated them, and **killed** them.
The king was **enraged** and sent his **troops**,
  destroyed those murderers, and burned their **city**.
Then he said to his servants, 'The feast is **ready**,
  but those who were invited were not **worthy** to come.
Go out, therefore, into the main **roads**
  and invite to the feast whomever you **find**.'

Remember, this is a story with some exaggerated details whose color and texture help the story do its work.
Pharisees = FAYR-uh-seez

The tone is upbeat and joyful.

The king is trying harder, but there is no hint of the anger that will follow.

Convey the dismissive and abusive attitude of the ungrateful guests.

The response is swift and unambiguous.

The king's voice should show regret, yet a determination to fill the banquet hall and not let the bounty go to waste.

TO KEEP IN MIND

Tell the story: The reading of Scripture is a storytelling moment. Storytellers are people of imagination. They help us to see, hear, feel, and smell the elements of the story because they themselves experience these sensory aspects of a story.

Paul ends with assurance that God will repay what he himself cannot, and God will meet their needs as they met his. Because he knows what God has given us in Christ, he can assert with confidence that God will give them everything they need. The final words of the text are a prayer. Let your sincere "Amen" follow a pause in which you thank God for the magnificent riches *you* have received.

GOSPEL   Like the First Reading, the beginning of the Gospel stresses the lavish preparations that were made and the invitations that were sent for a great banquet. We hear fanfare in the dispatching of servants and the call to "come to the feast." But the details stretch credulity. The hostility and violence of the invitees can only be understood as an allegory that reflects the situation faced by the Church of Matthew's day. He's making

sense of the destruction of Jerusalem and sees it as the consequence of Israel's rejection of Jesus and their hostility and violence toward the Christian community.

Underplay the first refusal of the invited guests, for the king invites again, his tone festive and excited. The king in no way anticipates a negative response, but the reactions of the invited guests should communicate their utter disregard for the king's preparations and generosity.

The servants went out into the **streets**
  and gathered **all** they found, bad and good **alike**,
  and the hall was **filled** with guests.
But when the king came in to **meet** the guests,
  he saw a man there not dressed in a **wedding** garment.
The king said to him, 'My friend, how is it
  that you came in here without a wedding garment?'
But he was reduced to **silence**.
Then the king said to his attendants, '**Bind** his hands and feet,
  and cast him into the **darkness outside**,
  where there will be **wailing** and grinding of **teeth**.'
Many are **invited**, but few are **chosen**."

[Shorter: Matthew 22:1–10]

There's an undertone of trouble in the narration.

He has nothing to say because, apparently, he made no effort to prepare.

The demands of the Kingdom are uncompromising.

Make good eye contact for this warning is meant for us as well.

THE 4 STEPS OF *LECTIO DIVINA* OR PRAYERFUL READING

1. *Lectio:* Read a Scripture passage aloud slowly. Notice what phrase captures your attention and be attentive to its meaning. Silent pause.

2. *Meditatio:* Read the passage aloud slowly again, reflecting on the passage, allowing God to speak to you through it. Silent pause.

3. *Oratio:* Read it aloud slowly a third time, allowing it to be your prayer or response to God's gift of insight to you. Silent pause.

4. *Contemplatio:* Read it aloud slowly a fourth time, now resting in God's word.

Naive no more, the "enraged" king sends an army to destroy and burn. Take a significant pause after the description of that graphic violence. As the destruction begins, so does the banquet. Because the king ordered that "whomever you find" be "invited to the feast," the banquet is filled with "bad and good alike"—an obvious echo of the non-discriminating reach of the dragnet parable.

A new controversy (and some say a new parable) begins with the king's entrance into the feast. Anger and disappointment flare when he spots someone "not dressed in a wedding garment." He gives the guest opportunity for defense, but the king can't abide the man's rudeness. Speak "He was reduced to silence" slowly, suggesting his lack of defence. The man has not taken the (Eucharistic) banquet seriously; he does not have the awe of God that would have compelled him to prepare. Swift and terrible judgment follows. The tag line speaks to us all; it's a warning intended to help us recognize the divine invitations we may be ignoring.

TWENTY-NINTH SUNDAY IN ORDINARY TIME

LECTIONARY #145

READING I   Isaiah 45:1, 4–6

Isaiah = ī-ZAY-uh

Cyrus = SĪ-ruhs

Set off the unexpected name of "Cyrus." God speaks in a very positive tone of this pagan king.

God is directing Cyrus's success, but the reason is not yet stated.

Here is God's motive: the welfare of Israel!

"You" refers again to Cyrus.

God makes it clear that even in the clash of empires God's hand is at work accomplishing the divine will.

Knowing and making known the one true God was Israel's great contribution to human history.

A reading from the Book of the Prophet Isaiah

Thus says the LORD to his **anointed**, **Cyrus**,
  whose right hand I **grasp**,
subduing **nations** before him,
  and making kings **run** in his service,
opening **doors** before him
  and leaving the gates **unbarred**:
For the sake of **Jacob**, my servant,
  of **Israel**, my **chosen** one,
I have **called** you by your name,
  giving you a **title**, though you knew me **not**.
I am the LORD and there is no **other**,
  there is **no** God besides me.
It is **I** who arm you, though you know me **not**,
  so that toward the **rising** and the **setting** of the sun
people may **know** that there is none besides me.
I am the LORD, there is **no other**.

READING I Cyrus the Great, founder of the Persian Empire, without his even knowing it, becomes God's instrument for rebuilding Israel and its Temple and ending Israel's decades-long exile in Babylon. Without violating Cyrus's free will, and despite the fact the Cyrus knows him not, God uses Cyrus and guides his actions to bring about the divine plan for Israel. The reason is simple and several times repeated: "I am the Lord and there is

no other." God is sovereign Lord, with control over life from beginning to end: all that happens is under God's power.

And God can choose even a pagan who has no knowledge of him. In fact, God even calls this pagan "his anointed." In Hebrew this exalted title is the root of the word Messiah, a title typically reserved to Israel's kings but here conferred on Cyrus because he is God's special instrument. God's voice speaks assertively in the opening lines claiming Cyrus is where he is only "for the sake of Jacob . . . my chosen one."

But the comment is both a right- and left-handed compliment. Yes, you are mighty and great, God says, but only for my purposes. God speaks in thunder to this mighty king, letting him know there is a throne above his; and upon it God sits *alone*. This text reminds Israel that God is free to do whatever he chooses and use whomever he wants to accomplish his will. You further my designs, God tells Cyrus, but remember they are *my* designs. "It is *I* who arm you" so that all may know "that there is none besides me!" The king of Persia has heard from the King of kings.

For meditation and context:

TO KEEP IN MIND

Units of Thought: Running too many words together blurs meaning and fails to distinguish ideas. Punctuation does not always indicate clearly what words to group together or where to pause. Identify *units of thought* and use your voice to distinguish one from another.

Thessalonians = thes-uh-LOH-nee-uhnz

Speak the names slowly and with familiarity and affection.

Silvanus = sil-VAY-nuhs

Make eye contact, letting the assembly know these words are also true of them.

Don't elide "faith," "love," and "hope." They are three distinct virtues.

Paul is not boasting about his role in bringing them to Christ.

In pointing to his evangelical method, Paul instructs the Thessalonians on how they, too, should live the Gospel—not in word only, but in "power" and the "Holy Spirit."

RESPONSORIAL PSALM   Psalm 96:1, 3, 4–5, 7–8, 9–10 (7b)

R. Give the Lord glory and honor.

Sing to the LORD a new song;
  sing to the LORD, all you lands.
Tell his glory among the nations;
  among all peoples, his wondrous deeds.

For great is the LORD and highly
    to be praised;
  awesome is he, beyond all gods.
For all the gods of the nations are things
    of nought,
  but the LORD made the heavens.

Give to the LORD, you families of nations,
  give to the LORD glory and praise;
  give to the LORD the glory due his name!
Bring gifts, and enter his courts.

Worship the LORD, in holy attire;
  tremble before him, all the earth;
say among the nations: The LORD is king,
  he governs the peoples with equity.

READING II   1 Thessalonians 1:1–5b

A reading from the first Letter of Saint Paul to the Thessalonians

Paul, **Silvanus**, and **Timothy** to the church of the **Thessalonians**
    in God the **Father** and the Lord Jesus **Christ**:
    grace to you and **peace**.
We give **thanks** to God always for all of you,
    remembering you in our **prayers**,
    unceasingly calling to mind your work of **faith** and labor
        of **love**
    and endurance in **hope** of our Lord Jesus **Christ**,
    before our God and Father,
    knowing, brothers and sisters loved by God,
    how you were **chosen**.
For our gospel did not come to you in **word** alone,
    but also in **power** and in the Holy **Spirit** and with
        much conviction.

READING II | Paul sowed the seeds of faith among the Thessalonians. Because of this labor of love among them, Paul knows them, and they know him and his co-workers, Silvanus and Timothy (who has just returned to Paul with a report on the life of the Church in Thessalonica). These circumstances call for a tone of familiarity and affection. Speak Paul's words as you might speak to someone with whom you worked on an important project and who won your deepest respect.

After the greeting, Paul gives thanks for the Thessalonians themselves and enthuses about the way they live out the virtues of "faith," "love," and "hope." Note the ordering of the virtues: by naming it last, Paul places the stress on "hope" and expresses eschatological longing for Christ's second coming. Paul realizes that his preaching was responsible for the Thessalonians being "chosen" to know and love Christ. That awareness fills him with pride and affection for his "brothers and sisters loved by God." Without pride, Paul names how he and his comrades preached

not just in word but "with much conviction" and in the power of the Spirit. You must speak these truths with joy and a sense of wonder at what God has done, for this is a review, not of the obvious, but of the glorious mercy of God.

GOSPEL | The fact that the introduction to this pericope uses the words "plotted" and "entrap" tells us Jesus was no easy target. He earned a reputation for cleverness and this episode is one likely reason why "Pharisees" (who

GOSPEL   Matthew 22:15–21

A reading from the holy Gospel according to Matthew

The **Pharisees** went off
  and **plotted** how they might **entrap** Jesus in speech.
They sent their **disciples** to him, with the **Herodians**, saying,
  "**Teacher**, we know that you are a truthful man
  and that you teach the way of **God** in accordance
    with the **truth**.
And you are not concerned with anyone's **opinion**,
  for you do not regard a person's **status**.
Tell us, then, what is your opinion:
  Is it **lawful** to pay the census tax to Caesar or **not**?"
Knowing their **malice**, Jesus said,
  "Why are you **testing** me, you **hypocrites**?
Show me the coin that **pays** the census tax."
Then they **handed** him the Roman coin.
He said to them, "Whose **image** is this and whose **inscription**?"
They replied, "**Caesar's**."
At that he said to them,
  "Then **repay** to Caesar what **belongs** to Caesar
  and to **God** what belongs to **God**."

Your initial tone should suggest the storm that's brewing over Jesus.
Phariasees = FAYR-ih-seez

This is manipulative but transparent posturing.
Herodians = her-OH-dee-uhnz

By answering, Jesus will either alienate the people who oppose the tax or the authorities who imposed it.

That they produce the coin immediately shows they participated in the Roman system of finance.

If you play by Rome's rules by using their currency, then follow all the rules and pay the tax; but also render to God what is rightfully God's, that is, love of God and of neighbor.
Caesar's = SEE-zerz

TO KEEP IN MIND
Posture speaks: Make sure it says what you want it to. Don't let your face or body contradict the good news you announce. Remember, readers are allowed to smile!

were against) and "Herodians" (who were in favor) opposed each other regarding the question of paying taxes to Rome. By telling them to "render to Caesar" what is rightfully his, Jesus avoids answering their real question. Caesar has the power, but whether or not he has a right to it, Jesus does not say. But he clearly limits to Caesar only that authority that is legitimately his. Jesus makes it clear that there are things that belong to God and not to the state. If the state intrudes into this sacred territory, then the person of faith is no longer obliged to "render to Caesar."

Those words "plotted " and "entrap" signal the controversy that's about to unfold. The Pharisees are also clever, so they don't overplay their part; Jesus is to be flattered and tricked into a self-incriminating response since too overt a trap might spook the prey. So they speak calmly and, once the way has been greased with cloying praise, they pose their question matter-of-factly.

The narrator's tone betrays his bias against the Pharisees, especially on the line "Knowing their malice." With blunt reproach, Jesus poses his question and calls them "hypocrites." He doesn't wait for a response.

"Show me the coin," he demands. His follow-up questions are also crisp and challenging. The Pharisees are still posturing when they answer, "Caesar's." Pause here as if Jesus were surveying them and the crowd, seeing into their hearts. His pronouncement is deliberate and unrushed. "Yes," he tells them, "give Caesar what belongs to him. But beware, beware that you don't surrender to Caesar what rightfully belongs to God."

THIRTIETH SUNDAY IN ORDINARY TIME

LECTIONARY #148

READING I   Exodus 22:20–26

A reading from the Book of Exodus

Thus says the LORD:
"You shall not molest or oppress an **alien**,
    for you were once aliens **yourselves** in the land of **Egypt**.
You shall not wrong any **widow** or **orphan**.
If ever you wrong them and they **cry** out to me,
    I will surely **hear** their cry.
My wrath will **flare** up, and I will kill you with the sword;
    then your own **wives** will be widows, and your
        children **orphans**.

"If you lend **money** to one of your poor neighbors among
        my people,
    you shall not act like an **extortioner** toward him
    by demanding **interest** from him.
If you take your neighbor's cloak as a **pledge**,
    you shall **return** it to him before **sunset**;
    for this **cloak** of his is the only **covering** he has for his body.
What **else** has he to sleep in?
If he **cries** out to me, I will **hear** him; for I am **compassionate**."

Exodus = EK-suh-duhs

The voice of God is immediately strong and authoritative.

"See" the potential victims you name. Make each a specific injunction, not a series of generic proscriptions.

God's defense of the powerless will not spare those who thrive on injustice.

Renew your energy in this section and assume the attitude of a wise counselor.

Speak this injunction as wise advice, not as a threat.

These lines reveal the tender care that motivates God's advocacy for the disadvantaged.

READING I   Many who hear today's text may understand the word "alien" in a generic sense, referring to *anyone* who is unloved or cast out. After all, who has not, at one time or another, felt like a stranger—even among friends or in their own home? In a sense, "Egypt" is a place we've all visited, even if we've never left our place of birth. On the other hand, many will hear today's declaration that "you were once aliens" more literally, for they know first-hand the experience of leaving their homeland and settling in a foreign land. That *literal* sense better conveys the meaning of "alien" within the context of this reading.

This text comes from a section of Isaiah comprised of laws that deal with social conduct. Isaiah is not making metaphors; he is speaking explicitly about the treatment of orphans, widows, and aliens or immigrants who have made their way to a new land. God's warnings about wronging "widow or orphan," are presented in stark terms. The consequences for doing to others what you would not want done to yourself are dire. The strong language is not that of a vengeful God but of a God who is solicitous for the weakest and most defenseless. If the poor seem easy prey, God warns, know that they are *not* unprotected and their cries *don't* go unheard.

In the Gospel, Jesus tells us to love God and neighbor. Here we learn to love God *by* loving our neighbor. Therefore, we mustn't extort interest or deprive a poor neighbor of the necessities of life, like clothing or shelter. As you admonish, remember that the God who says "I am compassionate," also calls *us* to compassion.

273

For meditation and context:

Thessalonians = thes-uh-LOH-nee-uhnz

Beware of sounding pompous. Paul says, "You saw our example and you imitated us, thus becoming an example for many others!"

Macedonia = mas-eh-DOH-nee-uh

Achaia = uh-KAY-yuh

Paul is rightly proud of them, and your tone should convey that.

As he praises them, he also reminds them of the commitments they've made to abandon idols and to ready themselves for the ultimate day of judgment.

End on a note of hope.

RESPONSORIAL PSALM   Psalm 18:2–3, 3–4, 47, 51 (2)

R. I love you, Lord, my strength.

I love you, O LORD, my strength,
    O LORD, my rock, my fortress,
        my deliverer.

My God, my rock of refuge,
    my shield, the horn of my salvation,
        my stronghold!
Praised be the LORD, I exclaim,
    and I am safe from my enemies.

The LORD lives and blessed be my rock!
    Extolled be God my savior.
You who gave great victories to your king
    and showed kindness to your anointed.

READING II   1 Thessalonians 1:5c–10

A reading from the first Letter of Saint Paul to the Thessalonians

Brothers and sisters:
You **know** what sort of people we were among you for your **sake**.
And you became **imitators** of us and of the **Lord**,
    receiving the word in great **affliction**, with **joy** from the
        Holy **Spirit**,
    so that you became a **model** for all the believers
    in Macedonia and in Achaia.
For from **you** the word of the Lord has **sounded** forth
    not **only** in Macedonia and in Achaia,
    but in **every** place your faith in God has gone forth,
    so that we have no need to say **anything**.
For they themselves openly **declare** about us
    what sort of **reception** we had among you,
    and how you **turned** to God from **idols**
    to **serve** the living and **true** God
    and to await his **Son** from **heaven**,
    whom he **raised** from the **dead**,
    Jesus, who delivers us from the coming **wrath**.

READING II | Here, as elsewhere, Paul points to himself and his example and asks his readers to imitate him. No doubt Paul had a healthy ego, but this theme of *imitation* is no sign of arrogance. As the title of the spiritual classic *The Imitation of Christ* (Thomas á Kempis, 1380–1471) suggests, Christianity is all about imitation. We value role models and even name them "saints" because they provide invaluable examples for those of us who are less advanced in the spiritual life. Like other saints, Paul is keenly mindful that what he offers he first received as gift

from God. This mindfulness becomes an occasion for gratitude, not pride. Paul offers his example as gift to all whose hearts are open to receive it. To their credit, the Thessalonians received the Word and became imitators despite "great affliction." Paul's focus is on these believers, not himself, and he praises their faith and the Spirit-given "joy" that pervades their lives. His notion of "imitation" is rooted in the conviction that we are made one by sharing Christ's Cross and receiving his Holy Spirit.

The opening resounds with praise and declares how the example of the Thessalonians caused the Word to "sound forth." While praising them, Paul also slips in some teaching, outlining the essentials of Christian faith: one "living and true God" instead of many false "idols"; Jesus, God's Son raised from the dead and reigning in heaven; and the "coming wrath"—a reference to end time judgment against unrepentant sinners. The encouragement and teaching Paul weaves into these emotional lines is meant for every assembly of believers.

Don't rush this important set-up and motivation for their "testing."

Pharisees = FAYR-uh-seez

Sadducees = SAD-yoo-seez

His tone is genuine; he's probably debated this question before.

Be sure to scan the assembly as you announce this non-negotiable requirement.

Soften your tone for the "second" commandment. Look at different faces on "neighbor" and on "yourself."

This is a summary declaration spoken with conviction and authority.

TO KEEP IN MIND

Who really proclaims: "When the Sacred Scriptures are read in the Church, God himself speaks to his people, and Christ, present in his word, proclaims the gospel" (#29 GIRM).

GOSPEL   Matthew 22:34–40

A reading from the holy Gospel according to Matthew

When the **Pharisees** heard that Jesus had **silenced** the Sadducees,
    they gathered together, and **one** of them,
    a scholar of the **law**, **tested** him by asking,
    "**Teacher**, which **commandment** in the law is the **greatest?**"
He said to him,
"You shall **love** the Lord, your **God**,
    with all your **heart**,
    with all your **soul**,
    and with all your **mind**.
This is the greatest and the **first** commandment.
The **second** is like it:
    You shall love your **neighbor** as **yourself**.
The whole **law** and the prophets depend on these
        two commandments."

GOSPEL   Jesus reduces the Law to two commandments that, in fact, embody the entirety of the Law. All that's commanded by Moses and the prophets, Jesus insists, is contained in these two injunctions that are harder to keep in spirit than any dietary laws or regulations about burnt offerings. The parallel in Mark's Gospel account is more nuanced and moving, but by eliminating focus on the personalities, this simple passage powerfully proclaims the essence of the Law.

By silencing the Sadducees, Jesus has raised the hackles of the Pharisees, who have come to test him. Their less than honest motive spotlights Jesus's simple, non-defensive teaching. Jesus won't give the prioritized list they're looking for. All the commandments required equally strict observance, but the scholar's question was not new within Judaism, so his tone is sincere.

Jesus's reply is as much addressed to the crowds as to the scholar. Sustain eye contact with your assembly as you speak—not information, but persuasion: "Love . . . with all your heart . . . soul . . . mind." Jesus quotes Deuteronomy 6:5 to stress that love requires the assent of the whole person; we can hold nothing back in our relationship with God. Speak with authority when declaring this "the greatest and the first commandment."

Unlike Mark, Matthew doesn't tell us the scholar compliments Jesus's response. But your tone as you speak the second commandment and the last sentence can suggest that Jesus sees in the eyes of his listeners an awareness and openness that places them close to the Kingdom of God.

ALL SAINTS

LECTIONARY #667

READING I   Revelation 7:2–4, 9–14

A reading from the Book of Revelation

Revelation = rev-uh-LAY-shuhn

There is much information in the first sentence: who is speaking, what he saw, and where it came from. Don't rush.

I, **John**, saw another **angel** come up from the East,
    holding the **seal** of the living **God**.
He cried out in a loud **voice** to the four angels
    who were given power to **damage** the **land** and the **sea**,
    "Do **not** damage the land or the sea or the trees
    until we put the **seal** on the **foreheads** of the **servants**
        of our God."

Your tone signals that this is exalted, symbolic language.

Use a softer tone, as if confiding information.

This number is symbolic and represents the new people of Israel comprised of all the people of the earth.

I heard the **number** of those who had been marked with the seal,
    one **hundred** and forty-four **thousand** marked
    from every **tribe** of the children of **Israel**.

Distinguish the words "nation," "race," "people," and "tongue" from one another.

After this I had a vision of a great **multitude**,
    which no one could **count**,
    from every **nation**, **race**, **people**, and **tongue**.
They stood before the **throne** and before the **Lamb**,
    wearing **white** robes and holding palm branches in their hands.
They cried out in a loud **voice**:

Though they are not yet identified, your tone tells us these are noble, heroic figures.

Give their outcry a joyful, not strident, sound.

"**Salvation** comes from our **God**, who is seated on the **throne**,
    and from the **Lamb**."

All the **angels** stood around the throne
    and around the **elders** and the four living **creatures**.
They **prostrated** themselves before the throne,
    worshiped God, and exclaimed:

The angels are not idling "before the throne" but worshipping God.

READING I — Addressed to people anticipating persecution and martyrdom, apocalyptic writing offers encouragement and hope, but in highly symbolic language. Apocalyptic is visionary writing that sees life through divine eyes and describes realities in terms of how they fit together in God's grand scope. It names neither future events nor the days and times they will occur, but it does speak of ultimate fulfillment, of God's will triumphing over all forces of darkness and opposition, and of the faithful surviving great distress and finding salvation and peace within the harbor of God's Kingdom.

Such is John's grand vision here, a vision that has offered hope and comfort for two millennia to individuals and groups undergoing times of trial and persecution. The hope it offers is of final, not immediate, vindication. The vision reframes the hardships and opposition disciples will inevitably face and presents those hardships as cleansing agents that bleach our "robes" purest white. Those who remain faithful through hard times, who keep their eyes fixed on the prize, who follow their crucified Lord and embrace suffering as he did—these will wear white robes that represent purification and eternal life in Christ.

The nature of this writing makes the text a mood piece. Mood is created by the sound of your words more than by their meaning, for the same words can sound soothing or terrifying depending on how we use them. John's images are dramatic, expansive, and awesome: angels ready to "damage" the land, the heavenly court around God's throne, worshipping angels

Again, distinguish the words in this angelic litany, using each as a distinct note of praise to God.

The elder already knows the answer.

John is not flippant but humbly defers to the elder.

These lines are the reason this text is read today; they describe the great assembly of saints who stand before the throne of God.

For meditation and context:

"**Amen. Blessing** and **glory**, **wisdom** and **thanksgiving**,
   honor, **power**, and **might**
   be to our **God** forever and **ever**. **Amen**."
Then one of the **elders** spoke up and said to me,
   "Who **are** these wearing white robes, and where did they
      come from?"
I said to him, "My lord, **you** are the one who knows."
He said to me,
   "These are the ones who have **survived** the time
      of great **distress**;
   they have **washed** their robes
   and made them **white** in the **Blood** of the **Lamb**."

RESPONSORIAL PSALM   Psalm 24:1bc–2, 3–4ab, 5–6 (6)

R. Lord, this is the people that longs to see your face.

The LORD's are the earth and its fullness;
   the world and those who dwell in it.
For he founded it upon the seas
   and established it upon the rivers.

Who can ascend the mountain of the LORD?
   or who may stand in his holy place?
One whose hands are sinless, whose heart
   is clean,
   who desires not what is vain.

He shall receive a blessing from the LORD,
   a reward from God his savior.
Such is the race that seeks him,
   that seeks the face of the God of Jacob.

TO KEEP IN MIND
Importance of the Narrator:
The narrator is often the pivotal role of a passage. Timbre, pitch, rate, and energy can make the same words convey very different moods or meaning. Sometimes the narrator is objective, but often the narrator has great interest in the events and characters of a story.

---

and elders, and the great assembly of the saved! Study the text carefully so you can appear to be describing a vision that's unfolding before you as you speak.

   "Do not damage . . . " is a command given out of concern for those who will receive the "seal," an action that guarantees the protection of the one whose mark is imprinted. The praise that fills the throne room is a promise of "salvation" for the struggling Church that read this vision. Those in "white," the elder says, have "come out of the great ordeal"—anotherword of

hope for those facing persecution—and are washed in the "blood *of the Lamb*." The survivors are rendered pure and holy not by their own efforts but by the saving work of the Lamb.

READING II False teachers in the early Church claimed that believers were already perfected and had no need to strive for greater holiness. While that was an attractive and comforting belief, it was also a lie. This letter was addressed to a community embroiled in an ongoing battle against this false teaching,

which accounts for the letter's very direct, personal, and urgent tone. The author rejoices in what "we are" but cautions against anticipating what "has not yet been revealed." Though the future continues to be a mystery, today's liturgy surrounds it with hope and eager expectation of victory and salvation. Our present exalted state as "children" is but a foretaste of the glory we will experience when we meet God face to face.

   What the false teachers of John's day got right is that we already live a life that

The first word sets the tone.

This is a clear and direct declaration that stands alone. Pause before the next sentence.

This is a clear and direct declaration that stands alone. Pause before the next sentence.

You share both what we *don't* know and what we *do* know. Speak the latter with enthusiasm.

The last sentence is more a command than a statement.

TO KEEP IN MIND

Endings: Your inflection of the last line of the reading should always signal that the reading is about to end. Then pause (three beats!) and make eye contact before announcing (from memory) "The word [Gospel] of the Lord." Always pronounce "the" as "thuh" except before words beginning with a vowel.

READING II   1 John 3:1–3

A reading from the first Letter of Saint John

Beloved:
See what **love** the Father has bestowed on us
    that we may be called the **children** of God.
Yet so we **are**.
The reason the world does not **know** us
    is that it did not know **him**.
Beloved, we **are** God's children **now**;
    what we **shall** be has not yet been **revealed**.
We do know that when it **is** revealed we shall be **like** him,
    for we shall **see** him as he is.
Everyone who has this hope based on **him** makes himself **pure**,
    as **he** is pure.

---

anticipates our future glory. As Paul often points out, though its fullness awaits the coming of the Kingdom, we've already begun to live the Resurrection. Hence, the profound joy that opens this reading. John is filled with awe at what God has made us: "children of God." We could easily substitute "Can you believe?" for the opening word "See" because the realization expressed here is almost too good to be true.

The author offers an explanation of why the world has not perceived this manifest truth: it does not recognize *us* because

if did not recognize *him*. He writes to spiritual children whom he wants to instruct and to disabuse of the false teachings heaped upon them. And the word "Beloved" is an unmistakable marker that points to the appropriate tone as you read. Specifics of what we shall become are unknown, what *is* known is that "we shall be . . . like . . . him." If "him" is the Lord we love, the one through whom we received adoption as sons and daughters of God, then surely that knowledge is meant to comfort and encourage. The final sentence states a logical consequence: if we are to become like Christ,

then the time to get started is now and the best way to begin is by making ourselves "pure" (the Gospel's "clean of heart") as Christ is pure.

GOSPEL   From Scripture scholars we know that these teachings of Jesus were radically opposed to the values of his day. But no one needs to tell us how radically opposed they are to the values of our own culture. No matter how familiar, these pronouncements continue

GOSPEL   Matthew 5:1–12a

A reading from the holy Gospel according to Matthew

When Jesus saw the **crowds**, he went up the **mountain**,
    and after he had **sat** down, his **disciples** came to him.
He began to **teach** them, saying:

    "Blessed are the **poor** in **spirit**,
        for theirs is the Kingdom of **heaven**.
    Blessed are they who **mourn**,
        for they will be **comforted**.
    Blessed are the **meek**,
        for they will inherit the **land**.
    Blessed are they who **hunger** and **thirst** for **righteousness**,
        for they will be **satisfied**.
    Blessed are the **merciful**,
        for they will be **shown** mercy.
    Blessed are the clean of **heart**,
        for they will see **God**.
    Blessed are the **peacemakers**,
        for they will be called **children** of God.
    Blessed are they who are **persecuted** for the sake
        of **righteousness**,
        for theirs is the Kingdom of **heaven**.
    Blessed are **you** when they **insult** you and **persecute** you
        and utter every kind of evil against you **falsely** because
        of **me**.
    Rejoice and be **glad**,
        for your reward will be **great** in heaven."

Take time setting the scene and let the verbs tell the story: "saw," "went," "sat," "began to teach."

Your proclamation could challenge, comfort, congratulate, or instruct. Deciding what approach you'll employ is your first task. Let your perception of your assembly's needs guide you.

Pause between the two halves of each beatitude.

You needn't try to capture the mood or tone of the individual virtue named in the beatitude. A consistent, authoritative delivery throughout will suffice.
Try making eye contact with a different section of the assembly at each beatitude.

Pause after the eighth beatitude. Then shift to a more direct, intense delivery, and note the change in pronoun from "they" to "you."

Don't overdramatize the final line. Keep the delivery simple and sincere.

---

to challenge. In form, the beatitudes consist of praise for a current state of blessedness or happiness and promise of future reward. Taken together, the beatitudes comprise a prescription for Kingdom living that outlines the virtues of a disciple.

In a culture that believed affliction and poverty were unmistakable signs of personal sin and divine displeasure, Jesus unashamedly extols the poor, sorrowing, and lowly. Essentially, in each beatitude he is alluding to the same group—the disenfranchised needy. Significantly, to the

notion of economic poverty Matthew adds "in spirit," a coda that connotes humility and detachment from wealth and says that anyone, no matter their economic status, who relies on God more than their wealth can be poor in spirit—thus sparing wealth the label of intrinsic evil. The first and last beatitudes bring a reward that is a present reality ("theirs *is* the Kingdom"), while the other beatitudes speak of *future* rewards.

"Righteousness" in the fourth beatitude refers to God's saving action, while in the eighth it means human conduct consonant with God's will. Those who "mourn"

grieve the reign of evil in the world; the "meek" will inherit the Kingdom, not property with geographic coordinates on the "earth;" the "merciful" show mercy to neighbor and *enemy* alike; the "clean of heart" are faithful to God's commands; "peacemakers," like the merciful, show love of neighbor. The elaboration of beatitude eight identifies the pursuit of righteousness with Jesus ("because of *me*") who has become the means of right relationship with God.

THE COMMEMORATION OF ALL THE FAITHFUL DEPARTED (ALL SOULS' DAY)

LECTIONARY #668

READING I   Wisdom 3:1–9

A reading from the Book of Wisdom

The souls of the **just** are in the hand of **God**,
   and no **torment** shall touch them.
They **seemed**, in the view of the **foolish**, to be **dead**;
   and their passing away was thought an **affliction**
   and their going forth from us, utter **destruction**.
But they are in **peace**.
For if before **men**, indeed, they be **punished**,
   yet is their hope full of **immortality**;
chastised a little, they shall be greatly **blessed**,
   because God **tried** them
   and found them **worthy** of himself.
As **gold** in the **furnace**, he **proved** them,
   and as sacrificial **offerings** he took them to **himself**.
In the time of their visitation they shall **shine**,
   and shall dart about as **sparks** through **stubble**;
they shall judge **nations** and rule over **peoples**,
   and the Lᴏʀᴅ shall be their King **forever**.
Those who **trust** in him shall understand **truth**,
   and the **faithful** shall abide with him in **love**:
because **grace** and **mercy** are with his **holy** ones,
   and his **care** is with his elect.

The melodic opening line is the foundation for all that follows. Speak with joyful confidence.

Let your tone convey that here appearances don't match the reality.

This is another line to be delivered with utter conviction.

The purification that may come after death is not to be feared but welcomed as God's gift that prepares one for final judgment. Speak with authority.

Energy builds and tempo quickens a bit as you offer the lovely image of souls shining like sparks.

There is hopeful energy in these lines, but also some key words you must highlight.
It is "those who *trust*" and "the *faithful*" who "understand" and "abide."

The final lines can be delivered at a slower pace, emphasizing the "grace," "mercy," and "care" that await God's elect.

The readings given here are suggestions. Any reading from the Lectionary for the Commemoration of All the Faithful Departed (#668) or the Masses for the Dead (#1011–1015) may be used. Ask your parish staff which readings to prepare.

READING I | **WISDOM 3:1–9.** These words offer profound comfort to anyone experiencing loss and grief. To the "foolish" that lack faith, death appears to be the final word and oblivion the fate of those who have died. But, in fact, the souls of the just are with God, not destroyed, but living in peace. "If before men . . . " suggests that this truth is not patently obvious; and it isn't. Such vision requires the eyes of faith, which the foolish don't possess.

With faith we see that even if "they are chastised a little" (some hear in that a suggestion of Purgatory), their ultimate reward is assured, for having purified them like "gold in the furnace," God will make them shine like "sparks" from a raging fire. Often applied to the martyrs, these verses also speak of the witness given by ordinary lives marked by the love of God and others. So the tone is peaceful and full of joy. When Wisdom was written, belief in an afterlife was far from settled, so the author's intent is to persuade as well as comfort. Today, many hearts still need comfort and persuasion, so proclaim with serene conviction.

For the *just*, the sufferings of life are but a means of purification that a cleansing God uses to prepare them for "their time of visitation" (that is, judgment). After their judgment, they will understand truth and receive grace and mercy in abundance. They will even "judge" nations. Wisdom

For meditation and context:

TO KEEP IN MIND

Pauses are never "dead" moments. Something is always happening during a pause. Practice will teach you how often and how long to pause. Too many pauses make a reading choppy; too few cause ideas to run into one another.

Look right at the assembly and speak with confidence and joy. You'll be more persuasive if you get in touch with the love God has poured out into *your* heart.

Marvel at the generosity of God.

The comparison serves to highlight God's mercy all the more and climaxes at "Christ died for us."

RESPONSORIAL PSALM   Psalm 23:1–3a, 3b–4, 5, 6 (1)

R. The Lord is my shepherd; there is nothing I shall want. orR. Though I walk in the valley of darkness, I fear no evil, for you are with me.

The LORD is my shepherd; I shall not want.
   In verdant pastures he gives me repose;
beside restful waters he leads me;
   he refreshes my soul.

He guides me in right paths
   for his name's sake.
Even though I walk in the dark valley
   I fear no evil; for you are at my side
with your rod and your staff
   that give me courage.

You spread the table before me
   in the sight of my foes;
you anoint my head with oil;
   my cup overflows.

Only goodness and kindness follow me
   all the days of my life;
and I shall dwell in the house of the LORD
   for years to come.

READING II   Romans 5:5–11

A reading from the Letter of Saint Paul to the Romans

Brothers and sisters:
Hope does not **disappoint**,
   because the love of God has been poured out into our **hearts**
   through the Holy **Spirit** that has been **given** to us.
For **Christ**, while we were still **helpless**,
   died at the appointed time for the **ungodly**.
Indeed, only with **difficulty** does one die for a **just** person,
   though perhaps for a **good** person
   one might even find **courage** to die.
But God **proves** his love for us
   in that while we were still **sinners** Christ **died** for us.
How much **more** then, since we are now **justified** by his **Blood**,
   will we be **saved** through him from the **wrath**.

offers "hope full of immortality," promising us who are left behind that the faithful loved ones we've lost await us in glory. Nothing is guaranteed unless we have surrendered to God and become "his holy ones." But it is never too late to pray that those we love are among God's "elect" and to win for ourselves that same hope of immortality.

READING II | **ROMANS 5:5–11.** Though the word "unconditional" is often bandied about freely, usually the love we know—and the love we give—is contingent. The word "if" is the fulcrum that vaults

such conditional love into our lives: "If you do this, I will love you." But that is not God's way, Paul says. In sending the greatest gift of all, his Son who would die for us, God set no conditions. And so it continues: God's love is given freely—all we need do is accept it.

There are occasions when human love breaks the barriers of self-interest, when some even give their lives for others. Such moments provide an image of God's love for us—a love that is constant and reliable, that doesn't ebb and flow with changing circumstances. God didn't wait for us to "clean up our act," or "get it all together" before saving us. No, God took the initiative

and completely transformed us. God reached right into our unworthiness and made us worthy.

These are the words of an evangelist in whom the Good News swells and demands proclamation. The "hope" of which Paul speaks is *assured*. We need not bite our nails and worry. Paul stresses how remarkable this is. Even the most altruistic human actions don't compare with what God has done. Christ gave his life for us even when we were still steeped in sin and wholly unworthy of such extravagant love. And if God did all that *before* we were justified, Paul says, imagine how much more

Renew your energy. Build on the previous point: if God loved us enough to save us while we were alienated, how much more will God bestow on us now that we have been reconciled through Christ?

Contrast the words "death" and "life."

Let your voice swell with boasting of the goodness of God!

Indeed, if, while we were **enemies**,
    we were reconciled to God through the **death** of his Son,
    how much more, once **reconciled**,
    will we be saved by his **life**.
Not only **that**,
    but we also **boast** of God through our Lord Jesus Christ,
    through whom we have now received **reconciliation**.

Or:

READING II   Romans 6:3–9

A reading from the Letter of Saint Paul to the Romans

Establish strong eye contact and speak directly and with conviction.

Paul is "making a case"; you must also.

There are many subordinate clauses that won't add up to a complete thought unless vocally you help us hear how they connect to each other.

Renew your energy for the beginning of the second paragraph.

Through the power of God's grace we now have the ability to resist the allure of sin.

Connect the phrase "a *dead* person" in this line with "we have *died*" in the next.

Help us to hear that this good news is also true of us.

Brothers and sisters:
Are you **unaware** that we who were **baptized** into Christ Jesus
    were baptized into his **death**?
We were indeed **buried** with him through baptism into **death**,
    so that, just as **Christ** was raised from the dead
    by the glory of the **Father**,
    we **too** might live in newness of life.

For if we have grown into **union** with him through a **death**
    like his,
    we shall also be **united** with him in the **resurrection**.
We know that our **old** self was crucified with him,
    so that our **sinful** body might be done **away** with,
    that we might no longer be in **slavery** to sin.
For a dead person has been **absolved** from sin.
If, then, we have **died** with Christ,
    we believe that we shall also **live** with him.
We know that Christ, **raised** from the dead, dies no **more**;
    death no longer has **power** over him.

God will do for us now that we live in the grace and reconciliation Christ won for us through his Death.

ROMANS 6:3–9. Paul is in the midst of a diatribe, a forceful piece of writing meant to denounce wrong-minded ideas. Specifically, he's attacking the notion some accused *him* of: promoting that Christians *should* sin to let grace prosper (see the two verses that precede the start of this text). But Paul asserts that God's goodness is not drawn out by sin; instead, it flows freely from his love for us. He then explains that what happened to Christ happens to all who are baptized in him. Christ died; we

die. Christ rose, we rise. We were "buried" in the waters of Baptism so that just as Christ was raised by the "glory of the Father" we too might be raised to new life.

In the second paragraph, Paul develops the analogy: if we were united to Christ by experiencing a death like his, we will be further "united" by sharing in his Resurrection. Our "old self" was crucified with Christ to free us from all that inclines us toward indulgence and sin. By letting our "sinful body" be nailed to the Cross of Christ, we were freed from "slavery to sin." No one can say Christianity is home to moral indulgence and indifference. That's

nonsense. "A dead person has been absolved from sin," Paul insists. And because we "died" with Christ in Baptism, sin and death no longer possess us. Though the fullness of that truth is a future rather than a present reality, by living now as faithful sons and daughters of God we move steadily toward that glorious future. Though Paul's writing takes the form of a diatribe, *your* assembly does not endorse sinning to let grace abound. So speak with joy and hope, assuring all that like Christ, "death no longer has power over [them]."

GOSPEL   John 6:37–40

A reading from the holy Gospel according to John

Jesus said to the **crowds**:
"Everything that the Father **gives** me will **come** to me,
　and I will **not** reject **anyone** who comes to me,
　because I came down from heaven not to do my **own** will
　but the will of the one who **sent** me.
And **this** is the will of the one who sent me,
　that I should not **lose** anything of what he **gave** me,
　but that I should **raise** it on the last **day**.
For **this** is the will of my **Father**,
　that everyone who **sees** the **Son** and **believes** in him
　may have eternal **life**,
　and I shall **raise** him up on the last **day**."

Imagine Jesus lifting his voice to address a large crowd.

These words that manifest Jesus's humility might be delivered in a softer tone.

He is answering an unspoken question.

Speak this last sentence very deliberately and with strength of conviction.

This final line should offer hope and comfort to all who pray for their faithful departed.

THE 4 STEPS OF *LECTIO DIVINA* OR PRAYERFUL READING

1. *Lectio:* Read a Scripture passage aloud slowly. Notice what phrase captures your attention and be attentive to its meaning. Silent pause.

2. *Meditatio:* Read the passage aloud slowly again, reflecting on the passage, allowing God to speak to you through it. Silent pause.

3. *Oratio:* Read it aloud slowly a third time, allowing it to be your prayer or response to God's gift of insight to you. Silent pause.

4. *Contemplatio:* Read it aloud slowly a fourth time, now resting in God's word.

GOSPEL   Today's Gospel text follows the Bread of Life discourse that comes on the heels of various "signs" performed by Jesus, including the multiplication of loaves and fishes. The miraculous signs drew crowds to him, but he chided them, saying that they sought him out not for himself but for his miracles. All this led to Jesus's assertion that he is the "bread of life" and that those who come to him will neither hunger nor thirst. Then Jesus continues with today's pericope, declaring that he rejects no one who comes to him because those who come were sent to him by the Father as his disciples. Here, we must understand the words "anyone who comes to me" as referring to those who have *faith* in him—"who see the Son and *believe* in him." Jesus then adds that his only agenda is to do God's will, and answers the unspoken question that God's will is to lose nothing of what God gave him. In Jesus we see the paradigm of Christian humility for he, the divine Son, submits his will entirely to the will of the Father.

Embedded in this short text are three key ideas: a call to faith in Jesus, that is, faith in him, his teachings, and his miraculous signs; the great mystery of the resurrection of all believers, a resurrection of which we acquire a foretaste here on earth but which we will experience fully only in the Kingdom; and Jesus's hope-filled assertion that God desires all human beings to come to eternal salvation. Proclaim this text with hopeful energy and with conviction born of your own belief that everyone who has belonged to Christ will be raised to "eternal life . . . on the last day."

THE DEDICATION OF THE LATERAN BASILICA

LECTIONARY #671

Ezekiel = ee-ZEE-kee-uhl

READING I   Ezekiel 47:1–2, 8–9, 12

A reading from the Book of the Prophet Ezekiel

Make sure we hear that this vision is guided by an "angel."

Proclaim with energy at a good pace, but without racing. The details ("toward the east," "south of the altar") are not as important as the flow of life-giving water. Put your emphasis on the water and its effects on the desert of Arabah and on the Dead Sea. Again, these details don't require emphasis; read at a good clip but with joyous energy.

The **angel** brought me
   back to the **entrance** of the temple,
   and I saw **water** flowing out
   from beneath the **threshold** of the temple toward the **east**,
   for the **façade** of the temple was toward the east;
   the water flowed down from the southern side of the temple,
   south of the **altar**.
He led me outside by the **north** gate,
   and around to the **outer** gate facing the east,
   where I saw **water** trickling from the southern side.
He **said** to me,
   "This water flows into the eastern district down upon
      the **Arabah**,
   and empties into the **sea**, the **salt** waters, which it makes **fresh**.

Arabah = AYR-uh-buh

The energy in your voice should suggest the transformative power of the waters.

Here you can slow your pacing to create the wonderful images of abundant life the waters will create.

Remember you are speaking of the life of God going forth and transforming all it touches.

Wherever the **river** flows,
   every **sort** of living creature that can **multiply** shall **live**,
   and there shall be abundant **fish**,
   for wherever this water comes, the **sea** shall be made **fresh**.
Along both **banks** of the river, **fruit** trees of every **kind**
      shall grow;
   their leaves shall not **fade**, nor their fruit **fail**.
Every month they shall bear **fresh** fruit,
   for they shall be **watered** by the flow from the **sanctuary**.

Deliver the last line slowly and with good eye contact.

Their fruit shall serve for **food**, and their leaves for **medicine**."

READING I Disasters and destruction have a way of becoming seedbeds of hope that grow visions of new life—life that surpasses what was known before the time of trial. Such was the time of the Babylonian exile. Though Jerusalem and its Temple lay in ruin, a vision was growing within the heart of the prophet Ezekiel that spoke not only of restoration but of an abundance of life like never seen before. And the source of this life is God's holy Temple.

As God's dwelling place on earth, the Temple had great significance for the people of Israel. Its stately columns and its gold, its massive walls and elaborate decoration were not tributes to human artifice but a dim reflection of the grandeur of God. This God who chose to make a home among them was worthy of the best artifice and the best materials and the grandest proportions human hands could fashion. This Temple would be home to the Lord of life, and from its heart would flow the waters of life that would heal and restore all they touched.

Such news must be shared with joy. In our own times of desolation, words like these should instill hope. Announce with conviction that the desert region of the Arabah would be brought to resurgent life and the "stagnant waters" of what we know as the Dead Sea would become "fresh" and life-giving. The message of this reading is the same as that of today's feast: great temples remind us of the greatness of God, but they cannot hold that greatness for it spills out to all the lands beyond, bringing sustenance and healing to all.

For meditation and context:

Corinthians = kohr-IN-thee-uhnz

From the start, speak with strength and conviction. Given the context, stress the world "building" and all it implies.

Other teachers, like Apollos, are adding to the structure, but they must do so with great care.

This is the heart of the reading. Make eye contact and speak the line with authority.

This question is not an accusation, but a call to greater awareness of their dignity. Sustain your eye contact.

Don't pull back from the threat of this line. It serves to emphasize the worth of the community of believers.

You have a wonderful set-up here: boldly declare the first line then, in a softer tone and with great sincerity, speak the final line.

RESPONSORIAL PSALM   Psalm 46:2–3, 5–6, 8–9 (5)

R. The waters of the river gladden the city of God, the holy dwelling of the Most High!

God is our refuge and our strength,
  an ever-present help in distress.
Therefore, we fear not, though the earth
    be shaken
  and mountains plunge into the depths
    of the sea.

There is a stream whose runlets gladden the
    city of God,
  the holy dwelling of the Most High.
God is in its midst; it shall not be disturbed;
  God will help it at the break of dawn.

The Lord of hosts is with us;
  our stronghold is the God of Jacob.
Come! behold the deeds of the Lord,
  the astounding things he has wrought
    on earth.

READING II   1 Corinthians 3:9c–11, 16–17

A reading from the first Letter of Saint Paul to the Corinthians

Brothers and sisters:
You are God's **building**.
According to the grace of God **given** to me,
  like a wise master **builder** I laid a **foundation**,
  and another is **building** upon it.
But each one must be careful **how** he builds upon it,
  for no one can lay a foundation other than the one that
    is **there**,
  namely, Jesus **Christ**.

Do you not know that you are the **temple** of God,
  and that the **Spirit** of God **dwells** in you?
If anyone **destroys** God's temple,
  God will destroy that **person**;
  for the **temple** of God, which you **are**, is **holy**.

READING II In this reading, as on this feast, a building takes on symbolic significance. Paul tells the believers at Corinth that they are "God's building" and that their "foundation" is "Jesus Christ." Essentially, today's feast proclaims the same truth, for it focuses not simply on the walls of a great basilica in Rome but on the fact that this building is the symbolic home of all Catholics because it is the cathedral church of the pope, who is father and shepherd of us all. The Lateran is not defined by four walls but by the hearts and souls it encompasses and the oneness it represents.

Such was Paul's agenda in writing today's text. Addressing divisions that centered on the authority of various leaders within the community, Paul states unequivocally that their only foundation is Christ. It was Paul who laid that foundation by first teaching them of Christ. Others have built upon it, and now they are a structure strong and secure. No one can lay a new foundation, for the foundation they have will never weaken. Their task, Paul tells them, is to recognize what they have become—

"God's temple." The Lord lives within them. The Old Testament Temple was seen as God's dwelling place on earth, and therefore its destruction was a devastating blow. But God now has a new temple, "the temple of God, which you are," Paul assures them. This temple can only be destroyed if their faith in God is destroyed. And if anyone were to cause that to come about, "God will destroy that person."

Though written to resolve controversy, in today's context, Paul's words resound with hope and a joyful message of oneness in Christ.

GOSPEL   John 2:13–22

A reading from the holy Gospel according to John

The first two lines set the time and location.

Since the **Passover** of the Jews was **near**,
     Jesus went up to **Jerusalem**.

Your tone should immediately signal Jesus's displeasure.

He found in the **temple** area Those who sold **oxen**, **sheep**,
     and **doves**,
     as well as the **money**-changers seated there.

Don't hide Jesus's anger.

He made a **whip** out of cords
     and **drove** them all out of the temple area, with the sheep
       and oxen,

These details are significant for demonstrating Jesus's disapproval and the extent of his "zeal."

     and spilled the **coins** of the money-changers
     and **overturned** their tables,
     and to those who **sold** doves he said,
     "Take these **out** of here,
     and stop making my Father's house a **marketplace**."

Look about as you render this line.

His disciples recalled the words of **Scripture**,
     Zeal for your house will **consume** *me.*
At this the Jews answered and said to him,

Their tone is indignant and confrontational.

     "What **sign** can you show us for doing this?"
Jesus answered and said to them,

Pause before answering in Jesus's voice. His reply is measured and full of authority.

     "**Destroy** this temple and in **three** days I will **raise** it up."
The Jews said,

Now their tone mocks him.

     "This temple has been under construction for forty-six **years**,
     and you will raise it up in three **days**?"
But he was speaking about the temple of his **Body**.

Pause before narrating to let the ridicule echo. Then, in a softer tone, relate the reflection on this incident of the early faith community and the faith that resulted.

Therefore, when he was **raised** from the **dead**,
     his disciples **remembered** that he had said this,
     and they came to believe the **Scripture**
     and the word **Jesus** had spoken.

TO KEEP IN MIND
Careful preparation expresses your reverence for the Word.

GOSPEL   This familiar incident is especially relevant to this feast, which as we've seen in both the First and Second Readings, uses the figure of a building to focus on much larger issues. Like Ezekiel, Jesus laments the treatment of the Temple which, though not in ruin as during the exile, is ruined nonetheless by the disrespect of the merchants. Their services betray their lack of understanding about where they are and why they do what they do.

While Paul asks, "Do you not know that you are the temple of God?" Jesus asks, "Do you not realize you've turned my Father's house into a marketplace?" But a larger question underlies the confrontation. When "the people" ask him for a sign, Jesus replies, "Destroy this temple . . . and I will raise it up." Of course, he's speaking of "his body" and of his Resurrection and, as such, his words connect with those of Paul: the true Temple is Jesus's own *body*; as baptized Christians, *we* are Jesus's body, and therefore in Paul's words, God's temple.

Perhaps, the blindness of the merchants is less about selling and changing within the sacred precincts and more about reducing God's presence to a physical building and failing to recognize God present in his Word, his prophets and, now, in the person of Jesus. Jesus calls for greater respect for the Temple, but he also points to a time beyond the Temple when people will worship in "spirit and truth" (John 4:24). That worship will occur within the temple of his body, of which we are all a part. For the sake of *this* temple we value temples made of stone since they sacramentalize with bricks and mortar the invisible reality that calls for consuming "zeal."

THIRTY-THIRD SUNDAY IN ORDINARY TIME

LECTIONARY #157

READING I   Proverbs 31:10–13, 19–20, 30–31

Proverbs = PRAH-verbz

A reading from the Book of Proverbs

Let your tone suggest the difficulty of finding such an ideal spouse.

Note that each sentence is an independent unit, so end each one on a note of finality.

She is ambitious and hard-working.

Her motivation is not profit but the good of her family.

Distaff = a tool used in spinning that prevents unspun fibers from tangling.

Her concern goes beyond her family to the needy in her midst.

Pause before starting this sentence and create a strong contrast between the first and second line of the sentence.

End on a joyful note of praise.

> When one finds a **worthy wife**,
>   her value is far beyond **pearls**.
> Her **husband**, entrusting his **heart** to her,
>   has an **unfailing** prize.
> She brings him **good**, and not **evil**,
>   all the days of her **life**.
> She obtains wool and flax
>   and works with **loving** hands.
> She puts her hands to the **distaff**,
>   and her fingers ply the **spindle**.
> She reaches out her hands to the **poor**,
>   and extends her arms to the **needy**.
> Charm is **deceptive** and beauty **fleeting**;
>   the woman who fears the LORD is to be **praised**.
> Give her a **reward** for her labors,
>   and let her works **praise** her at the city gates.

READING I The poetry that comprises this text is spoken by the queen mother to her son the king advising him, in the verses that precede this portion, on the proper use of sex, alcohol, and royal power. She then moves into a description of an ideal wife, describing the kind of woman who will bring him honor and who can best support and assist him in his kingly responsibilities. That portion, which is today's text, is structured as an acrostic poem that uses consecutive letters of the Hebrew alphabet to begin each new line. Given the characters and plot lines in much of modern media, it would be easy to imagine a concerned mother today realizing that these media and real-life images paint women and wives as objects to be little valued and less trusted. Out of that concern the mother shares this sage advice.

But the link between this text and today's Gospel gives it an even larger purpose. Under the light of the Gospel, this passage reinforces the importance of using our time and resources well and profitably and in a manner that results in readiness for whatever may come. We can also discern the contours of Woman Wisdom (a personification of wisdom) in these lines, which make the text symbolic, a rendering of a home led by Woman Wisdom who brings peace, prosperity, and prominence to her husband and household.

Speak as the concerned and loving mother whose only motivation is her son's happiness. Her goal is to make attractive the notion of finding a "worthy wife" who is more valuable than "pearls" and brings good "all the days of her life." The opening line is better translated as "Who can find?" to suggest the great difficulty of finding someone with such virtues.

For meditation and context:

> **TO KEEP IN MIND**
>
> **Pauses** are never "dead" moments. Something is always happening during a pause. Practice will teach you how often and how long to pause. Too many pauses make a reading choppy; too few cause ideas to run into one another.

Thessalonians = thes-uh-LOH-nee-uhnz

Begin slowly; you're not speaking of calendar dates but of end-times and the signs that precede them, which calls for a sober tone.

You are reversing an expectation, so speak with emphasis.
Precisely when people least expect, the end will come. Speak as those claiming "Peace and security," then quicken the pace as you talk of "disaster" coming on like the onset of labor.
Pause after "labor" to solemnly announce that "they will not escape."

The mood shifts here; joyfully tell us not to fear because we're "not . . . of darkness."

Tell us confidently that we're "children of the day" who don't belong to the darkness of sin and fear.

Make eye contact as you share this final instruction.

RESPONSORIAL PSALM   Psalm 128:1–2, 3, 4–5 (1a)

R. Blessed are those who fear the Lord.

Blessed are you who fear the LORD,
   who walk in his ways!
For you shall eat the fruit of your handiwork;
   blessed shall you be, and favored.

Your wife shall be like a fruitful vine
   in the recesses of your home;
your children like olive plants
   around your table.

Behold, thus is the man blessed
   who fears the LORD.
The LORD bless you from Zion:
   may you see the prosperity of Jerusalem
   all the days of your life.

READING II   1 Thessalonians 5:1–6

A reading from the first Letter of Saint Paul to the Thessalonians

Concerning **times** and **seasons**, brothers and sisters,
   you have no need for anything to be **written** to you.
For you yourselves know very **well** that the day of the Lord
    will come
   like a **thief** at night.
When people are saying, "**Peace** and **security**,"
   then sudden **disaster** comes upon them,
   like **labor** pains upon a pregnant **woman**,
   and they will not **escape**.

But **you**, brothers and sisters, are not in **darkness**,
   for that day to overtake you like a **thief**.
For all of you are children of the **light**
   and children of the **day**.
We are **not** of the night or of darkness.
Therefore, let us not **sleep** as the rest do,
   but let us stay **alert** and **sober**.

The woman described is multi-faceted: she is resourceful, industrious, and concerned for the poor. You may know such a woman. If so, fix her image in your mind as you speak. The mother ends with a reminder of the fleeting nature of worldly beauty. Speak more soberly and slowly here as you remind this son that among a wife's worthiest attributes is her faith in God, a "work" that praises her and is its own "reward."

 READING II | Christians have been fascinated with end-times since the Church's beginnings. It's easy to dismiss such thought as the mindless speculation

of uninformed fanatics who seek what was never promised. And, indeed, such is often the case with doomsayers who predict the "end" is waiting around the calendar's next corner. But, in part, that fascination finds its roots in Scripture that speaks of "signs of the times" that ought not to be missed and that calls for readiness when the time of judgment comes. Each year, the final weeks of our liturgical cycle bring those readings to us in order to remind us that vigilance is necessary and that being always in a ready state is not optional for the faithful Christian.

However, those who claim knowledge of the time of the Lord's return forget that such knowledge cannot be had and that anyone who claims to have it is a fraud. So we live in tension, recognizing the need to be watchful and prepared but realizing that no matter what, the "day of the Lord" will inevitably come unexpectedly, "like a thief at night."

Use the clear, concise, direct prose to convey what is now a familiar theme in these closing weeks of the liturgical year. It was because of Paul's own teaching that the Thessalonians anticipate the imminent return of the Lord. But in a style that's both

GOSPEL   Matthew 25:14–30

A reading from the holy Gospel according to Matthew

Jesus told his disciples this **parable**:
"A man going on a journey
    called in his servants and entrusted his **possessions** to them.
To one he gave **five** talents; to another, **two**; to a third, **one**—
    to each according to his **ability**.
Then he went away.
Immediately the one who received **five** talents went and **traded**
        with them,
    and made **another** five.
Likewise, the one who received **two** made **another** two.
But the man who received **one** went off and dug a **hole**
        in the ground
    and **buried** his master's money.

"After a long time
    the master of those servants came **back**
    and settled **accounts** with them.
The one who had received **five** talents came forward
    bringing the **additional** five.
He said, 'Master, you gave me **five** talents.
See, I have made five **more**.'
His master said to him, 'Well **done**, my good and
        faithful servant.
Since you were faithful in **small** matters,
    I will give you **great** responsibilities.
Come, share your master's joy.'
Then the one who had received **two** talents also came forward
        and said,
    'Master, you gave me **two** talents.
See, I have made two **more**.'
His master said to him, 'Well **done**, my good and
        faithful servant.

Remember this is a story, so create the characters through your use of their dialogue and be attentive to the growing tension in the unfolding of the drama.

Introduce the three servants impartially.

The pace immediately quickens as the industrious servants get to work.

Pause and speak at a slower pace here as this servant ponders his strategy.

A significant amount of time has passed.

Consider the attitude you want to give each servant, whether confident or insecure.

The response of the master is exactly the same for the first two servants. There is no need to vary your delivery.

Find another "personality" for this second servant.

---

direct and familiar, Paul rebuffs that notion, telling them instead they don't need to talk about specific dates and times because they know quite well that the end is coming when they least expect.

But Paul has another even more important point: while they live in constant vigilance, the Thessalonians must focus on the now, aware that they have already begun living the future life they anticipate. Right now, because of Baptism, they are "children of the light . . . of the day." Already we experience that future life that will be fully ours only when we are wrapped within God's full embrace. A reveille call ends the passage with Paul telling us to do two things: be alert and be clearheaded.

GOSPEL Tempting as it might be to extrapolate a lesson about shrewd investment and capital gains, this parable obviously leads elsewhere. The owner's harsh treatment of the unprofitable servant is a key to the lesson found here. We are told that the servant buried his talent out of "fear." The constant admonition of Jesus, taken up by John Paul II throughout his ministry, was "be not afraid."

Fear causes much destructive behavior—of others and of self. Fear narrows and constricts; it dries up creativity, reduces magnanimity, and casts the other as a threat, making us leery and causing us to "do to others before they can do to us."

This is a parable about the Kingdom that says fear has no place within God's reign. Allowing himself to be controlled by fear is what brings judgment upon the "wicked, lazy servant." For the master, this fear is not a minor lapse but a serious fault that can't be overlooked. So the little he

A slower delivery will signal that the fate of this servant will contrast with that of his colleagues.

Since you were faithful in **small** matters,
    I will give you **great** responsibilities.
Come, **share** your master's joy.'
Then the one who had received the **one** talent came forward
      and said,
    'Master, I knew you were a **demanding** person,
    harvesting where you did not **plant**
    and **gathering** where you did not **scatter**;
    so out of **fear** I went off and buried your talent in the **ground**.
Here it is **back**.'

His master said to him in reply, 'You **wicked**, **lazy** servant!
So you **knew** that I harvest where I did not plant
    and gather where I did not scatter?
Should you not then have put my money in the **bank**
    so that I could have got it back with **interest** on my return?
Now then! **Take** the talent from him and give it to the one
      with **ten**.
For to everyone who **has**,
    more will be given and he will grow **rich**;
    but from the one who has **not**,
    even what he **has** will be taken away.
And **throw** this useless servant into the darkness **outside**,
    where there will be **wailing** and grinding of **teeth**.'"

[Shorter: Matthew 25:14–15, 19–21]

Because of the deeper motivation for the master's rage, don't overplay it or make it surface anger. His deep disappointment is over the laziness that now excludes the servant from the reward of the Kingdom.

This is not a punishment imposed by the master but a consequence dictated by the servant's behavior.

Speak this teaching directly to the assembly.

Speak the final lines with regret over his lost opportunity (and salvation).

TO KEEP IN MIND
Importance of the Narrator:
The narrator is often the pivotal role of a passage. Timbre, pitch, rate, and energy can make the same words convey very different moods or meaning. Sometimes the narrator is objective, but often the narrator has great interest in the events and characters of a story.

---

has is taken and given to the one whose assets are already plentiful.

This parable is familiar and the action repetitive, so you'll need your best storytelling skills to assure the assembly is still listening when the third servant takes the stage, since his dilemma constitutes the lesson of the parable. Characterization of the servants often renders the first and second confident while the third is timid. But in real life those who do well and work hard are sometimes insecure or unaware of their industriousness, while the lazy and less talented are sometimes brazen and outspoken.

In an upbeat, lively tone speak of the first and second servants who eagerly run to make their wise investments. Slow your rate for the third. Pause after "went off," as if he's considering what to do, and announce his hole-in-the-ground strategy. After a "long time" comes the ominous settling of accounts, catching the servants off guard. The first might seem unsure if what he's done will meet the master's expectations. The second might be thinking, I've made only "two thousand more." But the master rewards and praises lavishly.

The third servant says: "I knew you were tough, so I made sure not to lose your money. Here it is." When the master's anger is finally spent, he philosophizes about "the one who has" and "has not." The order to cast the servant into the darkness reflects the master's regret that the lazy servant proved unworthy of his trust—and of the Kingdom.

OUR LORD JESUS CHRIST, KING OF THE UNIVERSE

LECTIONARY #160

READING I   Ezekiel 34:11–12, 15–17

A reading from the Book of the Prophet Ezekiel

Thus says the Lord *God*:
   I **myself** will look after and tend my sheep.
As a **shepherd** tends his flock
   when he finds himself among his **scattered** sheep,
   so will **I** tend my sheep.
I will **rescue** them from every place where they were **scattered**
   when it was **cloudy** and **dark**.
I myself will **pasture** my sheep;
   I myself will give them **rest**, says the Lord God.
The **lost** I will **seek** out,
   the **strayed** I will bring **back**,
   the injured I will **bind** up,
   the **sick** I will **heal**,
   but the sleek and the strong I will **destroy**,
   shepherding them **rightly**.

As for **you**, my sheep, says the Lord God,
   I will **judge** between one sheep and another,
   between **rams** and **goats**.

Ezekiel = ee-ZEE-kee-uhl

Note that the entire passage is spoken in the voice of God.

Because the appointed shepherds neglected their responsibility, now *God* will shepherd the flock.

Throughout, God is convincing the flock that had been neglected that they will be neglected no more.

This is not a shopping list, but a moving litany of God's promises that reveal God's commitment and love.

This discipline, too, is motivated by love.

Slow your delivery, especially on the last line. God's love is not blind; it can discriminate and distinguish the sincere from the falsehearted.

READING I Though the calendar year has a month to go, the liturgical year ends today. Soon we will begin again as we did last year with a time of anticipation, preparing for the celebration of God's new beginning in Christ. But this time of anticipation awaits more than the birth of the infant of Bethlehem; it anticipates the return of Christ in his full glory at the end of time. So this day of ending and the season of new beginning that will follow share, at least in part, a common focus on the kingship of Christ.

Year ends typically prompt retrospective looks at where we've been in the twelve months past. But today's readings focus us forward. Faith always pushes toward the future, it feeds imaginations and presents a God who says, I will "tend my sheep"; a Son of God, we hear in Reading II, in whom "all [shall] be brought to life"; and a Son of Man, we learn in the Gospel, who will come again "in his glory."

All today's readings work together to engender great expectancy. Ezekiel energizes us by painting an image of God as one who looks after us like a shepherd. And in

Israelite imagination the images of shepherd and king were closely connected, probably stemming from David the shepherd king. Ezekiel prophesied during the exile, a trauma that befell Israel in part because her kings had been *false* shepherds who led their people astray. So God assumes the role of shepherd and rescues the "scattered," binds up the "injured," and destroys "the sleek and the strong."

Speak Ezekiel's poetic words tenderly, as if to people weary, frightened, and alone. Comfort and assure. It would be a tragedy to render this text as if it were a list! The

For meditation and context:

TO KEEP IN MIND

Prophets: In addition to troubling the comfortable, prophets comforted the troubled. With equal passion, the great seers spoke threat and consolation, indictment and forgiveness. You must do the same for the chosen people you call "parish."

Corinthians = kohr-IN-thee-uhnz

This is a solemn declaration that contains two ideas: Christ was raised; but he was only the first of many who will rise.

Be sure to balance "death/man" with "resurrection/man."

Balance "Adam" and "death" with "Christ" and "life."

Give clear emphasis to the ordering that Paul lays out: 1) "Christ"; 2) "those who belong to Christ"; 3) "the end."

Distinguish from each other the words "sovereignty," "authority," and "power."

Punctuate this powerful declaration of Jesus's ultimate triumph.

Declare the final sentence with joy; it expresses Paul's vision of universal harmony.

RESPONSORIAL PSALM   Psalm 23:1–2, 2–3, 5–6 (1)

R. The Lord is my shepherd; there is nothing I shall want.

The LORD is my shepherd; I shall not want.
    In verdant pastures he gives me repose.

Beside restful waters he leads me;
    he refreshes my soul.
He guides me in right paths
    for his name's sake.

You spread the table before me
    in the sight of my foes;
you anoint my head with oil;
    my cup overflows.

Only goodness and kindness follow me
    all the days of my life;
and I shall dwell in the house of the LORD
    for years to come.

READING II   1 Corinthians 15:20–26, 28

A reading from the first Letter of Saint Paul to the Corinthians

Brothers and sisters:
Christ has been **raised** from the **dead**,
    the **firstfruits** of those who have fallen asleep.
For since **death** came through **man**,
    the **resurrection** of the dead came **also** through man.
For just as in **Adam** all **die**,
    so too in **Christ** shall all be brought to **life**,
    but each one in proper **order**:
    Christ the **firstfruits**;
    then, at his **coming**, those who **belong** to Christ;
    then comes the **end**,
    when he hands over the **kingdom** to his God and **Father**,
    when he has destroyed every **sovereignty**
    and every **authority** and **power**.
For he must **reign** until he has put all his enemies under his **feet**.
The **last** enemy to be destroyed is **death**.
When everything is **subjected** to him,
    then the Son **himself** will also be subjected
    to the one who subjected everything to **him**,
    so that **God** may be **all** in **all**.

---

actions God promises are guarantees of care and affection, so speak them tenderly. Take frequent pauses, building with slow intensity from one phrase to the next. The pronoun "I" is spoken eleven times, a clear sign of how intimately God is involved.

The closing reference to judgment is not a threat but a caution, motivated by love. The stern ending does not contradict the tender lines that went before because the God who judges also desires that *all* should enter the sheepfold.

READING II   Today's readings help us look forward toward a time of fulfillment. But before looking ahead to the end of Jesus's reign over the world as we know it and to the beginning of a whole new order in which God will be "all in all," Paul takes a backward glance, at Adam and our beginnings.

His opening is a flourish of good news proclaimed energetically: Christ is raised, the first to rise of those who have "fallen asleep." But then he draws a breath and considers how we arrived at this point and the formula is simple: first came Adam and

death, then came Jesus and Resurrection. We sense joyous energy in Paul's assertion that just as we died with Adam, so we all *live* with Christ. But it's a controlled enthusiasm that never blurs his logical progression: Christ first, then all. Besides affirming the fact of our *future* resurrection, Paul is also countering a false Gnostic notion that Christians had *already* been raised. For Paul, we begin to live a resurrection life here and now that we will enjoy in its fullness only after death when, at the second coming, Christ raises us all from our graves.

GOSPEL   Matthew 25:31–46

A reading from the holy Gospel according to Matthew

Jesus said to his **disciples**:
  "When the **Son of Man** comes in his **glory**,
    and all the **angels** with him,
    he will sit upon his glorious **throne**,
    and all the **nations** will be **assembled** before him.
And he will **separate** them one from another,
    as a **shepherd** separates the **sheep** from the **goats**.
He will place the **sheep** on his **right** and the **goats** on his **left**.
Then the king will say to those on his **right**,
    '**Come**, you who are blessed by my Father.
Inherit the kingdom prepared for you from the foundation
        of the world.
For I was **hungry** and you gave me **food**,
    I was **thirsty** and you gave me **drink**,
    a **stranger** and you **welcomed** me,
    naked and you **clothed** me,
    ill and you **cared** for me,
    in **prison** and you **visited** me.'
Then the righteous will answer him and say,
    'Lord, **when** did we see you hungry and **feed** you,
        or **thirsty** and give you **drink**?
When did we see you a **stranger** and **welcome** you,
        or **naked** and **clothe** you?
When did we see you **ill** or in **prison**, and **visit** you?'
And the king will say to them in reply,
    '**Amen**, I say to you, whatever you did
    for one of the **least** brothers of mine, you did for **me**.'

The opening lines of the parable require a majestic tone; you're describing something overwhelming.

The word "separate" immediately suggests judgment.
Sheep could endure the nighttime cold, but the less hearty goats had to be brought indoors each night.
"Left" and "right" suggest "positive" and "negative" attitudes.
The king's voice might be surprisingly gentle and loving.

Shift your focus from one face in the assembly to another as you speak of these acts of generosity.

The "righteous" demonstrate a naïve innocence.
The pacing is quicker on these repeated phrases.

This is a moment of both affirmation and instruction.

During the time between Christ's Ascension and his return in glory, we endure a time of constant combat with the enemies of Christ and of his Kingdom. For Paul the sequencing of events is significant: Christ rose first from the dead; at the second coming, the rest of us will rise; "then comes the end." That last is a solemn but hopeful statement, for the end is a time of fulfillment when Christ's Resurrection is finalized by our own. Royal and military imagery expresses Paul's vision of Christ's final victory over all enemies, of which the greatest is death.

In the end, when everything becomes submissive to Christ, Christ will hand over the Kingdom to the Father who had made all things submissive to the Son. Then the creator will relate directly with all creation and God will be fully God in all places and within all hearts.

GOSPEL The Solemnity of Our Lord Jesus Christ, King of the Universe presents highly unorthodox images of the king who reigns over us. Last year it was a king reigning from a cross; next year it will be a criminal standing before a human authority who wields the power of life and death. Today's figure comes from the heavens and sits on a "glorious throne," but he identifies so closely with the weakest and the poorest that he insists there is no distinction between him and them. This cosmic king brings countless angels and gathers all the nations of earth, so let your voice convey the splendor and magnitude of the judgment.

But we must ask who are these "least brothers of mine" with whom the Son of Man identifies? The most common answer is anyone who suffers hunger, nakedness,

The tone of these lines is: "How could you not have seen me or cared enough to help?" Don't look at individuals this time but over their heads.

Then he will say to those on his **left**,
  '**Depart** from me, you accursed,
  into the eternal **fire** prepared for the devil and his **angels**.
For I was **hungry** and you gave me no **food**,
  I was **thirsty** and you gave me no **drink**,
  a **stranger** and you gave me no **welcome**,
  naked and you gave me no **clothing**,
  ill and in **prison**, and you did not **care** for me.'

Their tone suggests they think the king must be mistaken.

Then they will answer and say,
  'Lord, **when** did we see you hungry or thirsty
  or a **stranger** or **naked** or ill or in **prison**,
  and not **minister** to your needs?'

But the king's response says there is *no* mistake!

He will answer them, '**Amen**, I say to you,
  what you did not do for one of these **least** ones,
  you did not do for **me**.'

The voice of the narrator returns announcing the fate of the "goats" and "sheep."

And these will go off to eternal **punishment**,
  but the **righteous** to eternal **life**."

TO KEEP IN MIND

Who really proclaims: "When the Sacred Scriptures are read in the Church, God himself speaks to his people, and Christ, present in his word, proclaims the gospel" (#29 GIRM).

---

or other forms of deprivation. But according to many scholars, a more likely response is Christian evangelists who suffer for the sake of the Gospel. That analysis makes this less a moral lesson and more an assertion of Jesus's oneness with those who represent him. The oneness is such that to reject the messenger is to reject the one who sent him or her.

Of course, the parable does also lend itself to ethical interpretation. You might surprise your assembly with the gentle and compassionate sound of the king's voice that speaks reward to the "sheep" before they even know why they deserve it.

Enumerate their good deeds by speaking the various corporal works of mercy to different faces in the assembly, convincing them that goodness never goes unnoticed. Naive in their goodness, the "sheep" are genuinely puzzled about *how* they were so considerate of their king. The king's response is powerful and poignant *assurance* that in *this* kingdom king and disciples are synonymous.

Speaking to the condemned, the king's voice assumes a rueful tone, seemingly asking, "How could you have been so blind and uncaring?" Each "I" could as easily be a "we" because he's speaking of the

ignored "hungry," "thirsty," "ill," and "imprisoned" of the world. As you read, imagine the "least ones" themselves crying aloud for recognition and justice. This litany will be more compelling as a revelation of the unheeded cries of the poor than as an accusation.

Stung but unconvinced, the "goats" protest they could never have been so heartless to the king. But the king responds again with assurance that even if *we* forget how connected we are to one another, the king *never* forgets.